CALIFORNIA EDITION

HOUGHTON MIFFLIN

Math Steps

HOUGHTON MIFFLIN

Boston • Atlanta • Dallas • Denver • Geneva, Illinois • Palo Alto • Princeton

Grateful acknowledgment is given for the contributions of

Student Book

Rosemary Theresa Barry
Karen R. Boyle
Barbara Brozman
Gary S. Bush
John E. Cassidy
Dorothy Kirk
Sharon Ann Kovalcik
Bernice Kubek
Donna Marie Kvasnok
Ann Cherney Markunas
Joanne Marie Mascha
Kathleen Mary Ogrin
Judith Ostrowski
Jeanette Mishic Polomsky
Patricia Stenger
Annabelle L. Higgins Svete

Teacher Book
Contributing Writers

Dr. Judy Curran Buck
Assistant Professor of Mathematics
Plymouth State College
Plymouth, New Hampshire

Dr. Anne M. Raymond
Assistant Professor of Mathematics
Keene State College
Keene, New Hampshire

Michelle Lynn Rock
Elementary Teacher
Oxford School District
Oxford, Mississippi

Dr. Richard Evans
Professor of Mathematics
Plymouth State College
Plymouth, New Hampshire

Stuart P. Robertson, Jr.
Education Consultant
Pelham, New Hampshire

Dr. Jean M. Shaw
Professor of Elementary Education
University of Mississippi
Oxford, Mississippi

Dr. Mary K. Porter
Professor of Mathematics
St. Mary's College
Notre Dame, Indiana

Dr. David Rock
Associate Professor,
Mathematics Education
University of Mississippi
Oxford, Mississippi

Printed in the U.S.A.

ISBN: 0-395-98008-0

10 11 12 13 14 15-B-05 04 03 02 01 00

Contents

UNIT 1 • TABLE OF CONTENTS

Addition and Subtraction Facts through 14

UNIT 1 • TABLE OF CONTENTS

We will be using this vocabulary:

addend one of the numbers added in an addition problem
sum result of an addition problem
difference result of a subtraction problem
fact family related addition and subtraction facts
order property Changing the order of the addends does not change the sum.
$3 + 2 = 5; 2 + 3 = 5$
grouping property Changing the grouping of the addends does not change the sum.
$3 + (1 + 2) = 6; (3 + 1) + 2 = 6$

Dear Family,

During the next few weeks our math class will be learning and practicing addition and subtraction facts through 14.

You can expect to see homework that provides practice with addition and subtraction facts.

As we learn about related facts and fact families you may wish to keep the following sample as a guide.

Related Facts

$9 + 5 = 14$ $14 - 5 = 9$

Fact Family

$$\begin{array}{r} 4 \\ +\,2 \\ \hline 6 \end{array} \qquad \begin{array}{r} 2 \\ +\,4 \\ \hline 6 \end{array} \qquad \begin{array}{r} 6 \\ -\,2 \\ \hline 4 \end{array} \qquad \begin{array}{r} 6 \\ -\,4 \\ \hline 2 \end{array}$$

Knowing addition facts can help children learn the related subtraction facts.

Sincerely,

Name ____________________

$$\begin{array}{r} 5 \\ +\ 4 \\ \hline 9 \end{array} \quad \begin{array}{c} \leftarrow \text{addend} \rightarrow \\ \leftarrow \text{addend} \rightarrow \\ \leftarrow \text{sum} \rightarrow \end{array} \quad \begin{array}{r} 4 \\ +\ 5 \\ \hline 9 \end{array}$$

You can add the **addends** in any order.
You will get the same **sum**.
This is called the **order property**.

Write the addends in a different order. Find the sums.

1. $\begin{array}{r} 3 \\ +\ 5 \\ \hline 8 \end{array}$ $\begin{array}{r} 5 \\ +\ 3 \\ \hline 8 \end{array}$

2. $\begin{array}{r} 1 \\ +\ 6 \\ \hline \end{array}$ $\begin{array}{r} \\ +\ \ \\ \hline \end{array}$

3. $\begin{array}{r} 2 \\ +\ 8 \\ \hline \end{array}$ $\begin{array}{r} \\ +\ \ \\ \hline \end{array}$

4. $\begin{array}{r} 6 \\ +\ 3 \\ \hline \end{array}$ $\begin{array}{r} \\ +\ \ \\ \hline \end{array}$

5. $\begin{array}{r} 7 \\ +\ 2 \\ \hline \end{array}$ $\begin{array}{r} \\ +\ \ \\ \hline \end{array}$

6. $\begin{array}{r} 4 \\ +\ 6 \\ \hline \end{array}$ $\begin{array}{r} \\ +\ \ \\ \hline \end{array}$

Solve. Match.

7.

0 + 8 = 8	4 + 1 = ☐
1 + 4 = 5	2 + 4 = ☐
4 + 2 = 6	8 + 0 = 8
3 + 6 = 9	6 + 3 = ☐

Solve.

8.

6 + 3 = 9

3 + 6 = 9

9.

___ + ___ = ___

___ + ___ = ___

10.

3 + 7 = ☐

___ + ___ = ☐

11.

2 + 5 =

___ + ___ = ☐

12.

3 + 1 = 1 + ☐

13.

5 + 2 = 2 + ☐

Problem Solving Reasoning

14. Does it matter in what order you add the numbers? Why or why not? ______________________

____

★ Test Prep

Mark the number that goes in the box to make the sentence true.

15

4 + 5 = 5 + ☐

5	4	3	2
○	○	○	○

Name ____________________

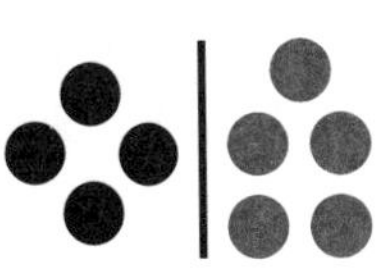

$4 + 5 = 9$

$9 - 5 = 4$

If you know the addition fact, it is easy to remember the subtraction fact. They are **related**.

Complete. Then write a related addition or subtraction fact.

1. $3 + 2 = \boxed{5}$
   5 − 2 = 3
2. $8 + 1 = \square$
   ____
3. $2 + 5 = \square$
   ____
4. $4 + 2 = \square$
   ____
5. $5 + 4 = \square$
   ____
6. $4 - 3 = \boxed{1}$
   1 + 3 = 4
7. $10 - 2 = \square$
   ____
8. $5 - 4 = \square$
   ____
9. $8 - 2 = \square$
   ____
10. $6 - 1 = \square$
    ____
11. $3 + 5 = \square$
    ____
12. $3 + 3 = \square$
    ____
13. $4 + 6 = \square$
    ____
14. $9 - 3 = \square$
    ____
15. $7 - 3 = \square$
    ____

Complete. Then write a related addition or subtraction fact.

16. $\begin{array}{r} 4 \\ +5 \\ \hline 9 \end{array}$ $\begin{array}{r} 9 \\ -5 \\ \hline 4 \end{array}$

17. $\begin{array}{r} 9 \\ -3 \\ \hline 6 \end{array}$ $\begin{array}{r} 6 \\ +3 \\ \hline 9 \end{array}$

18. $\begin{array}{r} 6 \\ +2 \\ \hline \end{array}$ $-$ ___

19. $\begin{array}{r} 3 \\ +4 \\ \hline \end{array}$ $-$ ___

20. $\begin{array}{r} 7 \\ +3 \\ \hline \end{array}$ $-$ ___

21. $\begin{array}{r} 8 \\ -2 \\ \hline \end{array}$ $+$ ___

22. $\begin{array}{r} 7 \\ -5 \\ \hline \end{array}$ $+$ ___

23. $\begin{array}{r} 5 \\ -1 \\ \hline \end{array}$ $+$ ___

Practice your facts. Add or subtract.

24. $\begin{array}{r} 8 \\ +2 \\ \hline \end{array}$

25. $\begin{array}{r} 5 \\ +5 \\ \hline \end{array}$

26. $\begin{array}{r} 9 \\ -4 \\ \hline \end{array}$

27. $\begin{array}{r} 7 \\ -2 \\ \hline \end{array}$

28. $\begin{array}{r} 8 \\ +1 \\ \hline \end{array}$

★ Test Prep

Mark next to the related fact.

29. 3 + 4 = 7

○ 8 − 1 = 7 ○ 7 − 2 = 5

○ 7 − 4 = 3 ○ 6 − 2 = 4

Name ______________________

You can write two related addition and two related subtraction facts. This is called a **fact family**.

	addition facts	subtraction facts
★★ ★ / ★★ ★ / ★ ★	5 + 3 = 8	8 − 3 = 5
	3 + 5 = 8	8 − 5 = 3

Complete the fact family.

1. 

4 + 3 = 7
3 + 4 = 7
7 − 3 = 4
7 − 4 = 3

2. 

5 + 4 = ☐
4 + 5 = ☐
9 − 4 = ☐
9 − 5 = ☐

3. 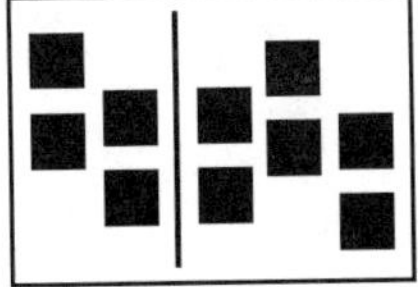

4 + 6 = ☐
6 + 4 = ☐
10 − 6 = ☐
10 − 4 = ☐

4.
3 + 5 = ☐
___ + ___ = ☐
___ − ___ = ☐
___ − ___ = ☐

5.
1 + 6 = ☐
___ + ___ = ☐
___ − ___ = ☐
___ − ___ = ☐

6.
7 + 2 = ☐
___ + ___ = ☐
___ − ___ = ☐
___ − ___ = ☐

You can write a fact family another way. Complete.

7. ♦♦ ♦♦ / ♦♦♦♦ ♦♦

$$\begin{array}{r} 4 \\ +\,6 \\ \hline 10 \end{array} \quad \begin{array}{r} 6 \\ +\,4 \\ \hline 10 \end{array} \quad \begin{array}{r} 10 \\ -\,6 \\ \hline 4 \end{array} \quad \begin{array}{r} 10 \\ -\,4 \\ \hline 6 \end{array}$$

8.

$$\begin{array}{r} 4 \\ +\,2 \\ \hline 6 \end{array} \quad \begin{array}{r} 2 \\ +\,4 \\ \hline 6 \end{array} \quad \begin{array}{r} 6 \\ -\,2 \\ \hline 4 \end{array} \quad \begin{array}{r} 6 \\ -\,4 \\ \hline 2 \end{array}$$

9.

$$\begin{array}{r} 3 \\ +\,7 \\ \hline \end{array} \quad \begin{array}{r} \\ + \quad \\ \hline \end{array} \quad \begin{array}{r} \\ - \quad \\ \hline \end{array} \quad \begin{array}{r} \\ - \quad \\ \hline \end{array}$$

10.

$$\begin{array}{r} 8 \\ +\,1 \\ \hline \end{array} \quad \begin{array}{r} \\ + \quad \\ \hline \end{array} \quad \begin{array}{r} \\ - \quad \\ \hline \end{array} \quad \begin{array}{r} \\ - \quad \\ \hline \end{array}$$

Problem Solving
Reasoning

11. How are all the number sentences in a fact family alike?

____

____

Quick Check

Solve.

1. $5 + 3 = 3 + \square$
2. $4 + 6 = 6 + \square$

Complete. Then write the related addition or subtraction fact.

3. $6 - 2 = \square$ ______________

4. $3 + 7 = \square$ ______________

Complete the fact family.

5.

$$\begin{array}{r} 7 \\ +\,2 \\ \hline \end{array} \quad \begin{array}{r} \\ + \quad \\ \hline \end{array} \quad \begin{array}{r} \\ - \quad \\ \hline \end{array} \quad \begin{array}{r} \\ - \quad \\ \hline \end{array}$$

Name ______________________________

Complete.

1. 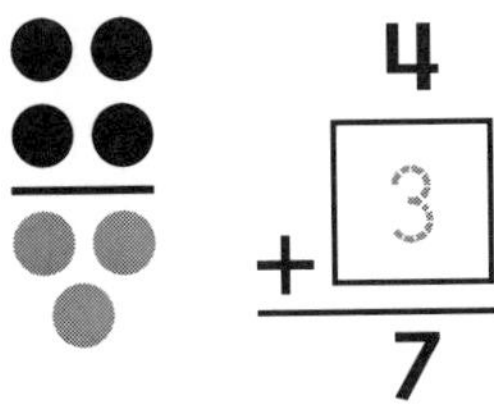

4 + [3] = 7	8 + [ ] = 10	4 + [ ] = 8

2.

3 + [ ] = 5	5 + [ ] = 9	3 + [ ] = 8	4 + [ ] = 10	0 + [ ] = 0	4 + [ ] = 7

3.

3 + [ ] = 7	2 + [ ] = 8	5 + [ ] = 10	2 + [ ] = 7	2 + [ ] = 6	6 + [ ] = 7

Complete.

4. 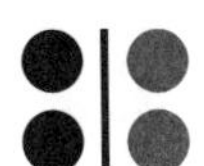

4.	2 + [2] = 4	2 + [ ] = 7	2 + [ ] = 8
5.	1 + [ ] = 5	1 + [ ] = 4	4 + [ ] = 9
6.	6 + [ ] = 9	1 + [ ] = 1	5 + [ ] = 8
7.	1 + [ ] = 3	6 + [ ] = 7	7 + [ ] = 8
8.	4 + [ ] = 6	3 + [ ] = 5	3 + [ ] = 7

Complete.

9.

4	2	5	6	6	5
+ ☐	+ ☐	+ ☐	+ ☐	+ ☐	+ ☐
6	5	8	10	8	7

10.

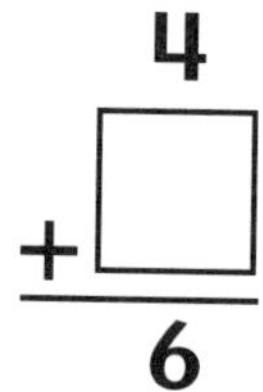

4	1	7	5	1	2
+ ☐	+ ☐	+ ☐	+ ☐	+ ☐	+ ☐
6	7	10	9	8	9

Practice your facts. Add or subtract.

11.

9	6	2	3	7	3
− 2	− 4	+ 6	+ 7	− 2	− 3

12.

3	9	10	2	5	2
+ 1	− 3	− 3	+ 7	− 4	+ 4

Problem Solving Reasoning

13. What related subtraction fact could you use to help you find

7 + ☐ = 10? ____________________

★ Test Prep

Decide on an answer. Mark the space for your answer.
If the answer is **not here**, mark the space for **NH**.

14 7 + ☐ = 9

4	3	2	1	NH
○	○	○	○	○

Name ______________________________

Problem

There are **5** balls outside the box.
There are **8** balls in all.
How many balls are in the box?

1 Understand

I need to find out how many balls are in the box.

2 Decide

I can draw a picture to solve the problem.

3 Solve

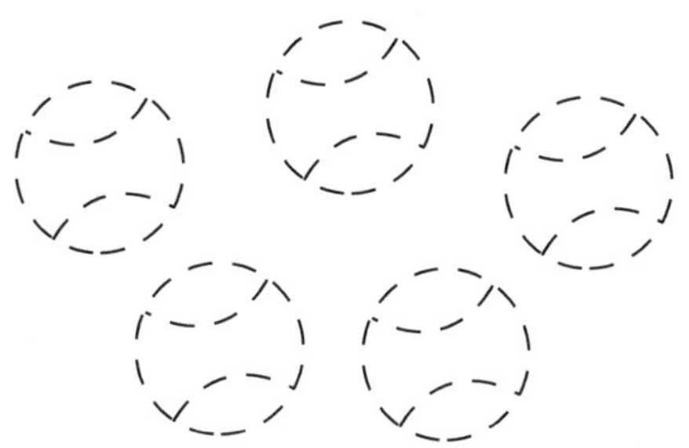

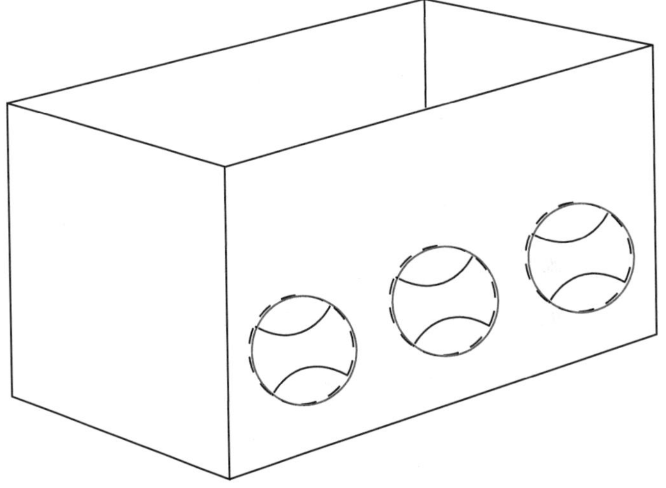

There are **3** balls in the box.

4 Look back

I know **5 + 3 = 8**.
My answer makes sense.

Draw a picture to solve.

1. There are **4** balls outside the box.
There are **7** balls in all.
How many balls are in the box?

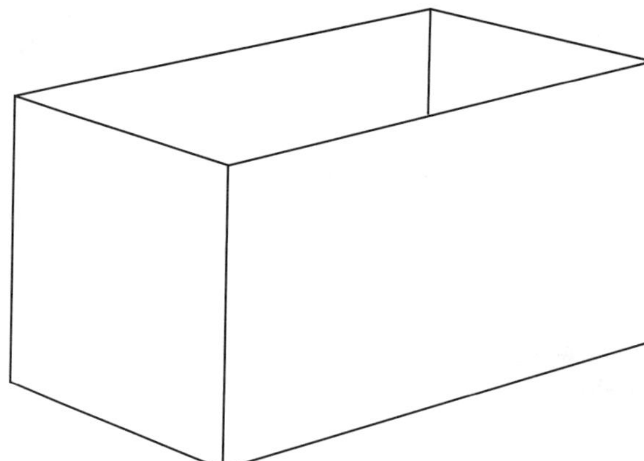

There are _____ balls in the box.

2. There are **6** balls outside the box.
There are **10** balls in all.
How many balls are in the box?

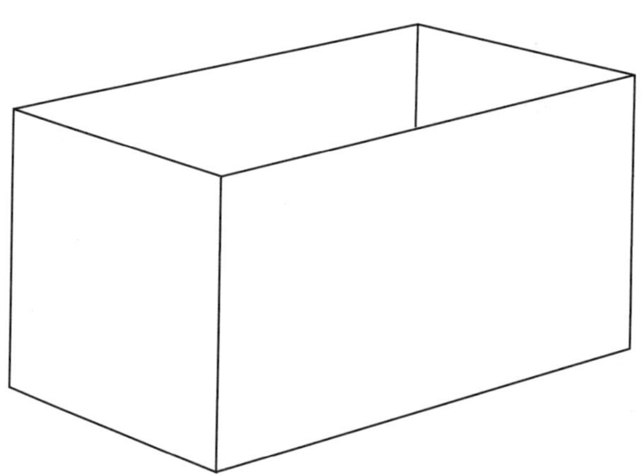

There are _____ balls in the box.

3. There are **2** balls outside the box.
There are **8** balls in all.
How many balls are in the box?

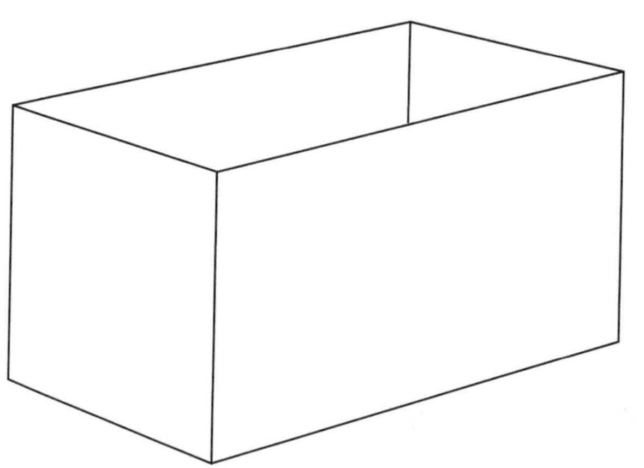

There are _____ balls in the box.

Tell why your answer makes sense.

____

____

Remember that for every fact there is a related addition or subtraction fact.

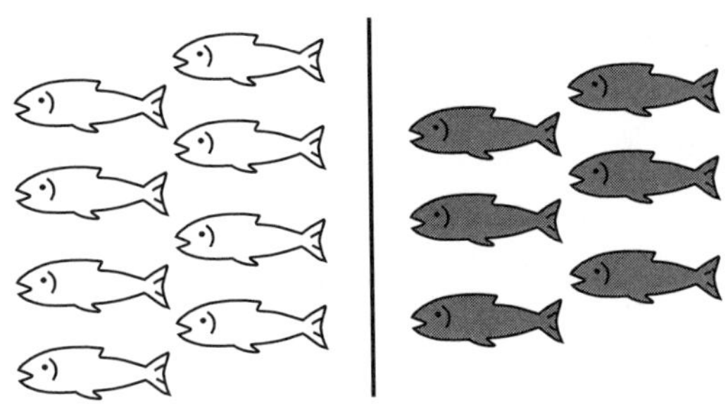

8 + 6 = 14
14 − 6 = 8

Complete. Then write a related addition or subtraction fact.

1. 5 + 8 = 13
13 − 8 = 5

2. 14 − 7 = 7
7 + 7 = 14

3. 8 + 4 = ☐
______

4. 12 − 9 = ☐
______

5. 13 − 7 = ☐
______

6. 14 − 5 = ☐
______

7. 5 + 7 = ☐
______

8. 11 − 6 = ☐
______

9. 6 + 8 = ☐
______

Complete. Then write a related addition or subtraction fact.

10. $\begin{array}{r} 6 \\ +8 \\ \hline 14 \end{array}$ $\begin{array}{r} 14 \\ -8 \\ \hline 6 \end{array}$

11. $\begin{array}{r} 13 \\ -4 \\ \hline 9 \end{array}$ $\begin{array}{r} 9 \\ +4 \\ \hline 13 \end{array}$

12. $\begin{array}{r} 5 \\ +9 \\ \hline \end{array}$ $\begin{array}{r} \\ - \\ \hline \end{array}$

13. $\begin{array}{r} 12 \\ -7 \\ \hline \end{array}$ $\begin{array}{r} \\ + \\ \hline \end{array}$

14. $\begin{array}{r} 6 \\ +4 \\ \hline \end{array}$ $\begin{array}{r} \\ - \\ \hline \end{array}$

Practice your facts. Add or subtract.

15. 1 + 8 = ____	18. 13 − 7 = ____	21. 5 + 7 = ____
16. 14 − 6 = ____	19. 4 + 8 = ____	22. 14 − 7 = ____
17. 9 + 3 = ____	20. 2 + 9 = ____	23. 3 + 8 = ____

Problem Solving Reasoning Solve. You can draw a picture.

24. There are **5** tops outside the box.
There are **13** tops in all.
How many tops are in the box?

There are ____ tops in the box.

★ Test Prep

Mark next to the related fact.

8 + 3 = 11

○ 11 − 3 = 8 ○ 8 − 3 = 5

○ 8 − 5 = 3 ○ 11 − 4 = 7

Name ____________________

Complete the fact family.

1.

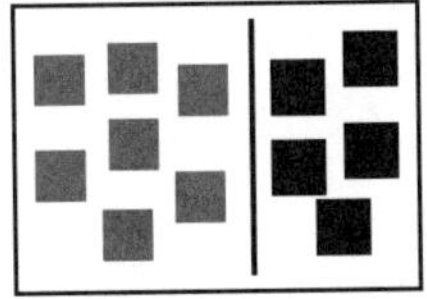

7 + 5 = 12

5 + 7 = 12

12 − 5 = 7

12 − 7 = 5

2.

___ + ___ = ☐

___ + ___ = ☐

___ − ___ = ☐

___ − ___ = ☐

3.

4 + 8 = ☐

___ + ___ = ☐

___ − ___ = ☐

___ − ___ = ☐

4.

6 + 5 = ☐

___ + ___ = ☐

___ − ___ = ☐

___ − ___ = ☐

5.

5 + 8 = ☐

___ + ___ = ☐

___ − ___ = ☐

___ − ___ = ☐

6.

3 + 9 = ☐

___ + ___ = ☐

___ − ___ = ☐

___ − ___ = ☐

Write the fact family.

7. 9, 5, 14

$$\begin{array}{r}9\\+5\\\hline 14\end{array}\quad\begin{array}{r}5\\+9\\\hline 14\end{array}\quad\begin{array}{r}14\\-9\\\hline 5\end{array}\quad\begin{array}{r}14\\-5\\\hline 9\end{array}$$

8. 6, 8, 14

$$\begin{array}{r}6\\+8\\\hline \end{array}\quad\begin{array}{r}\\+\\\hline \end{array}\quad\begin{array}{r}\\-\\\hline \end{array}\quad\begin{array}{r}\\-\\\hline \end{array}$$

Problem Solving
Reasoning

9. How are all the number sentences in a fact family alike?

____

____

Quick Check

Complete.

1. 3 + ☐ = 10

Complete. Write a related subtraction fact.

2. 6 + 7 = ☐

____

Write the fact family.

3. 7, 4, 11

$$\begin{array}{r}+\\\hline \end{array}\quad\begin{array}{r}+\\\hline \end{array}\quad\begin{array}{r}-\\\hline \end{array}\quad\begin{array}{r}-\\\hline \end{array}$$

Name ______________________________

You can group and add in any order.
You always get the same sum.
This is called the **grouping property**.

Add these first.

$(5 + 2) + 6 =$

$7 + 6 = 13$

Add these first.

$5 + (2 + 6) =$

$5 + 8 = 13$

Use the pictures.
Complete the number sentences.

1.

$(3 + \underline{5}) + 4 =$

$\underline{8} + 4 = \boxed{12}$

$3 + (5 + \underline{4}) =$

$3 + \underline{9} = \boxed{12}$

2.

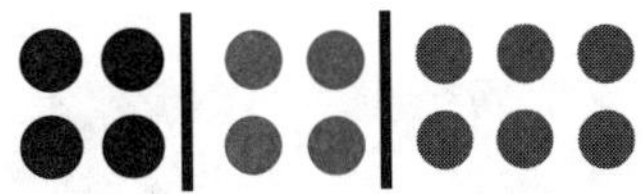

$(4 + \_\_\_\_) + 6 =$

$\_\_\_\_ + 6 = \square$

$4 + (4 + \_\_\_\_) =$

$4 + \_\_\_\_ = \square$

Complete the number sentences.

3. $(3 + 6) + 3 =$ ☐ $3 + (6 + 3) =$

9 $+ 3 =$ ☐ ___ + ___ = ☐

4. $(6 + 1) + 5 =$ $6 + (1 + 5) =$

___ $+ 5 =$ ☐ $6 +$ ___ = ☐

5. $(8 + 1) + 2 =$ $8 + (1 + 2) =$

___ + ___ = ☐ ___ + ___ = ☐

Group and then add.

6.

5	2	6	4	6	5
2 > 6	7	2	4	1	4
+ 4	+ 3	+ 6	+ 4	+ 5	+ 5

Problem Solving
Reasoning

7. Does it matter which two numbers you add first?

Why or why not? ______________________________

____

★ Test Prep

Decide on an answer. Mark the space for your answer.
If the answer is **not here**, mark the space for **NH**.

8 $(5 + 2) + 6 =$ ☐

11 ○ 12 ○ 13 ○ 15 ○ NH ○

Name ____________________

STANDARD

Use a fact you know to help add three addends.

```
  2 \
  8 / 10
+ 3
----
 13
```

I know **2 + 8 = 10**.

If I make a ten, it's easier to add.

Add. Look for a fact you know to help.

1.

3	4	4	1	5	7
5 } 10	1	8	7	4	3
+ 5	+ 6	+ 2	+ 3	+ 5	+ 2

2.

8	1	2	2	8	4
4	9	3	4	1	2
+ 0	+ 2	+ 6	+ 0	+ 4	+ 2

3.

3	3	1	0	5	6
4	6	1	5	2	3
+ 3	+ 2	+ 8	+ 4	+ 6	+ 1

4.

5	3	4	3	6	2
5	5	6	4	2	8
+ 3	+ 2	+ 2	+ 0	+ 1	+ 0

Complete.

5.

2 ⟩ 4	2	1	4	6	7
2	4	3	3	1	0
+ 5	+ ☐	+ ☐	+ ☐	+ ☐	+ ☐
9	11	9	12	10	12

6.

4	1	2	3	4	0
1	6	5	2	2	8
+ ☐	+ ☐	+ ☐	+ ☐	+ ☐	+ ☐
13	14	10	9	13	9

Practice your facts. Add or subtract.

7.

13	8	13	6	13	13
− 7	+ 3	− 9	+ 7	− 6	− 8

8.

6	9	11	12	5	14
+ 5	+ 4	− 2	− 8	+ 8	− 7

★ Test Prep

Decide on an answer. Mark the space for your answer.
If the answer is **not here**, mark the space for **NH**.

9

5
2
+ 6
☐

11	12	13	14	NH
○	○	○	○	○

Name ______________________________

Ring the facts that name the number on the house.

1. 11

9 + 2	8 + 3
8 + 4	7 + 5
5 + 8	6 + 5
6 + 7	3 + 7
4 + 7	9 + 3

2. 14

6 + 8	7 + 5
8 + 3	4 + 8
9 + 3	7 + 7
5 + 9	10 + 4
3 + 9	4 + 7

3. 13

9 + 4	7 + 6
3 + 6	4 + 9
8 + 5	5 + 8
9 + 3	7 + 5
8 + 4	6 + 7

Make the facts name the number on the umbrella.

4.

4 + 9	____ + 6
6 + ____	____ + 4
5 + ____	____ + 7
9 + ____	____ + 5
3 + ____	____ + 8

5.

6 + ____	____ + 2
8 + ____	____ + 6
5 + ____	____ + 9
9 + ____	____ + 5
7 + ____	____ + 4

6.

6 + ____	____ + 9
4 + ____	____ + 8
5 + ____	____ + 7
3 + ____	____ + 4
2 + ____	____ + 6

Ring the ways to name the number.

7. 13	4 + 2 + 3	3 + 7 + 3	4 + 6	5 + 4 + 4
8. 14	6 + 3 + 5	4 + 2 + 4	1 + 8 + 5	7 + 6

Problem Solving
Reasoning

9. How many different ways can you name **10**? List them.

____

____

____

Quick Check

Solve.

1. $6 + (2 + 2) = \square$

2. $\begin{array}{r} 3 \\ 3 \\ + 2 \\ \hline \end{array}$

3. $\begin{array}{r} 4 \\ 5 \\ + 3 \\ \hline \end{array}$

Ring the ways to name 12.

4. 8 + 4	6 + 5
7 + 7	6 + 6
9 + 2	5 + 7
2 + 10	3 + 8

Name ______________________________

2 is not equal to **5**

$2 \neq 5$

3 is equal to **3**

$3 = 3$

Use = or ≠.

1.

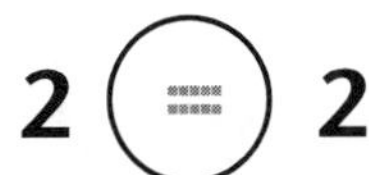

2 (=) 2

14 ◯ 14

11 ◯ 7

9 ◯ 9

12 ◯ 13

2.

Think 8.

4 + 4 (≠) 5

2 + 8 ◯ 9

7 + 5 ◯ 12

7 + 3 ◯ 14

10 − 5 ◯ 3

Use = or ≠.

3. 2 + 3 (≠) 4
 11 − 7 ◯ 4
 14 − 7 ◯ 5

4. 3 + 4 ◯ 7
 5 + 6 ◯ 4
 9 − 6 ◯ 3

5. 6 − 4 ◯ 3
 7 + 2 ◯ 9
 13 − 5 ◯ 2

Use + or −.

6.

14	8	9	12	10	0
(−) 8	◯ 4	◯ 2	◯ 3	◯ 4	◯ 9
6	12	7	9	6	9

7. 5 ◯ 9 = 14 13 ◯ 4 = 9 9 ◯ 4 = 5

Use = or ≠.

8. 2 + 6 (=) 14 − 6
 7 − 3 ◯ 2 + 2

9. 3 + 5 ◯ 8 − 4
 13 − 9 ◯ 2 + 7

★ Test Prep

Which of these is not true? Mark the space next to your answer.

10

○ 8 ≠ 3 + 3 ○ 12 − 9 ≠ 4
○ 13 = 4 + 9 ○ 6 + 6 = 14

Name ______________________________

Tim has **5** shells.

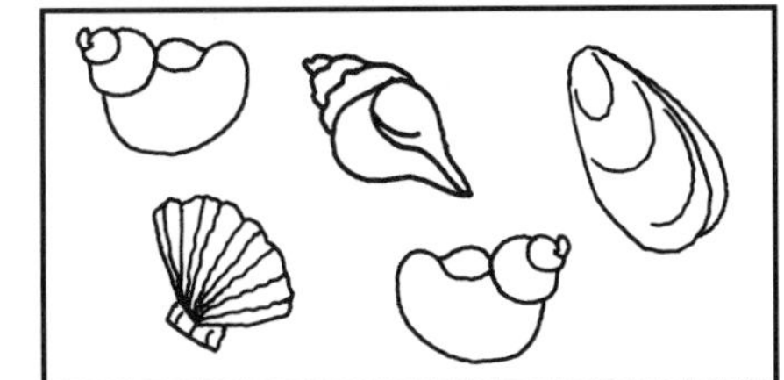

5 is greater than **3**. $5 > 3$

Sue has **3** shells.

3 is less than **5**. $3 < 5$

Use $>$ or $<$.

1.	9 ($>$) 6	12 ($<$) 14	13 ($>$) 10
2.	6 ◯ 8	13 ◯ 7	4 ◯ 5
3.	9 ◯ 12	7 ◯ 4	7 ◯ 9
4.	6 ◯ 9	4 ◯ 9	8 ◯ 14
5.	4 ◯ 8	7 ◯ 13	9 ◯ 5
6.	3 ◯ 6	12 ◯ 5	6 ◯ 12
7.	8 ◯ 5	6 ◯ 5	5 ◯ 3
8.	6 ◯ 7	9 ◯ 4	2 ◯ 8

Tim has **5** shells.

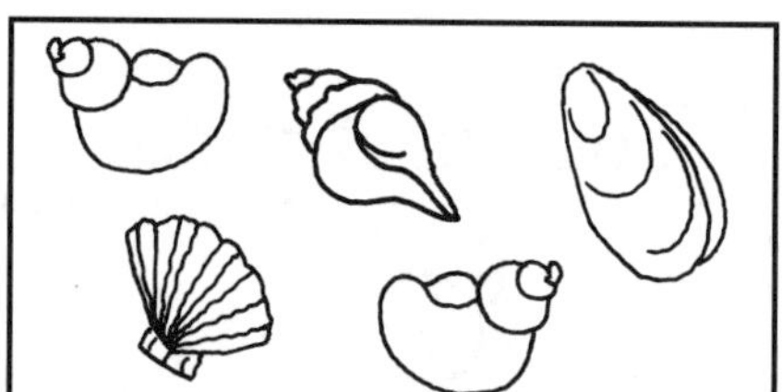

Sue has **5** shells.

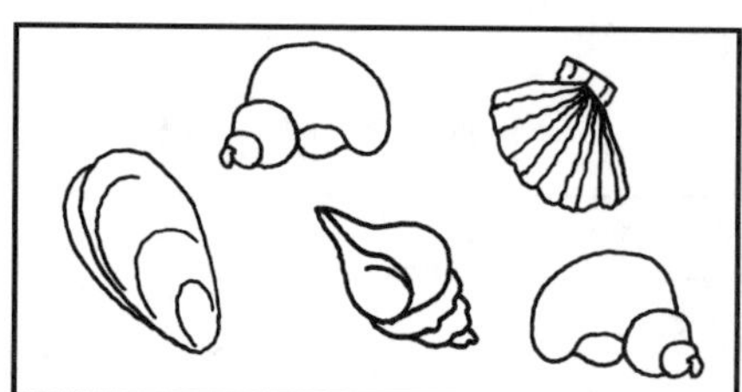

5 is equal to **5**. $5 = 5$

Use $>$, $<$, or $=$.

9. $14 \; (>) \; 6$ $\qquad 3 \; (=) \; 3$ $\qquad 8 \; (<) \; 12$

10. $11 \; \bigcirc \; 11$ $\qquad 14 \; \bigcirc \; 5$ $\qquad 9 \; \bigcirc \; 9$

11. $9 \; \bigcirc \; 13 - 4$ $\qquad 8 \; \bigcirc \; 2 + 4$ $\qquad 5 \; \bigcirc \; 8 - 3$

12. $12 \; \bigcirc \; 6 + 8$ $\qquad 10 \; \bigcirc \; 4 + 6$ $\qquad 14 \; \bigcirc \; 8 + 5$

Problem Solving
Reasoning

13. $3 + 3 \; (>) \; 6$

Is the answer correct? Why or why not? ______________________

____

★ Test Prep

Which of these is not true? Mark the space for your answer.

14

$11 > 9 + 2$	$7 = 7$	$5 < 8 + 4$	$14 = 8 + 6$
○	○	○	○

Name ____________________

STANDARD

Problem Solving Plan
1. Understand 2. Decide 3. Solve 4. Look back

Write + or −. Then solve.

1. Pam has **2** red balls.
Sue has **4** purple balls.
José has **3** orange balls.
How many balls do they have in all?

Think Do you need to add or subtract to find the answer?

add

2 (+) 4 (+) 3 = ____

Answer ____ balls

2. Ted has **10** tops.
7 spin away.
How many tops are left?

Think Do you need to add or subtract to find the answer?

____

10 ◯ 7 = ____

Answer ____ tops

3. There are **8** white cats.
There are **4** black cats.
There are **2** brown cats.
How many cats in all?

8 ◯ 4 ◯ 2 = ____

Answer ____ cats

4. There are **8** birds.
3 fly away.
How many birds are left?

8 ◯ 3 = ____

Answer ____ birds

5. There are **8** green fish.
There are **3** yellow fish.
How many fish in all?

8 ◯ 3 = ____

Answer ____ fish

6. There are **8** green fish.
There are **3** yellow fish.
How many more green fish are there than yellow fish?

8 ◯ 3 = ____

Answer ____ more green fish

Solve.

7. There are **5** boys and **4** girls at the party. How many children are there in all?

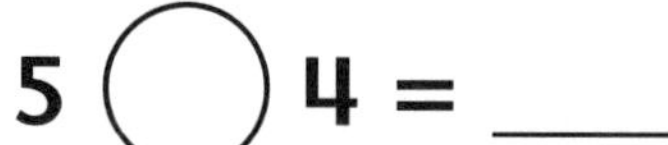

Answer _____ children

8. Mom has **10** apples. The children eat **8** of them. How many apples are left?

10 ◯ **8** = _____

Answer _____ apples

9. We have **3** red hats, **4** blue hats, and **2** green hats. How many hats are there in all?

Answer _____ hats

10. **Seven** of the children have white socks. **Two** of the children have blue. How many more children have white socks than blue socks?

_____ ◯ _____ = _____

Answer _____ more children

Extend Your Thinking

11. Draw a picture to match one of the problems.

Which problem did you choose? _______________

Does your picture show addition or subtraction? _______________

Name ____________________

Complete the tables.

1. Add 2.

8	10
0	2
4	6
7	9
5	7

2. Add 3.

7	
6	
5	
8	
9	

3. Add 5.

6	
4	
9	
3	
8	

4. Subtract 5.

10	5
14	
11	
13	
12	

5. Subtract 4.

11	
14	
10	
12	
8	

6. Subtract 7.

14	
11	
13	
10	
12	

Complete the rule.

7. Subtract 5.

9	4
11	6
12	7
14	9
13	8

8. Add ____.

6	12
8	14
3	9
5	11
4	10

9. Subtract ____.

14	7
10	3
9	2
13	6
11	4

Complete the rule.

10. Subtract ____.

12	9
9	6
10	7
13	10
11	8

11. Add ____.

9	13
4	8
7	11
10	14
6	10

12. Subtract ____.

14	6
13	5
12	4
11	3
10	2

Problem Solving
Reasoning

13. How can you check to see if your rule is correct?

____

____

Quick Check

Use $=$ or $\neq$.

1. $3 + 8$ ◯ 12

Use $>$, $<$, or $=$.

2. $14 - 7$ ◯ $3 + 3$

Complete the table.

3. Add 6.

6	
4	
7	

Name ____________________

Complete. Then write a related addition or subtraction fact.

1. 4 + 7 = ☐

______

2. 14 − 6 = ☐

______

3. 8 + 2 = ☐

______

Complete the fact family.

4. 7 + 2 = ___ + ___ − ___ − ___

5. 8 + 6 = ___ + ___ − ___ − ___

6. 7 + 6 = ___ + ___ − ___ − ___

7. 4 + 3 = ___ + ___ − ___ − ___

Solve.

8. 5 + 3

9. 8 + 4

10. 6 + 2

11. 9 + 5

12. 7 + 7

13. 6 + 6

14. 14 − 5

15. 12 − 7

16. 10 − 8

17. 11 − 7

18. 13 − 6

19. 12 − 8

Solve.

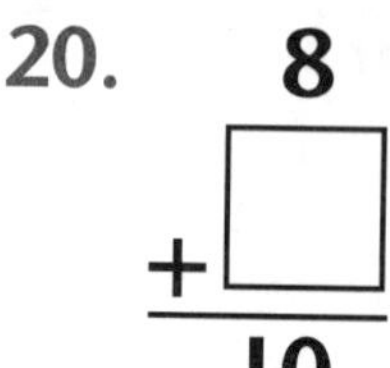

20. $\begin{array}{r} 8 \\ + \square \\ \hline 10 \end{array}$

21. $\begin{array}{r} 4 \\ + \square \\ \hline 9 \end{array}$

22. $\begin{array}{r} 5 \\ + \square \\ \hline 7 \end{array}$

23. $\begin{array}{r} 4 \\ + \square \\ \hline 8 \end{array}$

Use >, <, or =.

24. 7 ◯ 13

25. 9 ◯ 9

26. 5 ◯ 12

27. 4 + 4 ◯ 12 – 4

28. 14 ◯ 6 + 5

29. 8 ◯ 9 + 2

Add.

30. $\begin{array}{r} 4 \\ 1 \\ + 5 \\ \hline \end{array}$

31. $\begin{array}{r} 3 \\ 4 \\ + 2 \\ \hline \end{array}$

32. $\begin{array}{r} 6 \\ 4 \\ + 4 \\ \hline \end{array}$

33. $\begin{array}{r} 7 \\ 2 \\ + 4 \\ \hline \end{array}$

Problem Solving Reasoning Solve.

34. Luis has **7** books. He buys **6** more books. How many books does he have in all?

___ ◯ ___ = ___

___ books

35. Jackie has **8** toy cars. She gives **2** of them to a friend. How many cars does she have left?

___ ◯ ___ = ___

___ cars

Name ____________________

1

$6 + 7 = 13$

- ○ $6 + 8 = 14$
- ○ $13 - 8 = 5$
- ○ $13 - 7 = 6$
- ○ $7 + 7 = 14$

2

$$\begin{array}{r} 6 \\ + \square \\ \hline 10 \end{array}$$

8	7	6	4
○	○	○	○

3

$13 - 4 < 8$	$6 < 14$	$8 > 5 + 7$	$9 = 7$
○	○	○	○

4

8 tops	10 tops	12 tops	14 tops
○	○	○	○

Decide on an answer. Mark the space for your answer.
If the answer is **not here**, mark **NH**.

5

$8 + 5 = \square$

○ 9 ○ 10 ○ 11 ○ 12 ○ NH

6

$11 - 8 = \square$

○ 2 ○ 3 ○ 5 ○ 6 ○ NH

7

$$\begin{array}{r} 5 \\ +\ 4 \\ \hline \square \end{array}$$

○ 7 ○ 8 ○ 9 ○ 10 ○ NH

8

$$\begin{array}{r} 6 \\ +\ \square \\ \hline 14 \end{array}$$

○ 2 ○ 4 ○ 5 ○ 8 ○ NH

9

$$\begin{array}{r} 3 \\ 3 \\ +\ 7 \\ \hline \square \end{array}$$

○ 10 ○ 12 ○ 13 ○ 14 ○ NH

10

$12 \bigcirc 7 = 5$

○ + ○ − ○ > ○ < ○ NH

UNIT 2 • TABLE OF CONTENTS

Place Value through 100

We will be using this vocabulary:

before when ordering numbers, in front of

after when ordering numbers, next in order

between when ordering numbers, in the middle

Dear Family,

During the next few weeks our math class will be learning about place value through 100 and money amounts through 99¢.

You can expect to see homework that provides practice with place value and money amounts.

As we learn about place value and money amounts, you may wish to keep the following sample as a guide.

Place Value

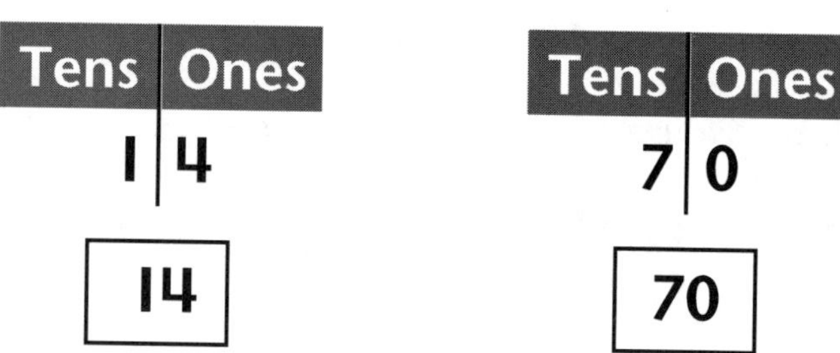

Money Amounts

In **50¢** there are **5** dimes.

In **50¢** there are **50** pennies.

Knowing place value can help children with their addition and subtraction exercises.

Sincerely,

Name ______________________________

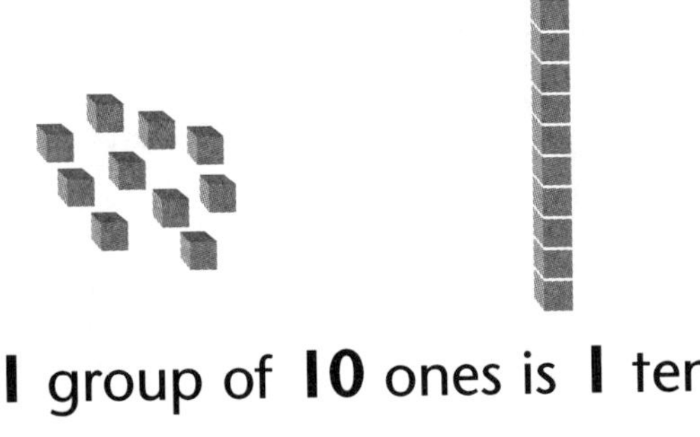

I group of **10** ones is **I** ten.

Complete.

1. ten

Tens	Ones
1	0

10

2. eleven

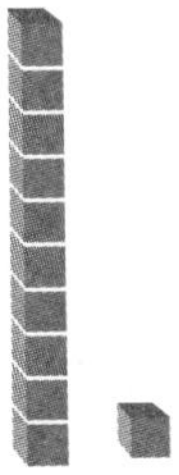

Tens	Ones

3. twelve

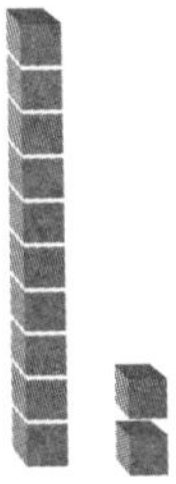

Tens	Ones

4. thirteen

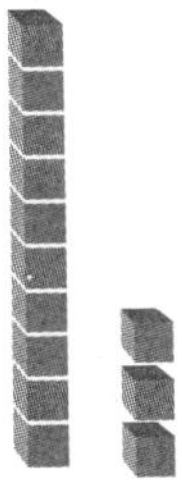

Tens	Ones

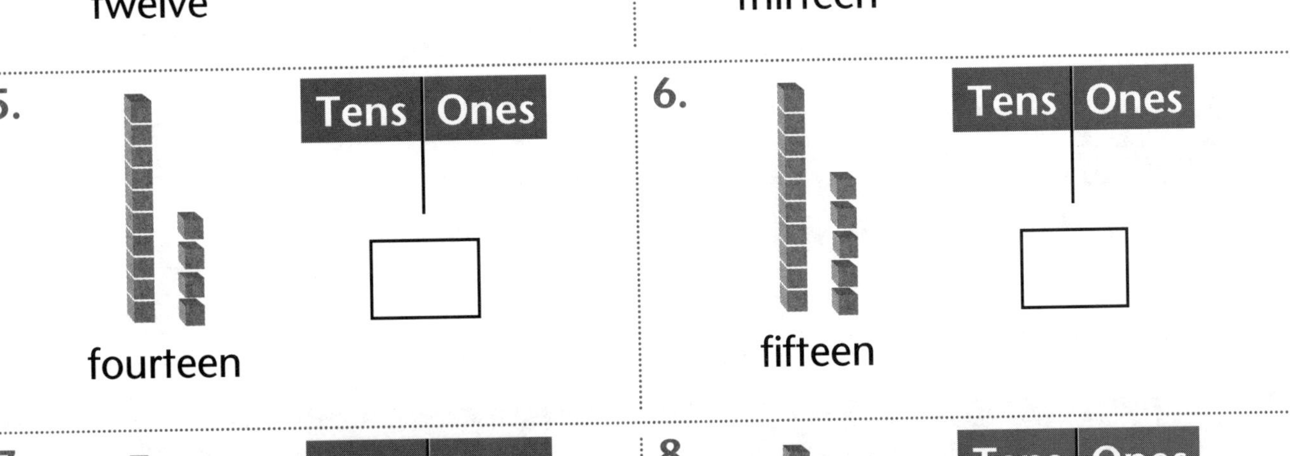

5. fourteen

Tens	Ones

6. fifteen

Tens	Ones

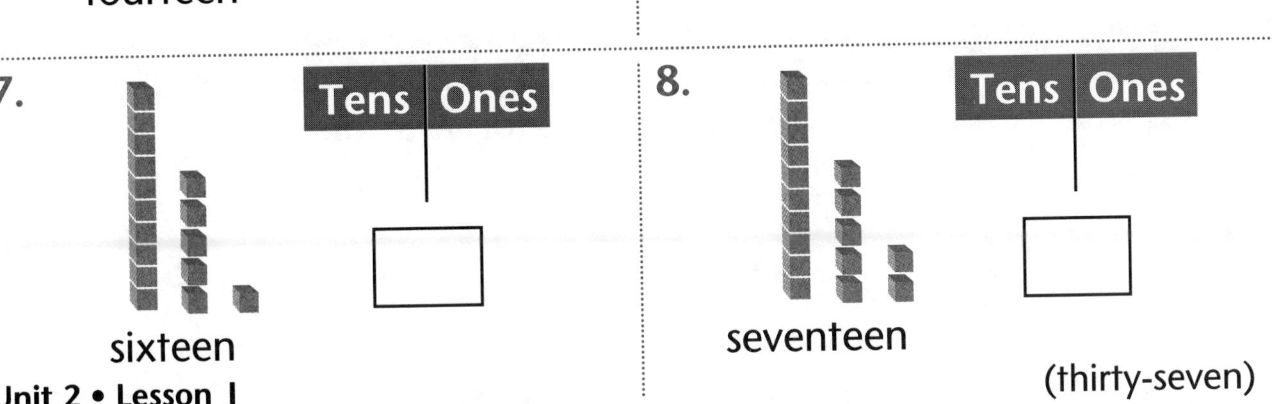

7. sixteen

Tens	Ones

8. seventeen

Tens	Ones

Complete.

9.

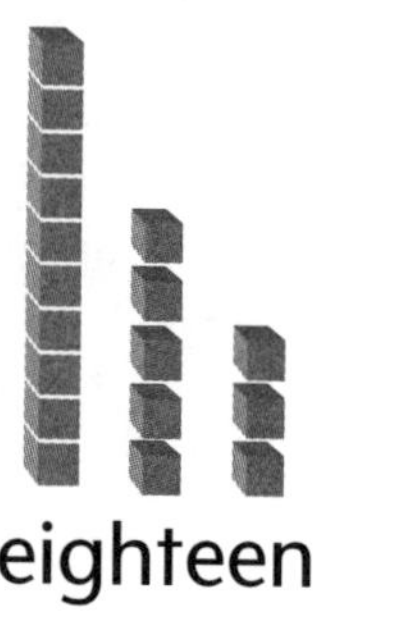

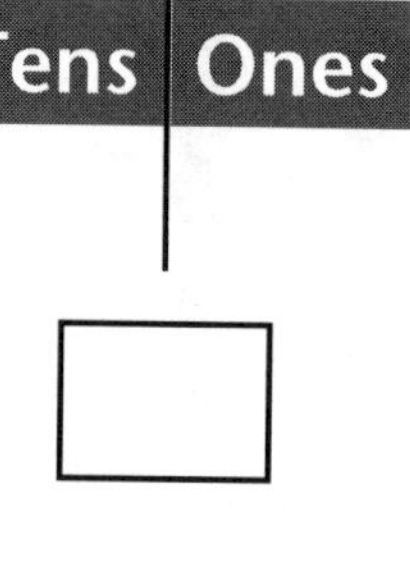

eighteen

10.

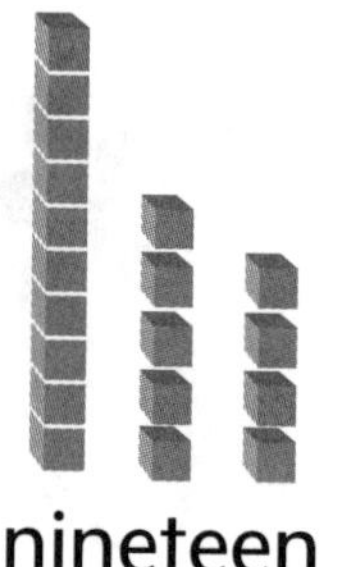

Tens | Ones

nineteen

What comes

11.

after?	before?	between?	before and after?
16, 17	17, 18	16, 17, 18	13, 14, 15
13, ____	____, 15	10, ____, 12	____, 18, ____

Ring the greatest number.

12. 19, 14, 7

Ring the least number.

13. 12, 11, 18

Use >, <, or =.

14. 10 (<) 15

15. 11 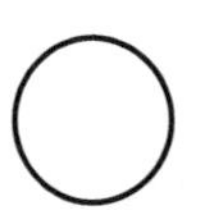 10

16. 12 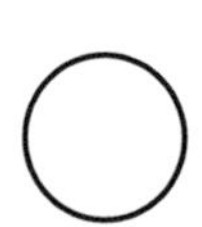 12

17. 13 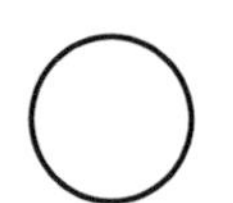 17

Problem Solving
Reasoning

18. Which number is greater, 13 or 15? Why? ____________________

____

★ Test Prep

What number is missing? Mark the space for your answer.

19

13, ____, 15

12	13	14	15
○	○	○	○

Name ____________________

Complete.

1\.
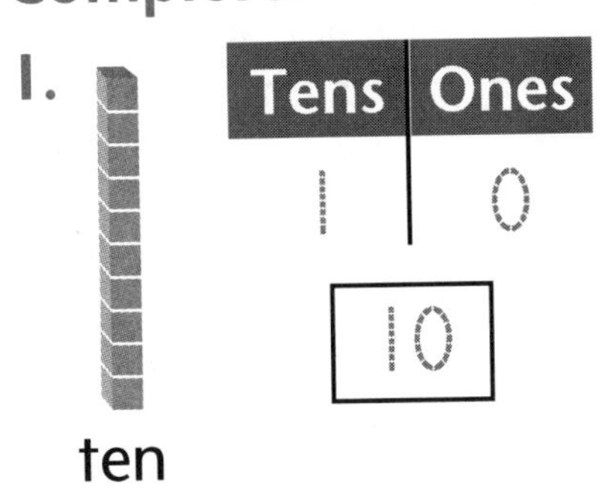

ten

2\.
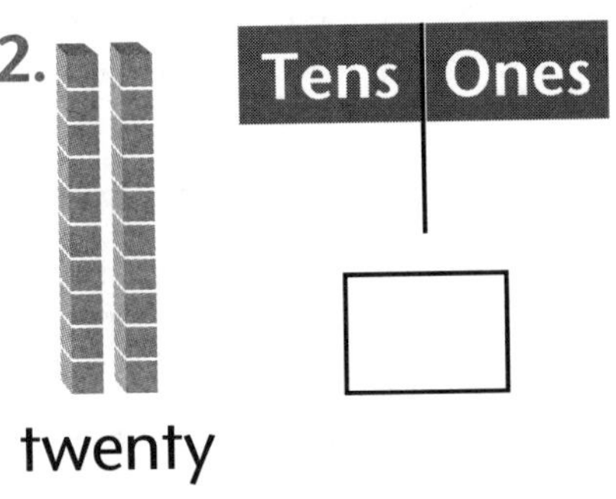

twenty

3\.
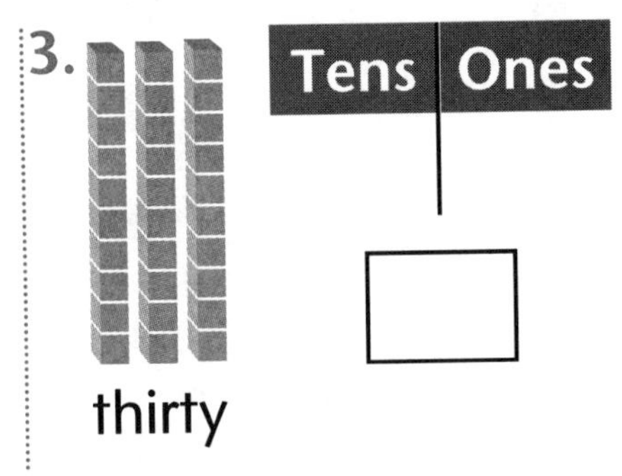

thirty

4\.
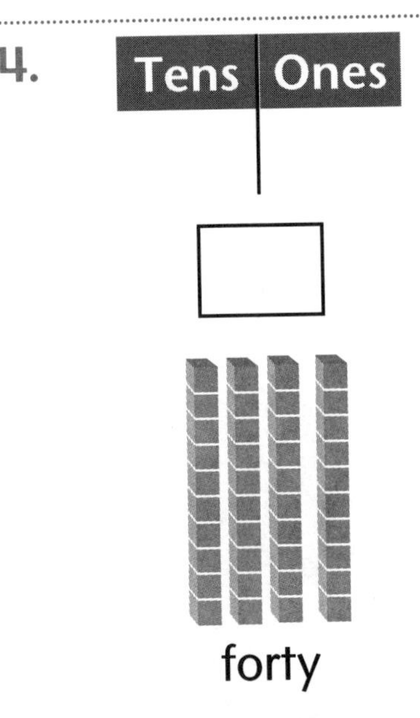

forty

5\.
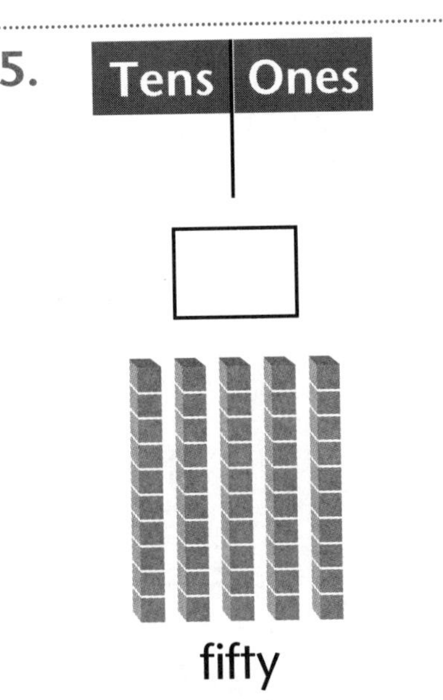

fifty

6\.
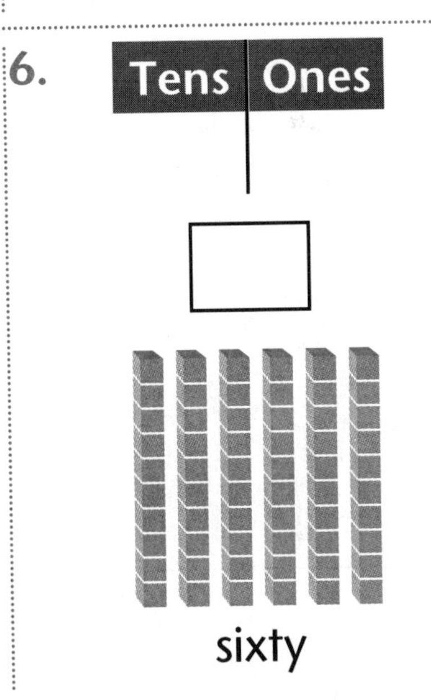

sixty

7\.
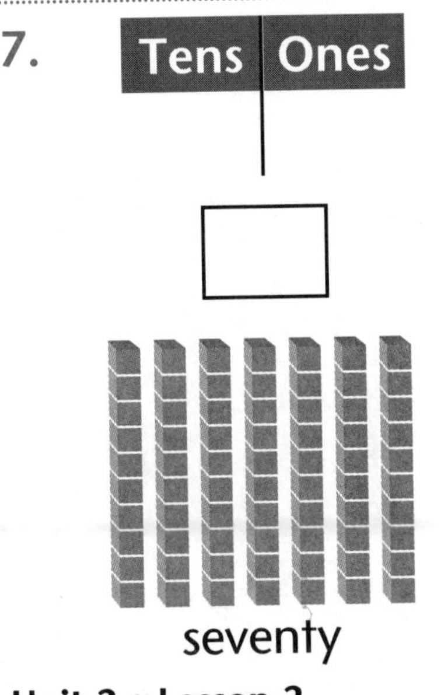

seventy

8\.
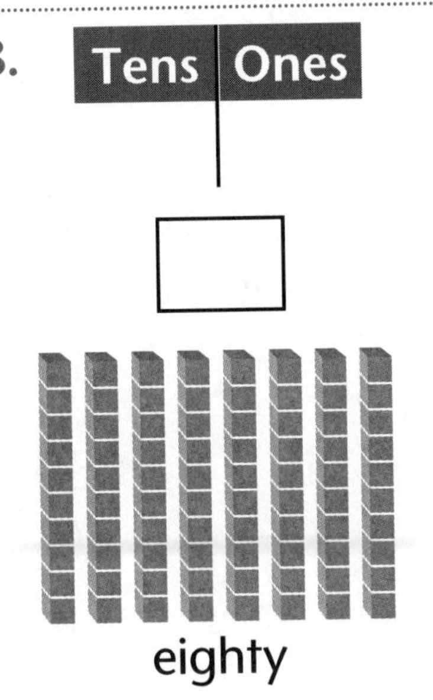

eighty

9\.
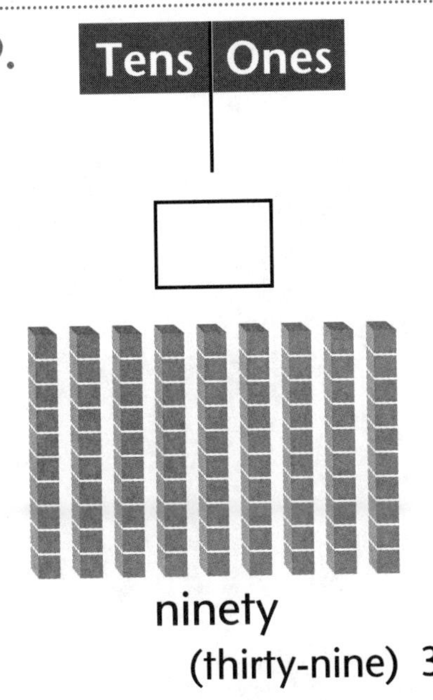

ninety

Complete.

10.

6	0	60
2	0	
9	0	
4	0	
1	0	
5	0	
8	0	
3	0	
7	0	

11.

	Tens	Ones
20	2	0
50		
90		
70		
60		
10		
40		
80		
30		

Problem Solving
Reasoning

12. Write the numbers in exercise 11 in order.

10 ____ ____ ____ ____ ____ ____ 80

★ Test Prep

What is the number? Mark the space for your answer.

13

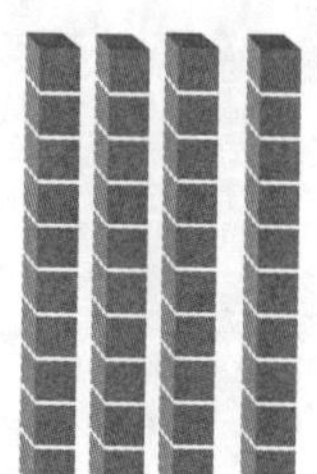

○ 20 ○ 30 ○ 40 ○ 50

Name ________________________________

Complete.

1.

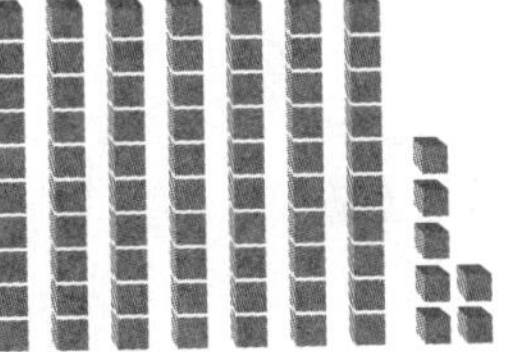

Tens	Ones
7	7

77

seventy-seven

2.

Tens	Ones
9	9

99

ninety-nine

3.

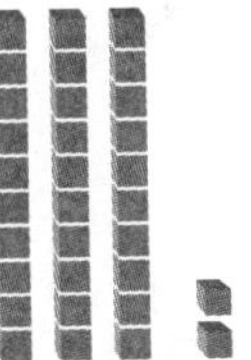

_____ tens and _____ ones = _____

thirty-two

4.

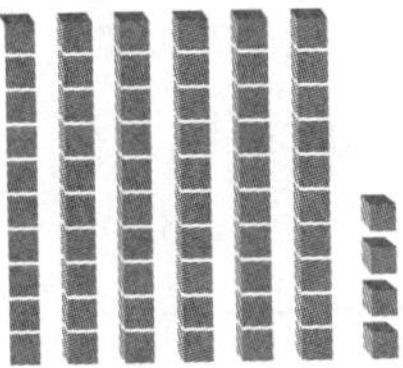

_____ tens and _____ ones = _____

sixty-four

Ring the value of the underlined digit.

5.

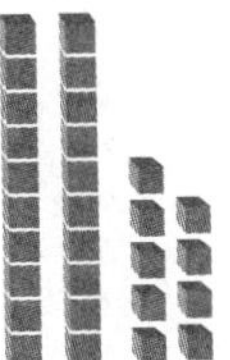

2<u>9</u>

99 ones   **20** tens   **9** ones

6.

<u>8</u>6

8 ones   **8** tens   **6** ones

7. 4<u>6</u>

60 ones   **4** ones   **6** ones

8. 9<u>0</u>

9 ones   **9** tens   **0** ones

Problem Solving Reasoning Fill in the blanks. Solve.

9.

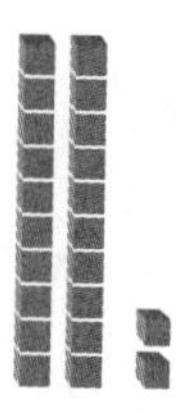

_____ tens _____ ones

10.

_____ tens _____ ones

How are these the same? Different? ______________________________

____

Quick Check

Write the number.

1.

10		30	40		60	70	80	

2.

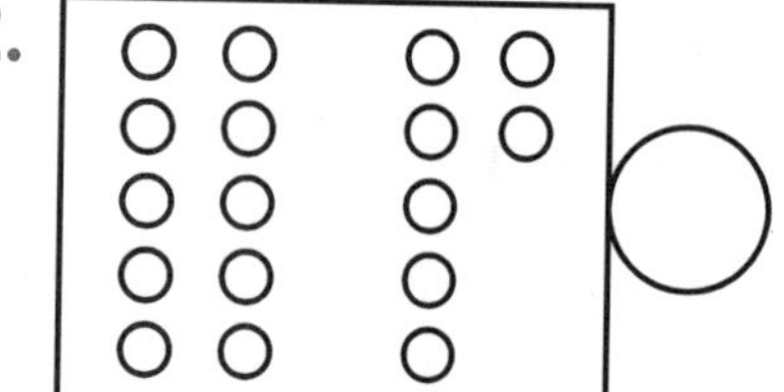

3.

Tens	Ones
4	3

= ___

Tens	Ones
8	7

= ___

4. Write how many tens and ones.

48 =

Tens	Ones

96 =

Tens	Ones

Name ____________________

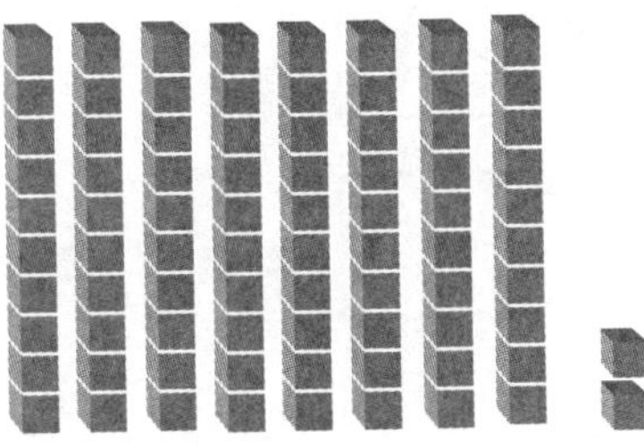

8 tens and **2** ones

80 + 2 = 82 or **8** tens **+ 2**

8 tens and **2** ones is the same as **80 + 2 = 82.**

Write the number three ways. You may use blocks.

1.

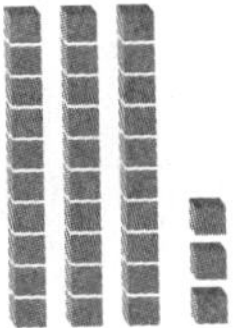

3 tens 3 ones

____ + ____

____

thirty-three

2.

____ tens ____ ones

____ + ____

____

seventy-two

3.

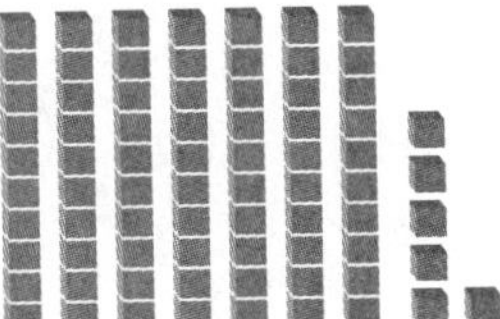

____ tens ____ ones

____ + ____

____

seventy-six

4.

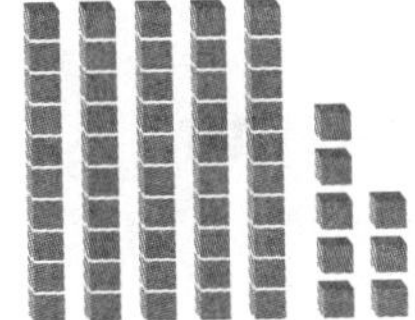

____ tens ____ ones

____ + ____

____

fifty-eight

Complete.

5. **2** tens and **1** one [20] + [ ] = [ ] or [ ] tens + **1**

6. **9** tens and **3** ones [ ] + [ ] = [ ] or **9** tens + [ ]

7. **4** tens and **9** ones [ ] + [ ] = [ ] or [ ] tens + **9**

8. **6** tens and **7** ones [ ] + [ ] = [ ] or **6** tens + [ ]

9. **20 + 3** = [2] tens and [3] ones = [ ] or twenty-three

10. **80 + 8** = [ ] tens and [ ] ones = [ ] or eighty-eight

11. **50 + 4** = [ ] tens and [ ] ones = [ ] or fifty-four

12. **70 + 5** = [ ] tens and [ ] ones = [ ] or seventy-five

13. **23** = [ ] tens and [ ] ones

14. **79** = [ ] tens and [ ] ones

15. **46** = [ ] tens and [ ] ones

16. **83** = [ ] tens and [ ] ones

17. **33** = [ ] tens and [ ] ones

18. **96** = [ ] tens and [ ] ones

19. **74** = [ ] tens and [ ] ones

20. **65** = [ ] tens and [ ] ones

★ Test Prep

Decide on an answer. Mark the space for your answer.
If the answer is **not here**, mark the space for **NH**.

21

40 + 3 = [ ]

23	36	43	53	NH
○	○	○	○	○

STANDARD

Name ______________________________

Count to 100. Complete the hundred chart.
Think about what numbers come before, after, and between.

1.

1	2		4					9	
		13		15			18		
21	22	23	24	25	26	27	28	29	30
31		33	34			37			
	42			45					
		53							
61					66				
	72							79	
81					86				
	92								100

Complete.

2. Skip-count by 2's. Ring those numbers.
3. Skip-count by 5's. Color those squares yellow.
4. Color the squares with 8 in the tens place blue.
5. Color the squares with 9 in the ones place red.

What comes before?

6. 80 , 81
___ , 30
___ , 56

7. 24 , 25
___ , 69
___ , 38

8. ___ , 40
___ , 81
___ , 26

What comes after?

9. 63, 64
89, ___
40, ___

10. 98, 99
85, ___
47, ___

11. 50, ___
64, ___
88, ___

What comes between?

12. 25, 26 , 27
49, ___ , 51
30, ___ , 32

13. 23, ___ , 25
38, ___ , 40
60, ___ , 62

14. 32, ___ , 34
58, ___ , 60
97, ___ , 99

Problem Solving Reasoning Use the hundred chart.

15. **10** more than **62**? ___

16. **10** less than **80**? ___

17. **10** less than **54**? ___

18. **10** more than **33**? ___

19. **1** more than **99**? ___

20. **1** less than **47**? ___

★ Test Prep

Which number is between 64 and 66?
Mark the space for your answer.

45	53	61	65
○	○	○	○

Name ______________________________

Problem

How many stamps are there?

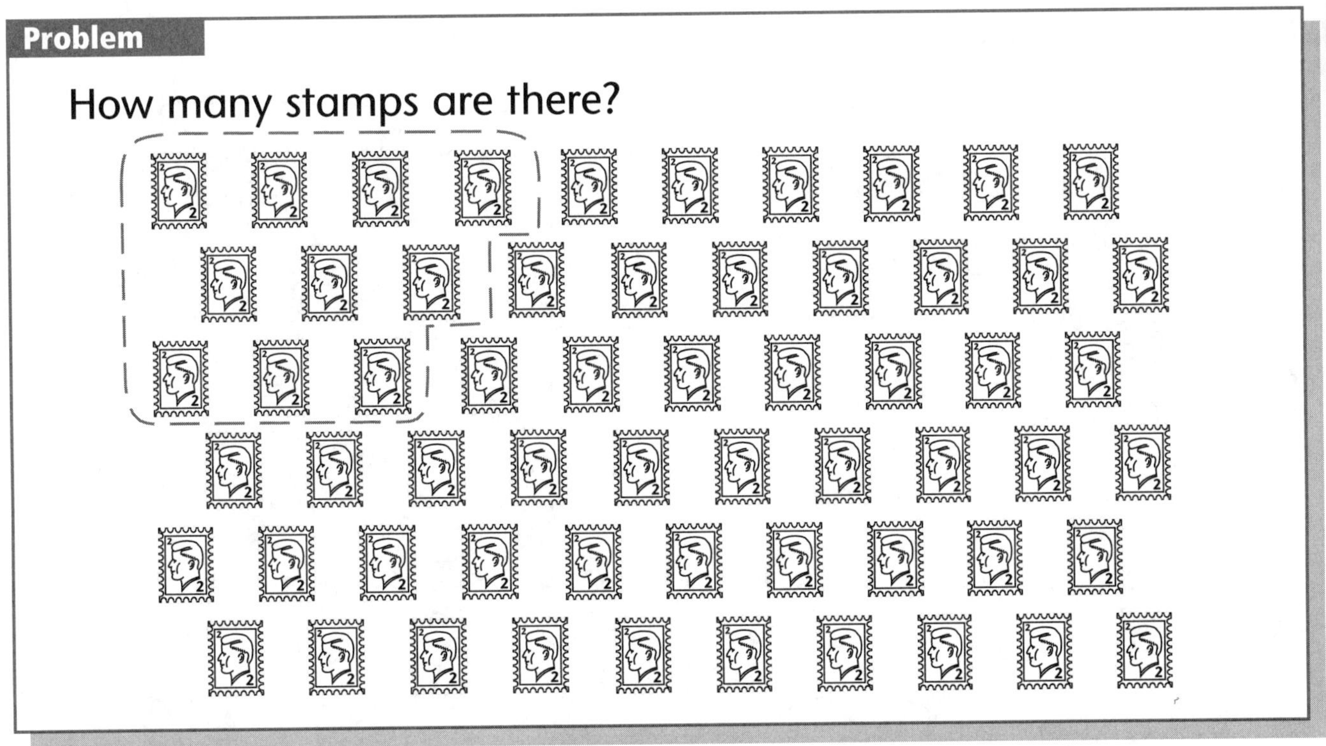

1 Understand

I need to find out how many stamps there are.

2 Decide

I can guess then check.

3 Solve

I'll think about **10** to help me guess.

My guess is ______ stamps.
I will ring groups of **10**.
I will count to check.

There are _____ stamps.

4 Look back

Does my answer make sense?

How many are there?
Guess, then check.

1.

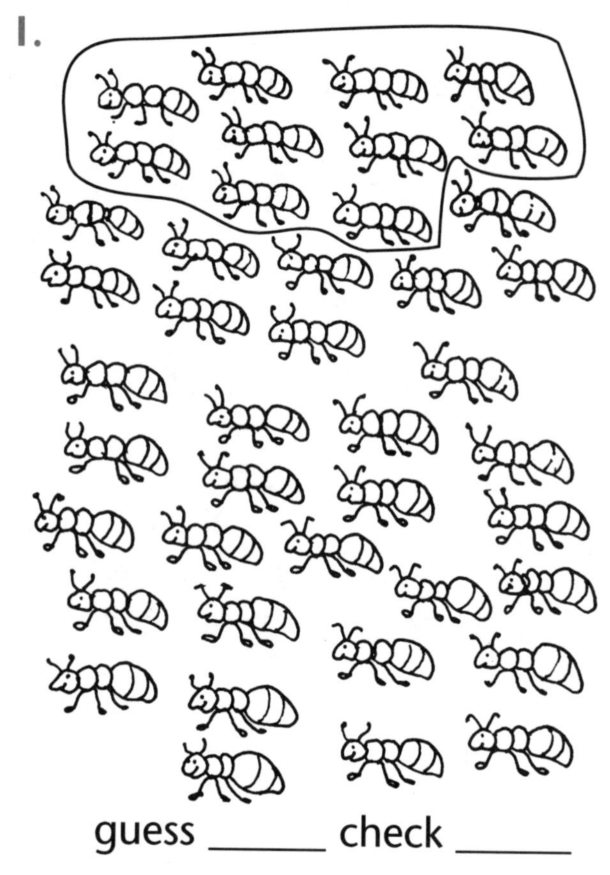

guess ______ check ______

2.

guess ______ check ______

3.

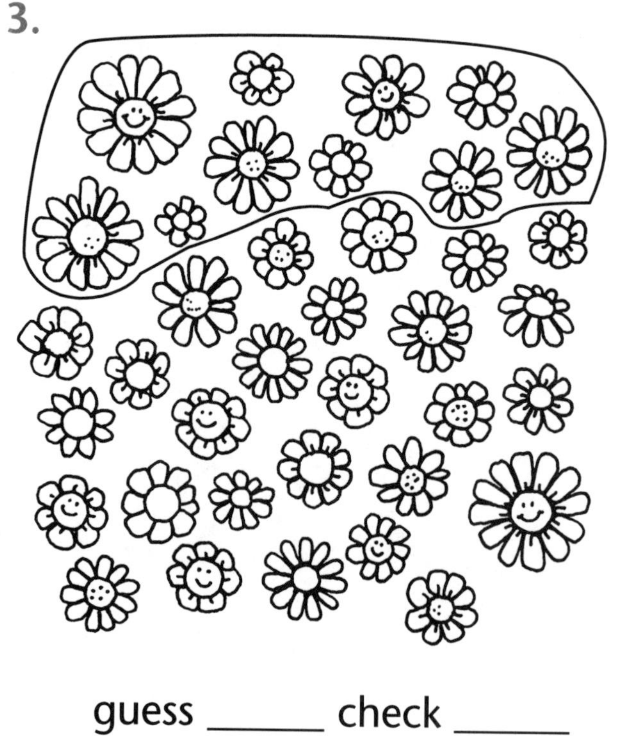

guess ______ check ______

4.

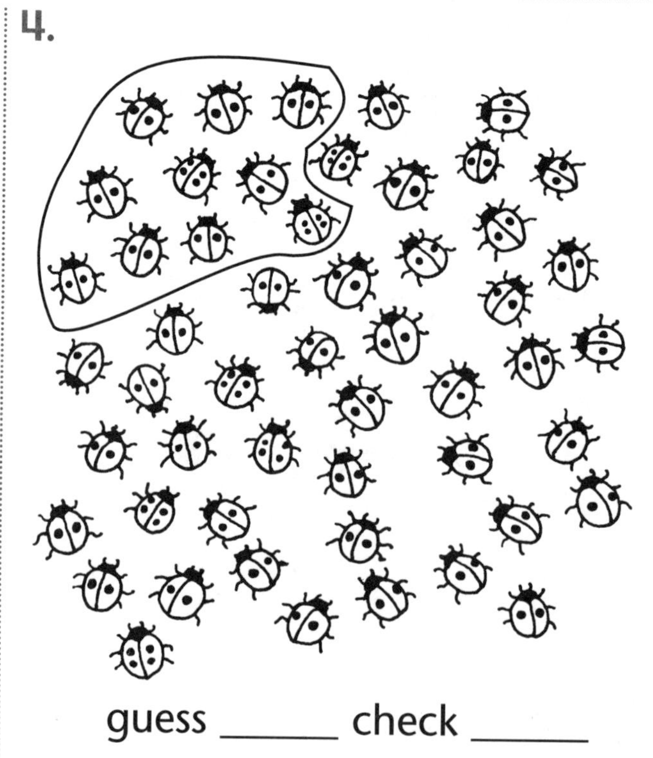

guess ______ check ______

Name ______________________________

Count by 2's.

1.

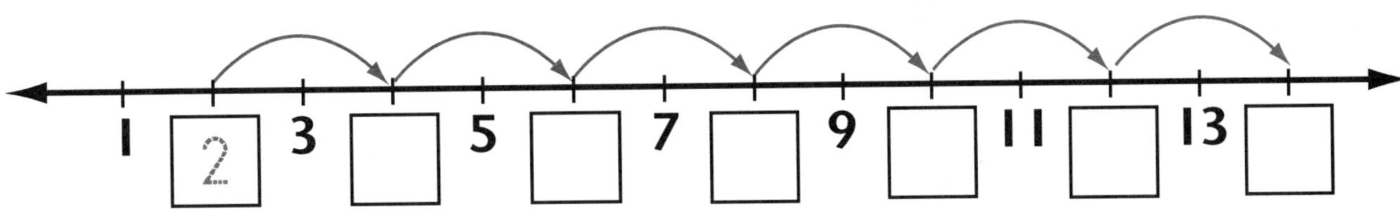

1 [2] 3 [ ] 5 [ ] 7 [ ] 9 [ ] 11 [ ] 13 [ ]

2. 2, __4__, 6, ____, ____, ____, 14, ____, ____, 20,

22, ____, 26, ____, ____, 32, ____, ____, ____, ____,

____, 44, ____, ____, ____, ____, 54, ____, ____, ____

Count by 3's.

3.

1 2 [3] 4 5 [ ] 7 8 [ ] 10 11 [ ] 13 14 [ ]

4. 3, 6, ____, ____, 15, ____, ____, 24, 27, ____,

33, ____, ____, ____, ____, 48, ____, ____, ____,

60, ____, 66, ____, ____, 75, ____, ____, ____

Count by 5's.

5.

5, 10, 15, ____, ____, ____, 30, ____, ____, 45, ____,

____, ____, 65, ____, ____, ____, 85, ____, ____

Count by 10's.

6.

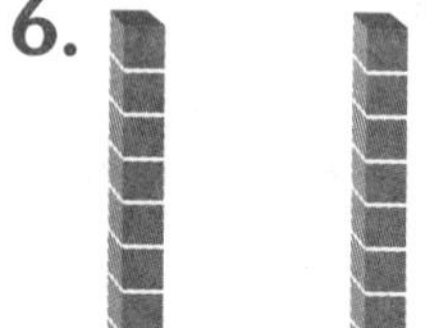
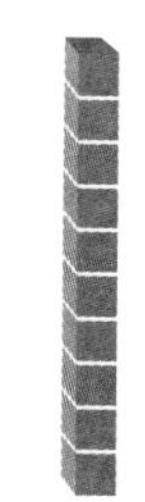
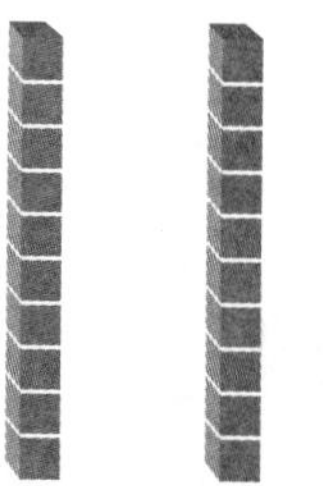
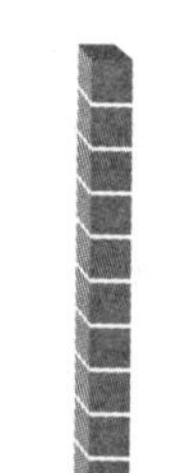
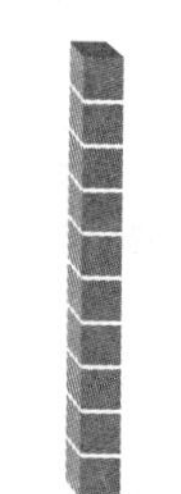
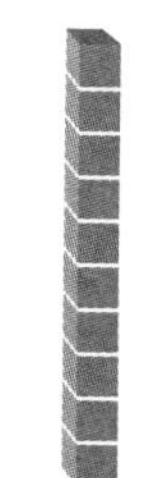

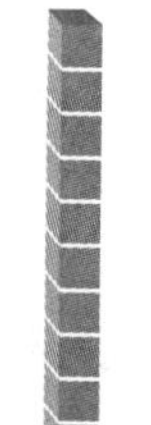
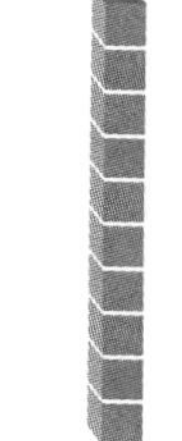

10, ____, ____, 40, ____, ____, ____, ____, ____, ____

Quick Check

Write the number.

1. 48 = ☐ tens and ☐ ones

☐ + ☐ = ☐

2. 53, ____, 55

Count by 2's.

3. ____, 14, ____, 18, 20, ____, ____

Name ____________________

We round numbers to the nearest ten to help us estimate. How do you round to the number 27?

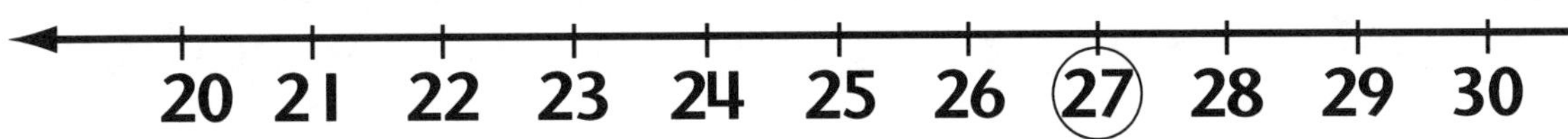

Find 27 on the number line.

27 is between 20 and 30.

27 is closer to 30 than to 20.

You round 27 to 30.

Find the number on the line.
Round the number to the nearest ten.

1.

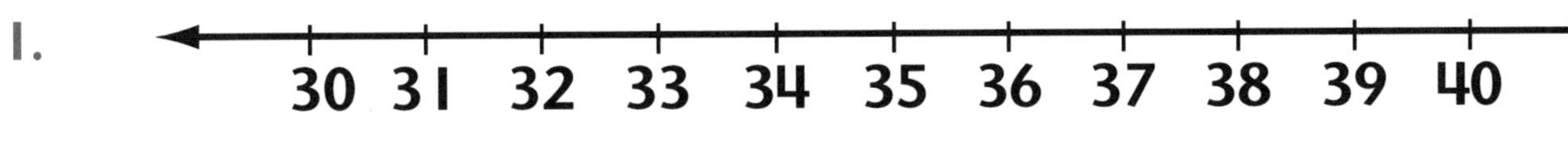

32 30 | 36 ____ | 38 ____ | 34 ____

37 ____ | 31 ____ | 33 ____ | 39 ____

2.

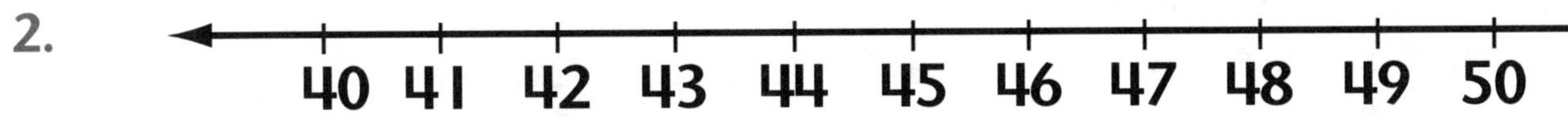

44 ____ | 48 ____ | 46 ____ | 43 ____

42 ____ | 49 ____ | 41 ____ | 47 ____

3.

60 61 62 63 64 65 66 67 68 69 70

66 ____ | 68 ____ | 63 ____ | 61 ____

62 ____ | 67 ____ | 64 ____ | 69 ____

Use the number line to help.
Round the number to the nearest ten.

4.

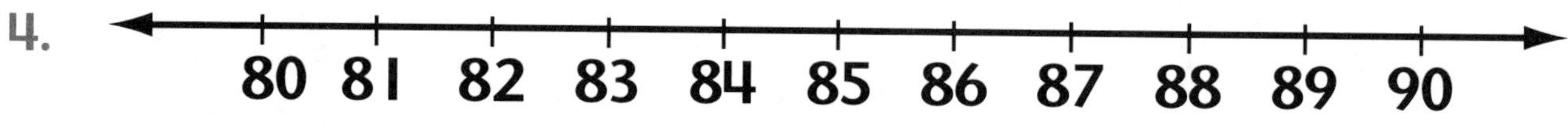

82 80	84 ____	88 ____	86 ____
89 ____	83 ____	81 ____	87 ____

5.

70 71 72 73 74 75 76 77 78 79 80

73 ____	71 ____	76 ____	79 ____
78 ____	72 ____	74 ____	77 ____

Problem Solving Reasoning

Solve.

6. Noah collects 38 flowers.
Tina collects 32 flowers.
Who collects the number of flowers closer to 30? ____________

7. Dee strings 54 beads.
John strings 56 beads.
Who strings the number of beads closer to 60? ____________

★ Test Prep

8 Round to the nearest ten. Mark the space for your answer.

86	80 ○	70 ○	76 ○	90 ○

Name ______________________________

Use the pictures to solve.
Write > or < .

1. Which number is greater?

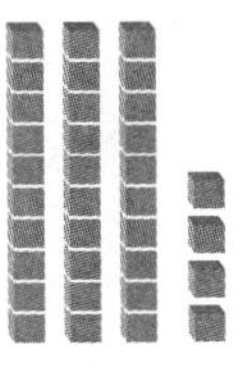

34

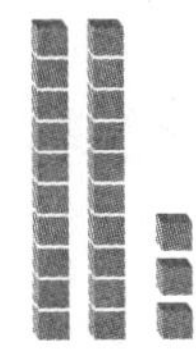

23

Think Are the tens the same? no

Which number has more tens? 34

Answer 34 (>) 23

34 is greater than 23

2. Which number is less?

42

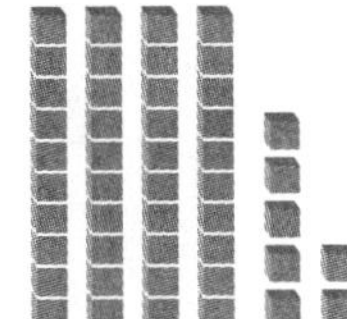

47

Think Are the tens the same? _____

The tens are the same so compare the ones.

Are the ones the same? _____

Which number has fewer ones? _____

Answer 42 ◯ 47

42 is __________ than 47

Use the pictures. Write the numbers.
Compare using >, <, or =.

3. 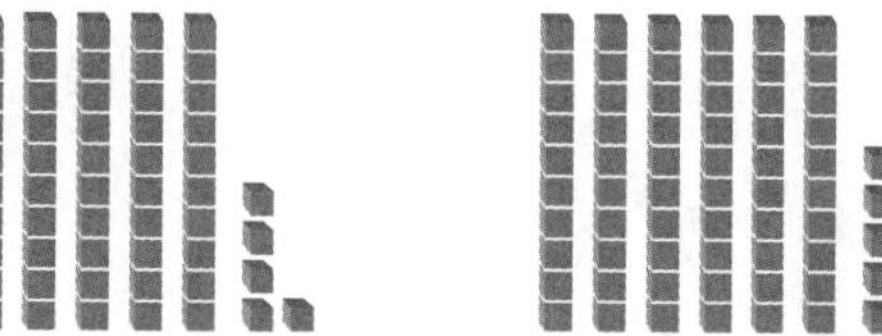

_____ _____

Answer _____ 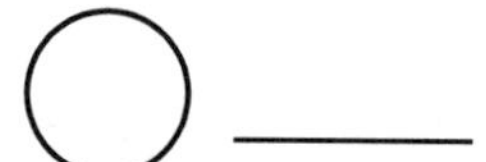 _____

4. 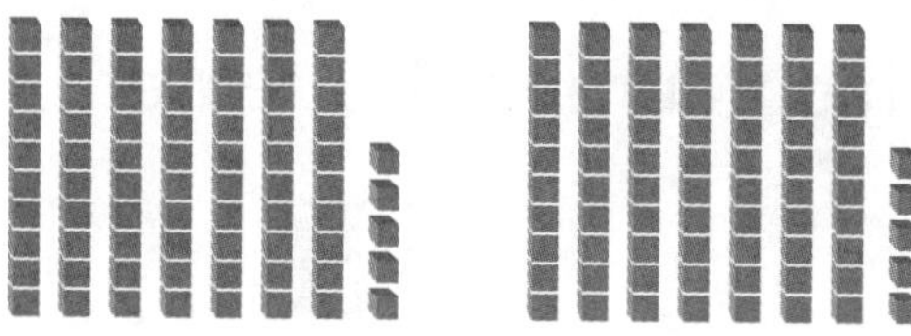

_____ _____

Answer _____ 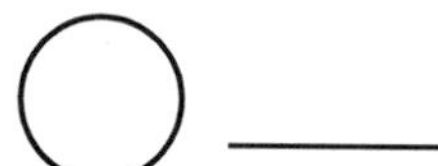 _____

Use the pictures. Write the numbers.
Write the numbers in order.

5. 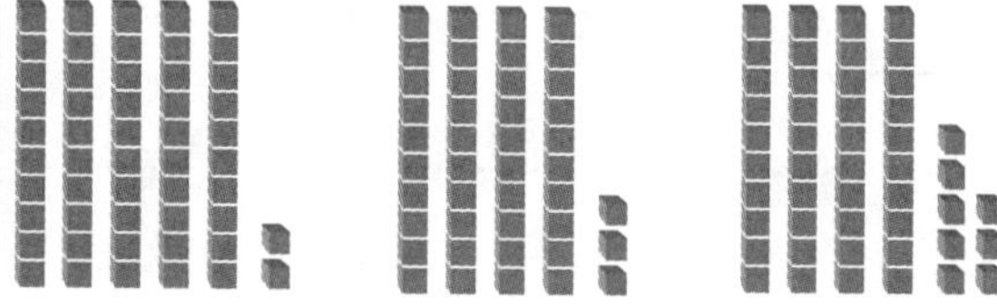

_____ _____ _____

Answer _____ _____ _____
least greatest

6. 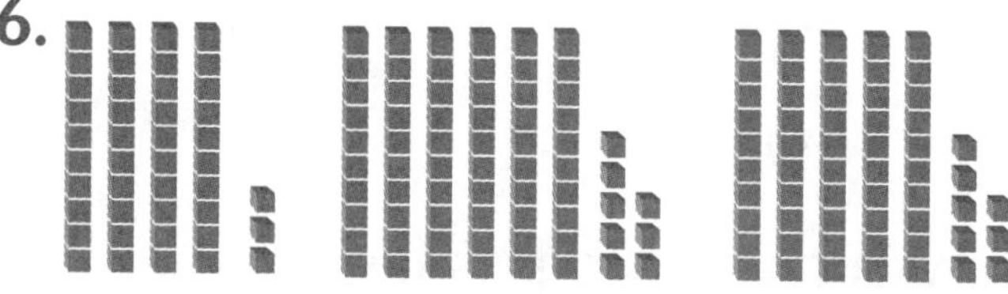

_____ _____ _____

Answer _____ _____ _____
greatest least

Extend Your Thinking

7. Circle the greatest number.

95 34 43 59

Explain how you know. _______________________________

____

Name ____________________

Complete.

1. 

In **10¢** there is __1__ dime.

In **10¢** there are __10__ pennies.

2. 

In **20¢** there are _____ dimes.

In **20¢** there are _____ pennies.

3.   

In **30¢** there are _____ dimes.

In **30¢** there are _____ pennies.

4.    

In **40¢** there are _____ dimes.

In **40¢** there are _____ pennies.

Count by 10's. Write the amount. Use the ¢.

5.  

__40¢__

6.   

_____

7.   

_____

8.   

_____

Ring the correct answer.

9. **4** dimes are worth

 **50¢** **20¢**

10. **1** dime is worth

50¢ **60¢** **10¢**

11. **7** dimes are worth

20¢ **90¢** **70¢**

12. **8** dimes are worth

50¢ **80¢** **90¢**

Write the amount. Use the ¢. Do you see a pattern?

13. one dime 10¢   four dimes ______   seven dimes ______

two dimes ______   five dimes ______   eight dimes ______

three dimes ______   six dimes ______   nine dimes ______

Problem Solving Reasoning Solve.

14. Shani has **3** dimes. Loni has **40¢**. Who has more money?

How do you know? ______________________________

____

____

★ Test Prep

What is the value of the coins? Mark the space for your answer.

36¢ ○   46¢ ○   50¢ ○   52¢ ○

Name ____________________

Think of the dime as 1 ten.

Complete.

1.

dimes 2 pennies 5

25¢

2.

dimes ☐ pennies ☐

☐¢

3.

dimes ☐ pennies ☐

☐¢

4.

dime ☐ pennies ☐

☐¢

5.

dimes ☐ pennies ☐

☐¢

6.

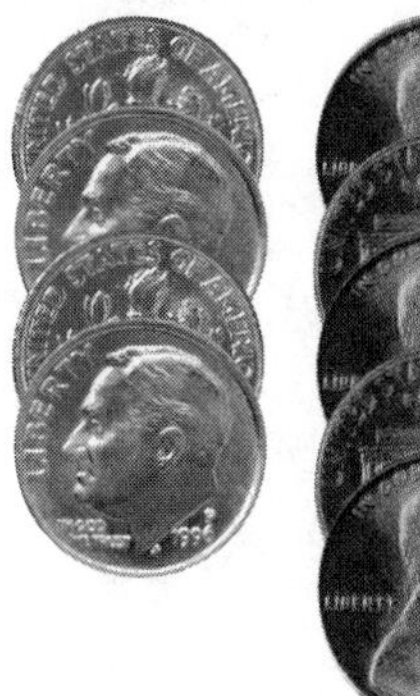

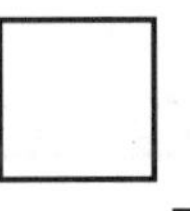

dimes ☐ pennies ☐

☐¢

Complete.

7. **25** cents

dimes [2] pennies [5]

25¢

8. **37** cents

dimes [ ] pennies [ ]

37¢

9. **60** cents

dimes [ ] pennies [ ]

60¢

Use > or <.

10.

70¢ (>) **30¢** **41¢** ( ) **14¢** **79¢** ( ) **97¢**

Complete.

11. In **85¢** there are __8__ dimes and __5__ pennies.

12. In **70¢** there are _____ dimes and _____ pennies.

✓ Quick Check

Solve.

Favorite Fruit

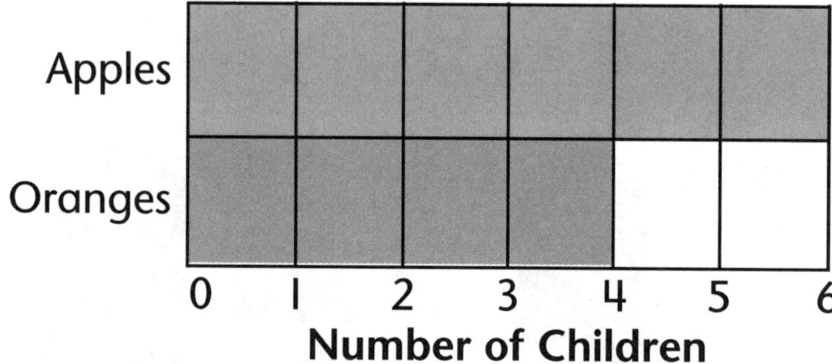

1. Read the graph.

   How many children like oranges? _____

2. In **50¢** there are _____ dimes.

3. In **63¢** there are _____ dimes

   and _____ pennies.

Name ____________________

Complete.

1.

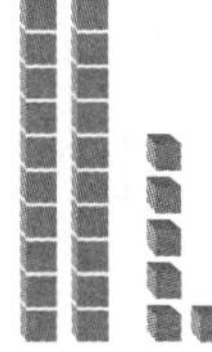

____ tens and ____ ones = ____

twenty-six

2.

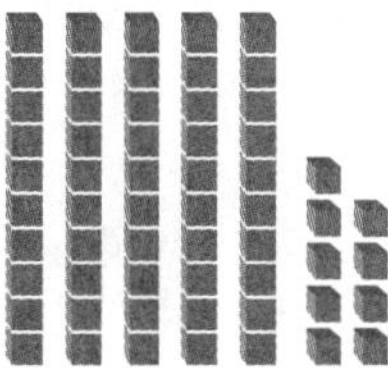

____ tens and ____ ones = ____

fifty-nine

Use >, <, or =.

3. **23** ◯ **59**

4. **36** ◯ **26**

5. **62** ◯ **24**

6. **16** ◯ **39**

7. **63¢** ◯ **83¢**

8. **91¢** ◯ **19¢**

9. **76¢** ◯ **76¢**

10. **46¢** ◯ **4¢**

Ring the greatest number.

11. **9** **20** **12**

Ring the least number.

12. **44** **55** **88**

What comes

before?	between?	after?
13. ____ , **18**	15. **16,** ____ , **18**	17. **16,** ____
14. ____ , **27**	16. **17,** ____ , **19**	18. **14,** ____

Complete.

19.

	Tens	Ones
53		
19		
26		

20.

Tens	Ones	
7	3	
9	9	
8	5	

Complete.

21. **2** tens and **3** ones = ☐ + ☐ = ☐

22. **8** tens and **6** ones = ☐ + ☐ = ☐

Count by 2's.

23.

10	12						24		

Count by 3's.

24.

3	6						24		

Match.

25. **8** dimes **5** pennies — **18¢**

26. **5** dimes **9** pennies — **59¢**

27. **1** dime **8** pennies — **85¢**

Problem Solving Reasoning

How many are there?
Guess then check.

28.

guess ______ check ______

Name ______________________________

1

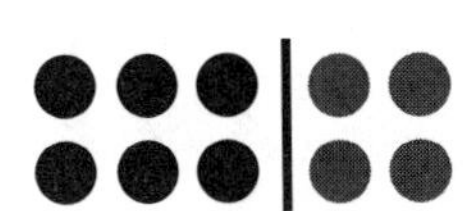

○ 6 + 3 = 9 ○ 4 + 7 = 11

○ 10 − 5 = 5 ○ 10 − 4 = 6

2

7 = 12 − 5	14 > 6 + 6	13 − 8 > 14	2 + 9 < 13
○	○	○	○

3

49		51

47	48	50	52
○	○	○	○

4

7 tens and 9 ones

77	79	85	97
○	○	○	○

5

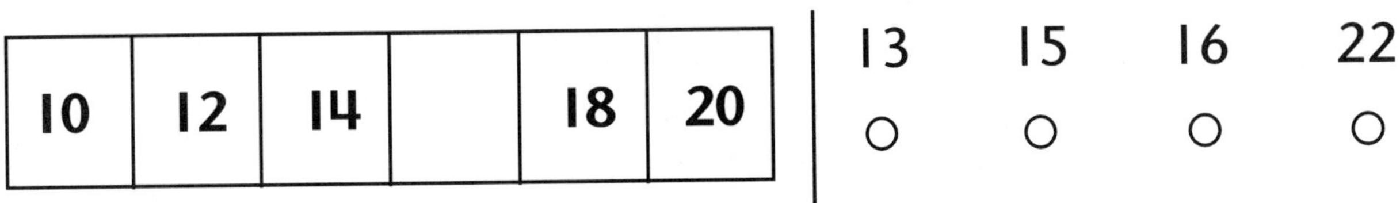

10	12	14		18	20

13	15	16	22
○	○	○	○

6

4 dimes	5 dimes	6 dimes	9 dimes
○	○	○	○

Decide on an answer. Mark the space for your answer.
If the answer is **not here**, mark the space for **NH**.

$$\begin{array}{r} 7 \\ +\square \\ \hline 8 \end{array}$$

5	4	2	1	NH
○	○	○	○	○

8

$$\begin{array}{r} 5 \\ +\ 7 \\ \hline \square \end{array}$$

12	10	7	5	NH
○	○	○	○	○

9

$$\begin{array}{r} 6 \\ 3 \\ +\ 2 \\ \hline \square \end{array}$$

12	9	8	5	NH
○	○	○	○	○

10

$$\begin{array}{r} 3 \\ 3 \\ +\ 3 \\ \hline \square \end{array}$$

3	6	7	9	NH
○	○	○	○	○

UNIT 3 • TABLE OF CONTENTS

Addition and Subtraction Facts through 20

We will be using this vocabulary:

addend one of the numbers added in an addition problem

sum result of an addition problem

fact family related addition and subtraction facts

order property Changing the order of the addends does not change the sum. $8 + 7 = 15$; $7 + 8 = 15$

grouping property Changing the grouping of the addends does not change the sum. $7 + (2 + 8) = 17$; $(7 + 2) + 8 = 17$

Dear Family,

During the next few weeks our math class will be learning and practicing addition and subtraction facts through 20. This is an extension of what we learned in Unit 1.

You can expect to see homework that provides practice with addition and subtraction facts.

As we learn about related facts and fact families, you may wish to keep the following sample as a guide.

Related Facts

$9 + 8 = 17$ $\quad$ $17 - 8 = 9$

Fact Family

$\begin{array}{r} 7 \\ +\,9 \\ \hline 16 \end{array}$ $\quad$ $\begin{array}{r} 9 \\ +\,7 \\ \hline 16 \end{array}$ $\quad$ $\begin{array}{r} 16 \\ -\,9 \\ \hline 7 \end{array}$ $\quad$ $\begin{array}{r} 16 \\ -\,7 \\ \hline 9 \end{array}$

Knowing addition facts can help children learn the related subtraction facts.

Sincerely,

Name ______________________________

Look at the picture and the facts.

$9 + 7 = 16$

$16 - 7 = 9$

Tell how they are related.

____

Complete. Then write a related addition or subtraction fact.

1. $7 + 8 = \boxed{15}$
   $15 - 8 = 7$

2. $16 - 8 = \boxed{8}$
   $8 + 8 = 16$

3. $5 + 9 = \square$
   ____

4. $6 + 8 = \square$
   ____

5. $15 - 9 = \square$
   ____

6. $7 + 7 = \square$
   ____

Complete. Then write a related addition or subtraction fact.

7.

$$\begin{array}{r} 8 \\ +\ 7 \\ \hline 15 \end{array} \qquad \begin{array}{r} 15 \\ -\ 7 \\ \hline 8 \end{array}$$

8.

$$\begin{array}{r} 14 \\ -\ 6 \\ \hline 8 \end{array} \qquad \begin{array}{r} 8 \\ +\ 6 \\ \hline 14 \end{array}$$

9.

$$\begin{array}{r} 9 \\ +\ 7 \\ \hline \end{array} \qquad \begin{array}{r} \\ -\ \_\_ \\ \hline \end{array}$$

10.

$$\begin{array}{r} 16 \\ -\ 8 \\ \hline \end{array} \qquad \begin{array}{r} \\ +\ \_\_ \\ \hline \end{array}$$

11.

$$\begin{array}{r} 15 \\ -\ 9 \\ \hline \end{array} \qquad \begin{array}{r} \\ +\ \_\_ \\ \hline \end{array}$$

12.

$$\begin{array}{r} 8 \\ +\ 8 \\ \hline \end{array} \qquad \begin{array}{r} \\ -\ \_\_ \\ \hline \end{array}$$

13.

$$\begin{array}{r} 6 \\ +\ 9 \\ \hline \end{array} \qquad \begin{array}{r} \\ -\ \_\_ \\ \hline \end{array}$$

14.

$$\begin{array}{r} 7 \\ +\ 9 \\ \hline \end{array} \qquad \begin{array}{r} \\ -\ \_\_ \\ \hline \end{array}$$

15.

$$\begin{array}{r} 10 \\ +\ 4 \\ \hline \end{array} \qquad \begin{array}{r} \\ -\ \_\_ \\ \hline \end{array}$$

16.

$$\begin{array}{r} 15 \\ -\ 8 \\ \hline \end{array} \qquad \begin{array}{r} \\ +\ \_\_ \\ \hline \end{array}$$

17.

$$\begin{array}{r} 16 \\ -\ 9 \\ \hline \end{array} \qquad \begin{array}{r} \\ +\ \_\_ \\ \hline \end{array}$$

Practice your facts. Complete.

18. 9 + ____ = 15

____ + 5 = 14

____ + 7 = 14

4 + ____ = 13

____ + 8 = 15

19. 16 = 9 + ____

15 = ____ + 6

15 = 9 + ____

16 = ____ + 7

14 = 8 + ____

20. 16 = ____ + 8

____ + 7 = 15

____ + 8 = 16

6 + ____ = 15

9 + ____ = 14

Complete the names for the number.

21. 

8 + ☐	6 + ☐	7 + ☐	9 + ☐

22. 

9 + ☐	7 + ☐	8 + ☐	10 + ☐

23. 

6 + ☐	7 + ☐	9 + ☐	8 + ☐

Use >, <, or =.

24. 13 ◯ 9 + 7

12 ◯ 6 + 5

25. 16 ◯ 7 + 8

10 ◯ 4 + 5

26. 8 ◯ 12 − 4

15 ◯ 8 + 4

Problem Solving Reasoning Solve.

27. Gina has **15** shells.
She gives away **8** shells.
How many shells does she have left?

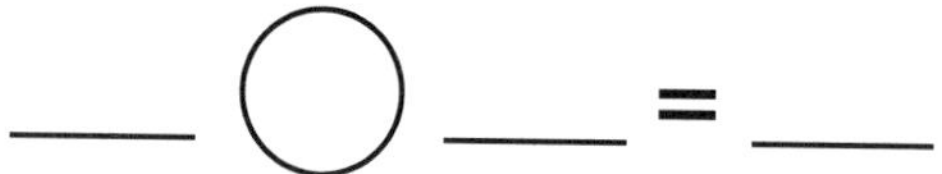

_____ shells

28. Arno has **8** blocks.
Lucy has **6** blocks.
How many blocks do they have in all?

____ ◯ ____ = ____

_____ blocks

29. How many shells are there?
Guess then check.

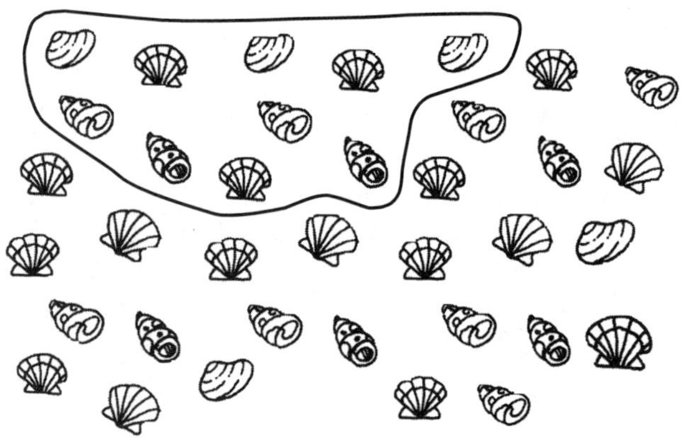

guess _____ check _____

30. How many blocks are there?
Guess then check.

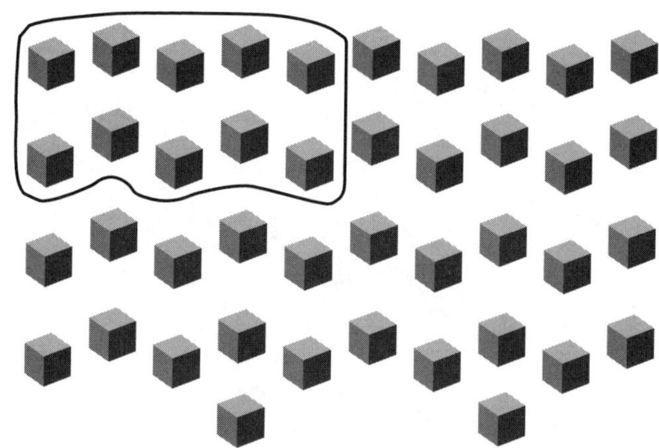

guess _____ check _____

★ **Test Prep**

Mark the related fact. Mark the space for your answer.

31

9 + 7 = 16

○ **16 − 7 = 9**

○ **6 + 8 = 14**

○ **9 − 6 = 3**

○ **8 + 7 = 15**

Name ______________________

Complete the fact family.

1.

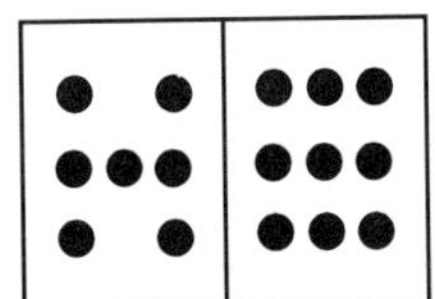

7 + 9 = [16]

9 + 7 = [16]

16 − 9 = [7]

16 − 7 = [9]

2.

8 + 7 = [15]

____ + ____ = [ ]

____ − ____ = [ ]

____ − ____ = [ ]

3.

7 + 6 = [ ]

____ + ____ = [ ]

____ − ____ = [ ]

____ − ____ = [ ]

4.

9 + 6 = [ ]

____ + ____ = [ ]

____ − ____ = [ ]

____ − ____ = [ ]

5.

4 + 9 = [ ]

____ + ____ = [ ]

____ − ____ = [ ]

____ − ____ = [ ]

6.

6 + 6 = [ ]

____ − ____ = [ ]

Write the fact family.

7. 7, 9, 16

$$\begin{array}{r} 7 \\ +9 \\ \hline 16 \end{array} \quad \begin{array}{r} 9 \\ +7 \\ \hline 16 \end{array} \quad \begin{array}{r} 16 \\ -9 \\ \hline 7 \end{array} \quad \begin{array}{r} 16 \\ -7 \\ \hline 9 \end{array}$$

8. 6, 8, 14

$$\begin{array}{r} 6 \\ +8 \\ \hline \end{array} \quad \begin{array}{r} + \\ \hline \end{array} \quad \begin{array}{r} - \\ \hline \end{array} \quad \begin{array}{r} - \\ \hline \end{array}$$

9. 9, 5, 14

$$\begin{array}{r} + \\ \hline \end{array} \quad \begin{array}{r} + \\ \hline \end{array} \quad \begin{array}{r} - \\ \hline \end{array} \quad \begin{array}{r} - \\ \hline \end{array}$$

10. 7, 7, 14

$$\begin{array}{r} + \\ \hline \end{array} \quad \begin{array}{r} - \\ \hline \end{array}$$

Problem Solving
Reasoning

11. Why are there only two facts for the fact family in exercise 10?

___

___

___

★ Test Prep

Which of these completes the fact family? Mark the space for your answer.

12

8 + 8 = 16

○ 8 + 7 = 15 ○ 16 − 8 = 8

○ 6 + 8 = 14 ○ 16 − 9 = 7

Name ____________________

STANDARD

Problem Solving Plan
1. Understand 2. Decide 3. Solve 4. Look back

Solve.

1. There are **15** cows.
There is **1** hen.
6 cows are black.
How many cows are not black?

Think Is there too much information?
I will ring what I do not need.

_____ ◯ _____ = ☐

Answer _____ cows

2. There are **6** horses in the barn.
There are **3** cows.
There are **8** horses in the field.
How many horses are there in all?

Think Is there too much information?
I will ring what I do not need.

_____ ◯ _____ = ☐

Answer _____ horses

Ring the information you do not need.
Solve.

3. There are **15** chickens.
7 chickens are white.
6 cats are black.
How many chickens are not white?

Answer ____ chickens

4. There are **8** baskets of white eggs.
There are **8** baskets of brown eggs.
José saw **3** birds.
How many baskets of eggs are there?

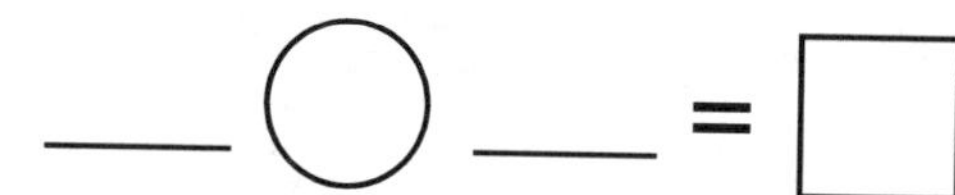

Answer ______ baskets of eggs

5. There are **9** big ducks.
There are **5** little ducks.
There are **7** little pigs.
How many ducks are there in all?

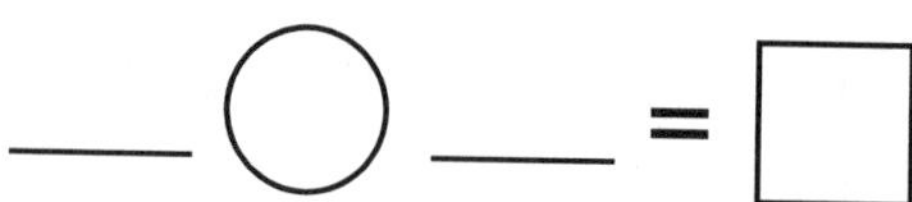

Answer ______ ducks

6. There are **16** horses.
8 chickens are white.
7 horses run away.
How many horses are left?

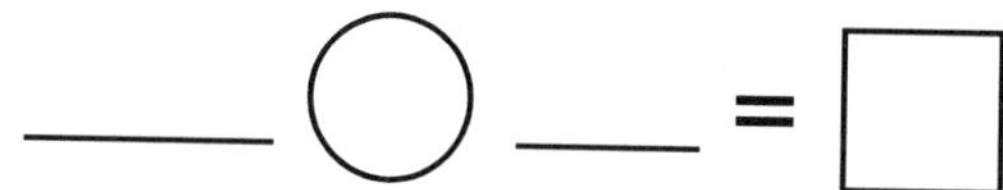

Answer ____ horses

Extend Your Thinking

7. How do you know your answer to exercise 6 is correct?
Draw or write to explain.

Name ___________________________

How does knowing the addition fact help you remember the subtraction fact?

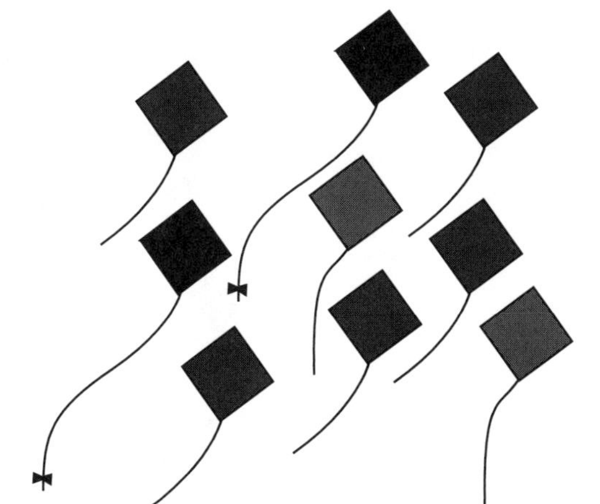

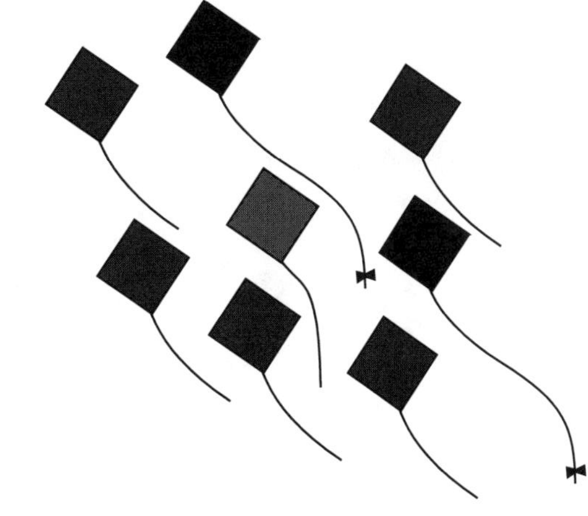

$9 + 8 = 17$

$17 - 8 = ?$

Complete. Then write a related addition or subtraction fact.

1. $16 - 9 = \boxed{7}$

   7 + 9 = 16

2. $7 + 9 = \square$

   ____

3. $8 + 8 = \square$

   ____

4. $17 - 9 = \square$

   ____

5. $15 - 8 = \square$

   ____

6. $6 + 9 = \square$

   ____

Complete. Then write a related addition or subtraction fact.

7.
$$\begin{array}{r} 7 \\ +\ 8 \\ \hline 15 \end{array} \qquad \begin{array}{r} 15 \\ -\ 8 \\ \hline 7 \end{array}$$

8.
$$\begin{array}{r} 17 \\ -\ 8 \\ \hline 9 \end{array} \qquad \begin{array}{r} 9 \\ +\ 8 \\ \hline 17 \end{array}$$

9.
$$\begin{array}{r} 7 \\ +\ 9 \\ \hline \end{array} \qquad \begin{array}{r} \\ -\ \\ \hline \end{array}$$

10.
$$\begin{array}{r} 9 \\ +\ 9 \\ \hline \end{array} \qquad \begin{array}{r} \\ -\ \\ \hline \end{array}$$

11.
$$\begin{array}{r} 16 \\ -\ 8 \\ \hline \end{array} \qquad \begin{array}{r} \\ +\ \\ \hline \end{array}$$

12.
$$\begin{array}{r} 15 \\ -\ 8 \\ \hline \end{array} \qquad \begin{array}{r} \\ +\ \\ \hline \end{array}$$

13.
$$\begin{array}{r} 13 \\ -\ 7 \\ \hline \end{array} \qquad \begin{array}{r} \\ +\ \\ \hline \end{array}$$

14.
$$\begin{array}{r} 9 \\ +\ 6 \\ \hline \end{array} \qquad \begin{array}{r} \\ -\ \\ \hline \end{array}$$

Practice your facts. Complete.

15. 9 + ____ = 16

____ + 8 = 18

9 + ____ = 14

16. 15 = 9 + ____

15 = ____ + 6

18 = ____ + 9

17. ☐ = 7 + 7

☐ = 5 + 8

14 = ____ + 5

Write the missing addends.

18.

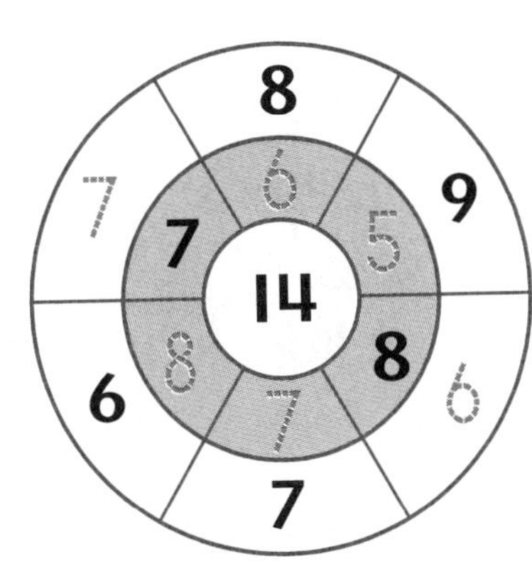

19.

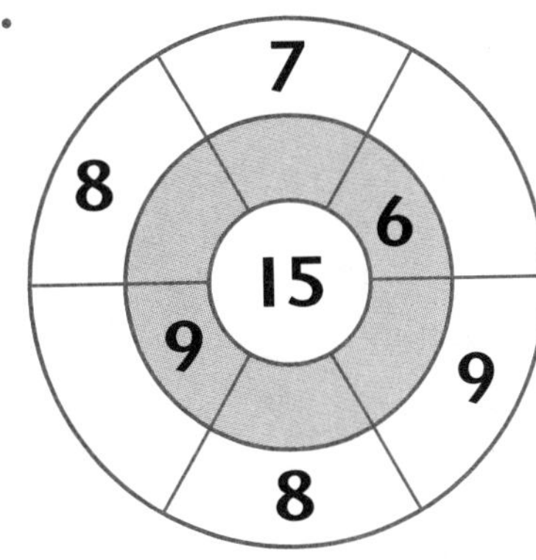

20.

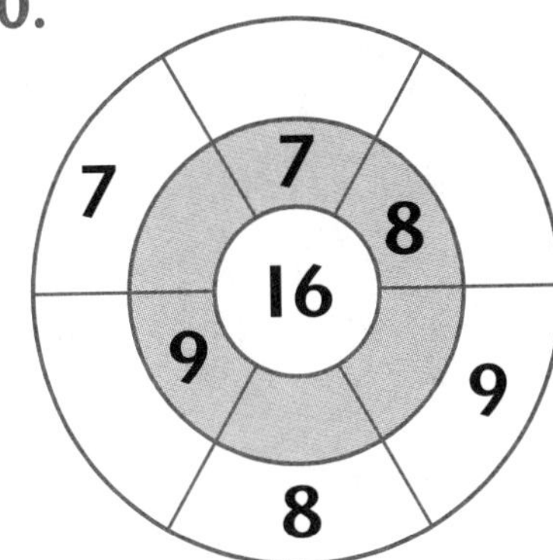

Use >, <, or =.

21. 4 + 7 ◯ 12

8 + 5 ◯ 13

10 − 7 ◯ 11

22. 16 − 9 ◯ 8

15 − 8 ◯ 5

9 + 9 ◯ 17

23. 8 + 6 ◯ 14

14 − 8 ◯ 6

7 + 6 ◯ 17

Problem Solving Reasoning Choose the operation. Solve.

24. Kodia has **17** balloons. She gives Dawn **9** balloons. How many balloons does Kodia have now?

____ ◯ ____ = ____

____ balloons

25. Aaron sees **8** blue kites in the sky. Jody sees **8** red kites in the sky. How many kites do Aaron and Jody see together?

____ ◯ ____ = ____

____ kites

Problem Solving Reasoning

Do you need all the information? Ring what you do not need. Solve.

26. There are **6** kites with long tails. There are **9** kites with short tails.
The kites are high in the sky.
How many kites are there in all?

____ ◯ ____ = ____

____ kites

27. Pablo sees **4** kites.
He sees **17** balloons.
9 balloons pop.
How many balloons does he see now?

____ ◯ ____ = ____

____ balloons

Quick Check

Complete. Match the related fact.

1. 18 − 9 = 9	9 + 8 = ☐
16 − 8 = 8	16 − 9 = ☐
7 + 9 = 16	8 + 8 = ☐
17 − 8 = 9	9 + 9 = ☐

Complete the fact family.

2. $\begin{array}{r} 7 \\ +8 \\ \hline \end{array}$ + ____   − ____   − ____

3. $\begin{array}{r} 9 \\ +8 \\ \hline \end{array}$ + ____   − ____   − ____

Name ____________________

Complete the fact family.

1.

★★★ ★★★
★★★ ★★
★★★ ★★★

9 + 8 = 17

8 + 9 = 17

17 − 8 = 9

17 − 9 = 8

2.

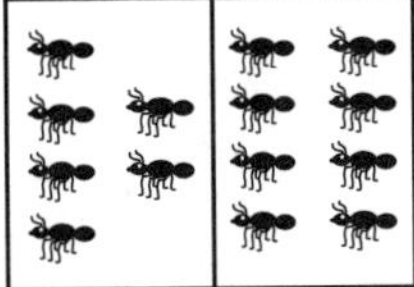

6 + 8 = ☐

___ + ___ = ☐

___ − ___ = ☐

___ − ___ = ☐

3.

9 + 7 = ☐

___ + ___ = ☐

___ − ___ = ☐

___ − ___ = ☐

4.

8 + 8 = ☐

___ − ___ = ☐

5.

9 + 6 = ☐

___ + ___ = ☐

___ − ___ = ☐

___ − ___ = ☐

6.

8 + 7 = ☐

___ + ___ = ☐

___ − ___ = ☐

___ − ___ = ☐

Write the fact family.

7. 8, 9, 17

$$\begin{array}{r} 8 \\ +9 \\ \hline 17 \end{array} \quad \begin{array}{r} 9 \\ +8 \\ \hline 17 \end{array} \quad \begin{array}{r} 17 \\ -9 \\ \hline 8 \end{array} \quad \begin{array}{r} 17 \\ -8 \\ \hline 9 \end{array}$$

8. 9, 9, 18

$$\begin{array}{r} 9 \\ +9 \\ \hline \end{array} \quad \begin{array}{r} - \\ \hline \end{array}$$

9. 9, 8, 17

$+$ ___ $+$ ___ $-$ ___ $-$ ___

10. 6, 9, 15

$+$ ___ $+$ ___ $-$ ___ $-$ ___

11. 4, 9, 13

$+$ ___ $+$ ___ $-$ ___ $-$ ___

12. 8, 6, 14

$+$ ___ $+$ ___ $-$ ___ $-$ ___

★ Test Prep

Which number sentence belongs to the fact family?
Mark the space next to your answer.

13

9, 7, 16

○ $16 - 8 = 8$

○ $16 - 7 = 9$

○ $7 + 8 = 15$

○ $9 + 8 = 17$

Name ____________________

Complete. Then write the fact another way.

1. 5 + 8 = [13]
8 + 5 = 13

2. 9 + 8 = [ ]
___ + ___ = 17

3. 6 + 9 = [ ]
___ + ___ = [ ]

4. 4 + 9 = [ ]
___ + ___ = [ ]

5. 8 + 7 = [ ]
___ + ___ = [ ]

6. 7 + 9 = [ ]
___ + ___ = [ ]

7. 6 + 8 = [ ]
___ + ___ = [ ]

8. 9 + 5 = [ ]
___ + ___ = [ ]

Complete the number sentence.

9. (7 + 2) + 8 =
9 + 8 = [ ]

10. 9 + (3 + 6) =
___ + ___ = [ ]

11. 6 + (4 + 5) =
___ + ___ = [ ]

12. 8 + (4 + 2) =
___ + ___ = [ ]

13. 3 + (5 + 4) =
___ + ___ = [ ]

14. 7 + (5 + 4) =
___ + ___ = [ ]

Complete. Then write the fact another way.

15. $\begin{array}{r} 9 \\ +\ 8 \\ \hline 17 \end{array}$ $\begin{array}{r} 8 \\ +\ \boxed{9} \\ \hline 17 \end{array}$

16. $\begin{array}{r} 7 \\ +\ 9 \\ \hline \end{array}$ $\begin{array}{r} 9 \\ +\ \boxed{} \\ \hline \end{array}$

17. $\begin{array}{r} 6 \\ +\ 8 \\ \hline \end{array}$ $\begin{array}{r} \\ + \\ \hline 14 \end{array}$

18. $\begin{array}{r} 6 \\ +\ 7 \\ \hline 13 \end{array}$ $\begin{array}{r} + \\ \hline \end{array}$

19. $\begin{array}{r} 7 \\ +\ 8 \\ \hline \end{array}$ $\begin{array}{r} + \\ \hline \end{array}$

20. $\begin{array}{r} 9 \\ +\ \boxed{} \\ \hline 12 \end{array}$ $\begin{array}{r} + \\ \hline \end{array}$

Group. Then find the sums.

21. $\begin{array}{r} 3 \\ 4 \\ +\ 7 \\ \hline \end{array}$ (3 + 4 grouped: 7) $\begin{array}{r} 5 \\ 4 \\ +\ 7 \\ \hline \end{array}$ $\begin{array}{r} 8 \\ 1 \\ +\ 4 \\ \hline \end{array}$ $\begin{array}{r} 6 \\ 3 \\ +\ 7 \\ \hline \end{array}$ $\begin{array}{r} 4 \\ 5 \\ +\ 6 \\ \hline \end{array}$ $\begin{array}{r} 3 \\ 6 \\ +\ 8 \\ \hline \end{array}$

Problem Solving
Reasoning

22. Show how you would group 4 + 6 + 8 = ☐ to add.

Explain why. ______________________________

____

★ Test Prep

23 Solve. Mark your answer.

8 + 5 + 2 = ☐

19	18	15	12
○	○	○	○

STANDARD

Name ______________________________

Complete the tables.

1. Add 5.

9	14
4	
8	
6	
7	

2. Add 6.

8	
10	
7	
5	
9	

3. Add 8.

7	
5	
8	
9	
6	

4. Subtract 9.

17	8
15	
18	
14	
12	

5. Subtract 8.

15	
13	
12	
17	
14	

6. Subtract 7.

16	
14	
12	
9	
13	

Complete the rule.

7. Subtract 5.

14	9
8	3
12	7
11	6
13	8

8. Add _____.

7	14
9	16
5	12
8	15
4	11

9. Subtract _____.

14	8
11	5
15	9
10	4
13	7

Solve.

10. $6 + \square = 14$

11. $8 + \square = 15$

12. $5 + \square = 12$

13. $9 + \square = 17$

Problem Solving Reasoning Solve.

14. Andy finds **16** frogs before and after school.
He finds **7** frogs before school.
How many frogs does he find after school?

____ frogs

Quick Check

Write the fact family.

1. **9, 8, 17**

+ ___   + ___   − ___   − ___

Solve.

2. $\begin{array}{r} 6 \\ 3 \\ +\ 7 \\ \hline \end{array}$

Complete the rule.

3. **Add ____.**

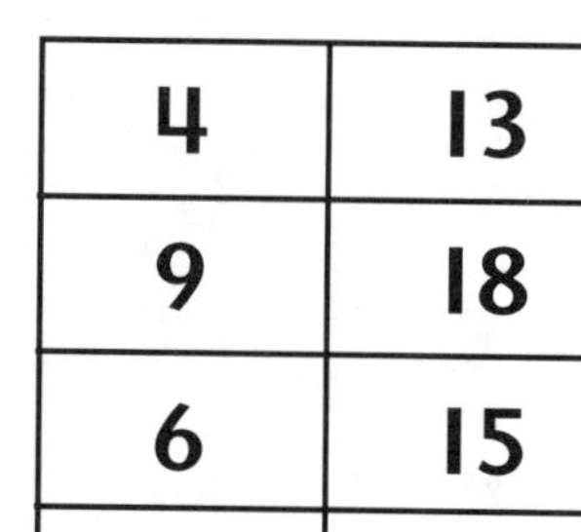

4	13
9	18
6	15
2	11

Name ____________________

Solve.

1. $10 + 1 =$ [11]

$10 + 2 =$ [ ]

$10 + 3 =$ [ ]

$10 + 4 =$ [ ]

$10 + 5 =$ [ ]

2. $11 - 1 =$ [10]

$12 - 2 =$ [ ]

$13 - 3 =$ [ ]

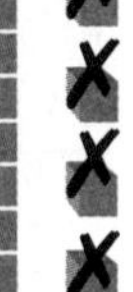

$14 - 4 =$ [ ]

$15 - 5 =$ [ ]

Problem Solving
Reasoning

3. What pattern do you see in exercise 2? ____________________

____

Solve.

4.
$20 - 10 =$ 10
$19 - 10 =$ ☐
$18 - 10 =$ ☐
$17 - 10 =$ ☐
$16 - 10 =$ ☐
$15 - 10 =$ ☐

5.
$10 + 10 =$ 20
$9 + 10 =$ ☐
$8 + 10 =$ ☐
$7 + 10 =$ ☐
$6 + 10 =$ ☐
$5 + 10 =$ ☐

Problem Solving Reasoning

Look at exercises 4 and 5.
Continue the patterns.

6.
14 – 10 = 4
____ – ____ = ☐
____ – ____ = ☐
____ – ____ = ☐

7.
4 + 10 = 14
____ + ____ = ☐
____ + ____ = ☐
____ + ____ = ☐

★ Test Prep

8. Solve. Mark the space under your answer.

$10 + \square = 19$

0	5	9	10
○	○	○	○

9.

$13 - \square = 10$

0	3	5	6
○	○	○	○

STANDARD

Name ______________________________

Problem

Julian sees **17** birds.
9 of the birds are red.
How many birds are not red?

1 Understand

I need to find out how many birds are not red.

2 Decide

I can write a number sentence to solve the problem.

3 Solve

17 − 9 = 8

There are 8 birds that are not red.

4 Look back

My answer makes sense
because 9 + 8 = 17.

Write a number sentence. Solve.

1. **7** children have big dogs.
9 children have little dogs.
How many children have dogs?

_____ children

Write a number sentence. Solve.

2. There are **12** dogs on the porch.
There are **9** cats in the tree.
How many more dogs are there than cats?

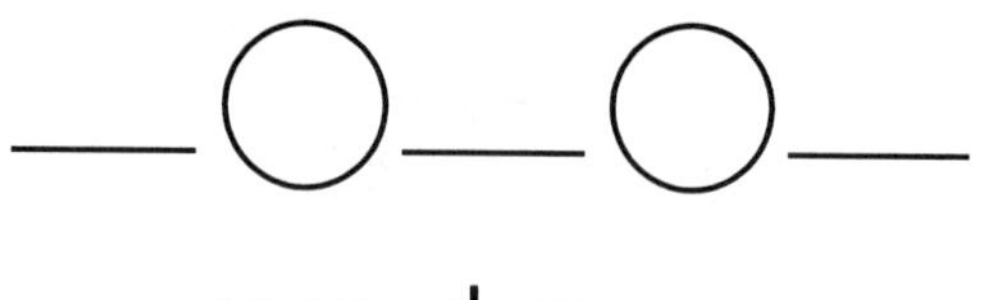

____ more dogs

3. There are **8** puppies in the yard.
7 more puppies come.
How many puppies are there now?

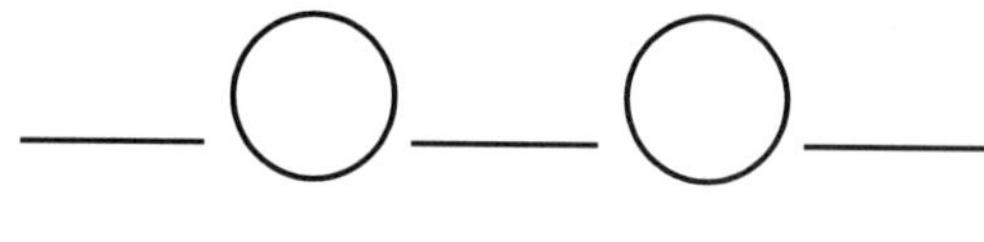

____ puppies

4. There are **18** birds on the fence.
9 fly away. How many are left?

____ birds

5. **4** red birds fly away.
4 blue birds fly away.
9 brown birds fly away. How many birds fly away?

____ birds

Write a story to go with the number sentence.

6. **9 + 8 = 17** ____________________

____

____

Name ____________________

Complete. Then write a related addition or subtraction fact.

1. 9 + 8 = ☐
   ____

2. 20 − 10 = ☐
   ____

3. 18 − 9 = ☐
   ____

Write the fact family.

4. 6, 8, 14

   + ___ + ___ − ___ − ___

5. 8, 7, 15

   + ___ + ___ − ___ − ___

6. 9, 7, 16

   + ___ + ___ − ___ − ___

7. 9, 9, 18

   + ___ − ___

Solve.

8. 5 + ☐ = 13

9. 7 + ☐ = 14

10. 8 + ☐ = 12

11. 10 + ☐ = 18

12. 8 + ☐ = 17

13. 5 + ☐ = 14

14. 7 + ☐ = 13

Use + or −.

15. 16 ◯ 9 = 7

16. 8 ◯ 5 = 13

17. 15 ◯ 8 = 7

18. 8 ◯ 4 = 4

Use >, <, or =.

19. 14 ◯ 17

20. 8 + 6 ◯ 12

21. 9 ◯ 9 + 2

22. 6+ 7 ◯ 13

23. 15 − 9 ◯ 6

24. 17 ◯ 11 − 5

Add.

25. $\begin{array}{r} 6 \\ 6 \\ +\ 6 \\ \hline \end{array}$

26. $\begin{array}{r} 5 \\ 6 \\ +\ 7 \\ \hline \end{array}$

27. $\begin{array}{r} 7 \\ 3 \\ +\ 9 \\ \hline \end{array}$

28. $\begin{array}{r} 8 \\ 4 \\ +\ 4 \\ \hline \end{array}$

Problem Solving Reasoning Write the number sentence. Solve.

29. Peg has **5** red hats, **4** blue hats, and **6** green hats.
How many hats does she have in all?

  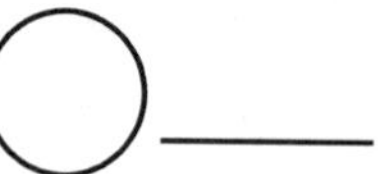

_____ hats

30. Sal sees **17** birds. **8** birds are on the fence.
How many birds are not on the fence?

_____ birds

Name ______________________________

1

19 < 16	10 < 8	13 = 11	13 > 9
○	○	○	○

2

77	79	87	97
○	○	○	○

3

9, 8, 17

○ 16 − 8 = 8 ○ 9 + 7 = 16

○ 17 − 8 = 9 ○ 8 + 7 = 15

4

13 animals	15 animals	17 animals	19 animals
○	○	○	○

5

7 more books ○

9 more books ○

8 more books ○

10 more books ○

6

7 + 6 = 13
○

7 + 9 = 16
○

13 − 7 = 6
○

16 − 9 = 7
○

Decide on an answer. Mark the space for your answer.
If the answer is **not here**, mark the space for **NH.**

7

8 + 9 = ☐

15	16	17	18	NH
○	○	○	○	○

8

Tens	Ones
8	**2**

89	82	68	28	NH
○	○	○	○	○

9

9 + (3 + 5) = ☐

19	18	17	16	NH
○	○	○	○	○

10

6 + 7 ○ 9 + 3

<	>	=	NH
○	○	○	○

UNIT 4 • TABLE OF CONTENTS

Geometry and Fractions

We will be using this vocabulary:

congruent the same size and the same shape
symmetrical having two parts that match

Dear Family,

During the next few weeks our math class will be learning about geometry and fractions.

You can expect to see homework that provides practice with geometric solids and plane figures. There will also be homework that provides practice with fractions.

As we learn about geometry and fractions, you may wish to keep the following sample as a guide.

Geometric Solids

Cone

Cube

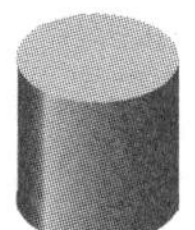
Cylinder

Rectangular Prism

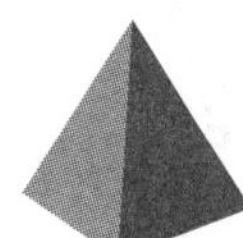
Square Pyramid

Sphere

Plane Figures

Square

Rectangle

Triangle

Circle

Fractions

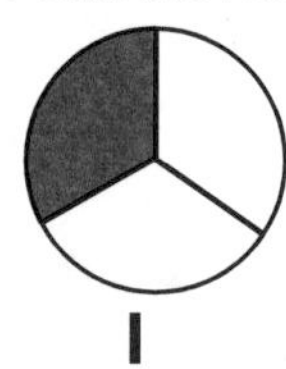
$\frac{1}{3}$

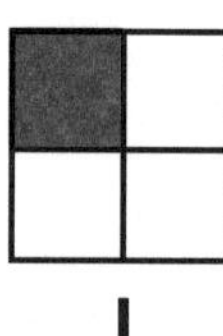
$\frac{1}{4}$

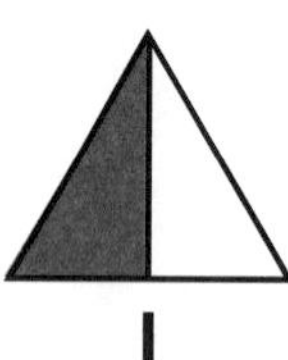
$\frac{1}{2}$

Sincerely,

Name ______________________________

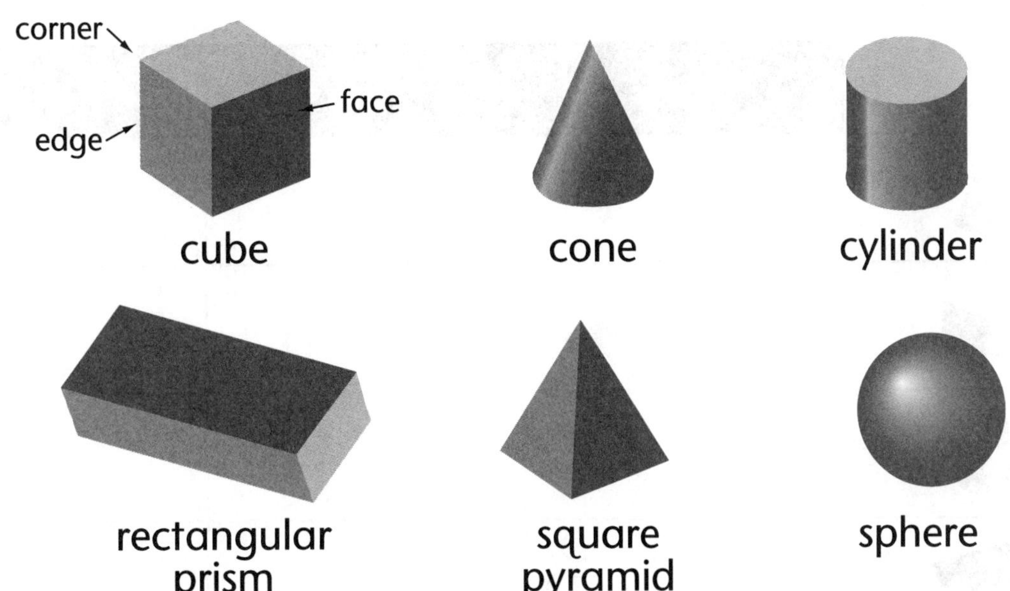

Look at the solids.
Write how many faces, edges, and corners.

	Name of Solid	Number of Flat Faces	Number of Edges	Number of Corners
1.	cube	6	12	8
2.	rectangular prism			
3.	square pyramid			
4.	sphere			

Problem Solving
Reasoning

Look around your classroom. Find an object that is shaped like a solid. Write clues about the object's shape and position in the room. Ask a friend to guess the object.

Complete the table.

		Slides	Stacks	Rolls
5.		yes	no	yes
6.				
7.				
8.				
9.				

Problem Solving
Reasoning

10. How are a cone and a cylinder alike? How are they different?

____

____

____

____

★ Test Prep

Mark the cube.

 ○ 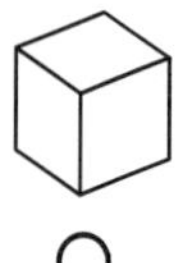 ○ 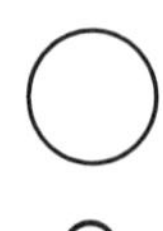 ○  ○

Name ______________________

These are plane figures.

Square

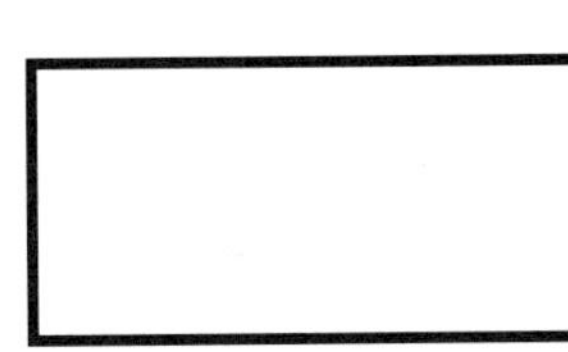
Rectangle

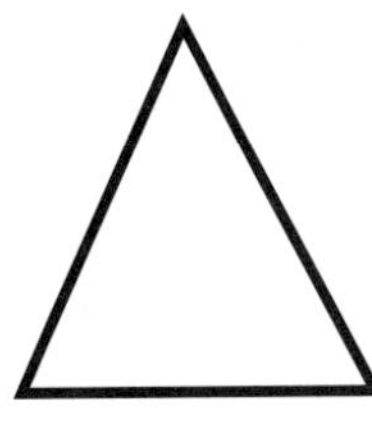
Triangle

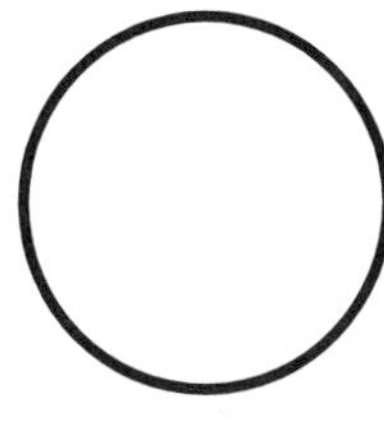
Circle

Describe the figures. How are they alike? How are they different?

Find an object that matches the shape of the solid. Trace around the face of the object to make a plane figure. What plane figure did you draw? Write the name.

1. 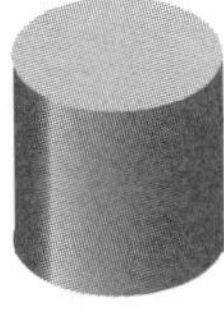

circle

2. 

____

3. 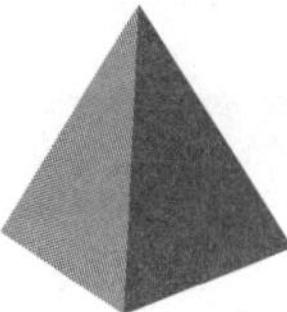

____

4. 

____

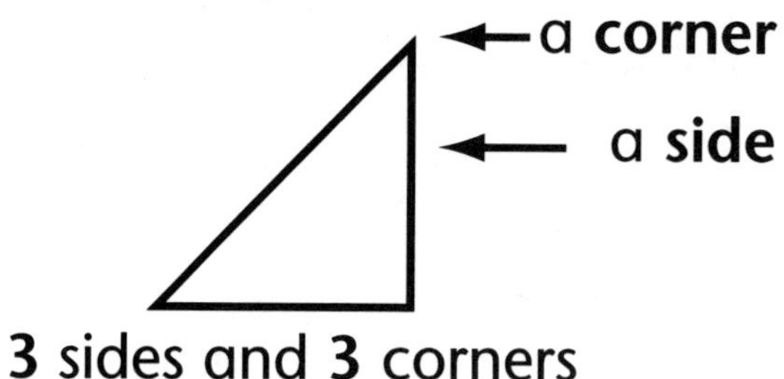

3 sides and **3** corners

How many sides?
How many corners?

5.

4 **sides**

4 **corners**

6.

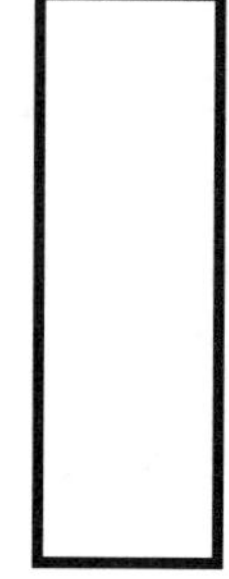

____ **sides**

____ **corners**

7.

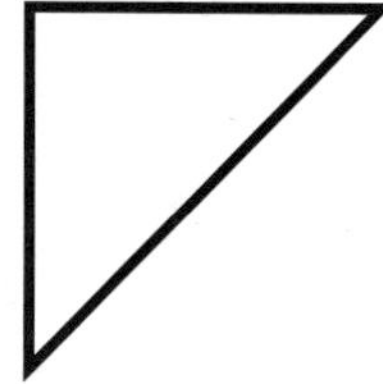

____ **sides**

____ **corners**

8.

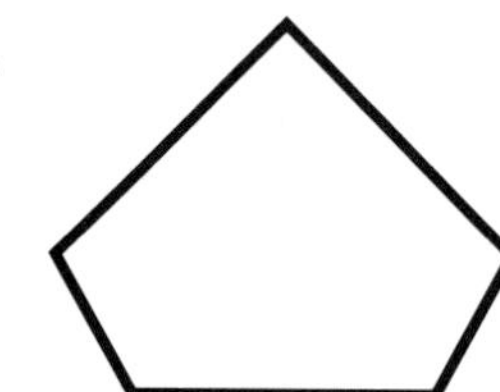

____ **sides**

____ **corners**

9.

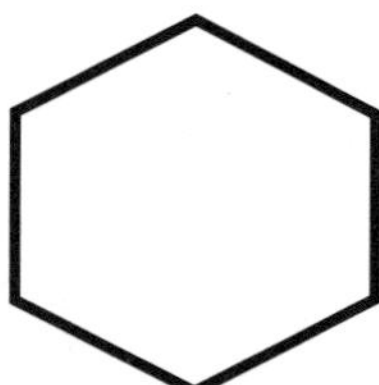

____ **sides**

____ **corners**

10.

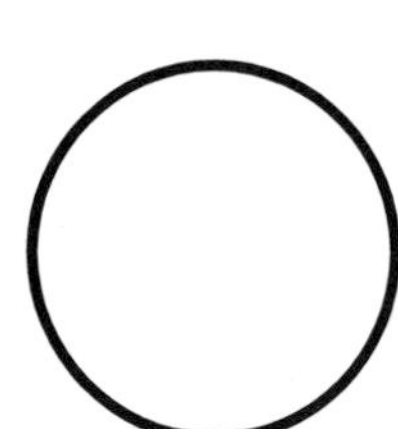

____ **sides**

____ **corners**

★ Test Prep

Mark what figure you will see if you trace the face of the solid.

11

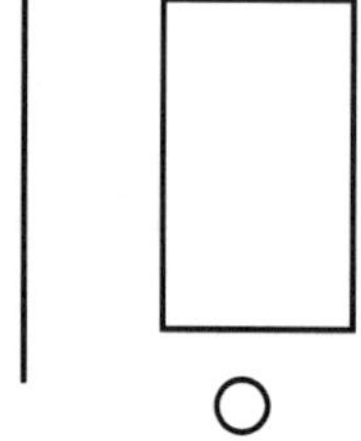
○

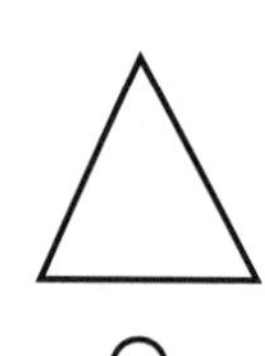
○

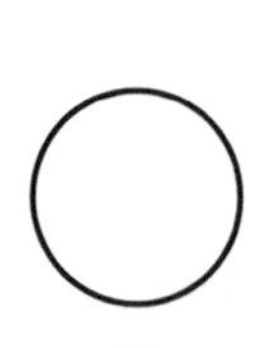
○

○

Name ______________________________

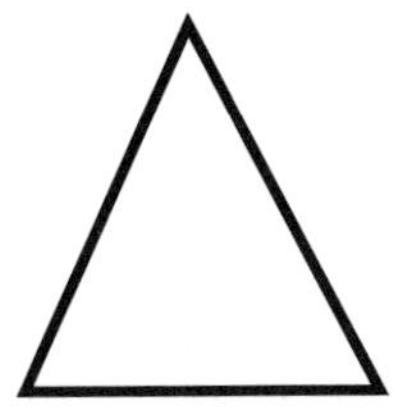
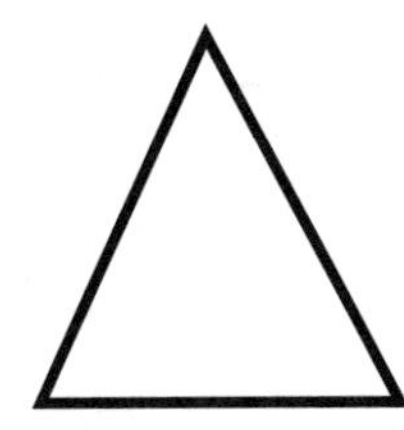

These two figures are **congruent**. They are the same size and the same shape.

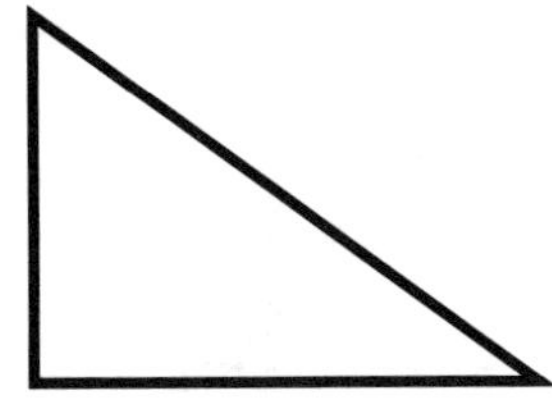
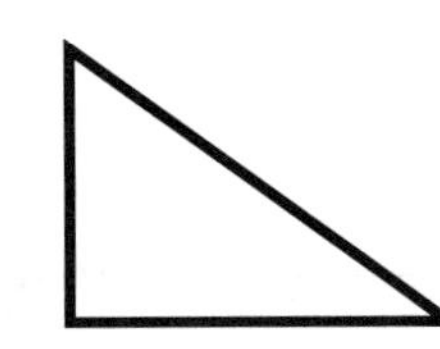

These two figures are not congruent. They are the same shape but not the same size.

Ring the figure that is congruent to the first figure.

1. 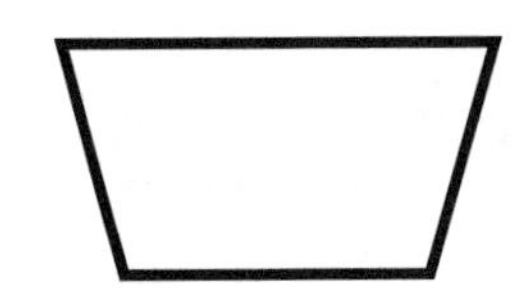 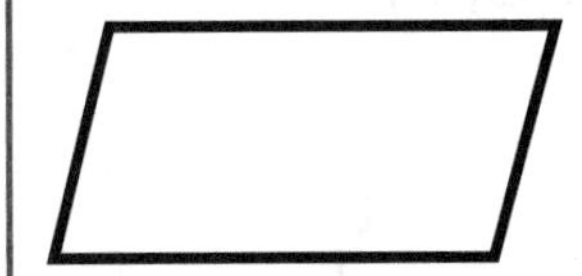 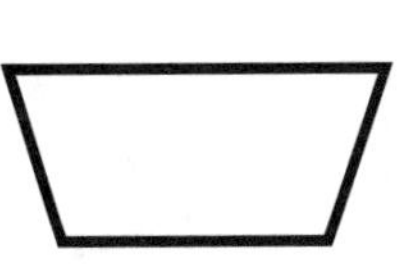 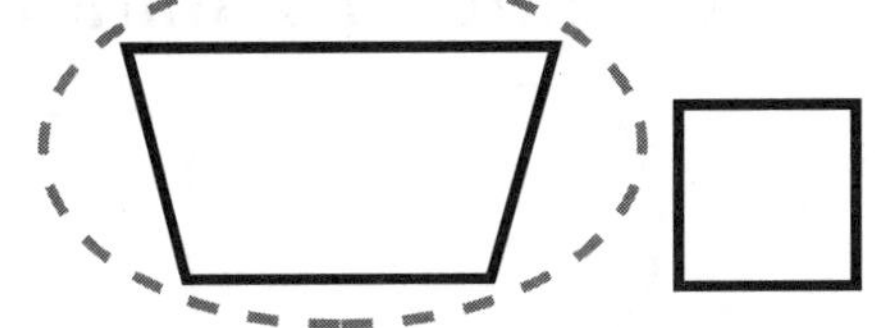

2. 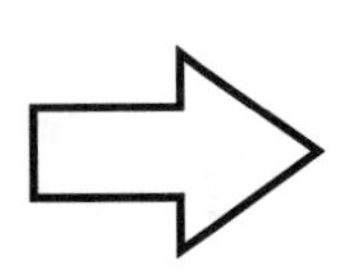 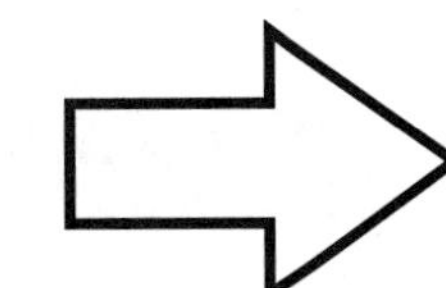 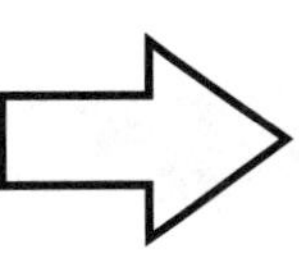 

3. 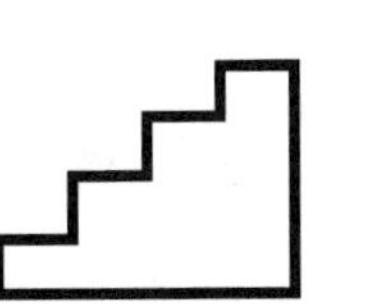 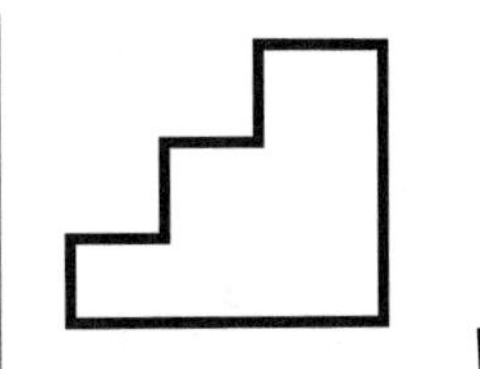 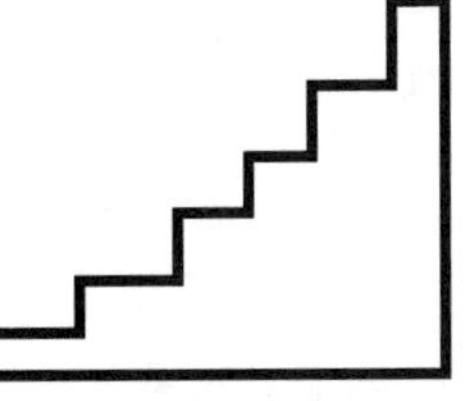 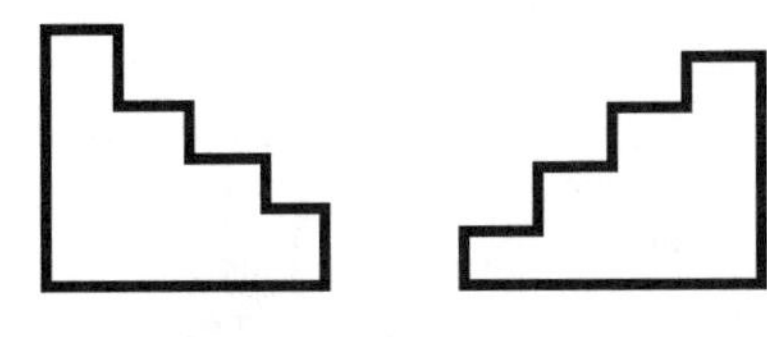

4. 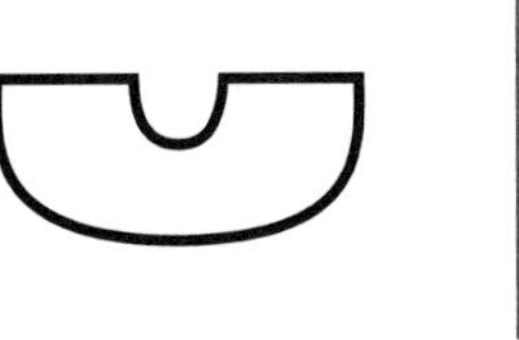   

5. 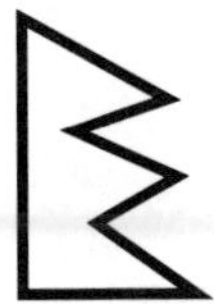   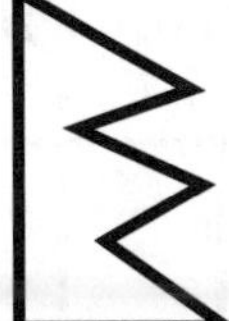 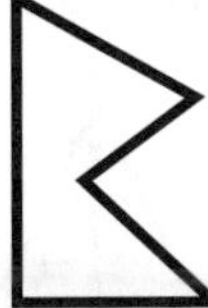

This figure is **symmetrical**.

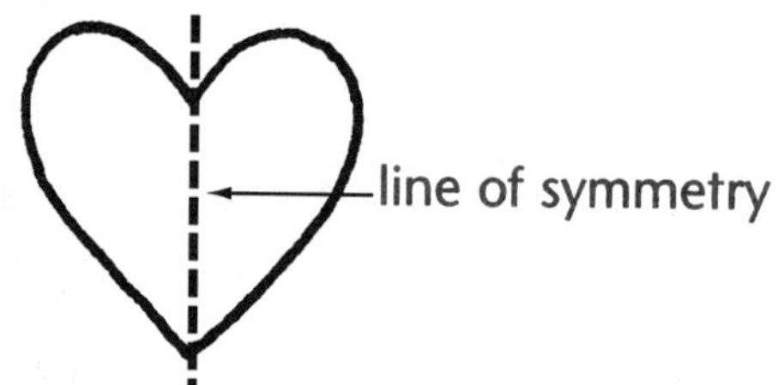

Both parts match.

This figure is not symmetrical.

Both parts do not match.

Ring the figures that are symmetrical.

6.  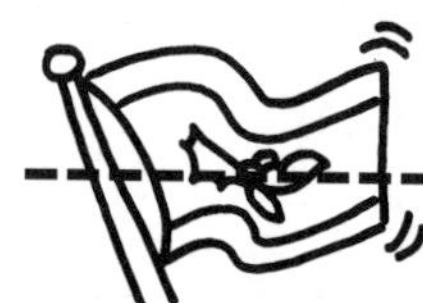 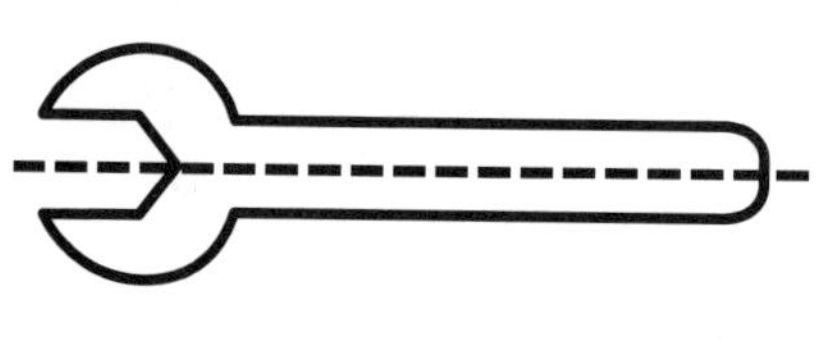 

Draw a line of symmetry on each figure.

7.   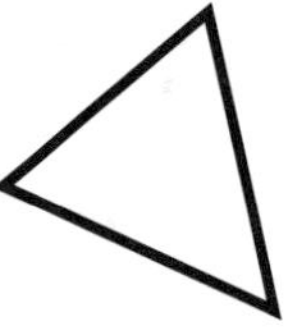 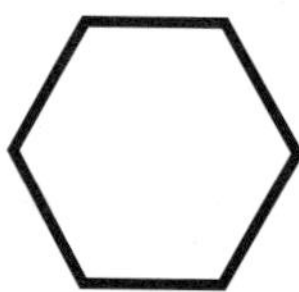 

Quick Check

Look at the picture.
Answer the questions.

cube 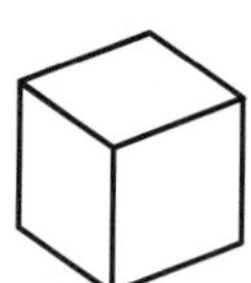

1. How many faces? _____ edges? _____

Name the figure that is the face of the cube.

2. ______________

Ring the symmetrical figures.

3.  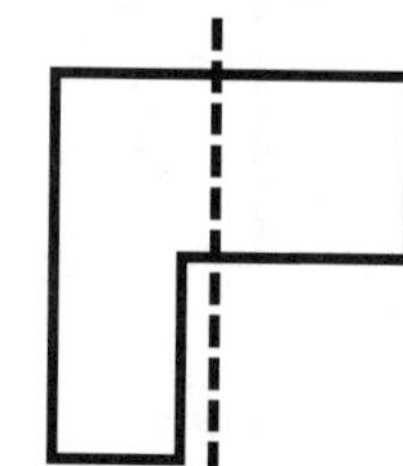 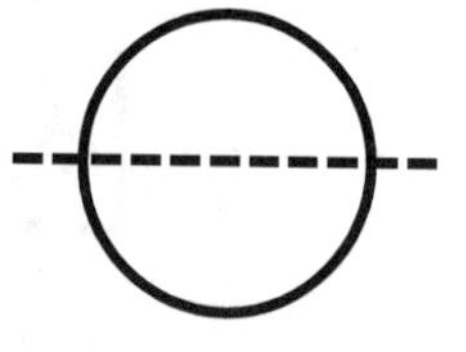

Name ____________________

STANDARD

Problem

Draw a line to make the rectangle into **2** squares.

1 **Understand**

I need to draw a line to make the rectangle into **2** squares.

2 **Decide**

I can draw lines on the picture of the rectangle until I find the line that makes **2** squares.

3 **Solve**

First Try

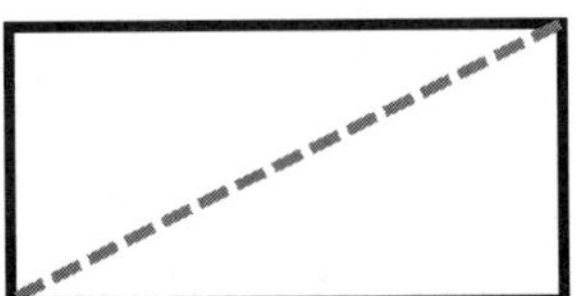

Second Try

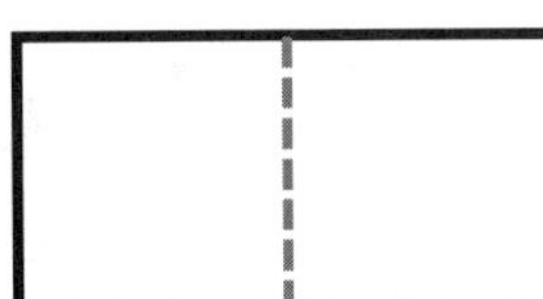

4 **Look back**

My second try was correct.
I know because a square has **4** sides and all the sides are the same length.

Draw a picture to solve.

1. Draw a line to make the square into **2** rectangles.

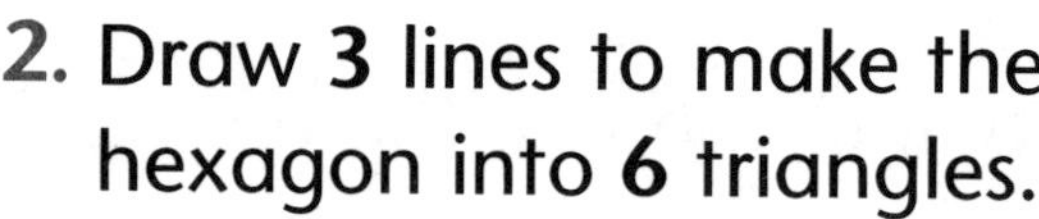

2. Draw **3** lines to make the hexagon into **6** triangles.

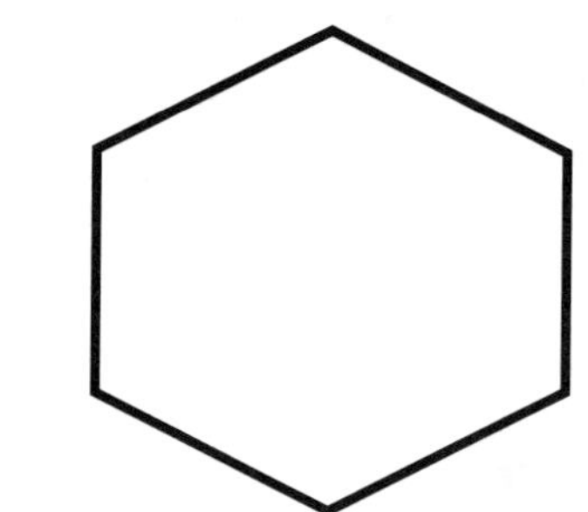

3. Draw **2** lines to make the trapezoid into **3** triangles.

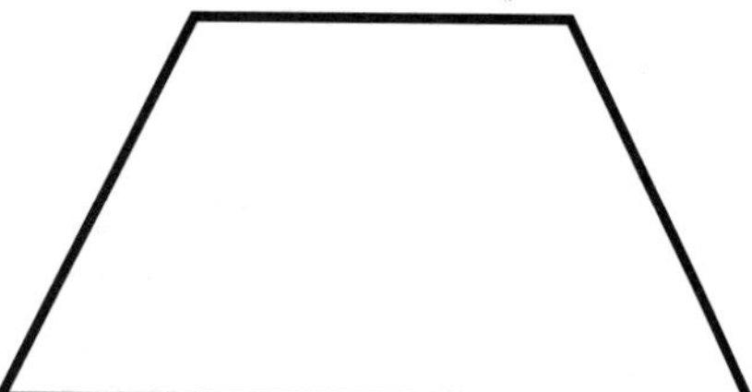

4. Draw a line to make the rectangle into **2** triangles.

5. Cut out a rectangle, a square, and a triangle. Then cut each figure to make **2** new figures. Draw the new figures.

STANDARD

Name ______________________________

Problem Solving Plan			
1. Understand	2. Decide	3. Solve	4. Look back

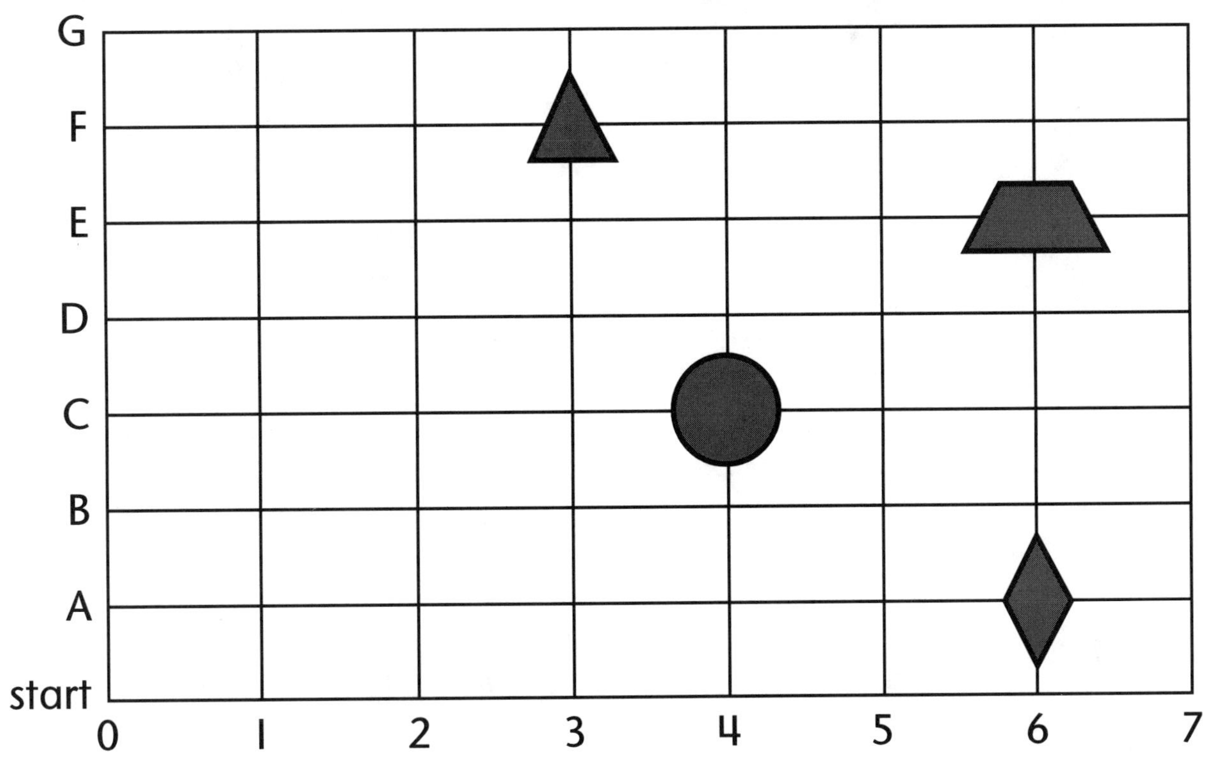

Use the picture. Solve.

1. Where is the ▲?
Think Find the figure.
Follow the line down.
Follow the line across.

Answer 3, F

2. Where is the ●?
Think Find the figure.
Follow the line down.
Follow the line across.

Answer ______

3. Where is the ⏢?
Think Find the figure.
Follow the line down.
Follow the line across.

Answer ______

4. Where is the ◆?
Think Find the figure.
Follow the line down.
Follow the line across.

Answer ______

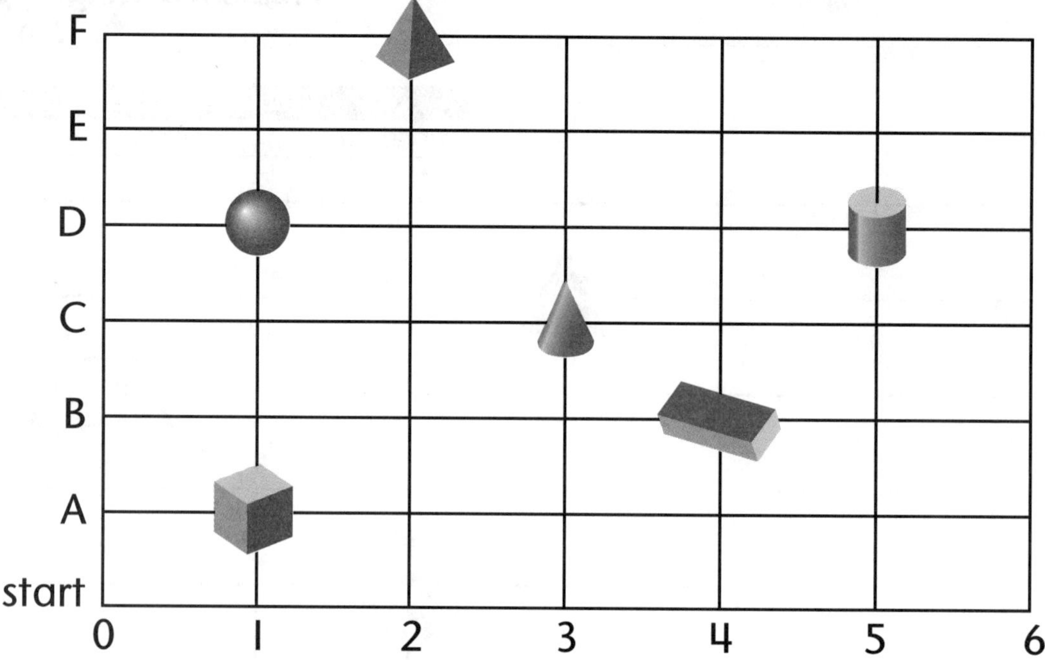

Use the picture. Solve.

5. Where is the 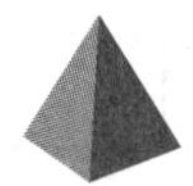 ?

Answer _____

6. Where is the  ?

Answer _____

7. Where is the  ?

Answer _____

8. Where is the  ?

Answer _____

9. Where is the  ?

Answer _____

10. Where is the  ?

Answer _____

Extend Your Thinking

Use the picture. Follow the direction.

11. Draw a square at 4, E.

Name ______________________________

We call $\frac{1}{2}$, $\frac{1}{3}$, and $\frac{1}{4}$ fractions.

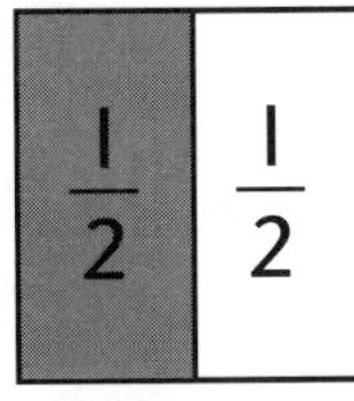

one half

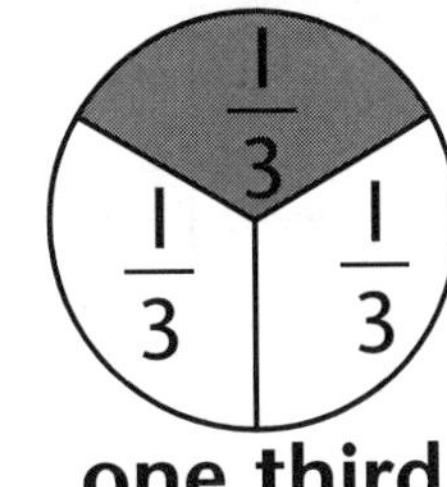

one third

1/4 1/4
1/4 1/4

one fourth

Here are some other fractions.

1/5 1/5 1/5 1/5 1/5

one fifth

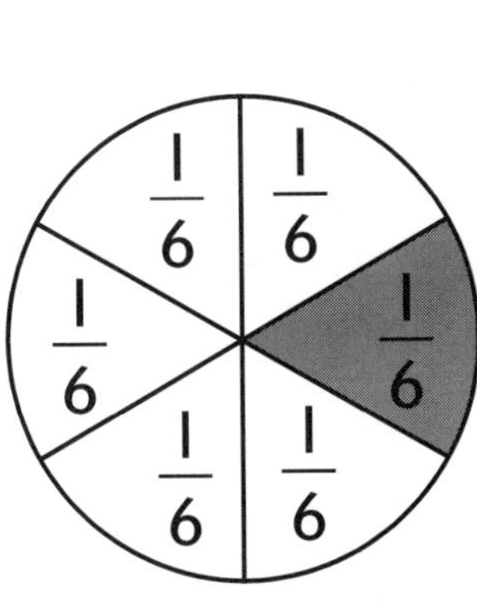

one sixth

1/8 1/8 1/8 1/8 1/8 1/8 1/8 1/8

one eighth

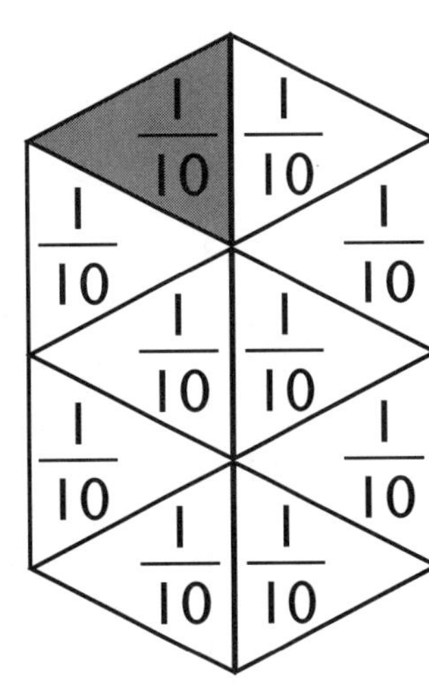

one tenth

1/12 1/12 1/12 1/12 1/12 1/12 1/12 1/12 1/12 1/12 1/12 1/12

one twelfth

Color one part. Ring the correct fraction.

1.

$\frac{1}{2}$ or $\frac{1}{4}$

2.

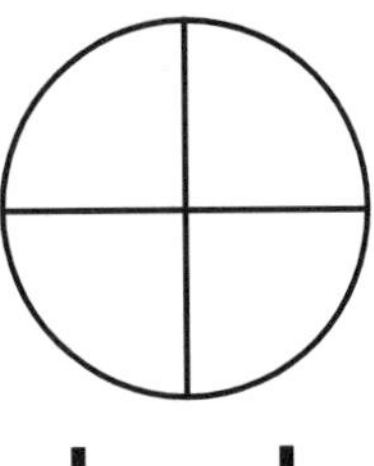

$\frac{1}{3}$ or $\frac{1}{4}$

3.

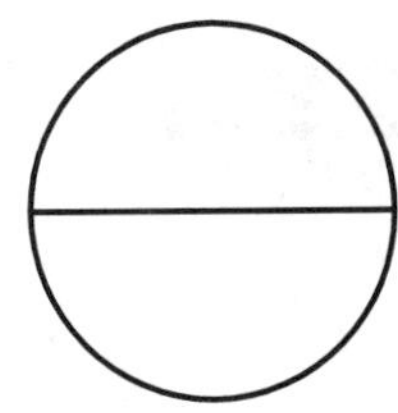

$\frac{1}{2}$ or $\frac{1}{3}$

4.

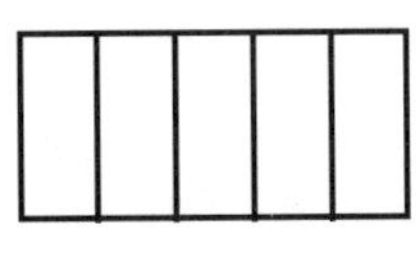

$\frac{1}{5}$ or $\frac{1}{6}$

5.

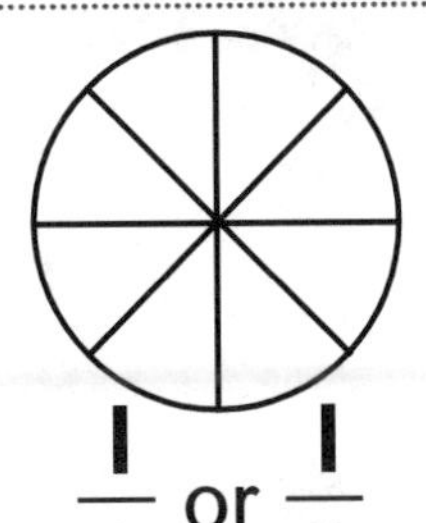

$\frac{1}{6}$ or $\frac{1}{8}$

6.

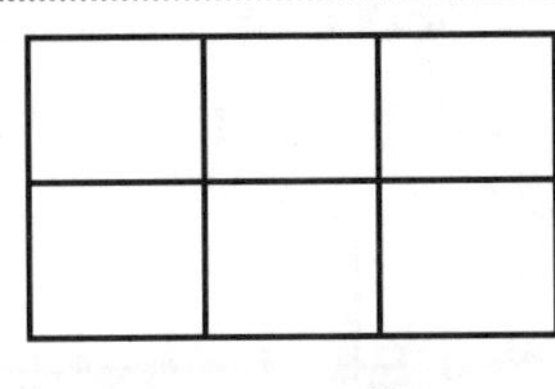

$\frac{1}{6}$ or $\frac{1}{10}$

Write the fraction in each part.

7.

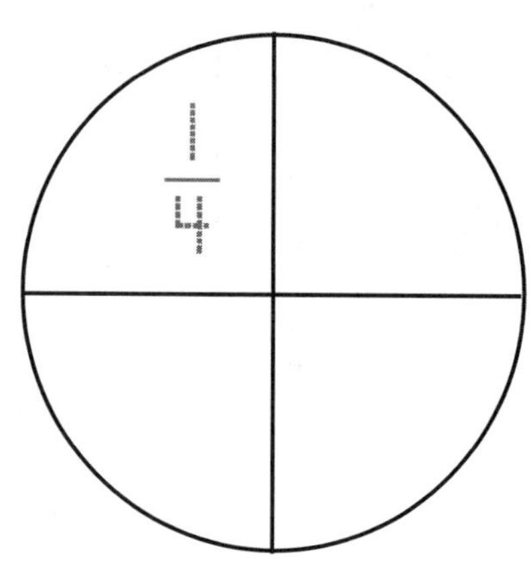

8.

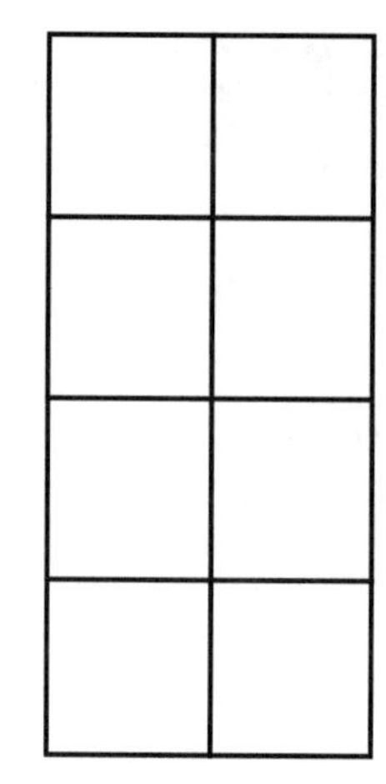

9.

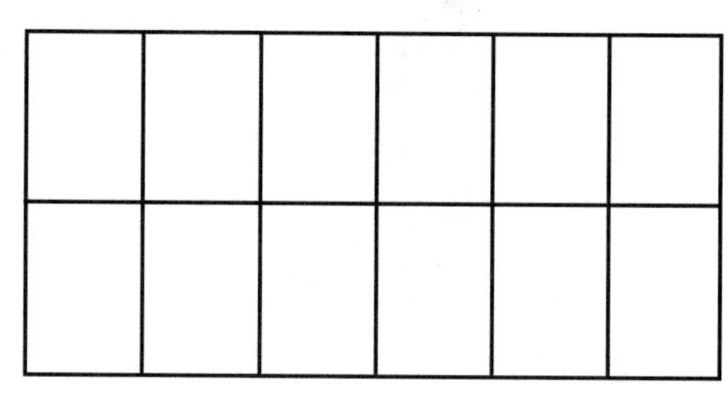

10.

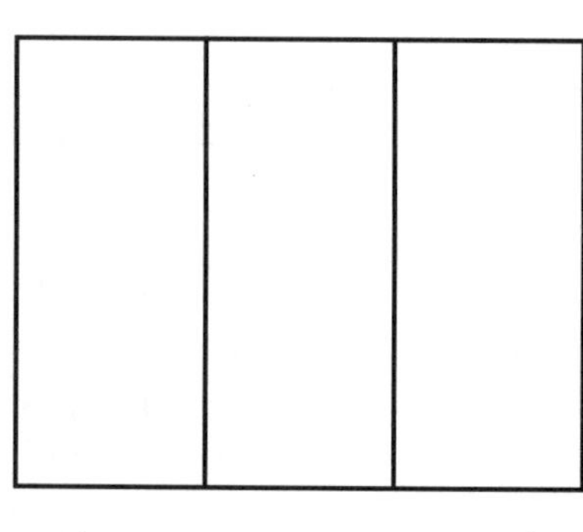

11.

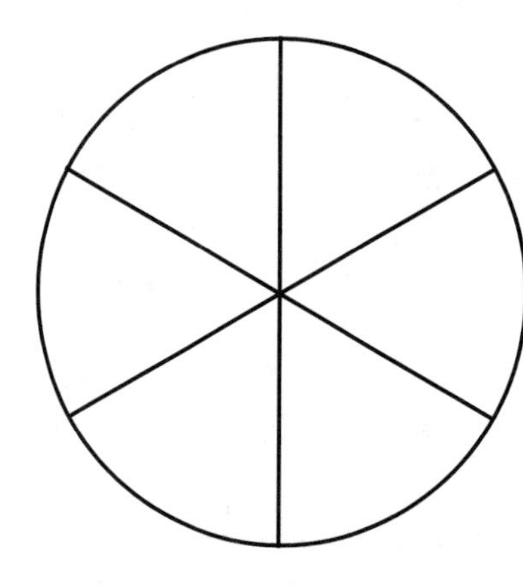

12.

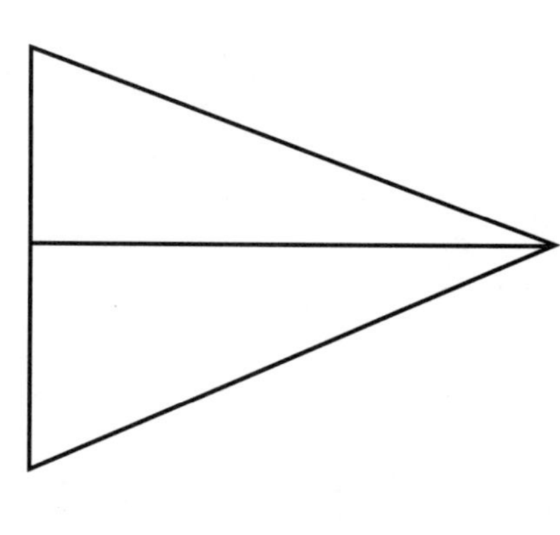

Problem Solving
Reasoning

13. Which is greater, $\frac{1}{6}$ or $\frac{1}{12}$ of a whole? Why? ______________

____

★ Test Prep

Mark the correct fraction.

14

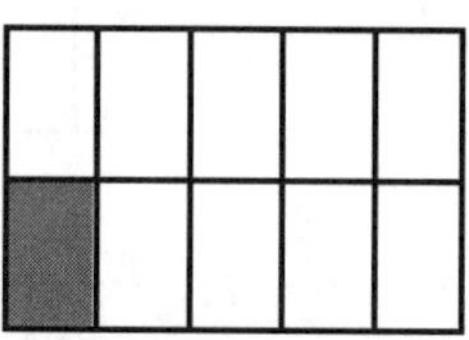

$\frac{1}{5}$	$\frac{1}{8}$	$\frac{1}{10}$	$\frac{1}{12}$
○	○	○	○

Name ______________________________

This figure has **8** equal parts.
5 of the **8** parts are colored.

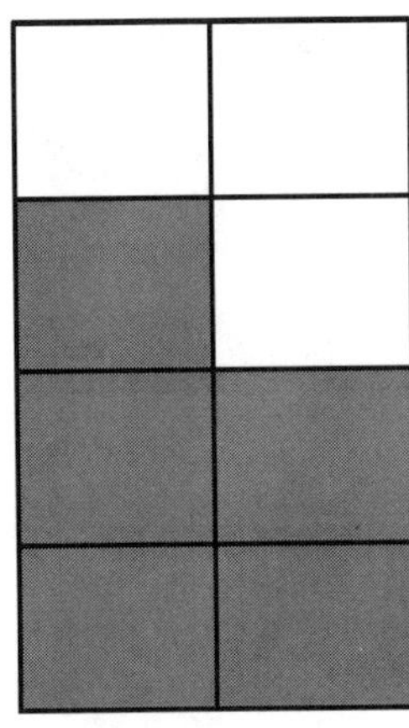

$\frac{5}{8}$ colored parts / equal parts

$\frac{5}{8}$ of the figure is colored.

Five eighths is colored.

Color to show the fraction.
Write the fraction.

1. two fifths

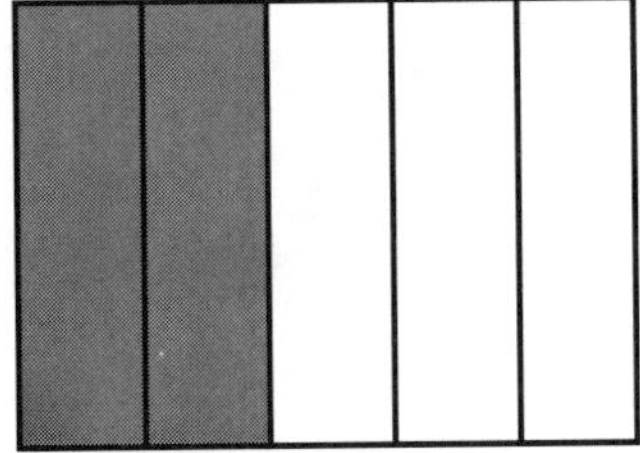

$\frac{2}{5}$

2. three tenths

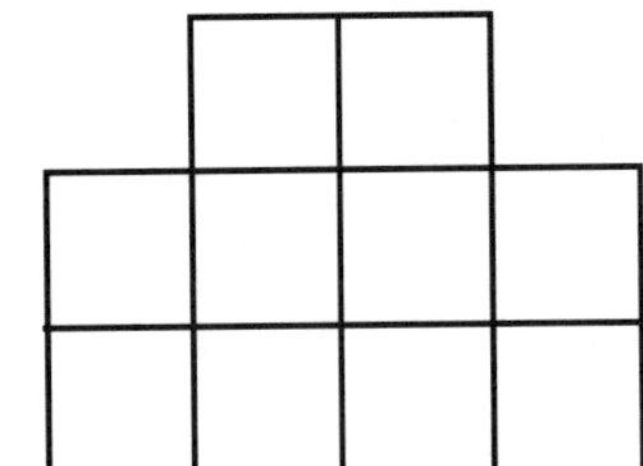

$\frac{\square}{\square}$

3. four ninths

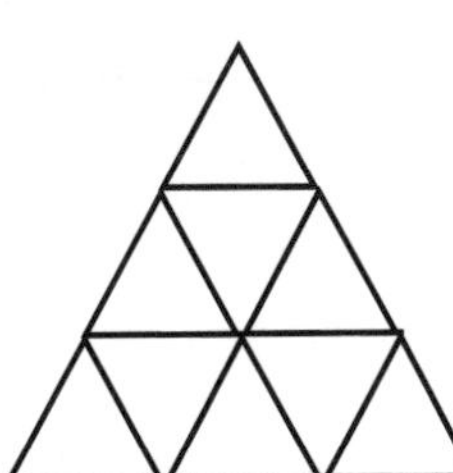

$\frac{\square}{\square}$

4. six sixths

$\frac{\square}{\square}$

5. If $\frac{4}{4}$ equals **1** or the whole, then what does $\frac{3}{3}$ equal?

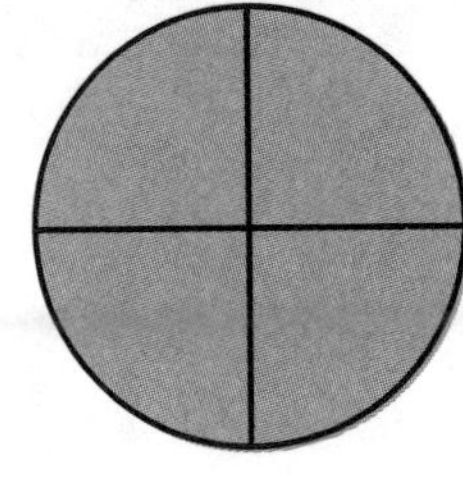

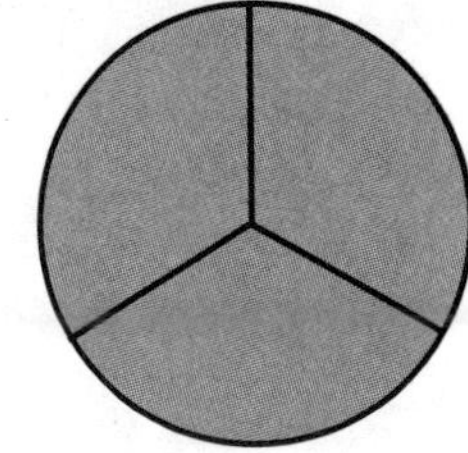

____

Ring the fraction that shows what part is colored.

6.

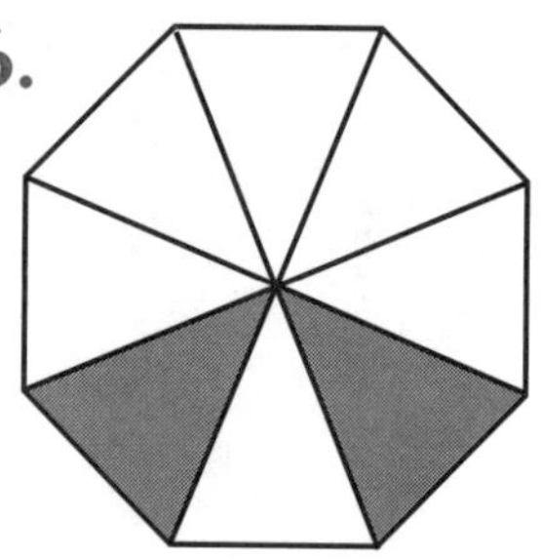

$\frac{6}{8}$ $\frac{2}{8}$ $\frac{1}{6}$

7.

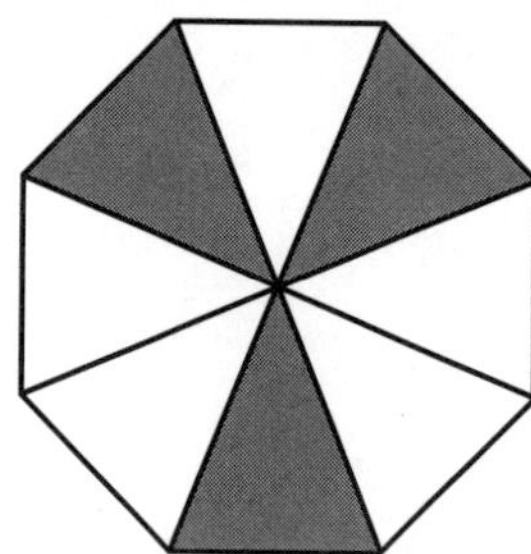

$\frac{3}{6}$ $\frac{5}{8}$ $\frac{3}{8}$

8.

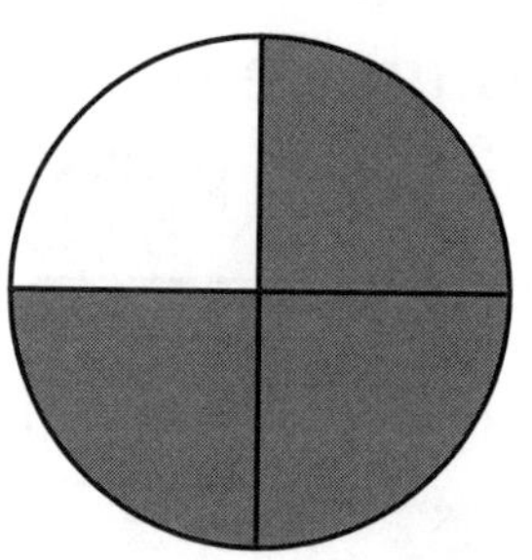

$\frac{3}{4}$ $\frac{2}{3}$ $\frac{1}{4}$

Ring the fraction that shows what part is not colored.

9.

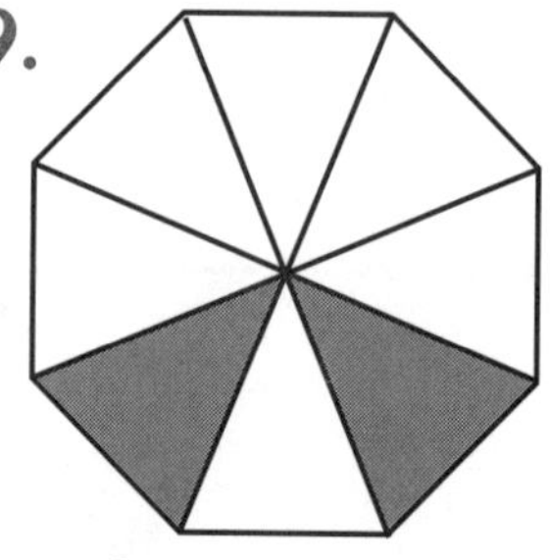

$\frac{6}{8}$ $\frac{2}{8}$ $\frac{1}{6}$

10.

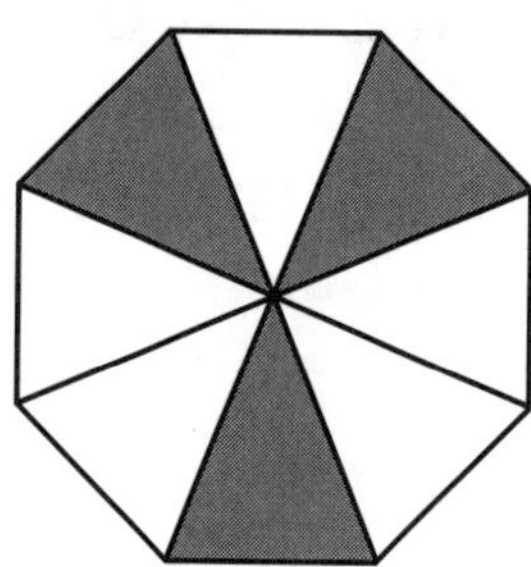

$\frac{3}{6}$ $\frac{5}{8}$ $\frac{3}{8}$

11.

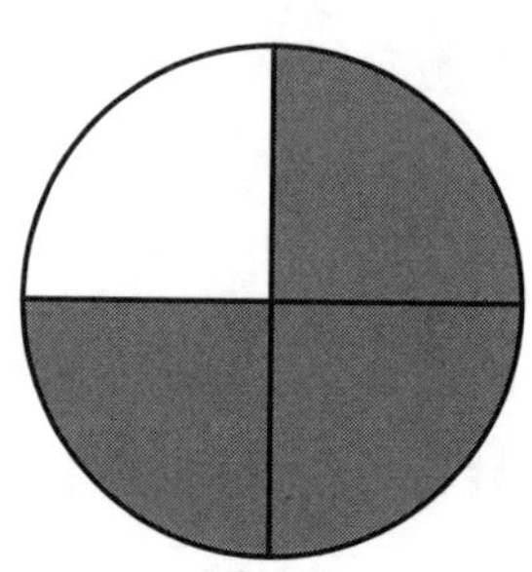

$\frac{3}{4}$ $\frac{2}{3}$ $\frac{1}{4}$

Problem Solving
Reasoning

12. Is $\frac{2}{4}$ greater than, less than, or equal to $\frac{1}{2}$? ____________

Draw a picture to show why.

★ Test Prep

Mark under the fraction that shows what part is colored.

13

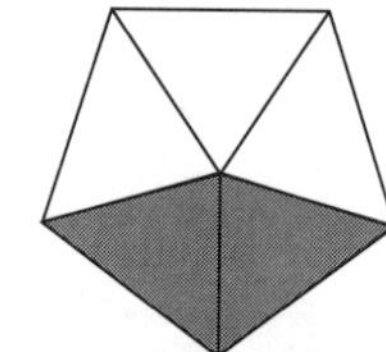

$\frac{1}{2}$	$\frac{3}{5}$	$\frac{2}{5}$	$\frac{1}{10}$
○	○	○	○

Name ____________________

Ring $\frac{1}{2}$ of the set. Complete.

1\. 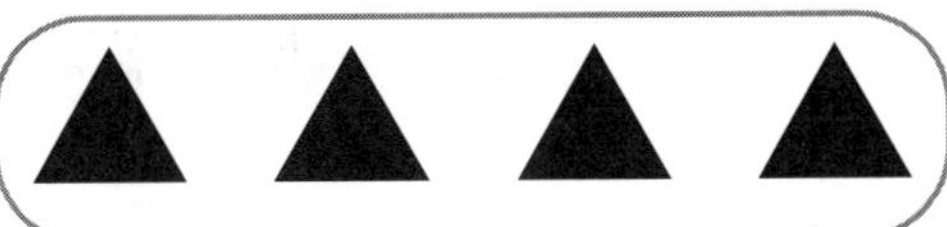

$\frac{1}{2}$ of **8** = 4

2\. 

$\frac{1}{2}$ of **10** = ____

3\. 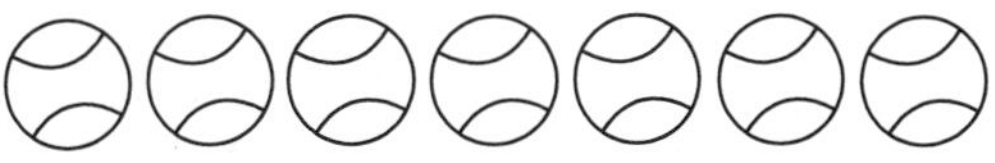

$\frac{1}{2}$ of **14** = ____

4\. 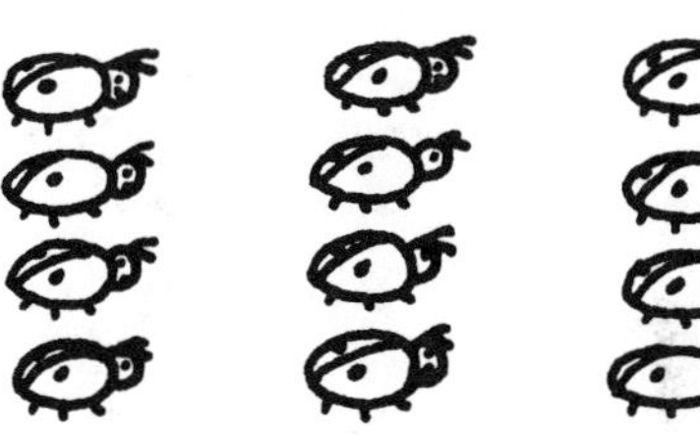

$\frac{1}{2}$ of **12** = ____

Ring $\frac{1}{4}$ of the set. Complete.

5\. 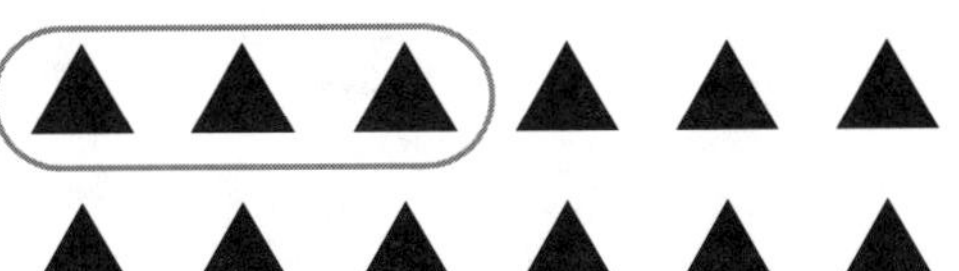

$\frac{1}{4}$ of **12** = 3

6\.    

$\frac{1}{4}$ of **4** = ____

7\. 

$\frac{1}{4}$ of **16** = ____

8\. 

$\frac{1}{4}$ of **8** = ____

Ring $\frac{3}{4}$ of the set. Complete.

9.    

$\frac{3}{4}$ of 4 = 3

10.

$\frac{3}{4}$ of 12 = ____

Ring $\frac{2}{3}$ of the set. Complete.

11. 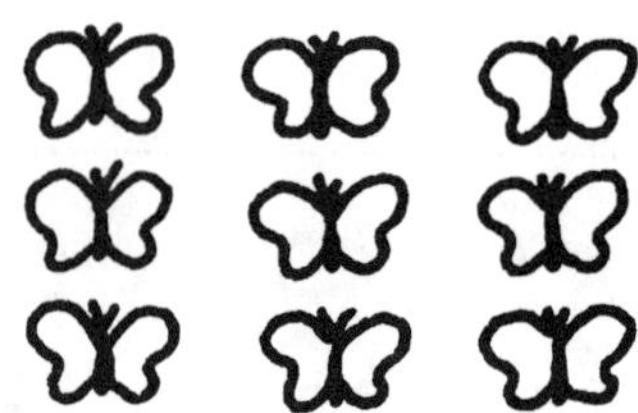

$\frac{2}{3}$ of 9 = ____

12. 

$\frac{2}{3}$ of 15 = ____

Quick Check

Write the fraction for the colored part.

1. 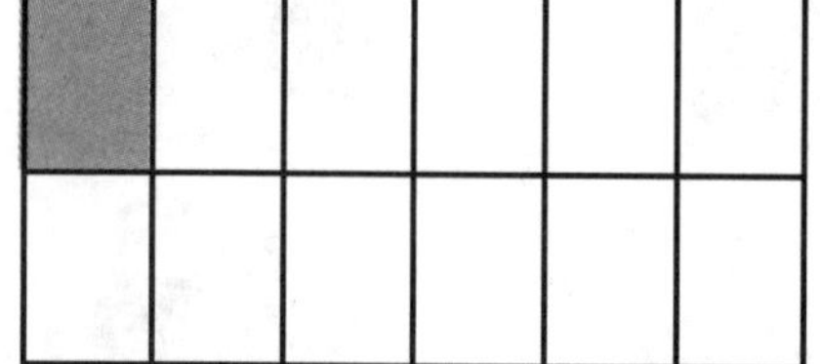 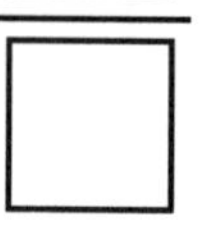

2. 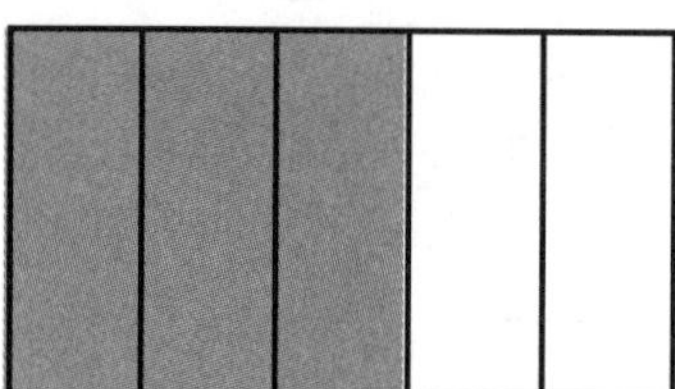

Ring $\frac{2}{3}$ of the set. Complete.

3. 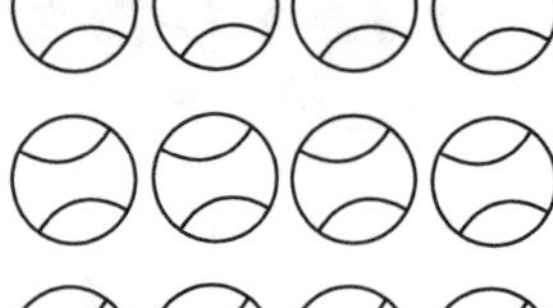
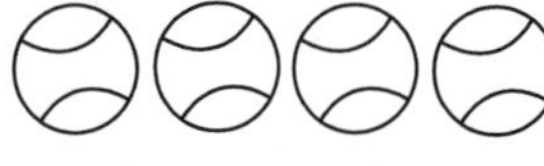

$\frac{2}{3}$ of 12 = ____

Name ____________________

Match.

1. cone
2. cube
3. square pyramid

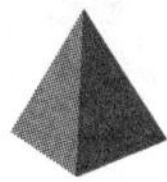

Look at the solids. Complete the table.

	Solid	Number of Flat Faces	Stacks	Rolls
4.				
5.				
6.				

Write how many sides and corners.

7. ____ sides ____ corners

8. ____ sides ____ corners

9. 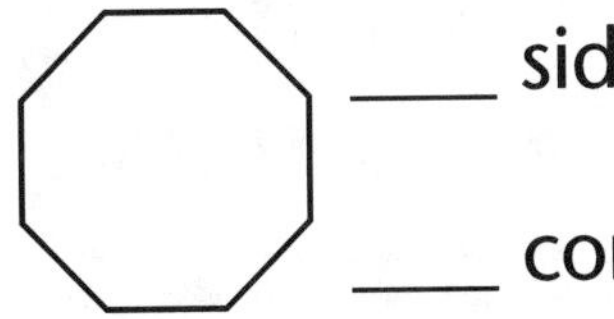 ____ sides ____ corners

Ring the figure that is congruent to the first figure.

10. 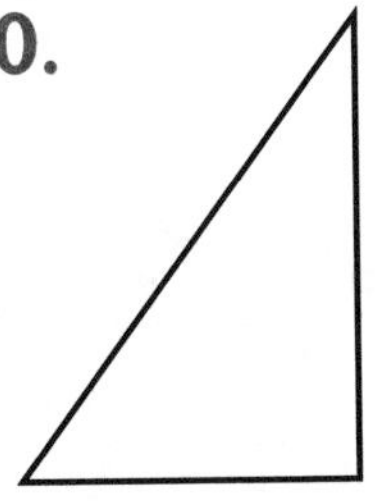

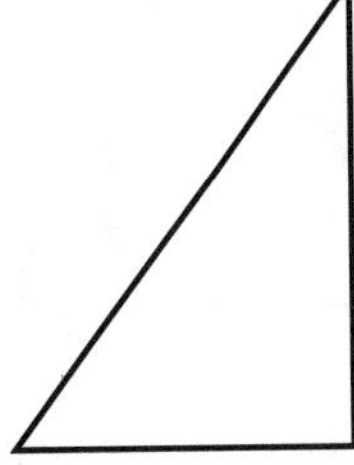

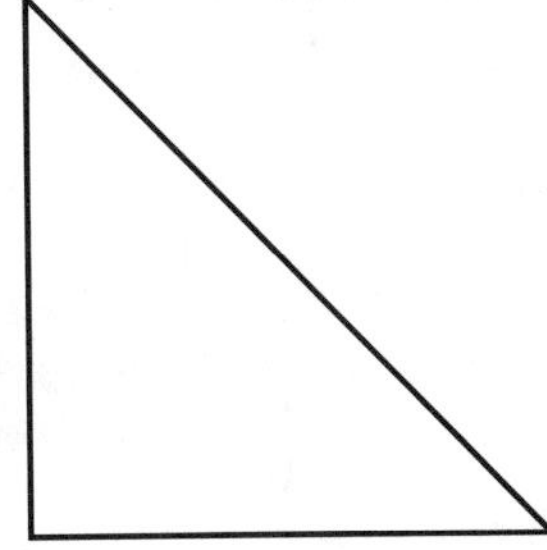

Color one part.
Ring the correct fraction.

11. 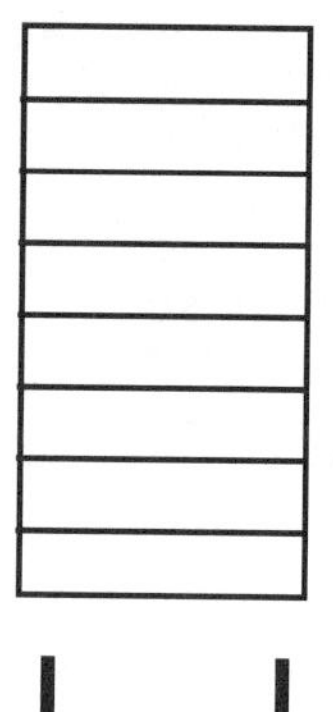

$\frac{1}{8}$ or $\frac{1}{10}$

12. 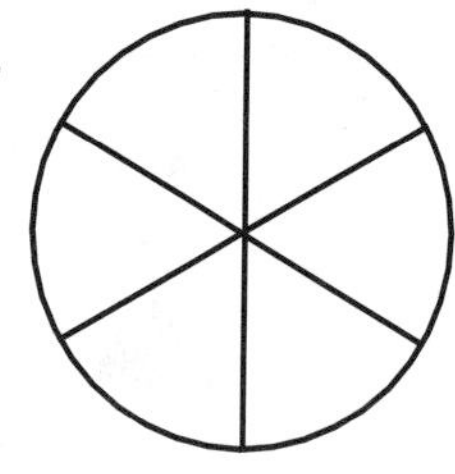

$\frac{1}{6}$ or $\frac{1}{8}$

13. 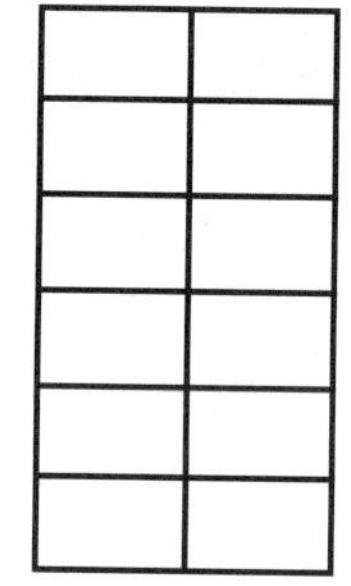

$\frac{1}{10}$ or $\frac{1}{12}$

14. 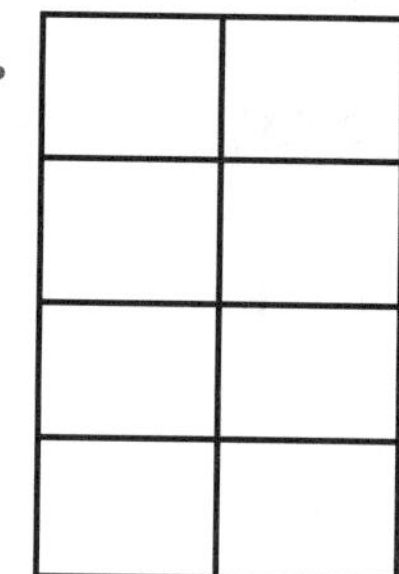

$\frac{1}{6}$ or $\frac{1}{8}$

Ring the fraction that shows what part is colored.

15. 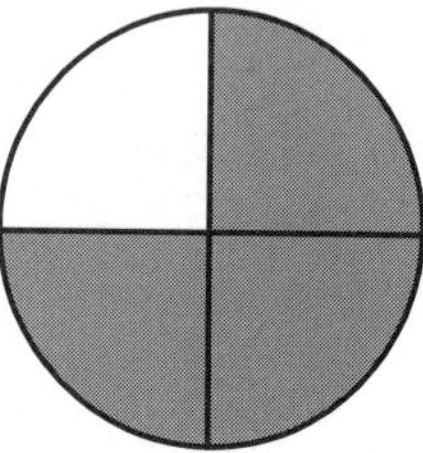

$\frac{1}{4}$ $\frac{2}{3}$ $\frac{3}{4}$

16. 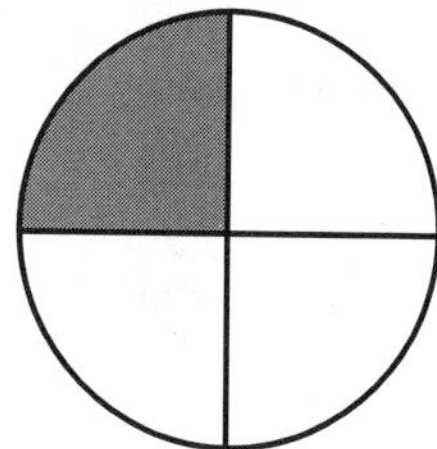

$\frac{1}{4}$ $\frac{2}{3}$ $\frac{3}{4}$

17. 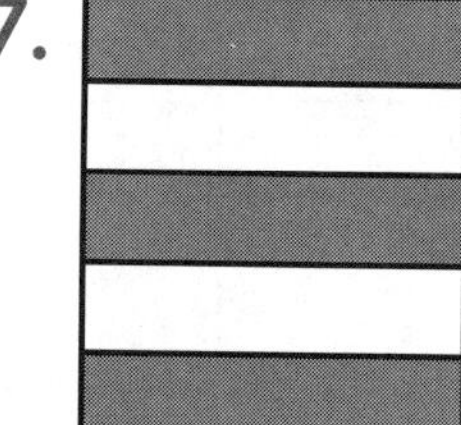

$\frac{4}{5}$ $\frac{3}{5}$ $\frac{5}{10}$

18. 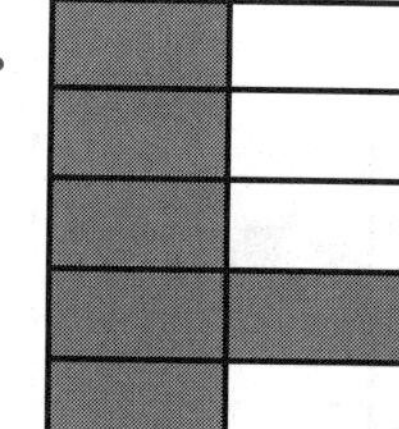

$\frac{6}{10}$ $\frac{4}{10}$ $\frac{2}{5}$

Ring $\frac{2}{3}$ of the set. Complete.

19. ✖✖✖✖✖
✖✖✖✖✖
✖✖✖✖✖

$\frac{2}{3}$ of 15 = ____

20. ◯◯◯
◯◯◯
◯◯◯

$\frac{2}{3}$ of 9 = ____

Problem Solving Reasoning Use the picture. Solve.

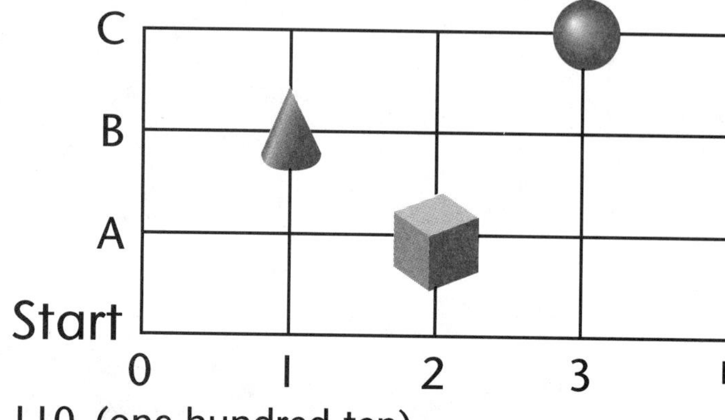

21. Where is the cube? ______

22. Where is the sphere? ______

23. Where is the cone? ______

Name ______________________________

1

78		80

○ 77 ○ 79 ○ 81 ○ 87

2

21	24	27		33	36

○ 26 ○ 28 ○ 30 ○ 39

3

$9 + 8 = 17$

○ $17 - 9 = 8$

○ $8 + 7 = 15$

○ $7 + 9 = 16$

○ $16 - 9 = 7$

4

○ $7 + 7 = 14$ ○ $7 + 8 = 15$ ○ $14 - 7 = 7$ ○ $14 - 5 = 9$

5

○

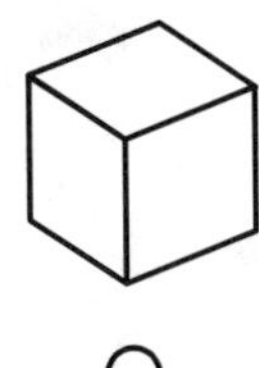
○

○

○

6

○ ○ ○ ○

7

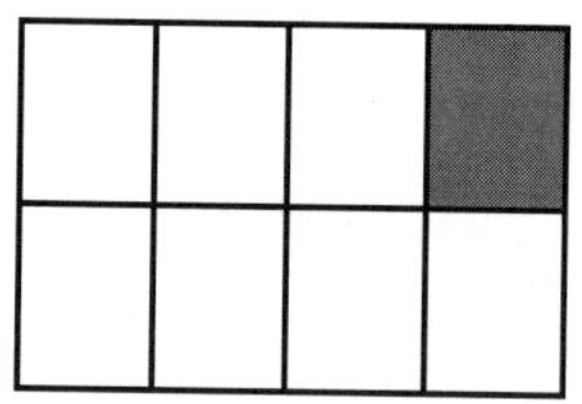

$\frac{1}{4}$ ○ $\frac{1}{8}$ ○ $\frac{1}{10}$ ○ $\frac{1}{12}$ ○

8

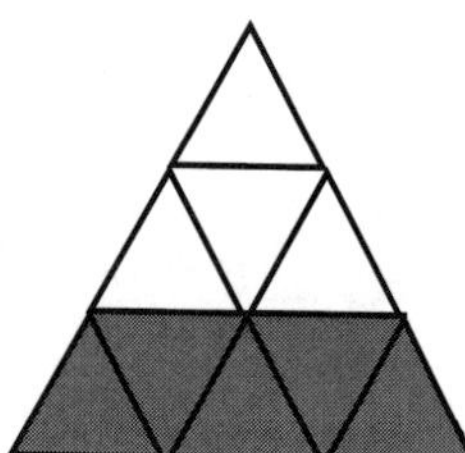

$\frac{1}{9}$ ○ $\frac{4}{9}$ ○ $\frac{5}{9}$ ○ $\frac{9}{9}$ ○

9

$\frac{1}{4}$ of **12** = ____

3 ○ 4 ○ 9 ○ 12 ○

10

$\frac{3}{4}$ of **8** = ____

3 ○ 4 ○ 6 ○ 8 ○

UNIT 5 • TABLE OF CONTENTS

Measurement

We will be using this vocabulary:

kilogram a unit for measuring mass
liter a unit for measuring how much liquid a container will hold
degree a unit of temperature

Dear Family,

During the next few weeks our math class will be learning about measurement.

You can expect to see homework that provides practice with estimating and measuring length, as well as with estimating weight, mass, and capacity. There will also be homework that provides practice with reading a thermometer.

As we learn about measuring length and standard units, you may wish to point out to your child everyday items that are about the same length as the standard units. This will help them remember the various lengths of the units.

Standard Units of Length	Everyday Referents
inch	small paperclip
foot (12 inches)	piece of writing paper
centimeter	pencil eraser
meter (100 centimeters)	giant step

Sincerely,

Name ______________________________

You can use paper clips to measure the length of a pencil.

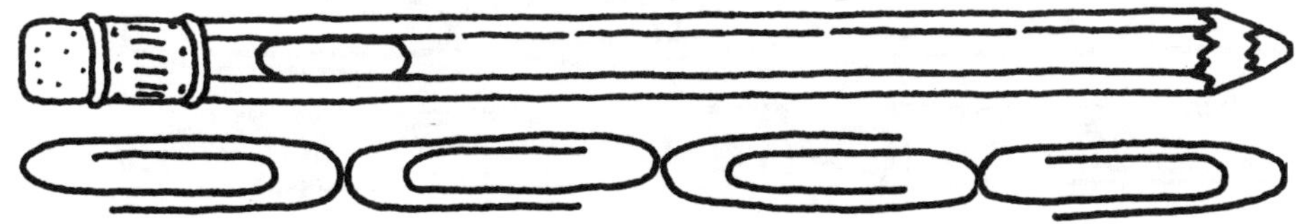

This pencil is about 4 paper clips long.

Estimate the length. Use paper clips to measure. Complete.

1.

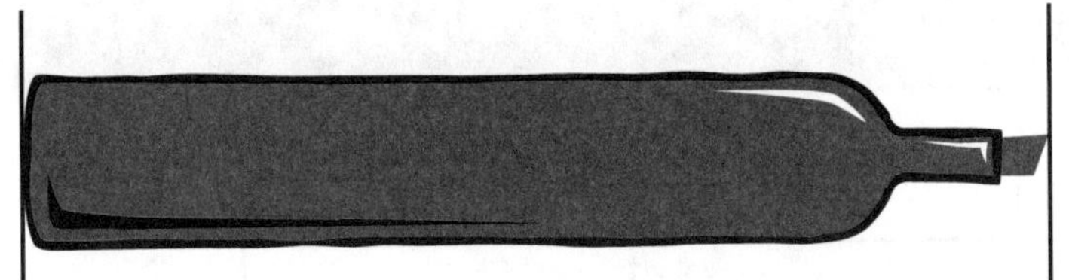

Estimate about _____ paper clips. **Measure** about _____ paper clips.

2.

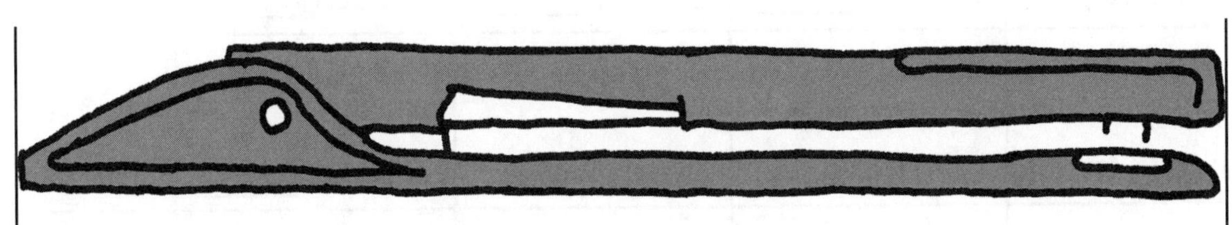

Estimate about _____ paper clips. **Measure** about _____ paper clips.

3.

Estimate about _____ paper clips. **Measure** about _____ paper clips.

You can measure the same object using different units.

This pencil is about 4 paper clips long or about 2 crayons long.

Complete the chart.
Estimate first. Then measure the object.

	Length in Paper Clips		Length in Crayons	
	Estimate	Measure	Estimate	Measure
4. paper	about ____	about ____	about ____	about ____
5. desk top	about ____	about ____	about ____	about ____
6. math book	about ____	about ____	about ____	about ____
7. ________	about ____	about ____	about ____	about ____

Problem Solving Reasoning

9. Barb measures the length of her shoe with paper clips. Then she measures with crayons. Does Barb use more paper clips or more crayons? Explain.

____

Name ____________________

This unit is 1 inch long.

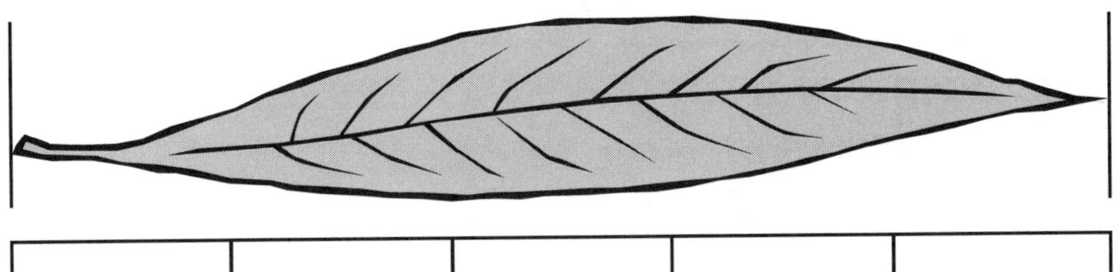

This leaf is about **5** inches long.

1. About how long is this leaf? Estimate.

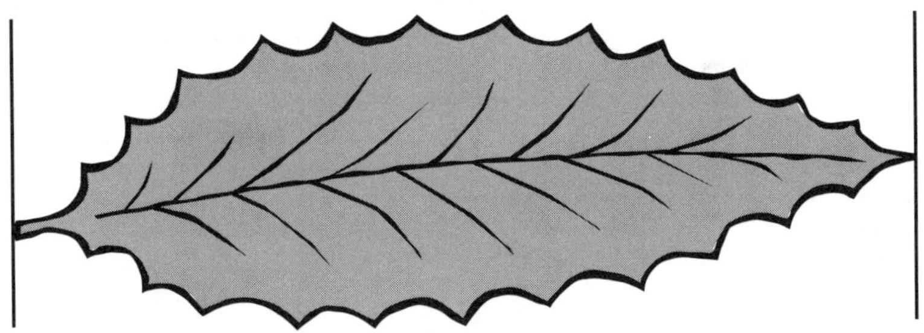

about ____ inches

Find these items in your classroom.
Estimate first, then measure. Use inch units.

		My Estimate in Inches	Measurement in Inches
2.	**the length of a marker**	about ____	about ____
3.	**the height of a cup**	about ____	about ____
4.	**the length of your shoe**	about ____	about ____
5.	**the width of a book**	about ____	about ____

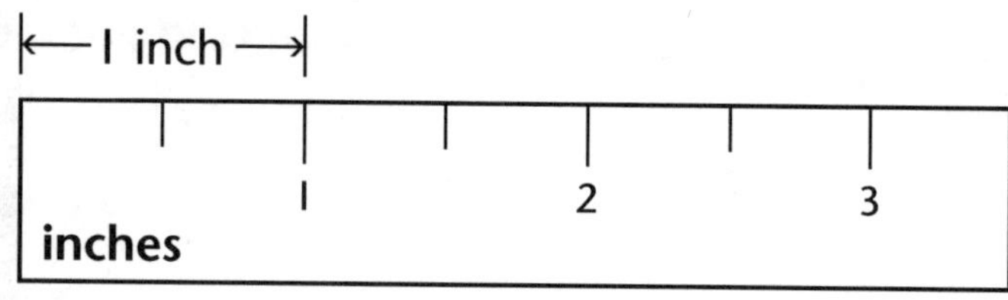

This is an inch ruler.
Each number marks **I** inch.

Use a ruler. How far has each ant gone?

6. about ☐ inches

7. about ☐ inches

Most inch rulers are **12** inches long.
12 inches = **I foot**

Use a ruler. Measure and record.

8. across your desk

   about _____ feet

9. across your teacher's desk

   about _____ feet

10. from your desk to the next desk

    about _____ feet

11. from the top of a table to the floor

    about _____ feet

★ Test Prep

About how many inches? Mark the space for your answer.
If the answer is **not here**, mark the space for **NH**.

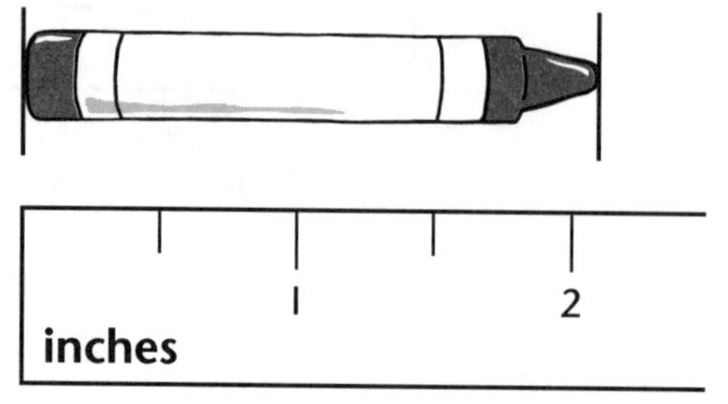

I	2	3	NH
○	○	○	○

Name ____________________

Problem Solving Plan

1. Understand 2. Decide 3. Solve 4. Look back

How long is the path?
Use an inch ruler to solve.

1.

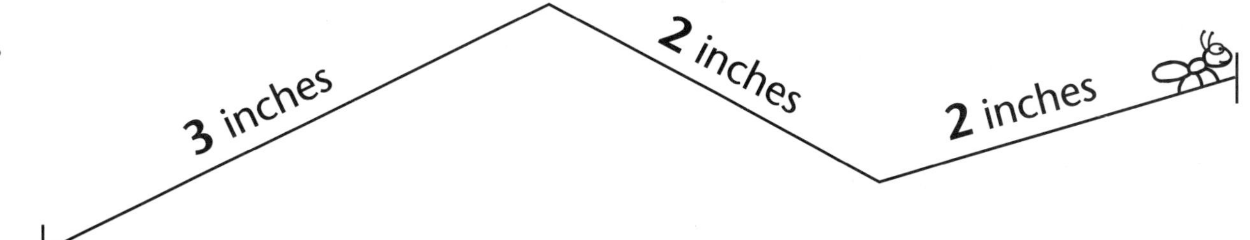

Think What is the length of each section of the path?

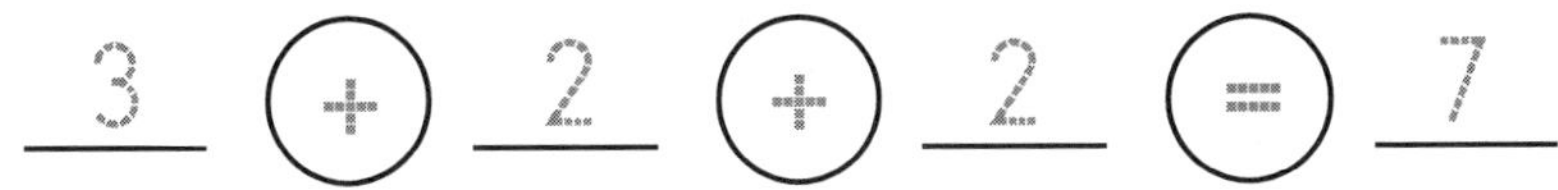

Answer about 7 inches

2.

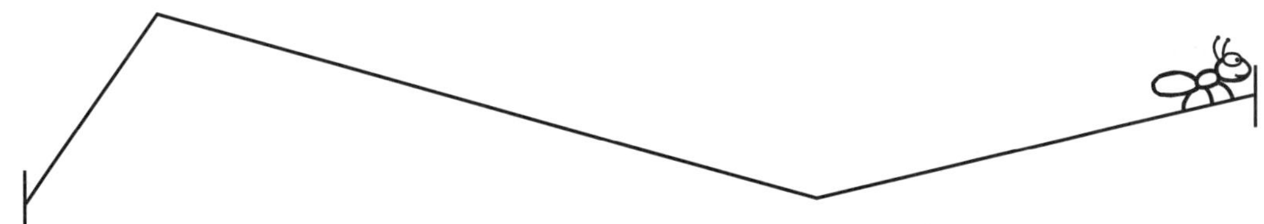

Think What is the length of each section of the path?

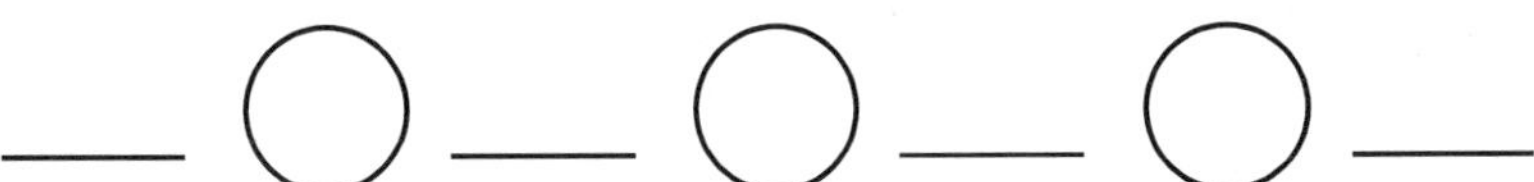

Answer about ____ inches

3.

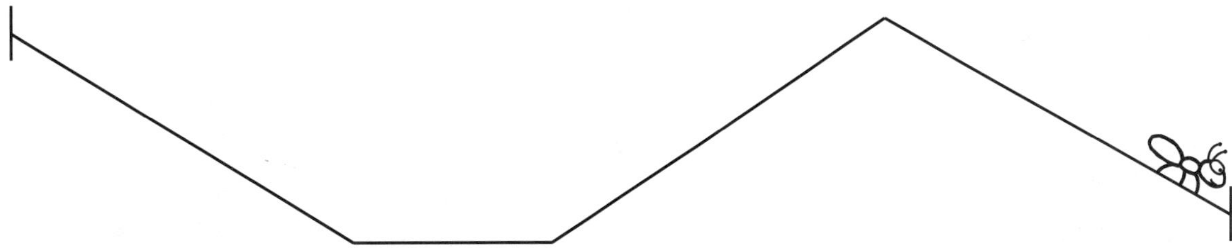

Think What is the length of each section of the path?

Answer about ____ inches

Perimeter is the length around all the sides of a figure. What is the perimeter of the figure? Use an inch ruler to solve.

4.

___ ◯ ___ ◯ ___ ◯ ___ ◯ ___

Answer about ____ inches

5.

___ ◯ ___ ◯ ___ ◯ ___ ◯ ___ ◯ ___

Answer about ____ inches

6.

___ ◯ ___ ◯ ___ ◯ ___ ◯ ___ ◯ ___

Answer about ____ inches

Extend Your Thinking

How could you measure the length of this path?

Name ______________________________

This unit is one centimeter long.

How is a centimeter different from an inch?

Use centimeter units to measure.

1\. about 10 centimeters.

2\. about _____ centimeters.

3\. about _____ centimeters.

Work with a partner.
Fill in the chart.
Estimate first, then measure.
Use a centimeter ruler.

1 2 3 4 5 6 7 8 9 10
centimeters

		My Estimate in Centimeters	Measurement in Centimeters
4.	the length of your thumb	about _____	about _____
5.	the length of your pencil	about _____	about _____
6.	the length of your math book	about _____	about _____
7.	the width of your math book	about _____	about _____
8.	the length of your shoe	about _____	about _____

A ruler 100 centimeters long is a meter stick.

100 centimeters = 1 meter

Use a meter stick.
Measure and record.

9. from your desk to the door

about _____ meters

10. from wall to wall

about _____ meters

11. from bottom to top of door

about _____ meters

12. across the chalkboard

about _____ meters

Quick Check

Measure and record.

1. Use small paper clips.

about ____ paper clips

2. Use an inch ruler.

about ____ inches

3. Use a centimeter ruler.

about ____ centimeters

Name ____________________

Problem

How many of the tiles do you need to cover this floor?

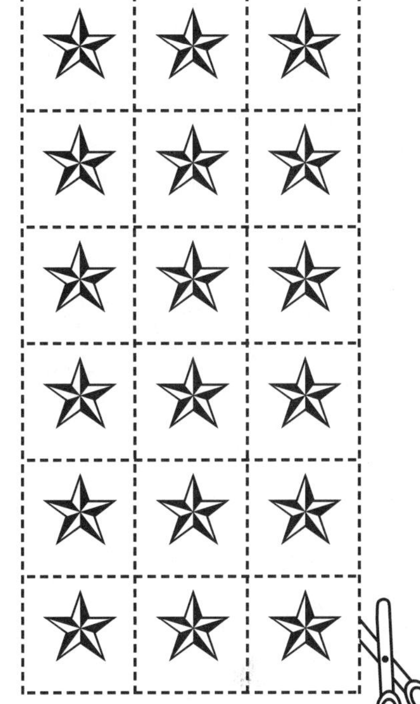

1 Understand

I need to find out how many tiles I need to cover the floor.

2 Decide

I can guess then check.

3 Solve

I'll make a guess.

My guess is ______ tiles.
I'll cut out the tiles and cover the floor.
I'll count the tiles to check how many I used.

I used __15__ tiles to cover the floor.

4 Look back

I know that I needed **15** tiles to cover the floor.
My answer makes sense.

How may tiles do you need?
Guess then check.

1.

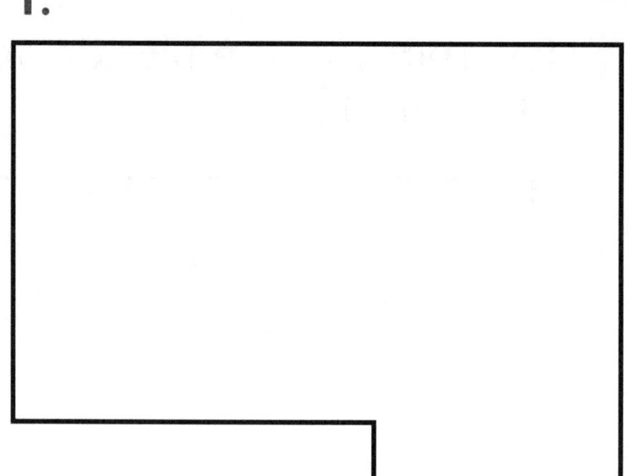

guess ______ check ______

2.

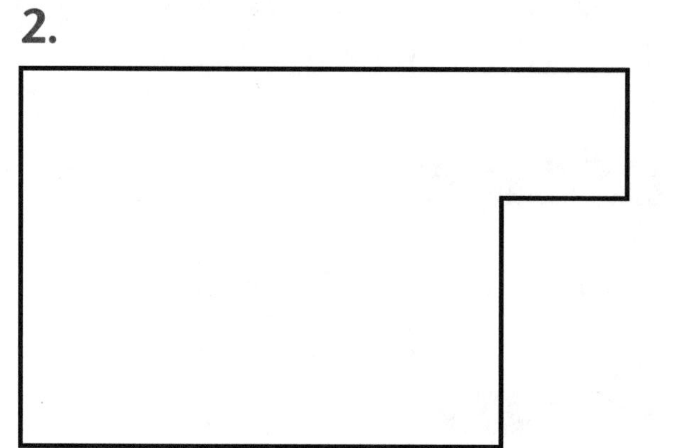

guess ______ check ______

3. Which floor has a larger area, the floor in problem 1 or in problem 2? Explain. ________________________________

____

____

Name ____________________

1 pound

A  weighs less than a pound.

A  weighs more than a pound.

Ring the best estimate.

1. 

less than a pound | about a pound | more than a pound

2. 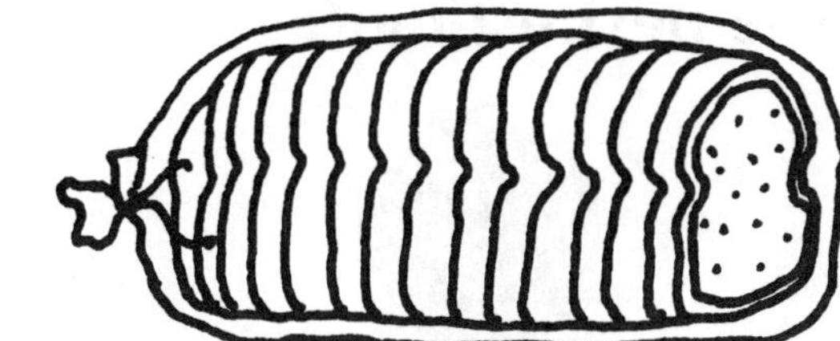

less than a pound | about a pound | more than a pound

3. 

less than a pound | about a pound | more than a pound

4. 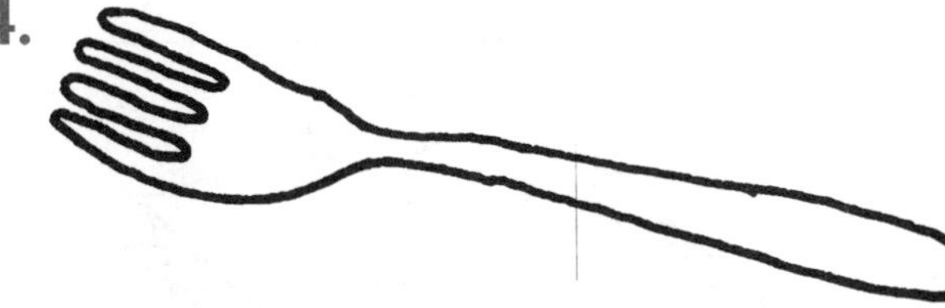

less than a pound | about a pound | more than a pound

★ Test Prep

Which one weighs more than a pound? Mark the best estimate.

5

 ○

 ○

 ○

 ○

A **kilogram** is a unit for measuring mass.

less than a kilogram

about a kilogram

more than a kilogram

Ring the best estimate.

1\.

less than a kilogram | about a kilogram | more than a kilogram

2\.

less than a kilogram | about a kilogram | more than a kilogram

3\.

less than a kilogram | about a kilogram | more than a kilogram

4\.

less than a kilogram | about a kilogram | more than a kilogram

★ Test Prep

Which one has a mass of less than a kilogram? Mark the best estimate.

5

○

○

○

○

Name ______________________________

2 cups = 1 pint

4 cups = 1 quart

2 pints = 1 quart

4 quarts = 1 gallon

Fill in the blank.

1. 4 cups = __2__ pints
2. 1 pint = ____ cups
3. ____ pints = 1 quart
4. ____ quarts = 1 gallon
5. 2 quarts = ____ cups
6. ____ cups = 1 quart
7. 4 pints = ____ quarts
8. ____ pints = 3 quarts

Quick Check

Ring the best estimate.

1.

less than a pound | about a pound | more than a pound

2.

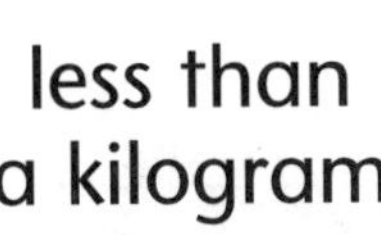
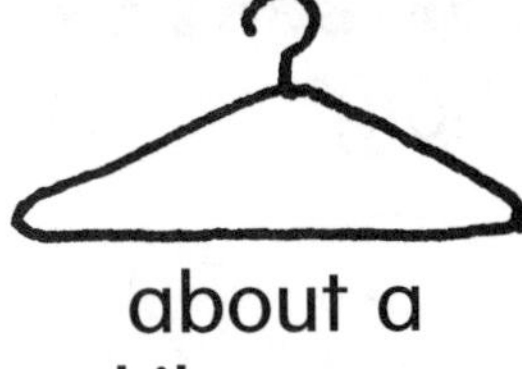

less than a kilogram | about a kilogram | more than a kilogram

Fill in the blank.

3. 8 cups = ____ quarts

Name ______________________________

A **liter** is a unit for measuring how much liquid a container will hold.

Try this experiment.

Find **5** jars or containers and label them **1–5**. Pour water from each one into a liter measure.

Which ones hold more than **1** liter?

Which ones hold less than **1** liter?

Does any jar hold the same as the liter measure?

		Less than 1 liter	1 liter	More than 1 liter
1.	**Jar 1**			
2.	**Jar 2**			
3.	**Jar 3**			
4.	**Jar 4**			
5.	**Jar 5**			

★ Test Prep

How much water does a large fish tank hold? Mark under your best estimate.

less than 1 liter	1 liter	more than 1 liter
○	○	○

Name ______________________________

Temperature can be measured in **degrees** Fahrenheit.

Read these Fahrenheit thermometers.

1. 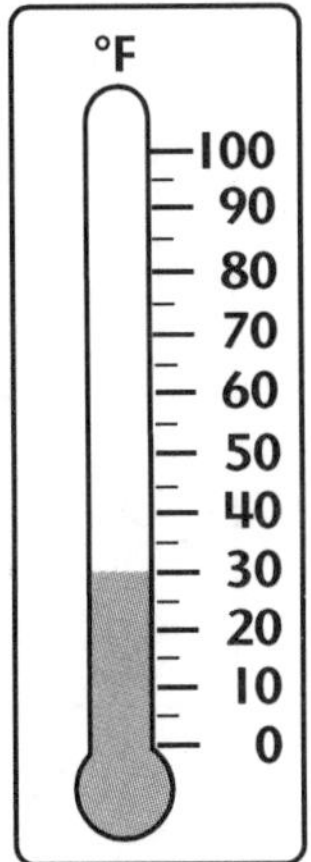

30 degrees

2. 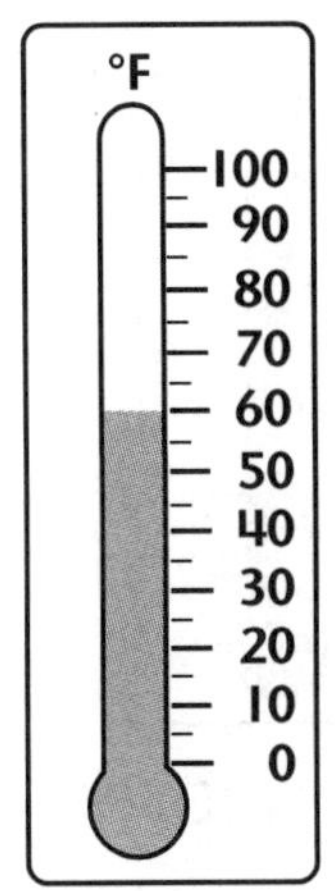

_____ degrees

3. 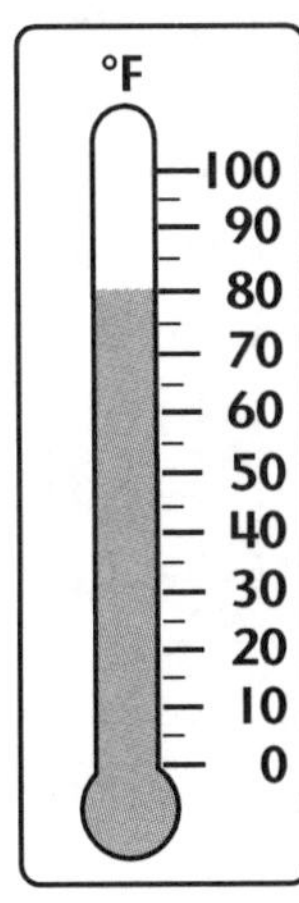

_____ degrees

4. 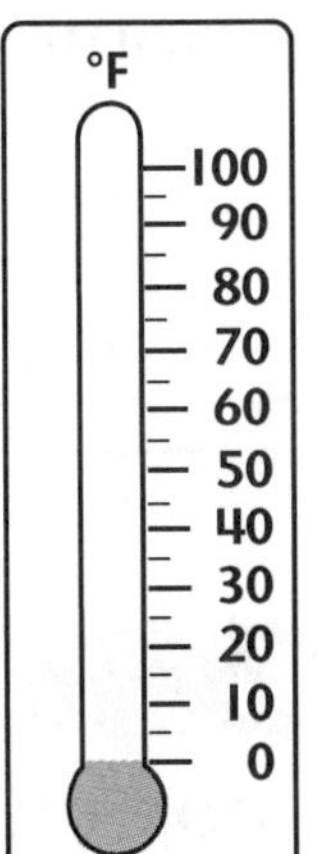

_____ degrees

5. 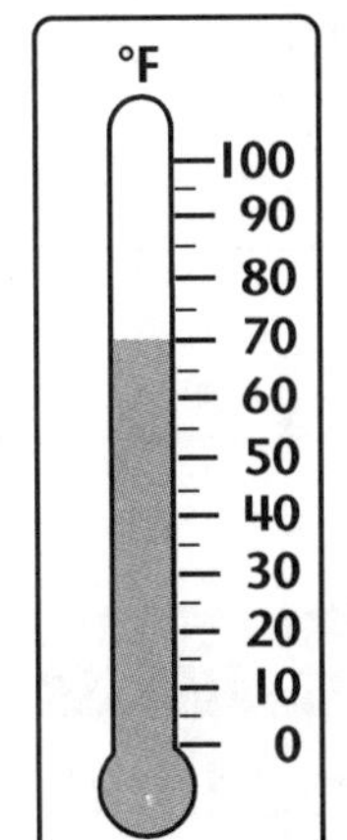

_____ degrees

6. 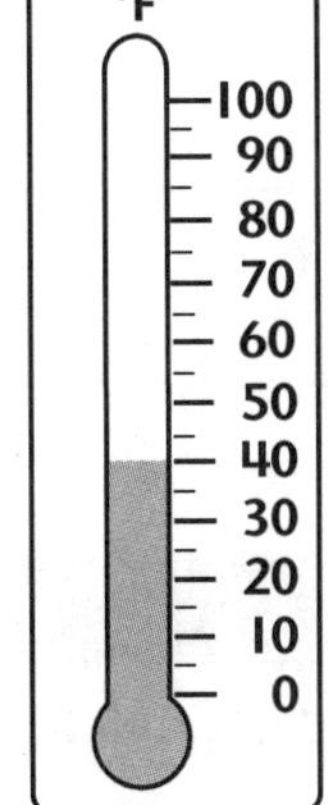

_____ degrees

Measure the temperature.

7. in your classroom _____

8. outside in the morning _____

9. outside at noon _____

Temperature can also be measured in **degrees** Celsius.

Read these Celsius thermometers.

10.

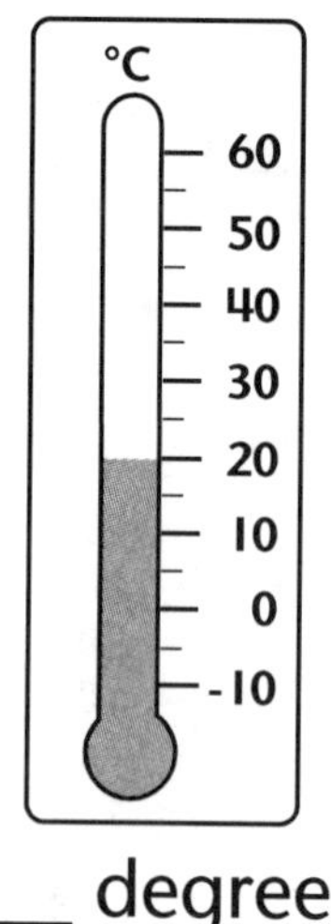

_____ degrees

11.

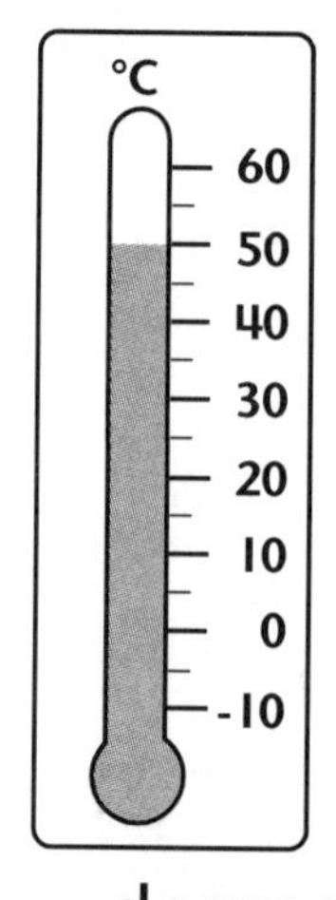

_____ degrees

12.

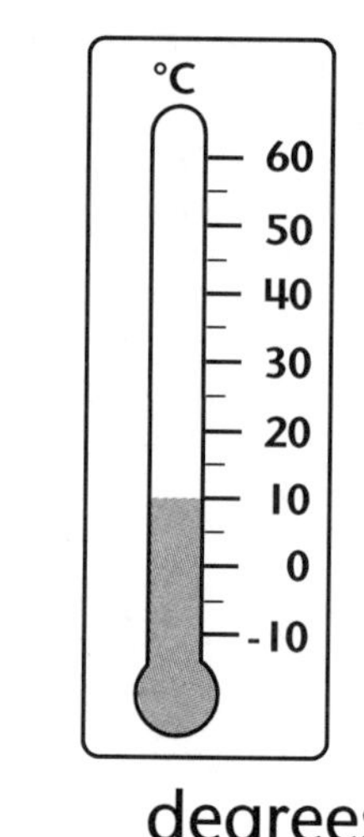

_____ degrees

Problem Solving
Reasoning

13. How are Celsius thermometers and Fahrenheit thermometers alike? ____

____

★ Test Prep

Read the Fahrenheit thermometer. Mark the correct temperature.

14

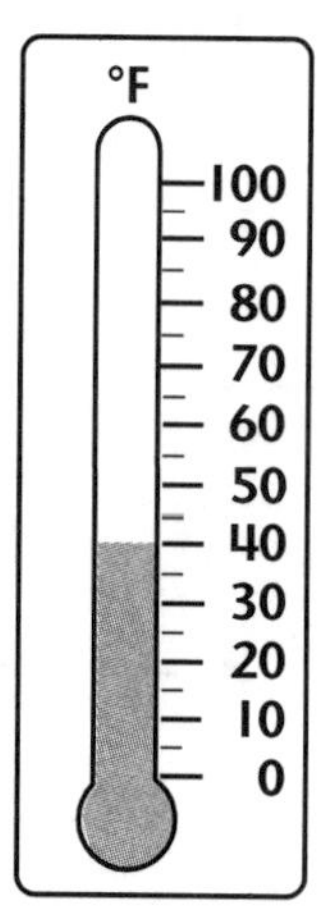

○ 20 degrees ○ 30 degrees

○ 40 degrees ○ 50 degrees

Name ______________________________

Measure with a centimeter ruler.

1.

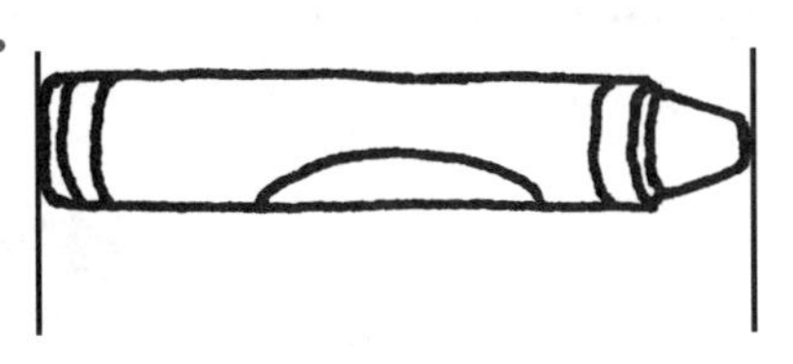

about _____ centimeters

2.

about _____ centimeters

Measure with an inch ruler.

3.

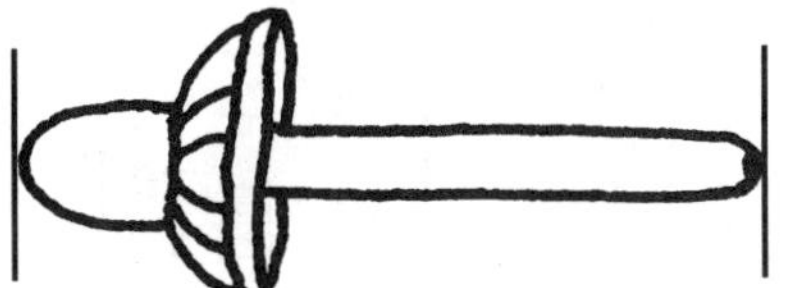

about _____ inches

4.

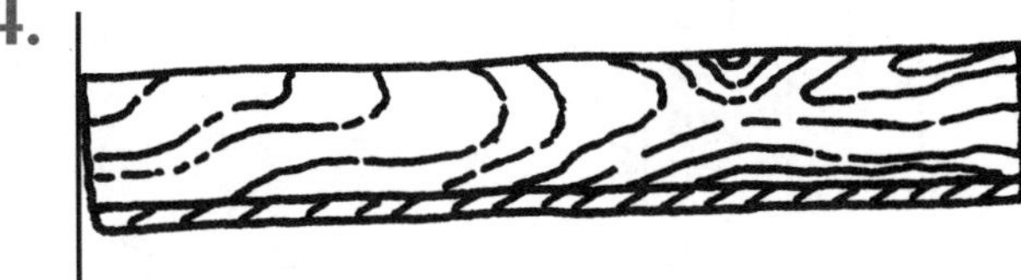

about _____ inches

Ring the best estimate.

5.

less than a pound | about a pound | more than a pound

6.

less than a pound | about a pound | more than a pound

7.

less than a kilogram | about a kilogram | more than a kilogram

8.

less than a kilogram | about a kilogram | more than a kilogram

Use an inch ruler. How far has each ladybug gone?

9. about ☐ inches

10. about ☐ inches

Read each Fahrenheit thermometer.

11. °F 100 90 80 70 60 50 40 30 20 10 0

_____ degrees

12. °F 100 90 80 70 60 50 40 30 20 10 0

_____ degrees

13. °F 100 90 80 70 60 50 40 30 20 10 0

_____ degrees

Problem Solving Reasoning

Use an inch ruler, then write a number sentence to solve.

14. What is the length of the path?

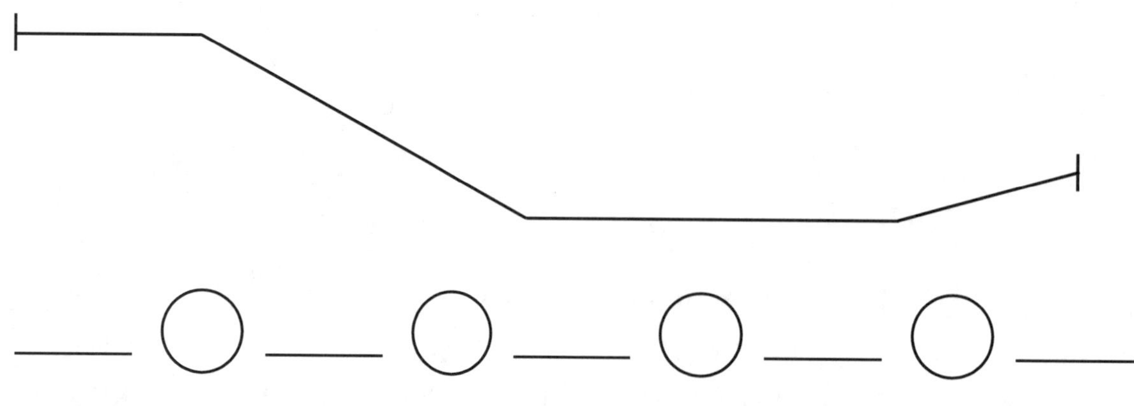

About _____ inches

Name ____________________

Complete.

1

66 ○ 68 ○ 80 ○ 86 ○

2

70¢ > 30¢ ○ 41¢ > 14¢ ○ 79¢ > 97¢ ○ 35¢ < 42¢ ○

3

○ 7 dimes and 6 pennies
○ 7 dimes and 8 pennies
○ 7 dimes and 7 pennies
○ 7 dimes and 9 pennies

4

17 pieces ○ 16 pieces ○ 19 pieces ○ 18 pieces ○

5

8 more rocks ○ 6 more rocks ○ 9 more rocks ○ 7 more rocks ○

Complete.

6

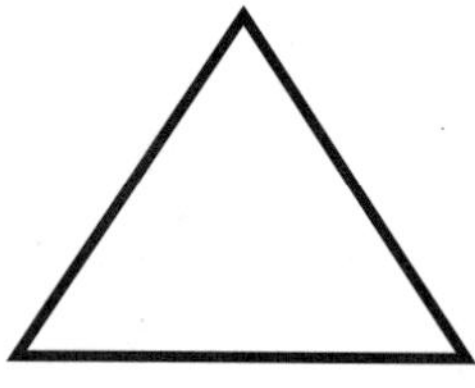

square ○ triangle ○ rectangle ○ circle ○

7

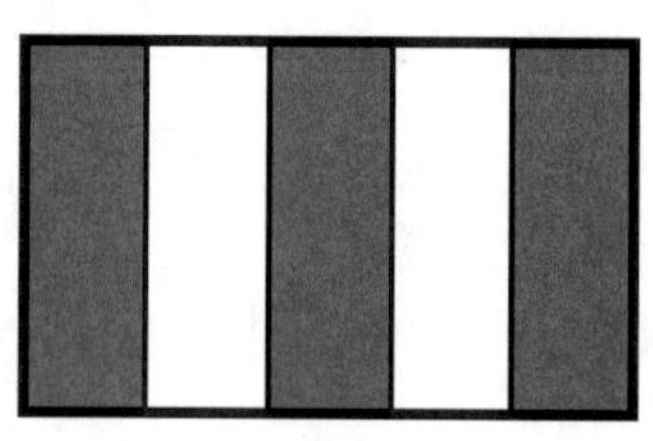

$\frac{1}{5}$ ○ $\frac{2}{5}$ ○ $\frac{3}{5}$ ○ $\frac{5}{5}$ ○

8

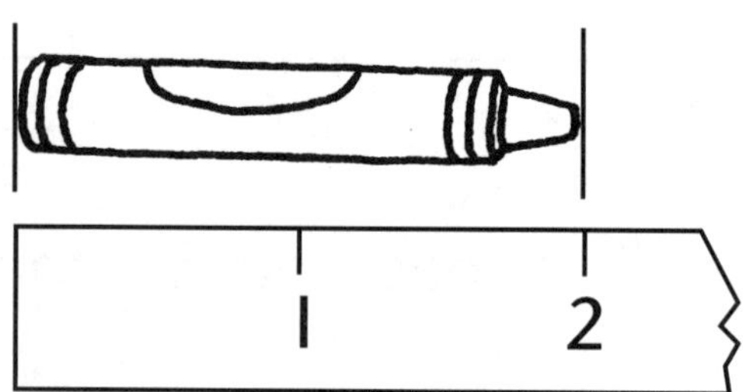

1 ○ 2 ○ 3 ○ 4 ○

Decide on an answer. Mark the space for your answer.
If the answer is **not here**, mark the space for **NH**.

9

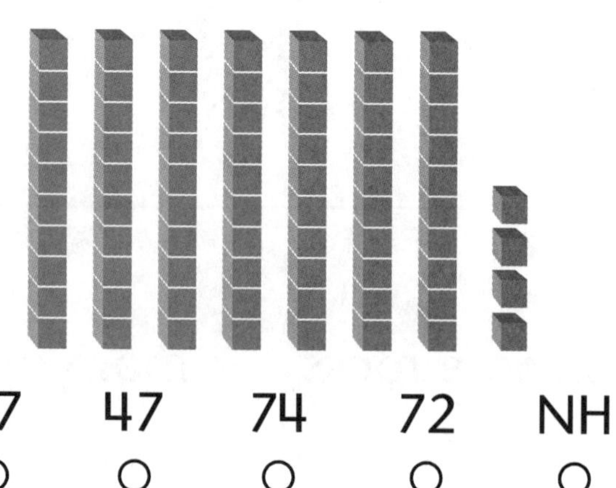

77 ○ 47 ○ 74 ○ 72 ○ NH ○

10

$9 + (4 + 3) = \square$

19 ○ 16 ○ 18 ○ 17 ○ NH ○

UNIT 6 • TABLE OF CONTENTS

2-Digit Addition

We will be using this vocabulary:

regroup group 10 ones into 1 ten

Dear Family,

During the next few weeks our math class will be learning about 2-digit addition with and without regrouping. (Other words for regrouping include carrying and trading.)

You can expect to see homework that provides practice with 2-digit addition. There will also be homework that provides practice with adding money.

As we learn about 2-digit addition, you may wish to keep the following as a guide.

Adding 2-digit Numbers

1. Look at the ones.
2. Can you regroup? If so, regroup.
3. Add the ones, then the tens.

Tens	Ones
1	
5	4
+ 3	8
9	2

Sincerely,

Name ______________________________

Use what you know to add tens.

4 tens + 2 tens = 6 tens

40 + 20 = 60

How does knowing **4 + 2 = 6** help you add **40 + 20**?

Add.

1. **2** tens + **6** tens = 8 tens

   20 + 60 = 80

2. **4** tens + **3** tens = ____ tens

   40 + 30 = ____

3. **5** tens + **4** tens = ____ tens

   50 + 40 = ____

4. **7** tens + **1** ten = ____ tens

   70 + 10 = ____

5. **20 + 30 =** ____

   30 + 10 = ____

   20 + 70 = ____

6. **30 + 30 =** ____

   60 + 30 = ____

   80 + 10 = ____

You can count on by 10's to find sums.
Use the hundred chart to help.

7. 18 + 20 = 38

Think 18. Count 28, 38.

8. 18 + 30 = ____

9. 18 + 40 = ____

10. 36 + 20 = ____

11. 37 + 20 = ____

12. 38 + 20 = ____

13. 44 + 50 = ____

14. 24 + 50 = ____

1	2	3	4	5	6	7	8	9	10
11	12	13	14	15	16	17	18	19	20
21	22	23	24	25	26	27	28	29	30
31	32	33	34	35	36	37	38	39	40
41	42	43	44	45	46	47	48	49	50
51	52	53	54	55	56	57	58	59	60
61	62	63	64	65	66	67	68	69	70
71	72	73	74	75	76	77	78	79	80
81	82	83	84	85	86	87	88	89	90
91	92	93	94	95	96	97	98	99	100

Circle the addend you count on from. Add.

15. 10 + 83 = 93

16. 30 + 21

17. 45 + 40

18. 20 + 50

19. 60 + 16

20. 71 + 10

21. 50 + 39

22. 12 + 70

You can round to the nearest ten to estimate sums.
Use the number line to round to the nearest ten.
Use mental math to estimate the sum.

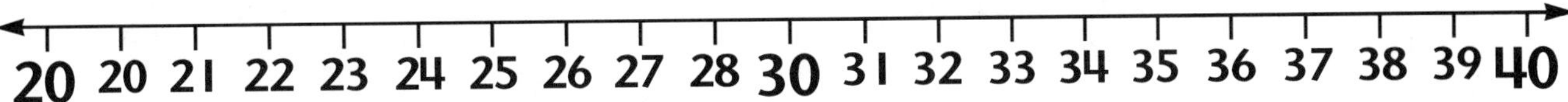

23. 23 + 39

23 is closer to 20.

29 is closer to 30.

20 + 30 = 50

23 + 39 is about 50.

24. 32 + 39

32 is closer to ______.

39 is closer to ______.

______ + ______ = ______

32 + 39 is about ______.

25. 24 + 29

______ + ______ = ______

24 + 29 is about ______.

26. 33 + 23

______ + ______ = ______

33 + 23 is about ______.

27. 22 + 37

______ + ______ = ______

22 + 37 is about ______.

28. 38 + 28

______ + ______ = ______

38 + 28 is about ______.

Problem Solving Reasoning

Estimate to solve.

29. Mei breings bunnies to the fair. She brings 22 white bunnies. She brings 12 brown bunnies. About how many bunnies are at the fair?

22 is closer to ______.

12 is closer to ______.

22 + 12 is about ______.

There are about ______ bunnies at the fair.

Name ____________________

Add.

1. 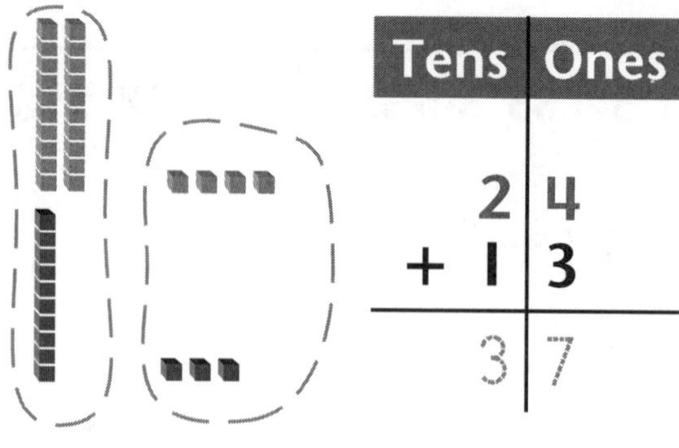

Tens	Ones
2	4
+ 1	3
3	7

2. 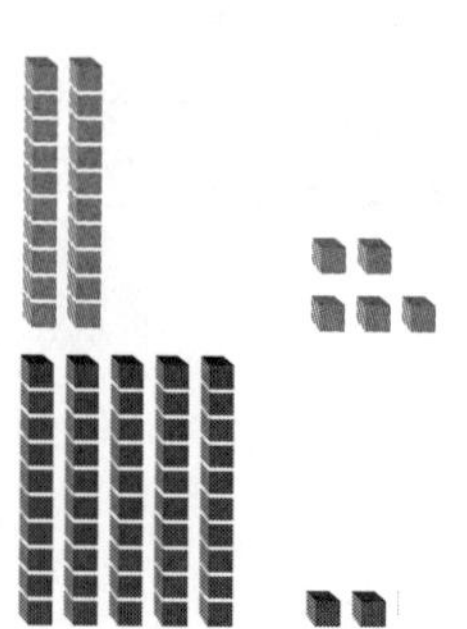

Tens	Ones
2	5
+ 5	2

3. 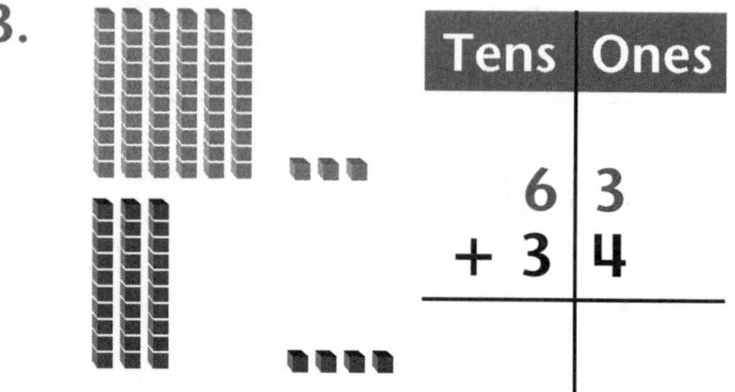

Tens	Ones
6	3
+ 3	4

4. 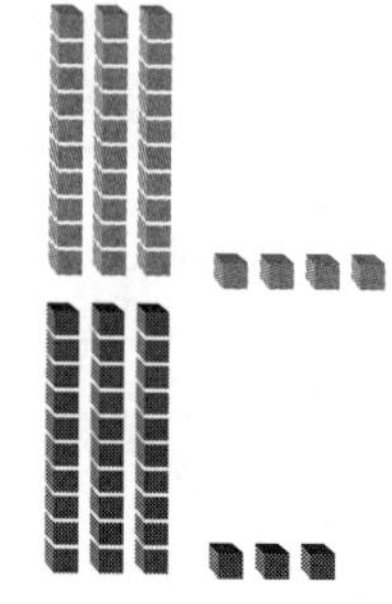

Tens	Ones
3	4
+ 3	3

5. 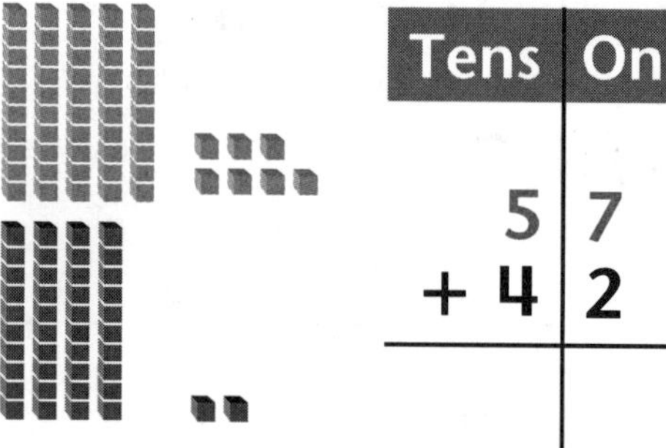

Tens	Ones
5	7
+ 4	2

6. 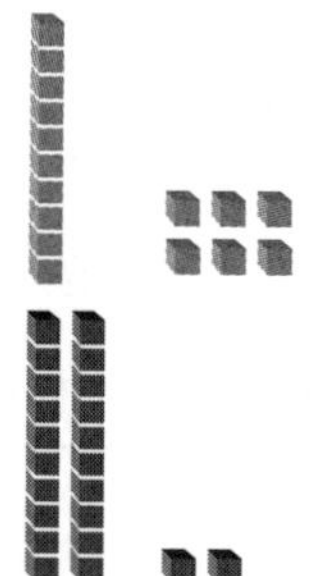

Tens	Ones
1	6
+ 2	2

7. 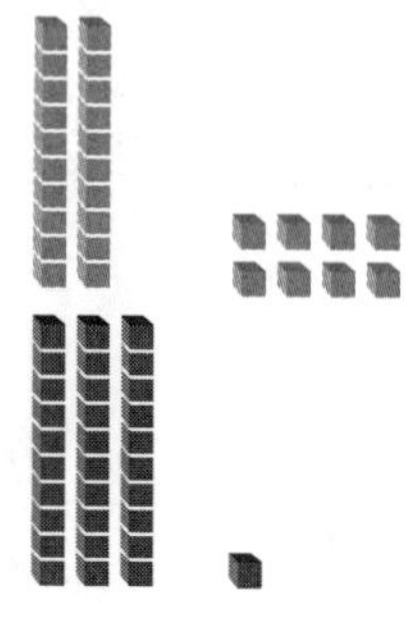

Tens	Ones
2	8
+ 3	1

8. 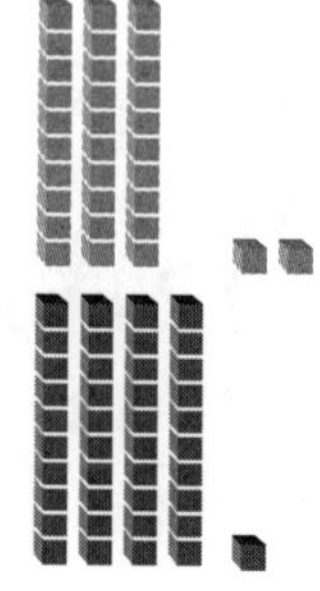

Tens	Ones
3	2
+ 4	1

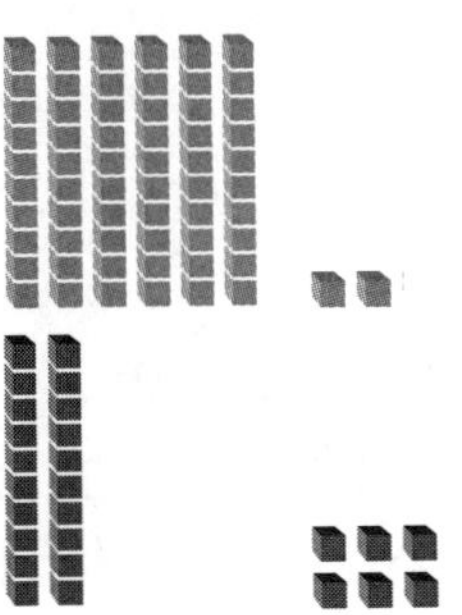

Tens	Ones
6	2
+ 2	6
8	8

$$\begin{array}{r} 62 \\ +26 \\ \hline 88 \end{array}$$ ← sum

Add.

9. $\begin{array}{r} 13 \\ +14 \\ \hline 27 \end{array}$ $\begin{array}{r} 26 \\ +11 \\ \hline \end{array}$ $\begin{array}{r} 35 \\ +12 \\ \hline \end{array}$ $\begin{array}{r} 65 \\ +11 \\ \hline \end{array}$ $\begin{array}{r} 54 \\ +13 \\ \hline \end{array}$

10. $\begin{array}{r} 46 \\ +42 \\ \hline \end{array}$ $\begin{array}{r} 34 \\ +21 \\ \hline \end{array}$ $\begin{array}{r} 18 \\ +61 \\ \hline \end{array}$ $\begin{array}{r} 27 \\ +62 \\ \hline \end{array}$ $\begin{array}{r} 93 \\ +6 \\ \hline \end{array}$

11. $\begin{array}{r} 35 \\ +44 \\ \hline \end{array}$ $\begin{array}{r} 36 \\ +12 \\ \hline \end{array}$ $\begin{array}{r} 87 \\ +2 \\ \hline \end{array}$ $\begin{array}{r} 30 \\ +12 \\ \hline \end{array}$ $\begin{array}{r} 40 \\ +11 \\ \hline \end{array}$

12. $\begin{array}{r} 54 \\ +31 \\ \hline \end{array}$ $\begin{array}{r} 65 \\ +4 \\ \hline \end{array}$ $\begin{array}{r} 82 \\ +16 \\ \hline \end{array}$ $\begin{array}{r} 60 \\ +10 \\ \hline \end{array}$ $\begin{array}{r} 70 \\ +12 \\ \hline \end{array}$

13. $\begin{array}{r} 13 \\ +22 \\ \hline \end{array}$ $\begin{array}{r} 24 \\ +30 \\ \hline \end{array}$ $\begin{array}{r} 12 \\ +54 \\ \hline \end{array}$ $\begin{array}{r} 40 \\ +10 \\ \hline \end{array}$ $\begin{array}{r} 10 \\ +11 \\ \hline \end{array}$

Problem Solving Reasoning

Solve.

14. Tony has **42** markers.
Xiao has **17** markers.
How many markers do they have in all?

_____ markers

15. Lisa grows **33** tomatoes.
Katarina grows **45** carrots.
How many vegetables do they grow in all?

_____ vegetables

16. Su Lin collects stamps.
She collects **40** red stamps and **30** blue stamps.
How many stamps has she collected?

_____ stamps

17. Kate tosses **2** counters on the game board to score points.
Her total score is **60** points.
Mark X where her counters may have landed.

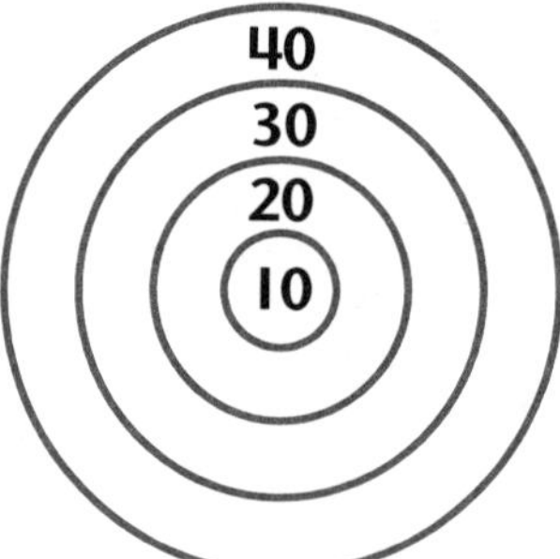

★ Test Prep

Solve. Mark the space for your answer.

$$\begin{array}{r} 54 \\ +32 \\ \hline \square \end{array}$$

75	86	22	96
○	○	○	○

Name ______________________________

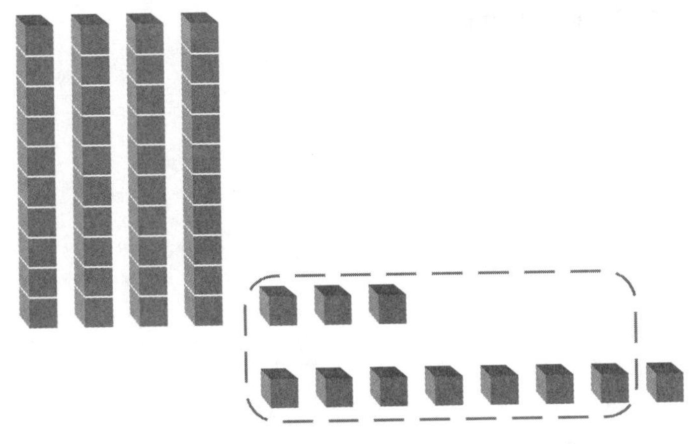

T	O
1	
4	3
+	8
5	1

This makes another ten.
So regroup.

Regroup and add.

1.

T	O
1	
2	2
+	9
3	1

2.

T	O
4	7
+	4

3.

T	O
5	5
+	6

4.

T	O
7	3
+	9

5.

T	O
4	6
+	4

6.

T	O
8	4
+	8

7.

T	O
3	4
+	6

8.

T	O
7	8
+	3

9.

T	O
3	9
+	2

Problem Solving
Reasoning

Use mental math. Think of the greater addend. Count on 1, 2, or 3 to find the sum.

$$\begin{array}{r} 2 \\ +\ 79 \\ \hline 81 \end{array}$$

Think 79.
Count 80, 81.
The sum is 81.

10. $\begin{array}{r} 87 \\ +\ 3 \\ \hline 90 \end{array}$ $\begin{array}{r} 3 \\ +18 \\ \hline \end{array}$ $\begin{array}{r} 39 \\ +\ 2 \\ \hline \end{array}$ $\begin{array}{r} 29 \\ +\ 3 \\ \hline \end{array}$ $\begin{array}{r} 2 \\ +\ 89 \\ \hline \end{array}$

11. $\begin{array}{r} 28 \\ +\ 3 \\ \hline \end{array}$ $\begin{array}{r} 1 \\ +\ 49 \\ \hline \end{array}$ $\begin{array}{r} 59 \\ +\ 3 \\ \hline \end{array}$ $\begin{array}{r} 3 \\ +\ 57 \\ \hline \end{array}$ $\begin{array}{r} 69 \\ +\ 1 \\ \hline \end{array}$

Quick Check

Add.

1. $\begin{array}{r} 50 \\ +35 \\ \hline \end{array}$

2. $\begin{array}{r} 41 \\ +\ 7 \\ \hline \end{array}$

3. $\begin{array}{r} 47 \\ +22 \\ \hline \end{array}$

4. $\begin{array}{r} 53 \\ +\ 8 \\ \hline \end{array}$

STANDARD

Name ____________________

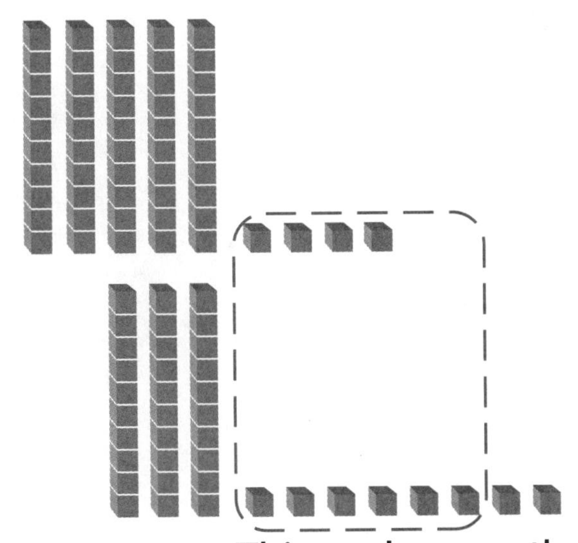

T	O
1	
5	4
+ 3	8
9	2

This makes another ten. So regroup.

Add. Start with the ones.

1.

T	O
1	
5	6
+ 2	5
8	1

2.

T	O
2	4
+ 5	7

3.

T	O
6	7
+ 2	3

4.

T	O
6	7
+ 2	4

5.

T	O
2	9
+ 1	2

6.

T	O
4	6
+ 1	6

7.

T	O
3	8
+ 2	3

8.

T	O
5	6
+ 1	6

9.

T	O
3	1
+ 1	9

Tens	Ones
1	
5	4
+ 3	6
9	0

$$\begin{array}{r} ^{1}\\ 54 \\ +\,36 \\ \hline 90 \end{array}$$

Find the sum.

10. $\begin{array}{r} 68 \\ +14 \\ \hline 82 \end{array}$
11. $\begin{array}{r} 39 \\ +23 \\ \hline \end{array}$
12. $\begin{array}{r} 48 \\ +14 \\ \hline \end{array}$
13. $\begin{array}{r} 44 \\ +26 \\ \hline \end{array}$
14. $\begin{array}{r} 53 \\ +19 \\ \hline \end{array}$
15. $\begin{array}{r} 22 \\ +29 \\ \hline \end{array}$
16. $\begin{array}{r} 44 \\ +28 \\ \hline \end{array}$
17. $\begin{array}{r} 37 \\ +44 \\ \hline \end{array}$
18. $\begin{array}{r} 64 \\ +28 \\ \hline \end{array}$
19. $\begin{array}{r} 17 \\ +33 \\ \hline \end{array}$
20. $\begin{array}{r} 43 \\ +19 \\ \hline \end{array}$
21. $\begin{array}{r} 23 \\ +28 \\ \hline \end{array}$
22. $\begin{array}{r} 45 \\ +27 \\ \hline \end{array}$
23. $\begin{array}{r} 29 \\ +32 \\ \hline \end{array}$
24. $\begin{array}{r} 56 \\ +26 \\ \hline \end{array}$
25. $\begin{array}{r} 67 \\ +24 \\ \hline \end{array}$

★ Test Prep

Solve. Mark the space for your answer.

26. $\begin{array}{r} 43 \\ +27 \\ \hline \square \end{array}$

60	69	70	80
○	○	○	○

Name ______________________________

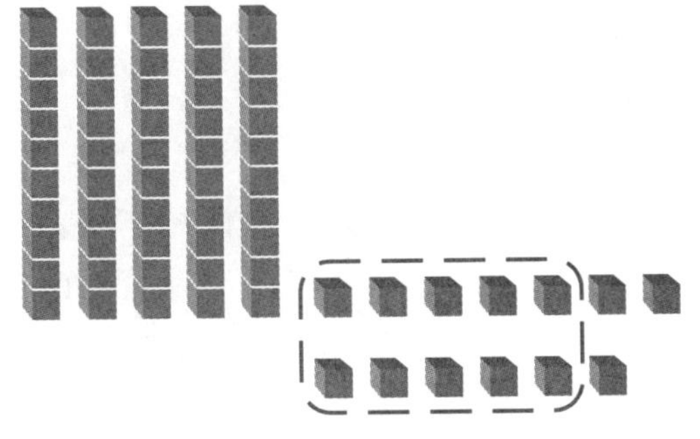

Another ten!

T	O
1	
5	7
+	6
6	3

Regroup and add.

1.

T	O
1	
4	8
+	6
5	4

2.

T	O
6	9
+	4

3.

T	O
2	7
+	7

4.

T	O
3	7
+	7

5.

T	O
4	4
+	9

6.

T	O
7	8
+	5

7.

T	O
2	5
+	8

8.

T	O
1	8
+	6

9.

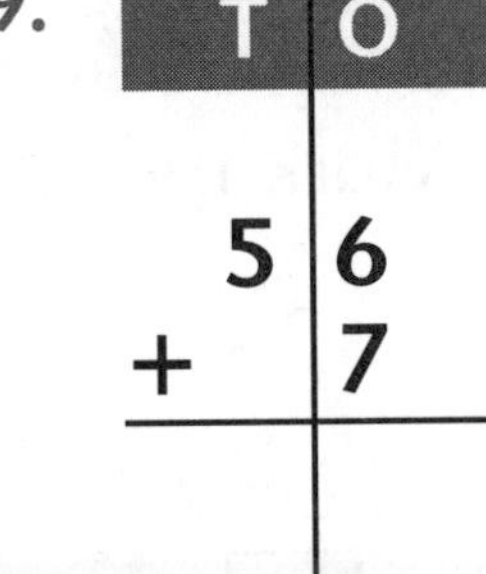

T	O
5	6
+	7

Add.

10.

T	O
6	8
+	6
7	4

68	74	57	35	42
+ 6	+ 8	+ 7	+ 7	+ 9
74				

11.

85	47	16	36	57	69
+ 8	+ 7	+ 7	+ 8	+ 5	+ 5

12.

65	39	79	54	17	49
+ 9	+ 2	+ 5	+ 7	+ 7	+ 5

Problem Solving Reasoning

Use mental math. Think of the greater addend. Count on 1, 2, or 3 to find the sum.

13.

37	2	3	38	1	77
+ 3	+79	+28	+ 3	+59	+ 3

★ Test Prep

Solve. Mark the space for your answer.

25
+ 9
☐

○ 24 ○ 34 ○ 35 ○ 38

Name ______________________________

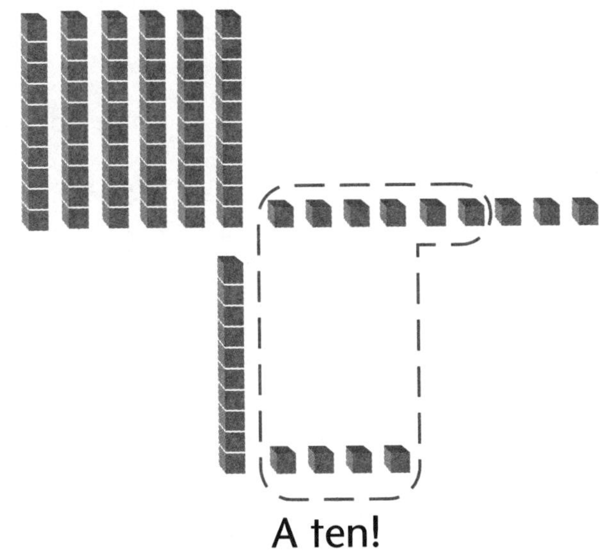

	T	O
	1	
	6	9
+	1	4
	8	3

Add. Start with the ones.

1.

	T	O
	1	
	4	9
+	3	5
	8	4

2.

	T	O
	5	8
+	1	5

3.

	T	O
	2	5
+	3	8

4.

	T	O
	1	9
+	1	4

5.

	T	O
	3	5
+	2	9

6.

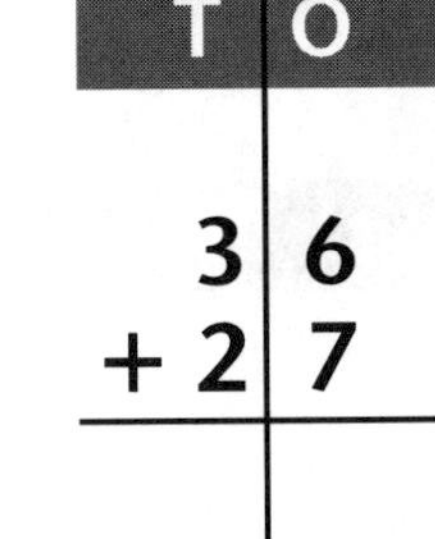

	T	O
	3	6
+	2	7

7.

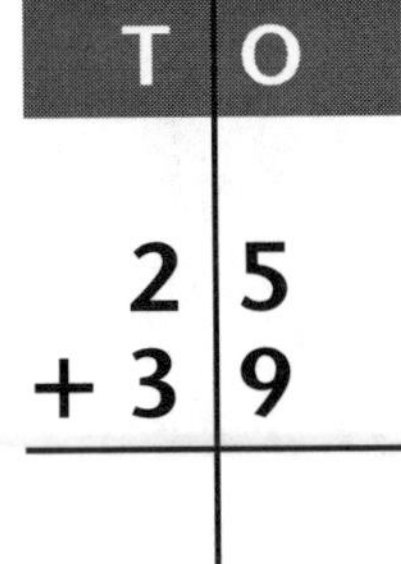

	T	O
	2	5
+	3	9

8.

	T	O
	3	6
+	1	8

9.

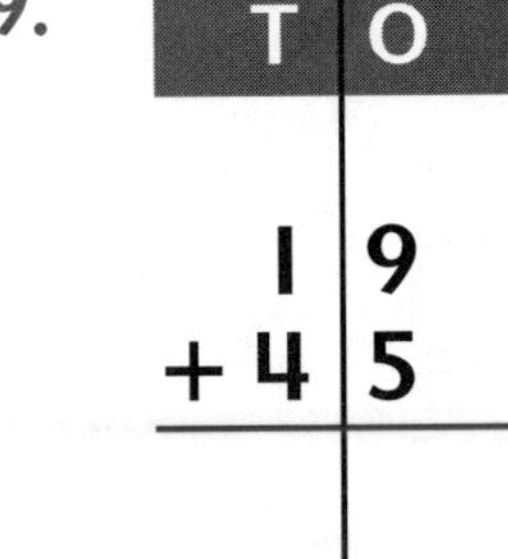

	T	O
	1	9
+	4	5

Add.

10.

T	O
1	
3	7
+ 2	7
6	4

$\begin{array}{r} 26 \\ +38 \\ \hline \end{array}$ $\begin{array}{r} 46 \\ +17 \\ \hline \end{array}$ $\begin{array}{r} 79 \\ +15 \\ \hline \end{array}$ $\begin{array}{r} 34 \\ +29 \\ \hline \end{array}$

11. $\begin{array}{r} 39 \\ +25 \\ \hline \end{array}$ $\begin{array}{r} 67 \\ +27 \\ \hline \end{array}$ $\begin{array}{r} 28 \\ +15 \\ \hline \end{array}$ $\begin{array}{r} 46 \\ +28 \\ \hline \end{array}$ $\begin{array}{r} 57 \\ +27 \\ \hline \end{array}$

12. $\begin{array}{r} 35 \\ +29 \\ \hline \end{array}$ $\begin{array}{r} 46 \\ +27 \\ \hline \end{array}$ $\begin{array}{r} 17 \\ +27 \\ \hline \end{array}$ $\begin{array}{r} 34 \\ +39 \\ \hline \end{array}$ $\begin{array}{r} 58 \\ +25 \\ \hline \end{array}$

Problem Solving
Reasoning

Solve.

13. There are **28** basketballs in the locker room.
There are **35** basketballs in the gymnasium.
How many basketballs are there in all? ______ basketballs

Quick Check

Add.

1. $\begin{array}{r} 57 \\ +24 \\ \hline \end{array}$

2. $\begin{array}{r} 78 \\ +\ 6 \\ \hline \end{array}$

3. $\begin{array}{r} 18 \\ +45 \\ \hline \end{array}$

4. $\begin{array}{r} 29 \\ +25 \\ \hline \end{array}$

STANDARD

Name ____________________

T	O
1	
2	9
+	6
3	5

T	O
1	
3	8
+	8
4	6

Add.

1. 27 + 9 = 6 (T O: 1 carried; 2 | 7, + 9, answer ones 6)   79 + 6   58 + 8   16 + 9   89 + 7

2. 37 + 8   27 + 9   26 + 9   69 + 6   88 + 7

3. 68 + 8   29 + 4   17 + 9   67 + 8   56 + 9

4. 28 + 7   37 + 9   47 + 9   19 + 6   38 + 7

5. 59 + 7   19 + 6   28 + 7   47 + 8   67 + 9

Add.

6.	36 +19 55	57 +19	38 +17	29 +46	38 +17
7.	19 +67	47 +18	58 +18	76 +19	37 +19
8.	76 +19	17 +49	68 +17	19 +47	79 +17
9.	29 +16	38 +48	47 +29	58 +38	67 +18

Problem Solving Reasoning Solve.

10. Kevin picks **36** apples. Dee picks **39** apples. How many apples do they pick in all?

____

11. The red team counts **28** caterpillars. The blue team counts **38** caterpillars. How many caterpillars are there in all?

____

★ Test Prep

Solve. Mark the space under your answer.

12. 48 + 18 = ☐

56	66	68	78
○	○	○	○

Name ____________________

T	O
1	
4	8
+	9
5	7

T	O
1	
3	9
+	9
4	8

Add.

1.	39 + 8 = 47	69 + 9	59 + 8	88 + 9	49 + 9
2.	39 + 9	68 + 9	58 + 9	29 + 8	78 + 9
3.	89 + 8	49 + 8	79 + 9	19 + 8	59 + 9
4.	38 + 9	89 + 9	18 + 9	69 + 8	29 + 9

Complete.

5. 8 + ____ = 17 18 − ____ = 9 9 + ____ = 17

6. 9 + ____ = 18 17 − ____ = 9 17 − ____ = 8

Add.

7. 49 + 28 = 77	58 + 19	68 + 29	69 + 19	58 + 39
8. 39 + 18	19 + 28	29 + 48	49 + 38	69 + 29
9. 39 + 29	19 + 29	19 + 19	78 + 19	38 + 29

Problem Solving Reasoning Solve.

10. There are **19** girls at the picnic. There are **18** boys at the picnic. How many children are at the picnic in all?

____

11. Cathy has **29** pins in her collection. Charlie has **29** pins in his collection, too. How many pins do they have in all?

____

★ Test Prep

Solve. Mark the space under your answer.

12. 29 + 19 = ☐

48	28	38	49
○	○	○	○

Name ____________________

Add. Use ¢.

1. 23¢ + 38¢ = 61¢   39¢ + 18¢ = ____   55¢ + 25¢ = ____   67¢ + 27¢ = ____   49¢ + 32¢ = ____

2. 47¢ + 29¢ = ____   53¢ + 19¢ = ____   66¢ + 27¢ = ____   29¢ + 67¢ = ____   68¢ + 22¢ = ____

How much for both?

3.

39¢ + 59¢ = 98¢

4.

\+ ____

5.

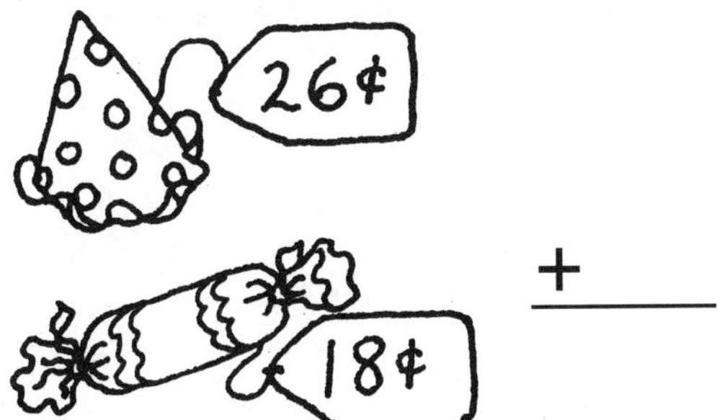

\+ ____

6.

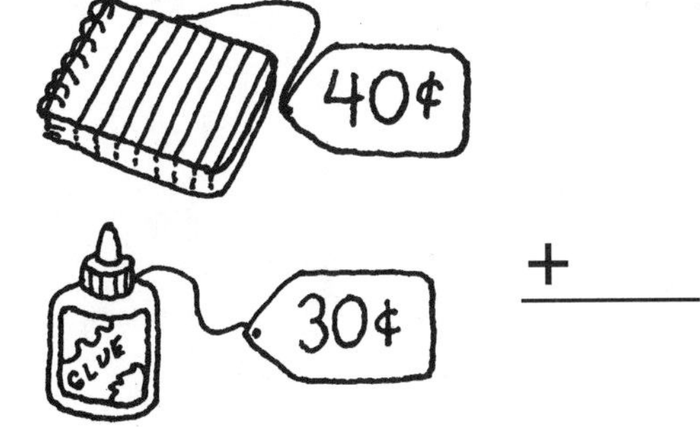

\+ ____

7.

\+ ____

8.

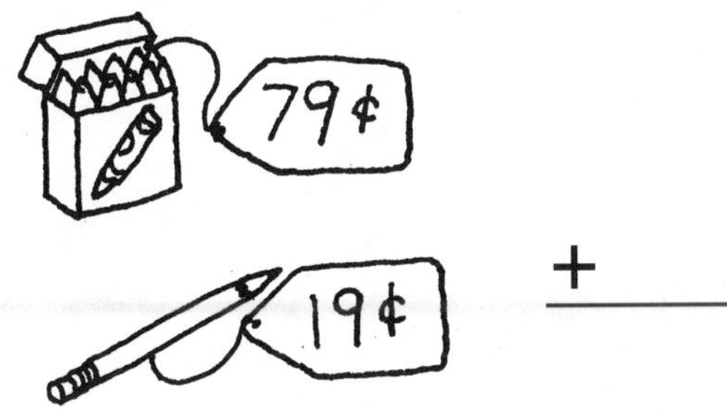

\+ ____

Find the sum.

9. $\begin{array}{r} 27¢ \\ + 18¢ \\ \hline \end{array}$ $\begin{array}{r} 39¢ \\ + 46¢ \\ \hline \end{array}$ $\begin{array}{r} 71¢ \\ + 19¢ \\ \hline \end{array}$ $\begin{array}{r} 26¢ \\ + 35¢ \\ \hline \end{array}$

10. $\begin{array}{r} 73¢ \\ + 17¢ \\ \hline \end{array}$ $\begin{array}{r} 92¢ \\ + 7¢ \\ \hline \end{array}$ $\begin{array}{r} 66¢ \\ + 26¢ \\ \hline \end{array}$ $\begin{array}{r} 29¢ \\ + 69¢ \\ \hline \end{array}$

Problem Solving
Reasoning

Solve.

11. Theo spends **63¢** for the ball.
He spends **29¢** for the balloon.
How much does Theo spend for both?

____

Quick Check

Solve.

1. $\begin{array}{r} 57 \\ + 8 \\ \hline \end{array}$

2. $\begin{array}{r} 53 \\ + 8 \\ \hline \end{array}$

3. $\begin{array}{r} 64 \\ + 19 \\ \hline \end{array}$

4. $\begin{array}{r} 66¢ \\ + 13¢ \\ \hline \end{array}$

Name ____________________

Add.

1. 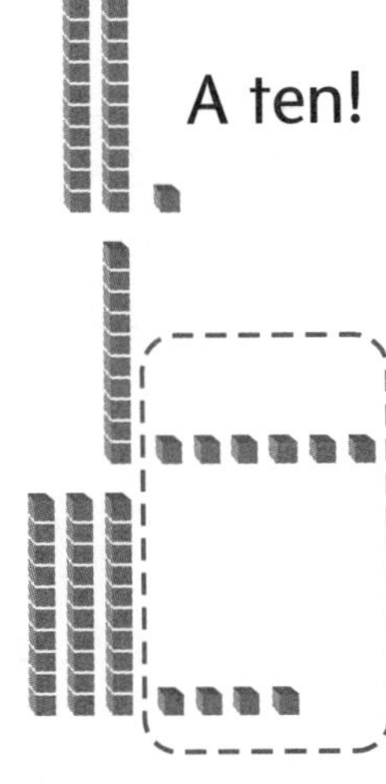

T	O
2	1
1	6
+ 3	4
7	1

>10

2. 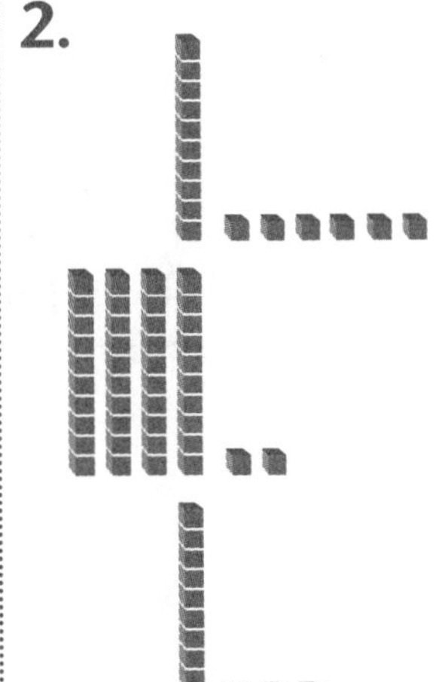

T	O
1	6
4	2
+ 1	3

>8

3.

32	43	41	62
14	14	25	12
+ 35	+ 25	+ 26	+ 18

4.

21	52	64	34
45	10	12	31
+ 16	+ 18	+ 16	+ 25

5.

43	36	43	34
12	10	20	42
+ 17	+ 46	+ 18	+ 16

6.

12	14	37	50
35	13	11	14
+ 23	+ 45	+ 24	+ 17

Add each column. Start with the ones.

7.

T	O
3	2
1	5
+ 2	6
7	3

8.

T	O
2	6
5	3
+ 1	3

9.

T	O
4	4
1	5
+ 3	4

Add.

10.

42	34	51	22	53
33	44	15	13	14
+ 18	+ 12	+ 23	+ 48	+ 23

11.

63	12	42	11	27
13	14	22	51	11
+ 16	+ 27	+ 28	+ 28	+ 53

Problem Solving Reasoning Write an addition story using three addends.

12. ____

____

★ Test Prep

Solve. Mark the space under your answer.
If the answer is **not here**, mark the space for **NH**.

13

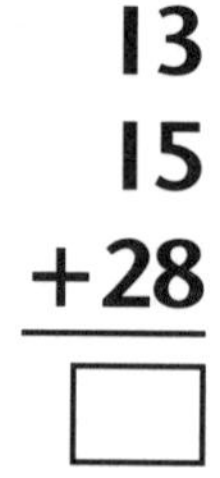

13
15
+28
☐

46	54	56	66	NH
○	○	○	○	○

STANDARD

Name ________________________________

Problem

Which two jars have a total of **60** beans?

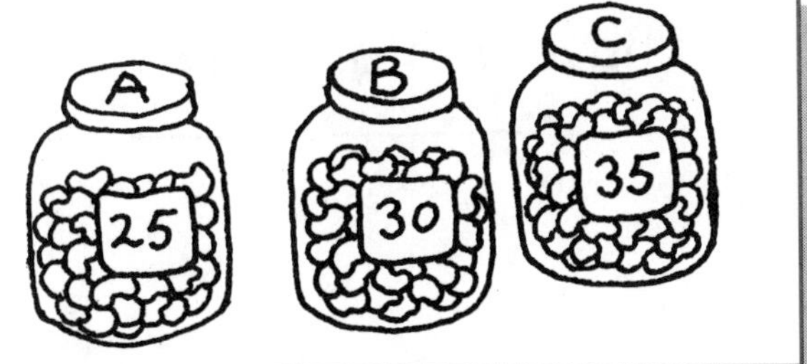

1 Understand

I need to find out which two jars have a total of **60** beans.

2 Decide

I can guess then check.

3 Solve

First guess: I'll guess Jar A and Jar B. I'll add to check.

$$\begin{array}{r} 25 \\ +\ 30 \\ \hline 55 \end{array}$$

beans. Too low. I'll guess again.

Second guess: I'll guess Jar B and Jar C. I'll add to check.

$$\begin{array}{r} 30 \\ +\ 35 \\ \hline 65 \end{array}$$

beans. Too high. I'll guess again.

Third guess: I'll guess Jar A and Jar C. I'll add to check.

$$\begin{array}{r} 25 \\ +\ 35 \\ \hline 60 \end{array}$$

beans. The guess checks!

Answer Jar <u>A</u> and Jar <u>C</u>

4 Look back

Does my answer make sense? Why?

Solve using guess and check. Show your work.

1. Which two jars have a total of **42** beans?

D 18

E 20

F 24

Answer Jar ____ and Jar ____

2. Which three jars have a total of **73** beans?

G 24

H 30

I 22

J 27

Answer Jar ____ and Jar ____ and Jar ____

Name ______________________________

Problem Solving Plan			
1. Understand	2. Decide	3. Solve	4. Look back

Is there enough information? Ring the answer.
Solve the problems that have enough information.

1. There are **17** red apple trees. There are more yellow apple trees than red apple trees. How many apple trees in all?

   Think Is there enough information?

   enough 

   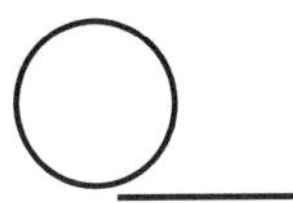

   _____ apple trees

2. Ashley sees **35** orange butterflies. Andrew sees **29** yellow butterflies. How many butterflies do they see in all?

   Think Is there enough information?

   enough not enough

   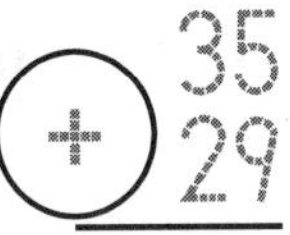

   64 butterflies

3. There are **12** big carrots. There are **9** little carrots. How many fewer little carrots?

   Think Is there enough information?

   enough not enough

   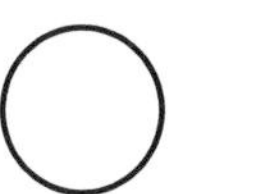

   _____ fewer little carrots

4. There are **28** white bears. There are **42** brown bears. How many black bears are there?

   Think Is there enough information?

   enough not enough

   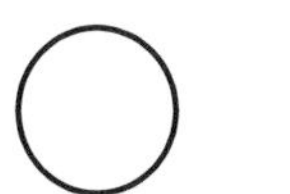

   _____ black bears

Is there enough information? Ring the answer. Solve the problems that have enough information.

5. Ling saw **24** elephants. She saw **14** bears. She saw **24** rabbits. How many animals did she see in all?

enough   not enough

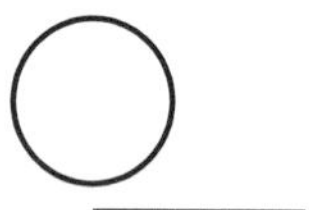

_____ animals

6. There are **16** birds in the first tree. There are **27** birds in the second tree. How many birds are in the third tree?

enough   not enough

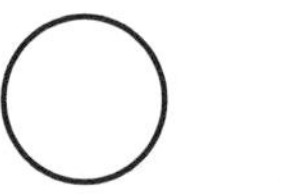

_____ birds

7. There are **36** red peanuts. There are **5** brown peanuts. How many peanuts in all?

enough   not enough

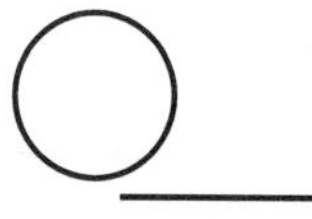

_____ peanuts

8. There are **11** blue fish in the pond. There are fewer red fish in the pond. How many red fish are there?

enough   not enough

_____ red fish

Extend Your Thinking

9. Choose a problem that does not have enough information. Rewrite it so that it has enough information. Solve.

Name ______________________

Unit 6 Review

Add.

1. 4 tens + 2 tens = ____ tens

   40 + 20 = ____

2. 3 tens + 5 tens = ____ tens

   30 + 50 = ____

3. 15 + 45 = ____

4. 40 + 35 = ____

Add.

5. 55 + 13

6. 36¢ + 24¢

7. 79 + 19

8. 47¢ + 19¢

9. 38 + 29

10. 45 + 27

11. 14 + 29

12. 15 + 39

13. 56 + 19

14. 45 + 13

15. 46 + 22 + 12

16. 16¢ + 23¢ + 18¢

17. 52 + 23 + 19

18. 42 + 34 + 17

19. 56 + 22 + 19

Problem Solving Reasoning

Is there enough information? Ring the answer. Solve the problems that have enough information.

20. There are 44 red apples.
There are 29 green apples.
How many apples are there?

enough   not enough

______ apples

21. There are 37 pears.
There are 16 bananas.
How many lemons are there?

enough   not enough

______ lemons

Name ______________________________

1

79		81

78 ○ 80 ○ 82 ○ 83 ○

2

30	35	40		50	55

39 ○ 41 ○ 45 ○ 60 ○

3

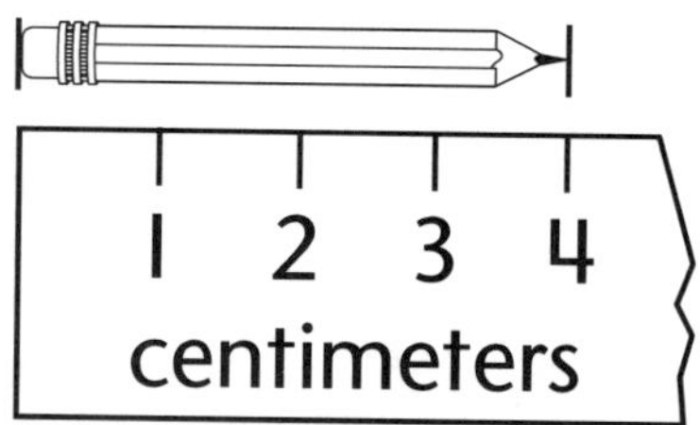

5 ○ 3 ○ 4 ○ 2 ○

Decide on an answer. Mark the space for your answer.
If the answer is **not here**, mark the space for **NH**.

4 **40** + **30** = ☐

60 ○ 65 ○ 70 ○ 75 ○ NH ○

5 **26** + **48** = ☐

63 ○ 74 ○ 64 ○ 73 ○ NH ○

6 **13** + **25** + **46** = ☐

85 ○ 74 ○ 75 ○ 80 ○ NH ○

7

X X X
X X X
X X X

$\frac{2}{3}$ of **9** = ☐

2 ○ 3 ○ 6 ○ 9 ○ NH ○

8

X X X X
X X X X
X X X X

$\frac{1}{3}$ of **12** = ☐

3 ○ 4 ○ 6 ○ 12 ○ NH ○

UNIT 7 • TABLE OF CONTENTS

2-Digit Subtraction

We will be using this vocabulary:

regroup a ten take apart 1 ten to make 10 ones

Dear Family,

During the next few weeks our math class will be learning about 2-digit subtraction with and without regrouping.

You can expect to see homework that provides practice with 2-digit subtraction. There will also be homework that provides practice with using money.

As we learn about 2-digit subtraction, you may wish to keep the following as a guide.

To subtract $\begin{array}{r} 62 \\ -\ 5 \\ \hline \end{array}$

1. Regroup a ten.

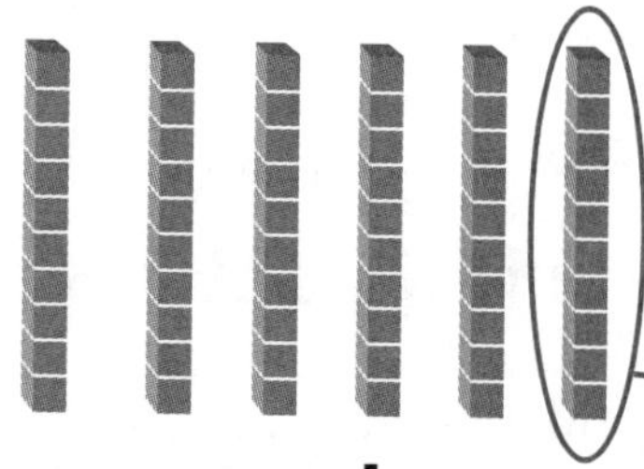

Take apart **1** ten to make **10** ones. **5** tens are left.

10 + 2 = 12 ones

2. Subtract.

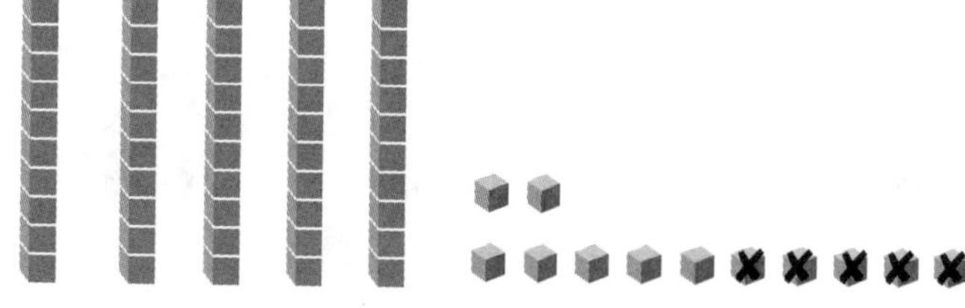

T	O
5	12
~~6~~	~~2~~
−	5
5	7

Sincerely,

Name ______________________________

Use mental math to subtract tens.

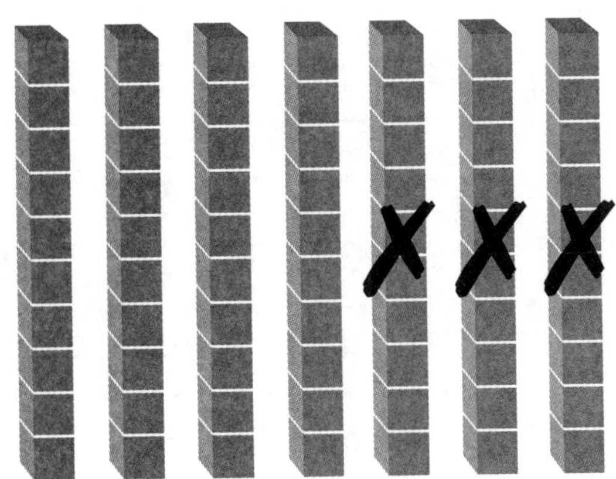

7 tens − **3** tens = **4** tens

70 − 30 = 40

How does knowing **7 − 3 = 4** help you subtract **70 − 30**?

____

Subtract.

1. **8** tens − **2** tens = 6 tens

   80 − 20 = 60

2. **9** tens − **4** tens = _____ tens

   90 − 40 = _____

3. **7** tens − **5** tens = _____ tens

   70 − 50 = _____

4. **5** tens − **1** ten = _____ tens

   50 − 10 = _____

5. **50 − 30 =** _____

6. **80 − 40 =** _____

7. **90 − 20 =** _____

8. **70 − 40 =** _____

9. **60 − 40 =** _____

10. **90 − 30 =** _____

Count back by 10's to find the difference. Use the hundred chart to help.

11. 66 − 30 = 36

Think 66.
Count back 56, 46, 36.

12. 66 − 40 = ____

13. 79 − 20 = ____

14. 78 − 20 = ____

15. 38 − 10 = ____

16. 52 − 40 = ____

1	2	3	4	5	6	7	8	9	10
11	12	13	14	15	16	17	18	19	20
21	22	23	24	25	26	27	28	29	30
31	32	33	34	35	36	37	38	39	40
41	42	43	44	45	46	47	48	49	50
51	52	53	54	55	56	57	58	59	60
61	62	63	64	65	66	67	68	69	70
71	72	73	74	75	76	77	78	79	80
81	82	83	84	85	86	87	88	89	90
91	92	93	94	95	96	97	98	99	100

Use the hundred chart.
Round to the nearest ten.
Subtract to estimate the difference.

17. 47 − 18

47 is closer to 50.

18 is closer to 20.

50 − 20 = 30

47 − 18 is about 30.

18. 71 − 27

71 is closer to ____.

27 is closer to ____.

____ − ____ = ____

71 − 27 is about ____.

19. 93 − 29

____ − ____ = ____

93 − 29 is about ____.

20. 89 − 42

____ − ____ = ____

89 − 42 is about ____.

Name ______________________________

Subtract.

1.

Tens	Ones
3	7
− 2	4
1	3

2. 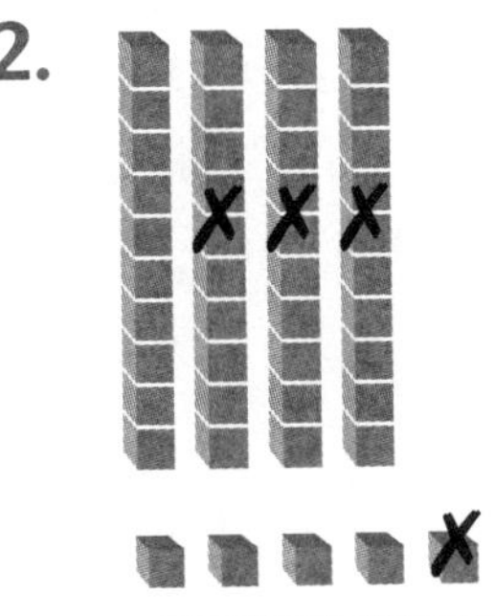

Tens	Ones
4	5
− 3	1

3. 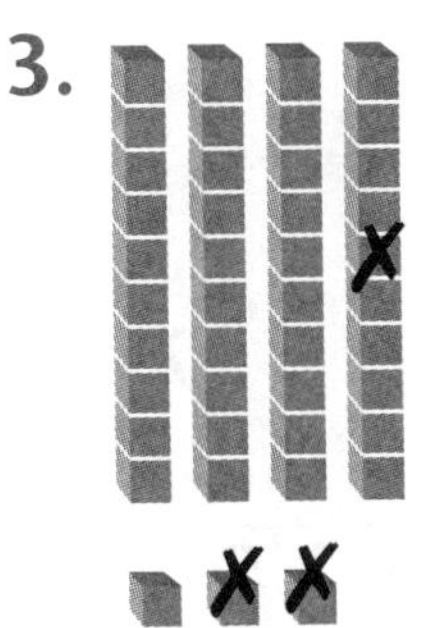

Tens	Ones
4	3
− 1	2

4. 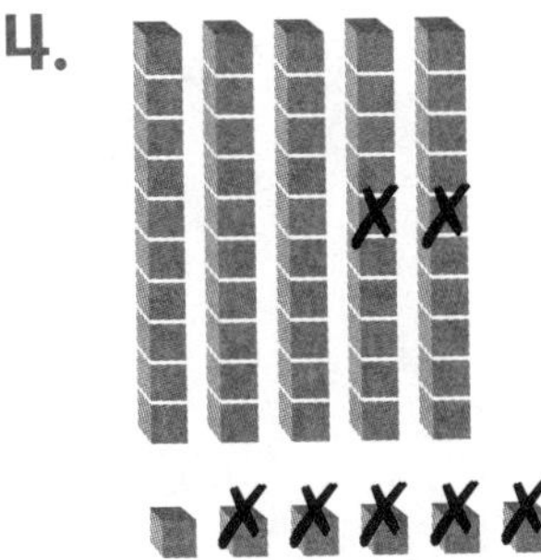

Tens	Ones
5	6
− 2	5

5. 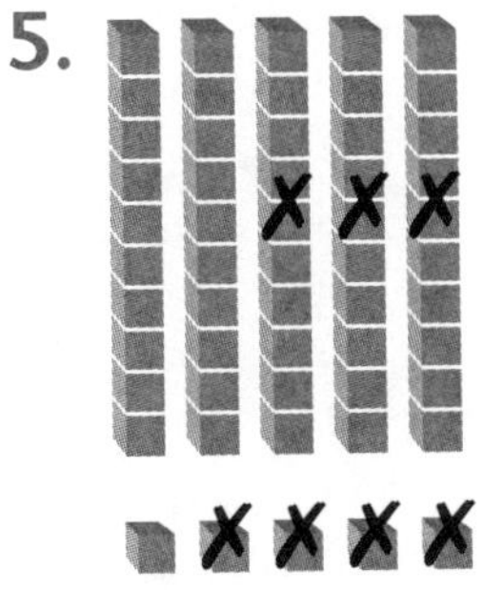

Tens	Ones
5	5
− 3	4

6. 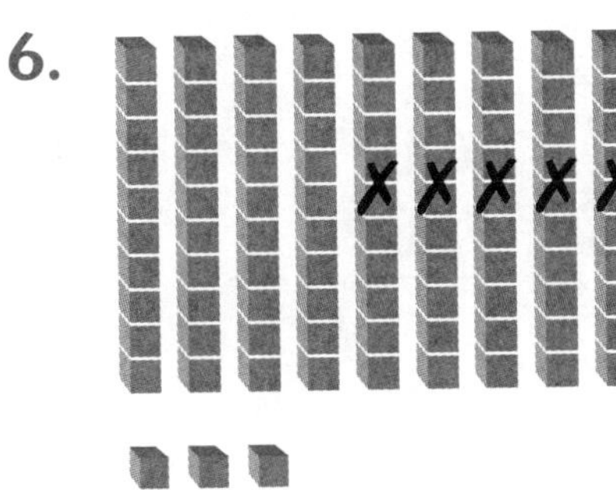

Tens	Ones
9	3
− 5	0

7. 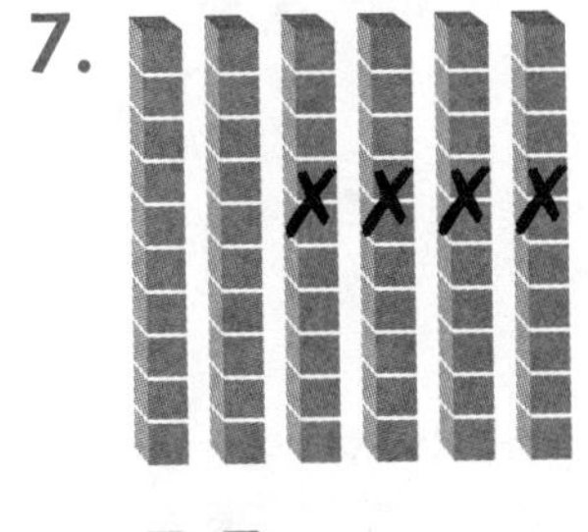

Tens	Ones
6	2
− 4	0

8. 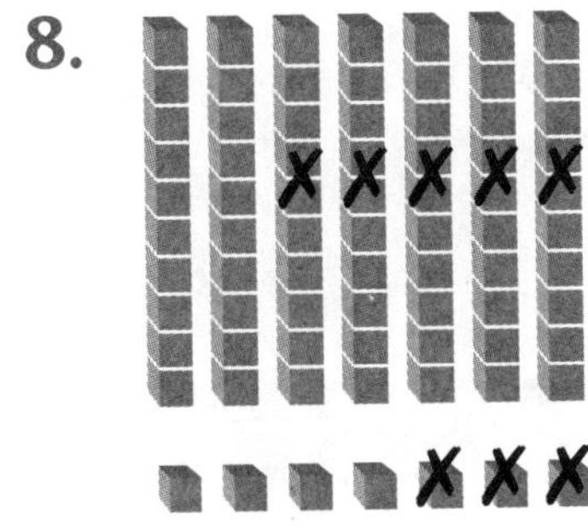

Tens	Ones
7	7
− 5	3

9. 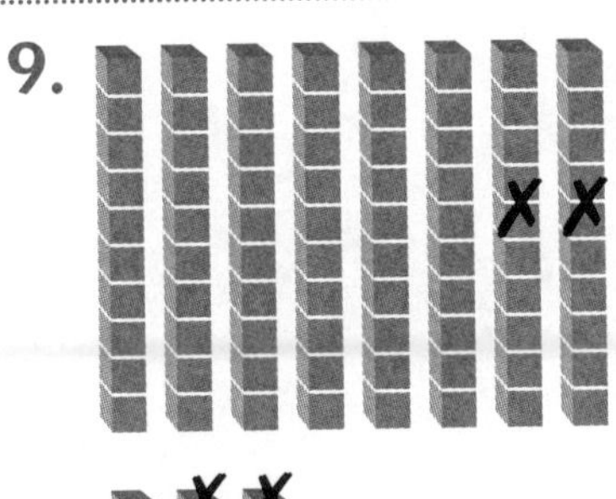

Tens	Ones
8	3
− 2	2

10. 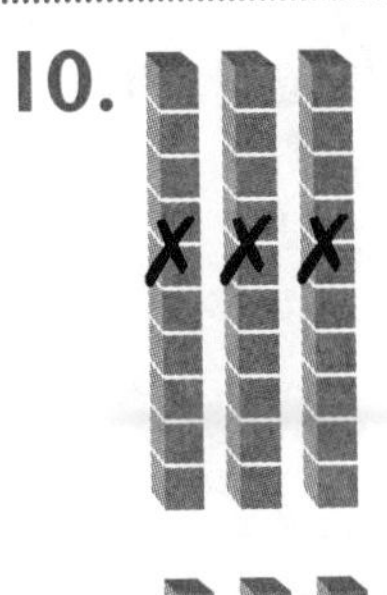

Tens	Ones
3	9
− 3	4

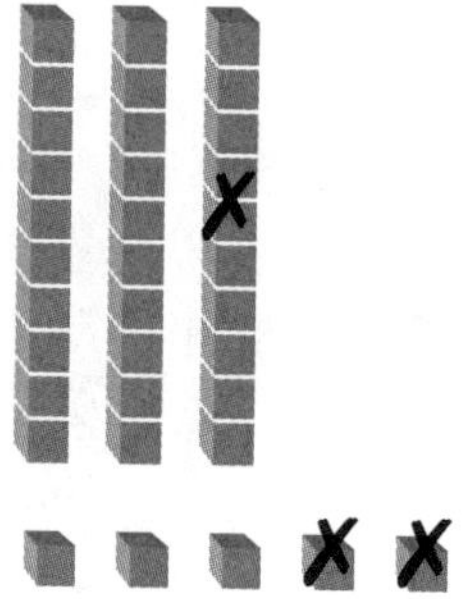

T	O
3	5
− 1	2
2	3

$$\begin{array}{r} 35 \\ -\ 12 \\ \hline 23 \end{array} \leftarrow \text{difference}$$

Subtract.

11.

T	O
2	7
− 1	3
1	4

T	O
3	6
− 1	2

T	O
4	5
− 2	4

T	O
6	6
− 1	5

T	O
7	7
− 3	4

12. $\begin{array}{r} 55 \\ -\ 23 \\ \hline \end{array}$ $\begin{array}{r} 60 \\ -\ 40 \\ \hline \end{array}$ $\begin{array}{r} 49 \\ -\ 28 \\ \hline \end{array}$ $\begin{array}{r} 20 \\ -\ 10 \\ \hline \end{array}$ $\begin{array}{r} 37 \\ -\ 16 \\ \hline \end{array}$

13. $\begin{array}{r} 98 \\ -\ 34 \\ \hline \end{array}$ $\begin{array}{r} 87 \\ -\ 51 \\ \hline \end{array}$ $\begin{array}{r} 76 \\ -\ 42 \\ \hline \end{array}$ $\begin{array}{r} 64 \\ -\ 31 \\ \hline \end{array}$ $\begin{array}{r} 59 \\ -\ 26 \\ \hline \end{array}$

★ Test Prep

Solve. Decide on an answer. Mark the space for your answer. If the answer is **not here**, mark the space for **NH**.

 14

$\begin{array}{r} 78 \\ -\ 26 \\ \hline \square \end{array}$

42	43	52	53	NH
○	○	○	○	○

Name ______________________________

Regroup a ten.

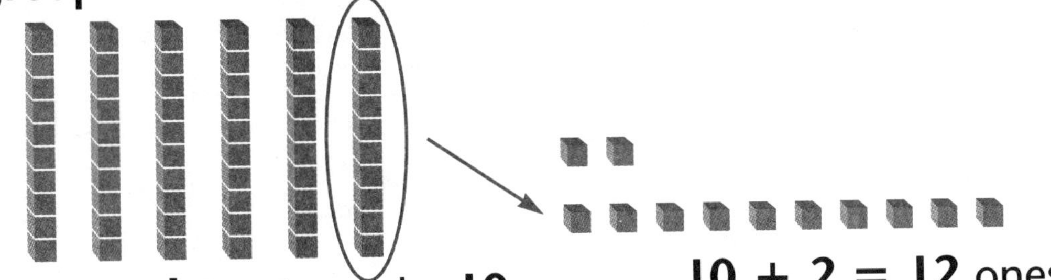

Take apart **1** ten to make **10** ones. **5** tens are left.

10 + 2 = 12 ones

Subtract.

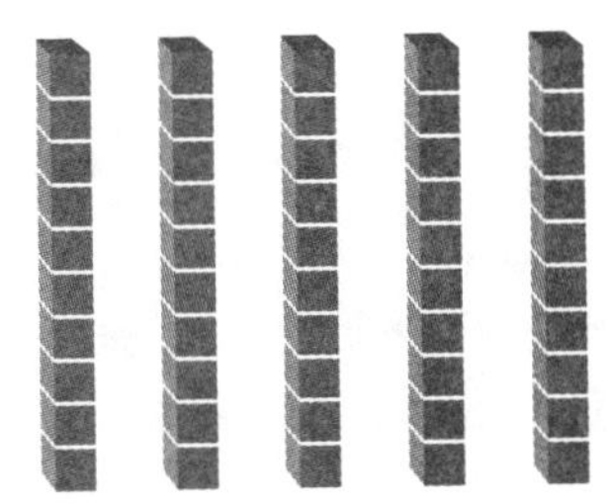

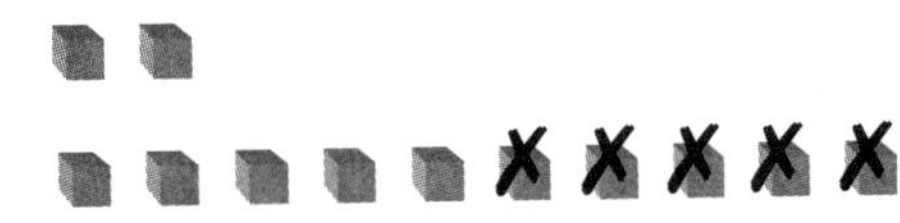

T	O
5	12
~~6~~	~~2~~
−	5
5	7

Subtract. Start with the ones.

1.

T	O
5	11
~~6~~	~~1~~
−	4
5	7

T	O
2	2
−	7

T	O
6	1
−	9

T	O
8	2
−	3

2.

T	O
8	2
−	8

T	O
7	1
−	7

T	O
2	1
−	8

T	O
5	2
−	5

3.

T	O
4	2
−	3

T	O
2	1
−	7

T	O
7	2
−	9

T	O
9	1
−	8

Find the differences.

4.

T	O
2	11
~~3~~	~~1~~
−	9
2	2

T	O
4	2
−	8

T	O
6	1
−	6

T	O
4	2
−	7

T	O
5	2
−	6

5. $\begin{array}{r} \overset{7}{\cancel{8}}\overset{12}{\cancel{2}} \\ -\ 7 \\ \hline 75 \end{array}$ $\begin{array}{r} 31 \\ -\ 9 \\ \hline \end{array}$ $\begin{array}{r} 41 \\ -\ 2 \\ \hline \end{array}$ $\begin{array}{r} 21 \\ -\ 5 \\ \hline \end{array}$ $\begin{array}{r} 61 \\ -\ 3 \\ \hline \end{array}$

Problem Solving Reasoning Use mental math. Count back 1, 2, or 3.

6. $\begin{array}{r} 51 \\ -\ 2 \\ \hline 49 \end{array}$ Think 51. Count back 50, 49. $\begin{array}{r} 61 \\ -\ 1 \\ \hline \end{array}$ $\begin{array}{r} 22 \\ -\ 1 \\ \hline \end{array}$ $\begin{array}{r} 81 \\ -\ 3 \\ \hline \end{array}$

Quick Check

Subtract.

1. $\begin{array}{r} 94 \\ -60 \\ \hline \end{array}$

2. $\begin{array}{r} 89 \\ -\ 6 \\ \hline \end{array}$

3. $\begin{array}{r} 74 \\ -54 \\ \hline \end{array}$

4. $\begin{array}{r} 62 \\ -\ 7 \\ \hline \end{array}$

Name ______________________

Regroup a ten.

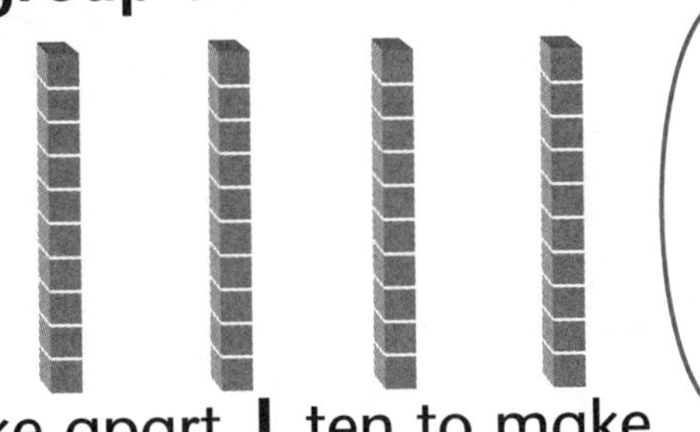

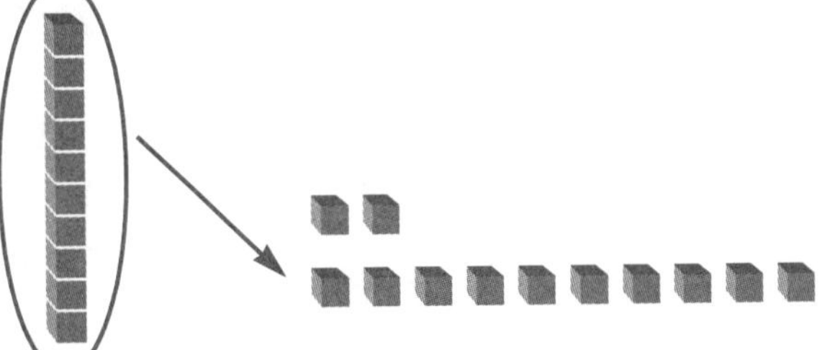

Take apart **1** ten to make **10** ones. **4** tens are left.

10 + 2 = 12 ones

Subtract.

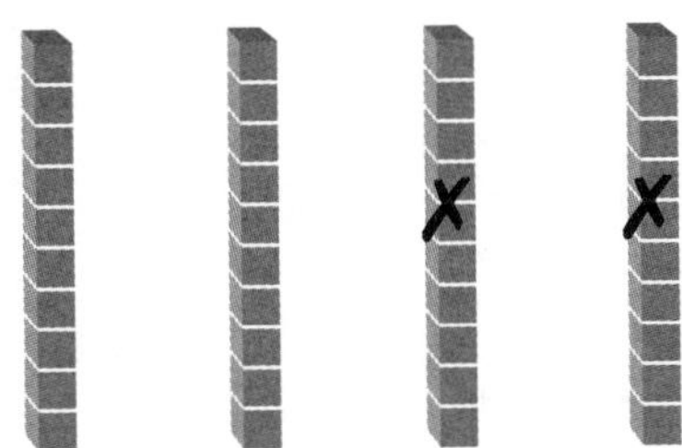

T	O
4	12
~~5~~	~~2~~
− 2	7
2	5

Subtract. Start with the ones.

1.

T	O
4	12
~~5~~	~~2~~
− 1	7
3	5

T	O
7	2
− 4	5

T	O
8	1
− 5	2

T	O
4	2
− 1	9

2.

T	O
6	2
− 4	8

T	O
7	2
− 4	4

T	O
6	2
− 4	3

T	O
8	1
− 5	6

3.

T	O
9	1
− 7	7

T	O
7	2
− 5	8

T	O
7	2
− 5	9

T	O
9	1
− 2	4

Find each difference.

4.

T	O
2	12
~~3~~	~~2~~
− 1	3
1	9

T	O
6	1
− 3	3

T	O
8	1
− 2	8

T	O
9	2
− 7	6

5. $\begin{array}{r} \overset{2}{\cancel{3}}\overset{12}{\cancel{2}} \\ -19 \\ \hline 13 \end{array}$ $\begin{array}{r} 92 \\ -73 \\ \hline \end{array}$ $\begin{array}{r} 42 \\ -15 \\ \hline \end{array}$ $\begin{array}{r} 91 \\ -29 \\ \hline \end{array}$ $\begin{array}{r} 62 \\ -26 \\ \hline \end{array}$

6. $\begin{array}{r} 72 \\ -48 \\ \hline \end{array}$ $\begin{array}{r} 81 \\ -26 \\ \hline \end{array}$ $\begin{array}{r} 92 \\ -64 \\ \hline \end{array}$ $\begin{array}{r} 91 \\ -33 \\ \hline \end{array}$ $\begin{array}{r} 51 \\ -18 \\ \hline \end{array}$

Problem Solving Reasoning

Solve. Use any strategy.

7. Jeffrey has **71** stamps in his collection. He sends **15** stamps to his pen pal in China. How many stamps does Jeffrey have left?

_____ stamps

8. Carmelita has **42** bowls in her pottery collection. She gives **19** bowls to her friend. How many bowls does Carmelita have left?

_____ bowls

★ Test Prep

Solve. Decide on an answer. Mark the space for your answer. If the answer is **not here**, mark the space for NH.

9 $\begin{array}{r} 82 \\ -46 \\ \hline \square \end{array}$

26	36	46	56	NH
○	○	○	○	○

Name ______________________

Regroup a ten.

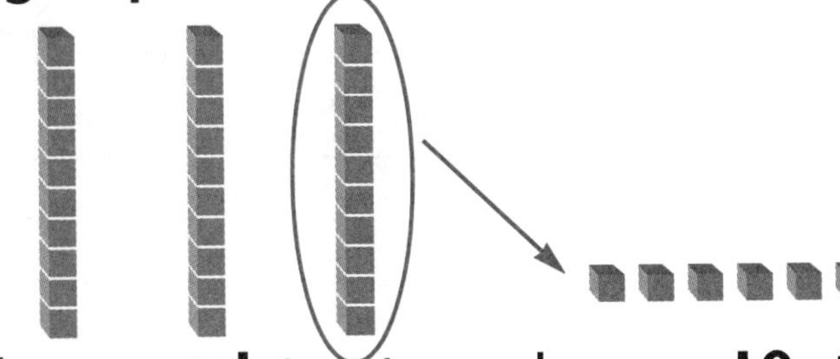

Take apart **1** ten to make **10** ones. **2** tens are left.

10 + 0 = 10 ones

Subtract.

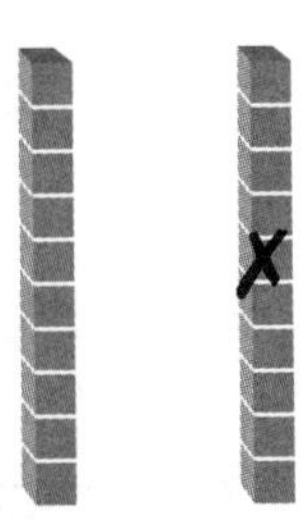

T	O
~~3~~ (2)	~~0~~ (10)
− 1	3
1	7

$$\begin{array}{r} \overset{2}{\cancel{3}}\overset{10}{\cancel{0}} \\ -13 \\ \hline 17 \end{array}$$

Subtract. Start with the ones.

1.

T	O
~~4~~ (3)	~~0~~ (10)
− 2	6
1	4

T	O
5	0
−	7

T	O
6	1
− 3	3

T	O
8	0
− 6	7

T	O
3	1
− 1	6

2. $\begin{array}{r} 52 \\ -33 \\ \hline \end{array}$ $\begin{array}{r} 40 \\ -29 \\ \hline \end{array}$ $\begin{array}{r} 30 \\ -17 \\ \hline \end{array}$ $\begin{array}{r} 92 \\ -66 \\ \hline \end{array}$ $\begin{array}{r} 80 \\ -\ 8 \\ \hline \end{array}$

3. $\begin{array}{r} 60 \\ -27 \\ \hline \end{array}$ $\begin{array}{r} 50 \\ -38 \\ \hline \end{array}$ $\begin{array}{r} 42 \\ -15 \\ \hline \end{array}$ $\begin{array}{r} 30 \\ -18 \\ \hline \end{array}$ $\begin{array}{r} 90 \\ -\ 7 \\ \hline \end{array}$

4. $\begin{array}{r} 80 \\ -55 \\ \hline \end{array}$ $\begin{array}{r} 90 \\ -67 \\ \hline \end{array}$ $\begin{array}{r} 70 \\ -\ 4 \\ \hline \end{array}$ $\begin{array}{r} 60 \\ -\ 9 \\ \hline \end{array}$ $\begin{array}{r} 42 \\ -17 \\ \hline \end{array}$

Now try these.

5. $\begin{array}{r} 71 \\ -43 \\ \hline \end{array}$ $\begin{array}{r} 92 \\ -64 \\ \hline \end{array}$ $\begin{array}{r} 60 \\ -\ 8 \\ \hline \end{array}$ $\begin{array}{r} 90 \\ -63 \\ \hline \end{array}$ $\begin{array}{r} 62 \\ -25 \\ \hline \end{array}$ $\begin{array}{r} 80 \\ -\ 7 \\ \hline \end{array}$

6. $\begin{array}{r} 51 \\ -29 \\ \hline \end{array}$ $\begin{array}{r} 50 \\ -17 \\ \hline \end{array}$ $\begin{array}{r} 96 \\ -81 \\ \hline \end{array}$ $\begin{array}{r} 70 \\ -45 \\ \hline \end{array}$ $\begin{array}{r} 80 \\ -\ 8 \\ \hline \end{array}$ $\begin{array}{r} 81 \\ -52 \\ \hline \end{array}$

7. $\begin{array}{r} 62 \\ -48 \\ \hline \end{array}$ $\begin{array}{r} 87 \\ -16 \\ \hline \end{array}$ $\begin{array}{r} 70 \\ -\ 4 \\ \hline \end{array}$ $\begin{array}{r} 60 \\ -\ 3 \\ \hline \end{array}$ $\begin{array}{r} 98 \\ -73 \\ \hline \end{array}$ $\begin{array}{r} 81 \\ -56 \\ \hline \end{array}$

Problem Solving Reasoning Solve. Use any strategy.

8. There are **40** children on the school bus. At the first stop, **7** children get off. How many children are left on the bus?

_____ children

9. There are **70** children at the picnic. After lunch, **22** children play kickball. How many children do not play kickball?

_____ children

★ Test Prep

Solve. Decide on an answer. Mark the space for your answer. If the answer is **not here**, mark the space for **NH**.

10 $\begin{array}{r} 90 \\ -24 \\ \hline \square \end{array}$

56	64	66	76	NH
○	○	○	○	○

Name ______________________________

Solve.

1. Had: **50¢**

   Bought: 25¢ 

   Had 25 ¢ left

2. Had: **62¢**

   Bought: 35¢ 

   Had ☐ ¢ left

3. Had: **21¢**

   Bought: 17¢  

   Had ☐ ¢ left

4. Had: **52¢**

   Bought: 12¢  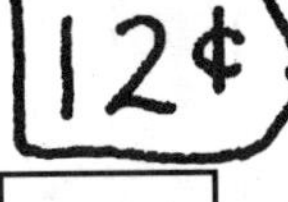

   Had ☐ ¢ left

5. Had: **60¢**

   Bought: 33¢ 

   Had ☐ ¢ left

6. Had: **72¢**

   Bought: 59¢  

   Had ☐ ¢ left

7. Had: **32¢**

   Bought: 21¢ 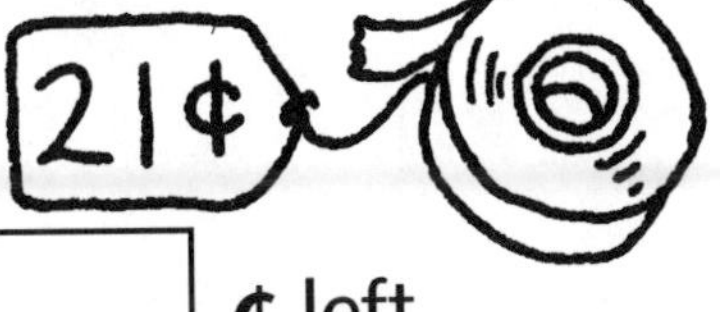 

   Had ☐ ¢ left

8. Had: **41¢**

   Bought: 31¢  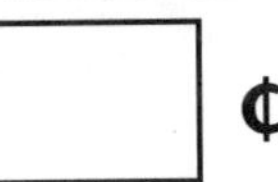

   Had ☐ ¢ left

Solve.

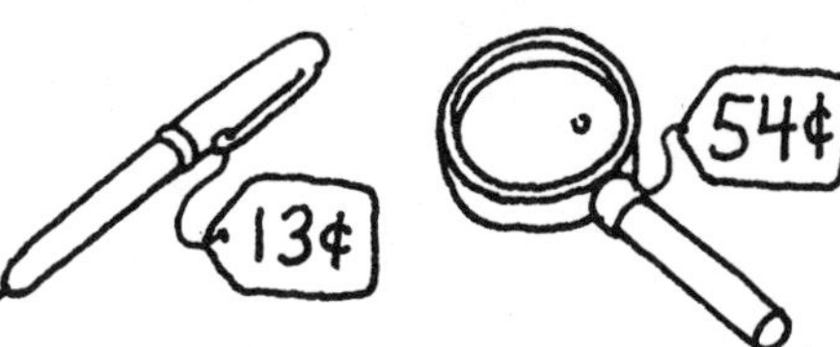

9. How much less does  cost than 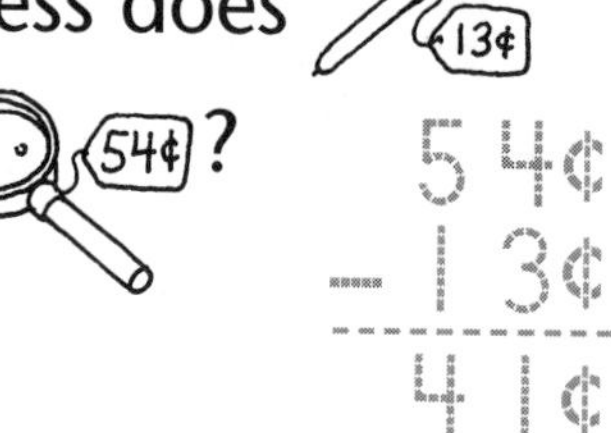?

$$\begin{array}{r} 54¢ \\ -\ 13¢ \\ \hline 41¢ \end{array}$$

10. How much more does  cost than (13¢) ?

11. How much more does  cost than 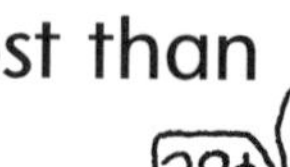 ?

12. How much less for  than for  ?

Problem Solving
Reasoning

Solve. Use any strategy you choose.

13. The pin costs **71¢.** The sticker costs **59¢.** How much more does the pin cost than the sticker? ______ ¢ more

 Quick Check

Subtract.

1. $\begin{array}{r} 81 \\ -\ 67 \\ \hline \end{array}$

2. $\begin{array}{r} 70 \\ -\ 14 \\ \hline \end{array}$

3. $\begin{array}{r} 52¢ \\ -\ 18¢ \\ \hline \end{array}$

4. $\begin{array}{r} 95¢ \\ -\ 42¢ \\ \hline \end{array}$

Name ______________________________

Regroup a ten.

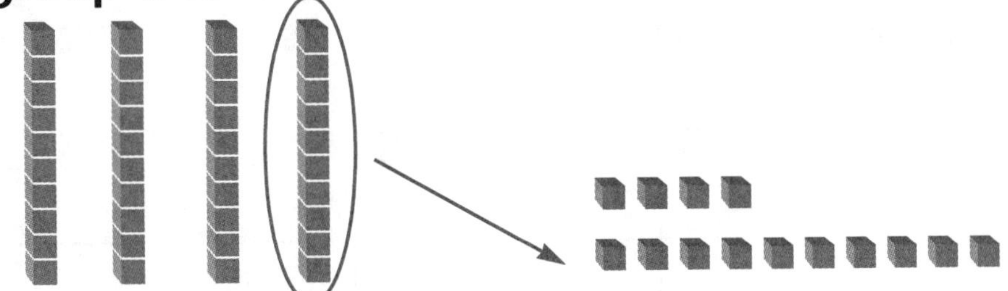

Take apart **1** ten to make **10** ones. **3** tens are left.

10 + 4 = 14 ones

Subtract.

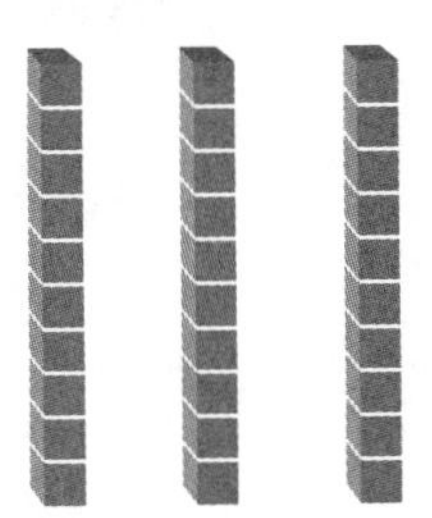

T	O
3	14
~~4~~	~~4~~
−	5
3	9

Subtract. Start with the ones.

1.

T	O
7	14
~~8~~	~~4~~
−	8
7	6

T	O
3	3
−	7

T	O
9	4
−	6

T	O
7	4
−	6

2.

T	O
6	4
−	9

T	O
2	4
−	7

T	O
8	3
−	5

T	O
4	4
−	9

3.

T	O
7	4
−	7

T	O
6	4
−	5

T	O
5	4
−	8

T	O
6	3
−	8

Subtract.

4.

T	O
~~3~~ 2	~~3~~ 13
−	5
2	8

T	O
~~6~~ 5	~~4~~ 14
−	6

T	O
~~3~~ 2	~~4~~ 14
−	7

T	O
~~9~~ 8	~~4~~ 14
−	5

T	O
5	2
−	7

5.

T	O
4	2
−	6

T	O
7	4
−	9

T	O
6	4
−	8

T	O
7	1
−	5

T	O
8	4
−	9

6. $34 - 8$ $94 - 7$ $74 - 5$ $91 - 7$ $23 - 6$ $63 - 9$ $54 - 6$

Problem Solving Reasoning

Use mental math. Count back 1, 2, or 3 to find the difference.

7. $54 - 3$ $63 - 2$ $44 - 1$ $73 - 1$ $34 - 2$ $23 - 3$

★ Test Prep

Solve. Mark the space for your answer.
If the answer is **not here**, mark the space for **NH**.

8. $63 - 9 = \square$

○ 44 ○ 54 ○ 55 ○ 64 ○ NH

Name ______________________________

Regroup a ten.

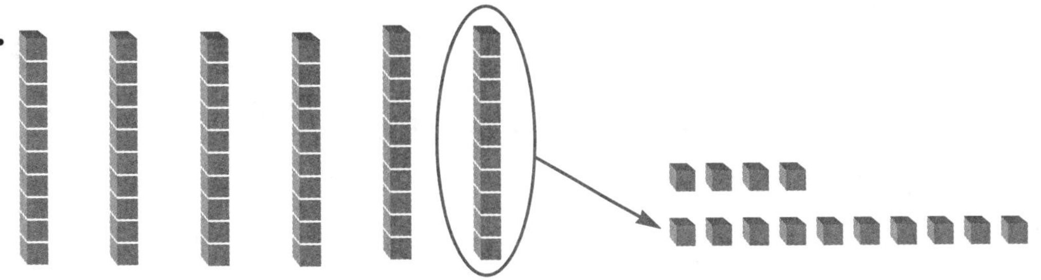

Take apart **1** ten to make **10** ones.
5 tens are left.

10 + 4 = 14 ones

Subtract.

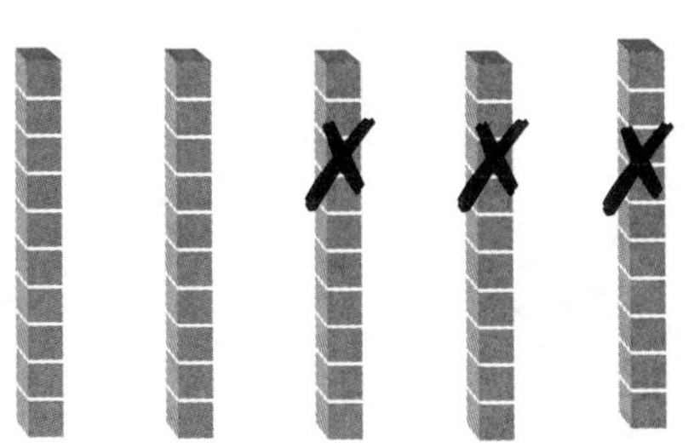

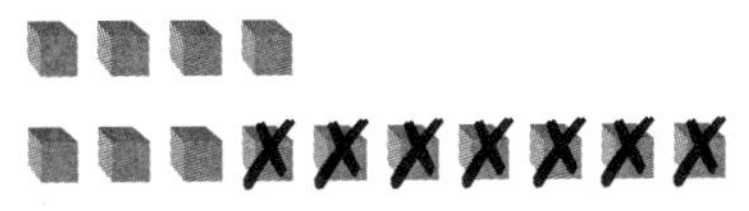

T	O
5	14
~~6~~	~~4~~
− 3	7
2	7

Subtract. Start with the ones.

1.

T	O
3	13
~~4~~	~~3~~
− 2	5
1	8

T	O
6	4
− 1	5

T	O
5	4
− 1	8

T	O
6	3
− 2	4

2.

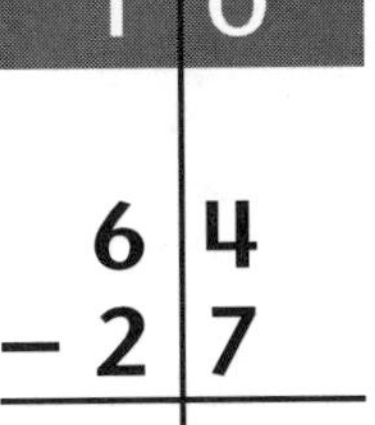

T	O
6	4
− 2	7

T	O
4	3
− 1	9

T	O
9	4
− 5	9

T	O
6	3
− 4	4

3.

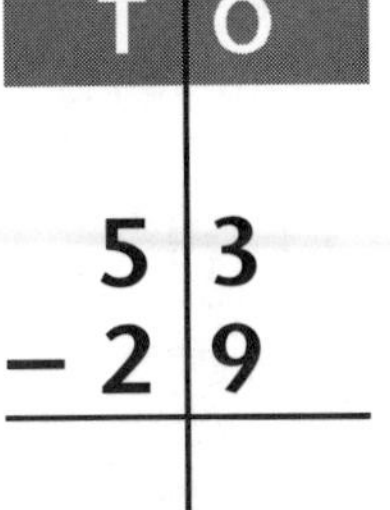

T	O
5	3
− 2	9

T	O
7	4
− 5	9

T	O
8	3
− 2	7

T	O
3	3
− 1	8

Subtract.

4.

34	63	94	73	34	93
− 15	− 24	− 68	− 56	− 19	− 65
19					

5.

93	80	73	34	73	44
− 19	− 17	− 56	− 19	− 57	− 28

6.

54	63	84	63	34	83
− 26	− 29	− 18	− 28	− 17	− 65

Problem Solving Reasoning Solve. Use any strategy.

7. There are **54** pigs. **28** pigs are playing in the mud. How many pigs are not playing in the mud?

_____ pigs

8. There are **23** horses. **17** horses are out in the field. How many horses are still in the stables?

_____ horses

★ Test Prep

Solve. Mark the space for your answer.
If the answer is **not here**, mark the space for **NH**.

9.

$$\begin{array}{r} 84 \\ -37 \\ \hline \square \end{array}$$

47	48	57	58	NH
○	○	○	○	○

STANDARD

Name ____________________

Problem Solving Plan			
1. Understand	2. Decide	3. Solve	4. Look back

Use the table. Answer the questions. Write a number sentence. Solve.

Books Seen at the Book Fair

Student	Number of Books
Kyle	24
Yoko	43
Cheryl	31
Evan	40

1. How many more books does Evan see than Kyle?

Think How many books does Evan see? 40

How many books does Kyle see? 24

  40
− 24
  16

40 (−) 24 = 16

Answer Evan sees 16 more books than Kyle.

2. How many more books does Yoko see than Kyle?

Think How many books does Yoko see? _____

How many books does Kyle see? _____

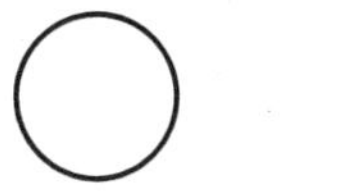

___ ◯ ___ = ___

Answer Yoko sees _____ more books than Kyle.

3. How many books do Yoko and Cheryl see together?

Think How many books does Yoko see? _____

How many books does Cheryl see? _____

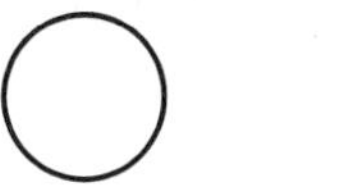

___ ◯ ___ = ___

Answer Yoko and Cheryl see _____ books.

Use the table. Write a number sentence. Solve.

Things Collected

Grade	Bottles	Cans
Second Grade	**90**	**49**
Third Grade	**72**	**64**

4. How many more bottles does the Second Grade collect than the Third Grade?

○ ____ ____ ○ ____ = ____

Answer The Second Grade collects _____ more bottles.

5. How many fewer cans does the Second Grade collect than the Third Grade?

○ ____ ____ ○ ____ = ____

Answer The Second Grade collects _____ fewer cans.

6. How many more bottles than cans does the Third Grade collect?

○ ____ ____ ○ ____ = ____

Answer The Third Grade collects _____ more bottles than cans.

Extend Your Thinking

7. Write your own question about the table.
Ask a friend to answer it. ________________________________

____

____

STANDARD

Name ______________________

Regroup a ten.

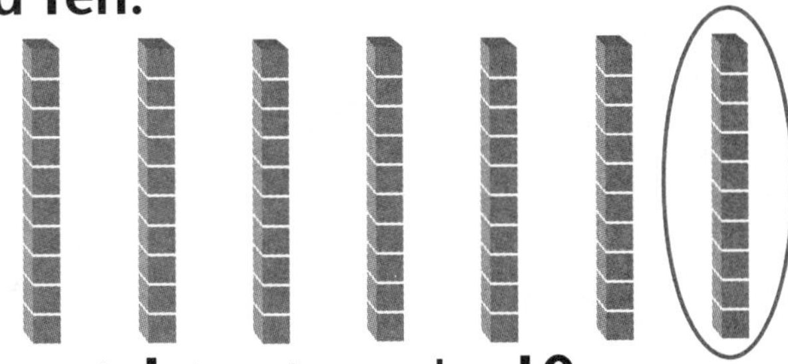

Take apart **1** ten to make **10** ones.
6 tens are left.

10 + 6 = 16 ones

Subtract.

T	O
6	16
7	6
− 4	7
2	9

Subtract. Remember to regroup.

1.

T	O
3	16
4	6
− 2	7
1	9

T	O
6	5
− 2	9

T	O
9	6
−	7

T	O
5	5
−	9

2.

T	O
6	6
−	9

T	O
4	6
− 1	7

T	O
8	6
− 5	9

T	O
7	5
−	9

3.

T	O
4	6
− 2	7

T	O
3	5
−	7

T	O
6	6
− 4	8

T	O
7	5
− 6	8

Subtract. Start with the ones.

4.

75	85	56	96	86
− 29	− 7	− 37	− 7	− 59
46				

5.

96	45	66	45	96
− 57	− 27	− 9	− 18	− 77

6.

75	42	95	86	71
− 19	− 19	− 28	− 8	− 58

 Quick Check

Subtract.

1. $\begin{array}{r} 54 \\ -\ 8 \\ \hline \end{array}$

2. $\begin{array}{r} 93 \\ -\ 37 \\ \hline \end{array}$

3. $\begin{array}{r} 85 \\ -\ 19 \\ \hline \end{array}$

4. $\begin{array}{r} 76 \\ -\ 47 \\ \hline \end{array}$

STANDARD

Name ____________________

Subtract. Start with the ones.

1.

T	O
6	17
7	7
− 2	9
4	8

T	O
8	18
9	8
− 6	9

T	O
7	17
8	7
− 1	8

T	O
4	18
5	8
−	9

2.

T	O
4	7
− 2	8

T	O
6	8
− 2	9

T	O
9	7
−	8

T	O
9	8
− 7	9

3.

T	O
4	8
− 2	9

T	O
6	7
− 3	8

T	O
5	8
− 1	9

T	O
4	7
−	9

4.

T	O
3	7
−	8

T	O
7	8
− 2	9

T	O
5	7
− 2	8

T	O
9	8
− 5	9

5.

T	O
8	8
− 6	9

T	O
5	7
− 3	8

T	O
7	8
−	9

T	O
6	7
− 3	9

Subtract.

6.

77	58	97	67	40
− 9	− 39	− 18	− 38	− 18
68				

7.

98	47	98	58	88
− 69	− 28	− 9	− 19	− 19

8.

87	68	48	47	50
− 18	− 29	− 9	− 29	− 39

Problem Solving
Reasoning

Write a number sentence. Solve.

9. Mario sees **48** red barns. Julie sees **29** white barns. How many more barns does Mario see?

___ ◯ ___ = ___

____ more barns

10. Julie sees **87** green tractors. Mario sees **58** white tractors. How many more tractors does Julie see?

___ ◯ ___ = ___

____ more tractors

★ Test Prep

Solve. Mark the space for your answer.
If the answer is **not here**, mark the space for **NH**.

88
−29
☐

58	59	68	69	NH
○	○	○	○	○

Name ______________________

You can check subtraction by adding.

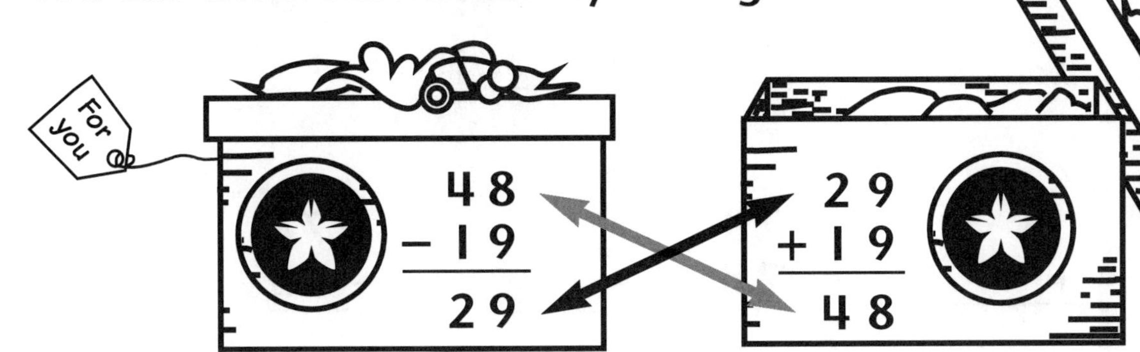

Subtract. Check by adding.

1. 32 − 19 = 13 | 13 + 19 = 32

2. 71 − 28 | + ___

3. 42 − 15 | + ___

4. 72 − 48 | + ___

5. 81 − 26 | + ___

6. 92 − 64 | + ___

7. 81 − 28 | + ___

8. 92 − 73 | + ___

9. 92 − 23 | + ___

10. 91 − 63 | + ___

11. 32 − 19 | + ___

12. 81 − 66 | + ___

13. 62 − 48 | + ___

14. 81 − 63 | + ___

15. 52 − 18 | + ___

Subtract. Check by adding.

68 − 42 = ___ ; ___ + ___	40 − 15 = ___ ; ___ + ___	54 − 19 = ___ ; ___ + ___
51 − 18 = ___ ; ___ + ___	73 − 28 = ___ ; ___ + ___	76 − 25 = ___ ; ___ + ___
32 − 19 = ___ ; ___ + ___	61 − 33 = ___ ; ___ + ___	85 − 27 = ___ ; ___ + ___
49 − 18 = ___ ; ___ + ___	56 − 19 = ___ ; ___ + ___	42 − 24 = ___ ; ___ + ___
75 − 26 = ___ ; ___ + ___	72 − 44 = ___ ; ___ + ___	74 − 19 = ___ ; ___ + ___

Problem Solving
Reasoning

31. How does adding help you check your subtraction?

___

★ Test Prep

Solve. Mark the space for your answer.
If the answer is **not here**, mark the space for **NH**.

83 − 25 = 58 ; □ + 25 = 83

25	48	58	83	NH
○	○	○	○	○

Name ____________________

You can rewrite the problem to find the sum.

Rewrite the problem. Find the sum or difference.

1. **28 + 25**

   1
   28
   +25
   53

2. **54 − 38**

   54
   −38

3. **56 + 36**

4. **46 + 32**

5. **53 − 19**

6. **52 − 49**

Solve.

7. **32 + 57 =** ____

8. **53 − 19 =** ____

9. **38 + 38 =** ____

Work Space

Rewrite the problem. Solve.

10.

25 + 16	25 − 16
1 25 +16 41	

11.

58 + 27	58 − 27

12.

69 + 19	69 − 19

13.

48 + 36	48 − 36

Quick Check

Solve.

1. $\begin{array}{r} 62 \\ -\ 7 \\ \hline \end{array}$

2. $\begin{array}{r} 86 \\ -38 \\ \hline \end{array}$

Subtract. Check by adding.

3. $\begin{array}{r} 44 \\ -\ 29 \\ \hline \end{array}$ $\quad + \underline{\quad\quad}$

4. $\begin{array}{r} 62 \\ -\ 37 \\ \hline \end{array}$ $\quad + \underline{\quad\quad}$

Rewrite the problem. Solve.

5. 67 − 29

Name ______________________

STANDARD

Problem

Valerie's house is **57** miles away from the beach.
Nico's house is **38** miles away from the beach.
How much farther away is Valerie's house than Nico's house from the beach?

1 Understand

I need to find out how much farther Valerie's house is from the beach than Nico's house.

2 Decide

Can I use simpler numbers to help?
Have I solved any problems like this before?

3 Solve

If I use simpler numbers, the problem would read:

Valerie's house is **60** miles away from the beach.
Nico's house is **40** miles away from the beach.
How much farther away is Valerie's house from the beach?

I will subtract to find about how much farther it is.

60 − 40 = 20

I think it is about 20 miles farther away.

Now I will subtract the actual amounts.

$$\begin{array}{r} 57 \\ -\ 38 \\ \hline 19 \end{array}$$

Answer It is **19** miles farther away.

4 Look back

Is my answer reasonable? Why or why not?

Solve. Use simpler numbers or other strategies. Show your work.

1. Jenna jumps rope **67** times on Monday. She jumps rope **49** times on Tuesday. How many more times does she jump rope on Monday?

   Work Space

   Answer ______ more times

2. Kirk has to read **46** pages in his chapter book. He reads **38** pages. How many pages does Kirk have left to read?

   Work Space

   Answer ______ pages

3. Tanya uses a magnet to pick up paper clips. The first time she picks up **63** paper clips. The second time she picks up **47** paper clips. How many more paper clips does she pick up the first time?

   Work Space

   Answer ______ more paper clips

4. Raphael and his aunt go apple picking. Together their apples weigh **62** pounds. His aunt's apples weigh **43** pounds. How much do Raphael's apples weigh?

   Work Space

   Answer ______ pounds

Name ____________________

Subtract.

1. 6 tens − 4 tens = _____ tens

60 − 40 = _____

2. 8 tens − 3 tens = _____ tens

80 − 30 = _____

3. 55 − 25 = _____

4. 75 − 30 = _____

Subtract.

5. $\begin{array}{r} 36 \\ -\ \ 9 \\ \hline \end{array}$

6. $\begin{array}{r} 58 \\ -49 \\ \hline \end{array}$

7. $\begin{array}{r} 21 \\ -\ \ 8 \\ \hline \end{array}$

8. $\begin{array}{r} 68¢ \\ -42¢ \\ \hline \end{array}$

9. $\begin{array}{r} 37 \\ -28 \\ \hline \end{array}$

10. $\begin{array}{r} 64 \\ -\ \ 7 \\ \hline \end{array}$

11. $\begin{array}{r} 92¢ \\ -73¢ \\ \hline \end{array}$

12. $\begin{array}{r} 71 \\ -29 \\ \hline \end{array}$

13. $\begin{array}{r} 38 \\ -17 \\ \hline \end{array}$

14. $\begin{array}{r} 72 \\ -39 \\ \hline \end{array}$

15. $\begin{array}{r} 84 \\ -47 \\ \hline \end{array}$

16. $\begin{array}{r} 30 \\ -\ \ 8 \\ \hline \end{array}$

17. $\begin{array}{r} 52 \\ -34 \\ \hline \end{array}$

18. $\begin{array}{r} 91 \\ -\ \ 6 \\ \hline \end{array}$

19. $\begin{array}{r} 56¢ \\ -27¢ \\ \hline \end{array}$

Problem Solving Reasoning

Use the table. Solve.

Cracker Boxes Sold

	Monday	Tuesday
Room 5	30	31
Room 6	29	28

20. How many boxes of crackers were sold on Monday?

_____ boxes

21. How many more boxes of crackers did Room 5 sell on Tuesday than Room 6?

_____ more boxes

Name ______________________________

1

8, 7, 15

○ 8 + 8 = 16 ○ 15 − 7 = 8
○ 9 + 7 = 16 ○ 16 − 8 = 8

2

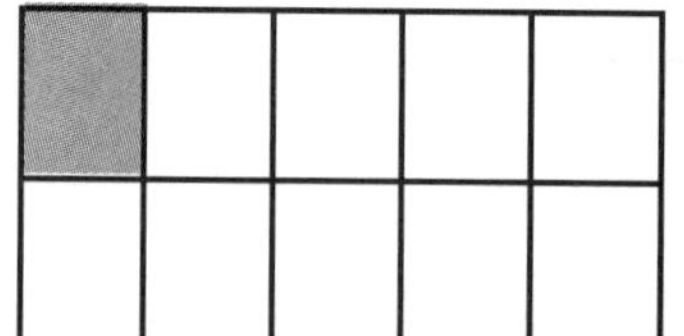

$\frac{1}{5}$	$\frac{1}{8}$	$\frac{1}{10}$	$\frac{1}{12}$
○	○	○	○

3

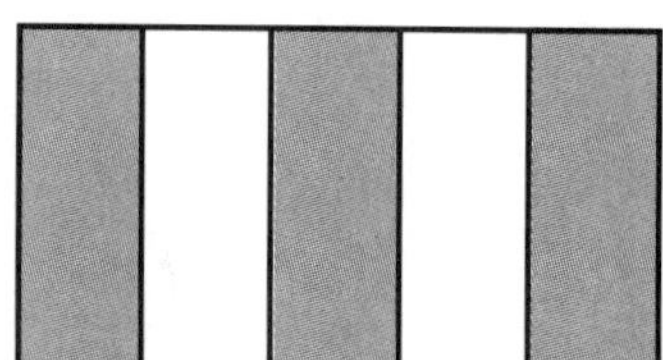

$\frac{1}{5}$	$\frac{3}{5}$	$\frac{4}{5}$	$\frac{5}{5}$
○	○	○	○

Solve.

4

25 + 35 = ☐

50	55	60	70	NH
○	○	○	○	○

5

80 − 30 = ☐

70	60	55	40	NH
○	○	○	○	○

6

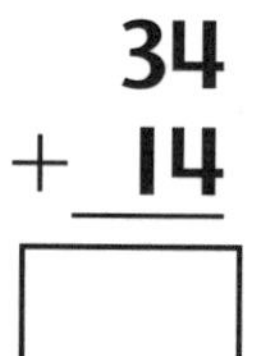

$$\begin{array}{r} 34 \\ +\ 14 \\ \hline \end{array}$$

38	44	48	58	NH
○	○	○	○	○

7

$$\begin{array}{r} 27 \\ +\ 48 \\ \hline \end{array}$$

65	75	76	86	NH
○	○	○	○	○

8

$$\begin{array}{r} 49 \\ -\ 28 \\ \hline \end{array}$$

31	29	21	11	NH
○	○	○	○	○

9

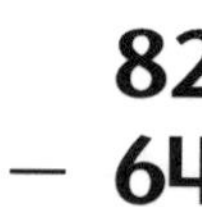

$$\begin{array}{r} 82 \\ -\ 64 \\ \hline \end{array}$$

28	27	18	17	NH
○	○	○	○	○

UNIT 8 • TABLE OF CONTENTS

Time and Money

We will be using this vocabulary:

half past 30 minutes after the hour
quarter past 15 minutes after the hour
quarter to 15 minutes before the next hour
A.M. the hours from midnight to noon
P.M. the hours from noon to midnight
midnight 12 A.M.
noon 12 P.M.

Dear Family,

During the next few weeks our math class will be learning about time and money.

You can expect to see homework that provides practice with reading and writing time. There will also be homework that provides practice with counting combinations of coins.

As we learn about time and money, you may wish to keep the following sample as a guide.

10 o'clock
10:00

half past 8
8:30

quarter past 4
4:15

quarter to 2
1:45

Sincerely,

Name ________________________________

Write the time.

1.

____ o'clock

2.

____ o'clock

3.

____ o'clock

4.

____ o'clock

5.

____ o'clock

6.

____ o'clock

What time does the clock show?

7.

9 o'clock

9:00

8.

_____ o'clock

_____:_____

9.

_____ o'clock

_____:_____

10.

_____ o'clock

_____:_____

11.

_____ o'clock

_____:_____

12.

_____ o'clock

_____:_____

13.

_____ o'clock

_____:_____

14.

_____ o'clock

_____:_____

★ Test Prep

Give the time. Mark the space for your answer.

12:00	2:00	4:00	5:00
○	○	○	○

Name ____________________

Tell the time two ways.

1.

half past 4

4:30

2.

half past ____

____ : ____

3.

half past ____

____ : ____

4.

half past ____

____ : ____

5.

half past ____

____ : ____

6.

half past ____

____ : ____

7.

half past ____

____ : ____

8.

half past ____

____ : ____

9.

half past ____

____ : ____

Show the time on the clock. Draw the hands.

10.

half past **2**

11.

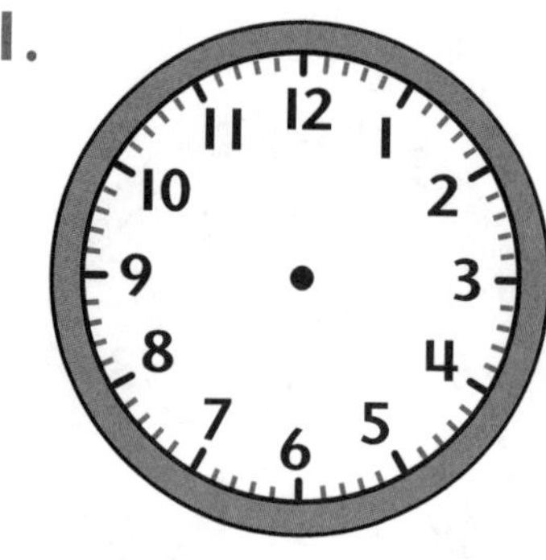

half past **4**

12.

half past **6**

13.

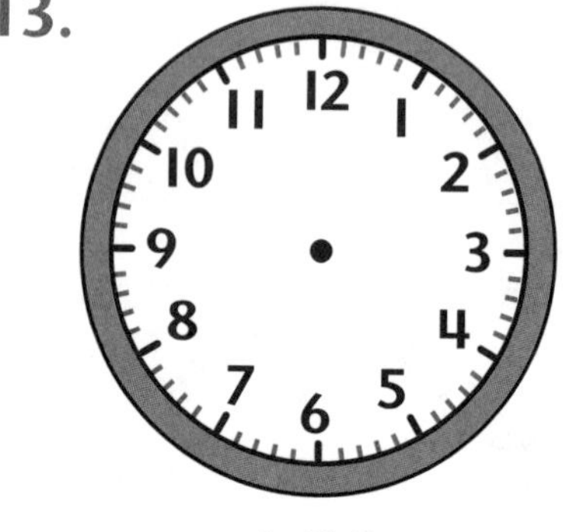

1:30

14.

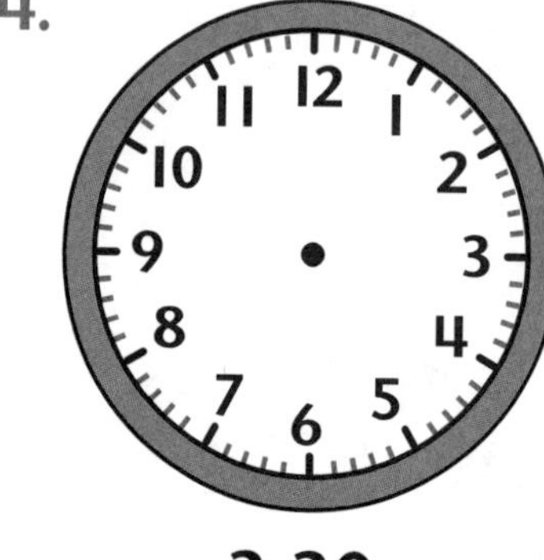

3:30

15.

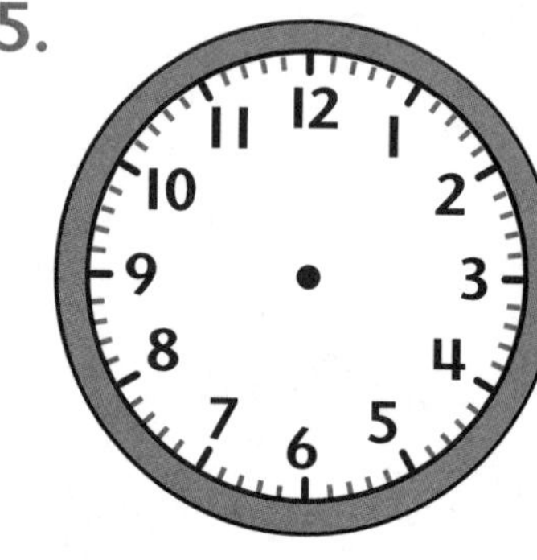

5:30

16.

11:30

17.

10:30

18.

12:30

★ Test Prep

Give the time. Mark the space for your answer.

19

7:30	6:45	8:30	6:30
○	○	○	○

Name ________________________________

This clock shows
15 minutes after 12
or
12:15.

Write the time.

1. 

1:15

2. 

___ : ___

3. 

___ : ___

4. 

___ : ___

5. 

___ : ___

6. 

___ : ___

15 minutes after 2
is the same as
quarter past 2
or
2:15.

Show the time. Draw the hands.

7. **6:15**

quarter past **6**

8. **8:15**

quarter past **8**

9. **10:15**

quarter past **10**

Quick Check

Write the time.

1.

____ o'clock

2.

____:____

Match.

3. quarter past **1** — **5:15**

quarter past **3** — **1:15**

quarter past **5** — **3:15**

Name ______________________

This clock shows
45 minutes after 11
or
11:45.

Write the time.

1.

7:45

2.

___ : ___

3.

___ : ___

4.

___ : ___

5.

___ : ___

6.

___ : ___

45 minutes after 2
is the same as
quarter to 3
or
2:45.

Show the time. Draw the hands.

7. 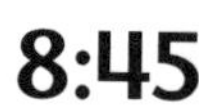

quarter to **9**

8. **5:45**

quarter to **6**

9. 

quarter to **10**

Problem Solving
Reasoning

10. If the hour hand is pointing to just before the **3**, and the minute hand is pointing to the **9**, what time is it? How do you know?

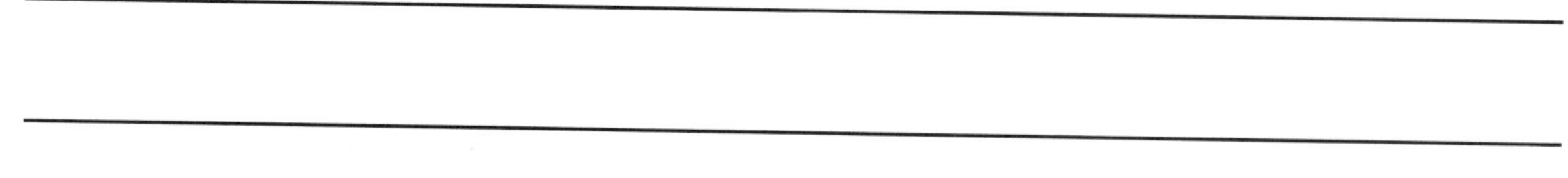

★ Test Prep

Which is the same? Mark the space for your answer.

11 quarter to **2**

11:45	12:45	1:45	2:45
○	○	○	○

Name ______________________________

There are **60** minutes in an hour. It takes **1** hour for the minute hand to go around the clock once.

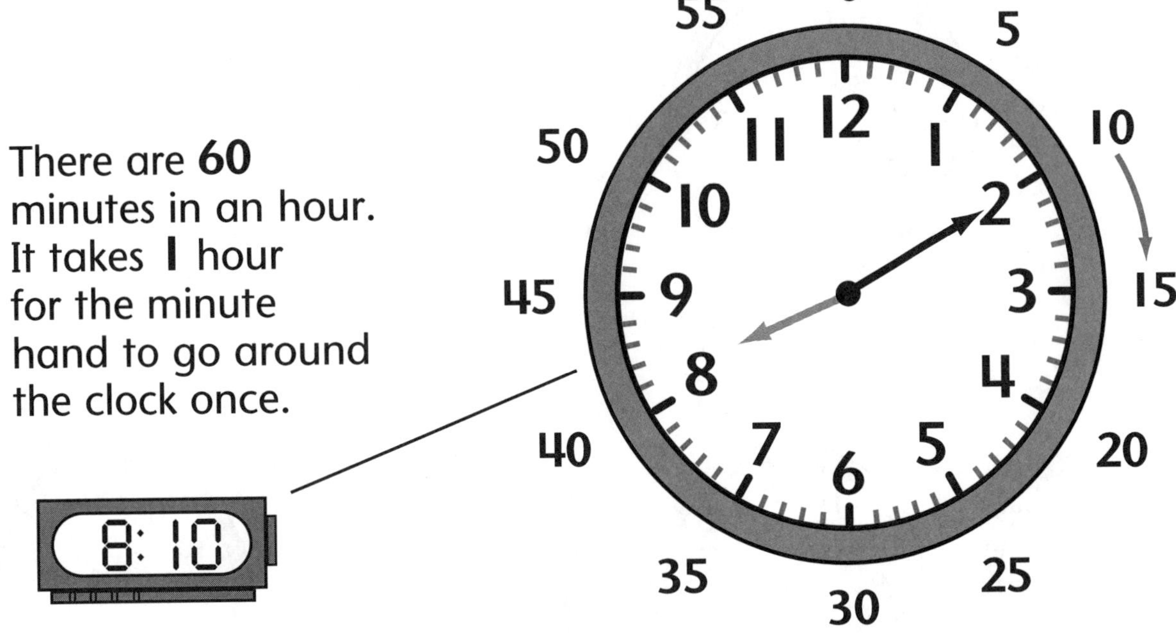

There are **60** seconds in a minute. It takes **5** minutes for the minute hand to go from number to number.

Match.

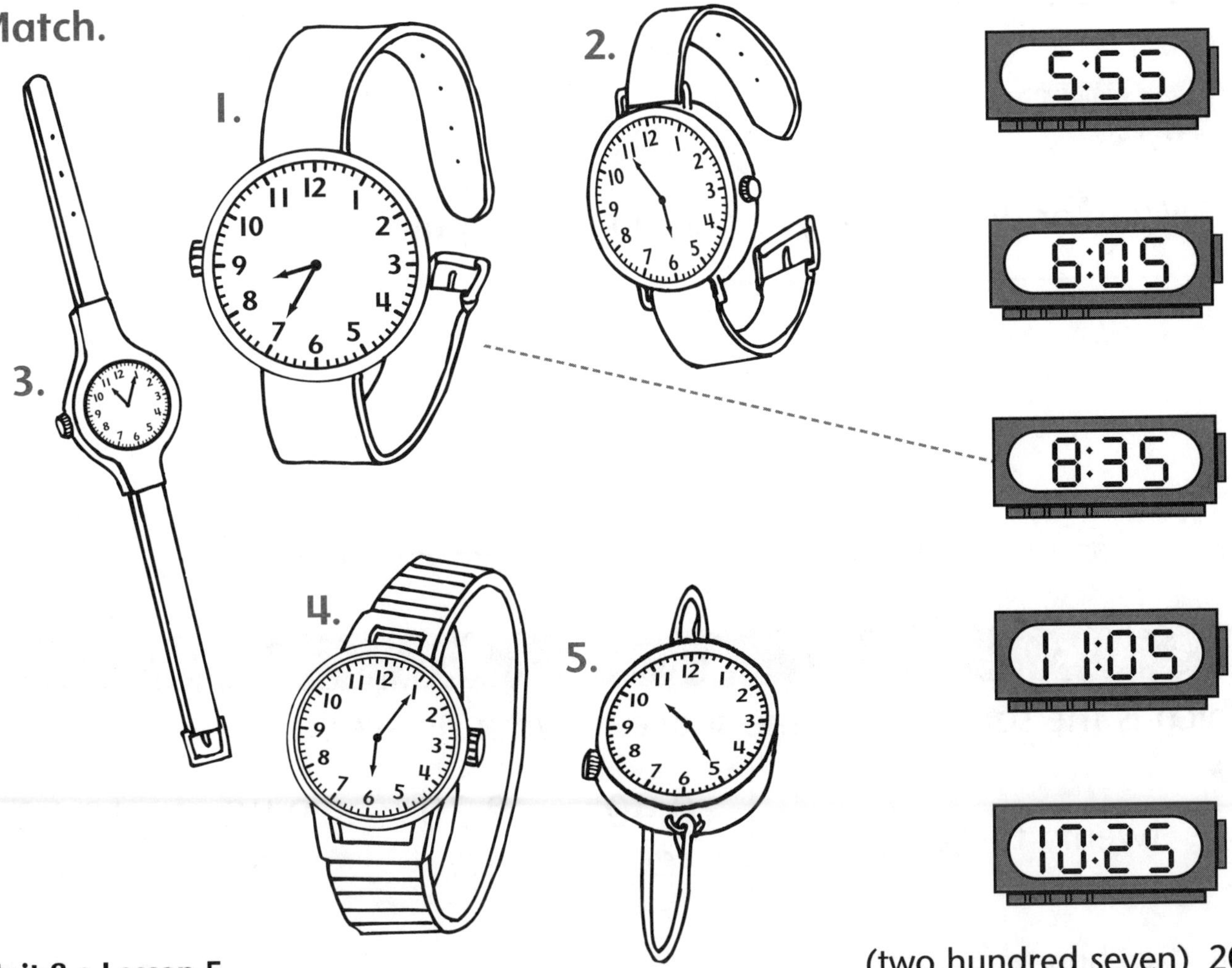

1.

2.

3.

4.

5.

5:55

6:05

8:35

11:05

10:25

40 minutes after 5
is the same as
twenty to 6
or
5:40.

Count by 5's. Write the time.

6. 

3:35

7. 

___:___

8. 

___:___

9. 

___:___

Problem Solving
Reasoning

10. Write or draw what you can do in a minute.

★ Test Prep

Which is the same? Mark the space for your answer.

twenty to **10**

10:40	9:30	9:40	10:20
○	○	○	○

Name ____________________

There are **24** hours in a day.
The hour hand goes around the clock two times each day.

I day

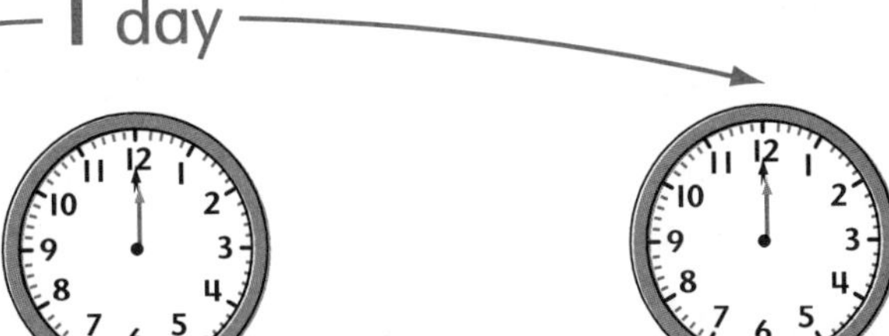

12 A.M. midnight

12 P.M. noon

12 A.M. midnight

The hours from midnight to noon are labeled **A.M.**

The hours from noon to midnight are labeled **P.M.**

6:00 A.M. is in the morning.

6:00 P.M. is in the evening.

Write the time. Solve.

1. Renee was at school from

8:00 **A.M.**

to

2:00 **P.M.**

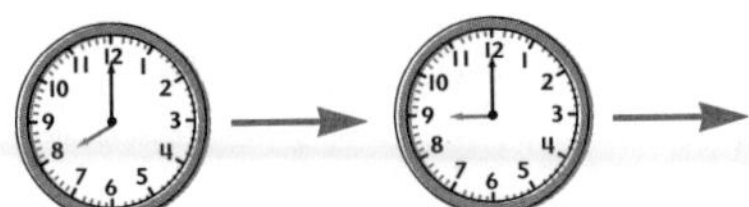 →  →  →  → 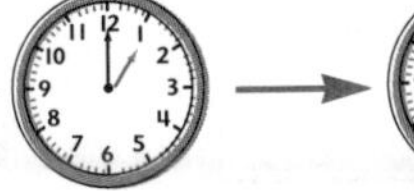 → 

She was at school for __6__ hours.

Write the time. Solve.

2. Renee did homework from

to

____:____ P.M. ____:____ P.M.

She did homework for ____ hour and ____ minutes.

3. Renee watched T.V. from

to

____:____ P.M. ____:____ P.M.

She watched T.V. for ____ minutes.

Quick Check

Write the time.

1.

____:____

2.

____:____

3. Stephen played from

to

____:____ A.M. ____:____ P.M.

He played for ____ hours and ____ minutes.

Name ______________________________

Problem Solving Plan			
1. Understand	2. Decide	3. Solve	4. Look back

Eric's Saturday Plan

7:30 A.M.	Wake up
8:00 A.M.	Eat breakfast
8:30 A.M.	Clean room
9:00 A.M.	Go to Nathan's house
12:00 P.M.	Go home and have lunch
1:30 P.M.	Go to club meeting
3:30 P.M.	Play soccer
6:00 P.M.	Eat supper
7:00 P.M.	Watch T.V.
8:45 P.M.	Go to sleep

Use the schedule. Solve.

1. What time will Eric eat breakfast?
   Think Find Eat breakfast on the schedule.
   Follow across to the time.

   Answer 8:00 A.M.

2. What will Eric do at **9:00** A.M.?
   Think Find **9:00** A.M. on the schedule.
   Follow across.

   Answer ______________________________

3. About how much time will Eric spend at Nathan's house?
   Think What time will he go to Nathan's?
   What time will he go home?

   Answer about ______ hours

Eric's Saturday Plan	
7:30 A.M.	Wake up
8:00 A.M.	Eat breakfast
8:30 A.M.	Clean room
9:00 A.M.	Go to Nathan's house
12:00 P.M.	Go home and have lunch
1:30 P.M.	Go to club meeting
3:30 P.M.	Play soccer
6:00 P.M.	Eat supper
7:00 P.M.	Watch T.V.
8:45 P.M.	Go to sleep

Use the schedule. Solve.

4. What will Eric do at **8:30** A.M.?

   Answer ____________________

5. What time will Eric go home for lunch?

   Answer ____________________

6. For about how long will Eric be home before he goes to his club meeting?

   Answer about ______ hour ______ minutes

Extend Your Thinking

7. Make up your own question about the schedule and show how you solve it. ____________________

Name ______________________________

One Year

January

Su	M	T	W	Th	F	Sa
						1
2	3	4	5	6	7	8
9	10	11	12	13	14	15
16	17	18	19	20	21	22
23	24	25	26	27	28	29
30	31					

February

Su	M	T	W	Th	F	Sa
		1	2	3	4	5
6	7	8	9	10	11	12
13	14	15	16	17	18	19
20	21	22	23	24	25	26
27	28					

March

Su	M	T	W	Th	F	Sa
			1	2	3	4
5	6	7	8	9	10	11
12	13	14	15	16	17	18
19	20	21	22	23	24	25
26	27	28	29	30	31	

April

Su	M	T	W	Th	F	Sa
						1
2	3	4	5	6	7	8
9	10	11	12	13	14	15
16	17	18	19	20	21	22
23	24	25	26	27	28	29
30						

May

Su	M	T	W	Th	F	Sa
	1	2	3	4	5	6
7	8	9	10	11	12	13
14	15	16	17	18	19	20
21	22	23	24	25	26	27
28	29	30	31			

June

Su	M	T	W	Th	F	Sa
				1	2	3
4	5	6	7	8	9	10
11	12	13	14	15	16	17
18	19	20	21	22	23	24
25	26	27	28	29	30	

July

Su	M	T	W	Th	F	Sa
						1
2	3	4	5	6	7	8
9	10	11	12	13	14	15
16	17	18	19	20	21	22
23	24	25	26	27	28	29
30	31					

August

Su	M	T	W	Th	F	Sa
		1	2	3	4	5
6	7	8	9	10	11	12
13	14	15	16	17	18	19
20	21	22	23	24	25	26
27	28	29	30	31		

September

Su	M	T	W	Th	F	Sa
					1	2
3	4	5	6	7	8	9
10	11	12	13	14	15	16
17	18	19	20	21	22	23
24	25	26	27	28	29	30

October

Su	M	T	W	Th	F	Sa
1	2	3	4	5	6	7
8	9	10	11	12	13	14
15	16	17	18	19	20	21
22	23	24	25	26	27	28
29	30	31				

November

Su	M	T	W	Th	F	Sa
			1	2	3	4
5	6	7	8	9	10	11
12	13	14	15	16	17	18
19	20	21	22	23	24	25
26	27	28	29	30		

December

Su	M	T	W	Th	F	Sa
					1	2
3	4	5	6	7	8	9
10	11	12	13	14	15	16
17	18	19	20	21	22	23
24	25	26	27	28	29	30
31						

Use the calendar to answer the questions.

1. How many months are in a year? ______

2. What is the seventh month of the year? ____________

3. How many days are there in January? ______ in February? ______

4. What day of the week is June 11th? ____________

Problem Solving Reasoning

5. There are **52** weeks in a year.

About how many weeks are there in each month? ________________

Explain how you found your answer. ________________________

____

eleventh **11th**	twelfth **12th**	thirteenth **13th**	fourteenth **14th**	fifteenth **15th**
sixteenth **16th**	seventeenth **17th**	eighteenth **18th**	nineteenth **19th**	twentieth **20th**

Copy the calendar in your room.

6.

Sunday	Monday	Tuesday	Wednesday	Thursday	Friday	Saturday

Write how many.

7. Sundays ____ **8.** Tuesdays ____ **9.** Days in a week ____

10. What is the **fifteenth** day in this month? ____________

11. What is the **twentieth** day in this month? ____________

★ Test Prep

What day of the week is the **nineteenth**?

12

January

S	M	T	W	Th	F	S
					1	2
3	4	5	6	7	8	9
10	11	12	13	14	15	16
17	18	19	20	21	22	23
24	25	26	27	28	29	30
31						

○ Sunday ○ Tuesday

○ Wednesday ○ Friday

Name ______________________________________ 

I nickel
or
5 cents
5¢

I dime
or
10 cents
10¢

Count the money.

I.  

5 ¢, 10 ¢, 15 ¢ 15 ¢ total

2.  

_____¢, _____¢ _____¢ total

3.   

_____¢, _____¢, _____¢, _____¢ _____¢ total

4.     

_____¢, _____¢, _____¢, _____¢, _____¢ _____¢ total

5.    

_____¢, _____¢, _____¢, _____¢ _____¢ total

How much money?

6.  

Think 10¢, 20¢

20 ¢

7.  

_____ ¢

8.  

_____ ¢

9.   

_____ ¢

Problem Solving
Reasoning

10. If you have **4** dimes and **2** nickels, how much money do you have? How do you know?

____

____

____

____

★ Test Prep

How much money? Mark the space for your answer.

11

15¢	20¢	25¢	30¢
○	○	○	○

Name ______________________________

Count by **10**'s. Then count on by **5**'s. Then count on by **1**'s.

10¢, 20¢, 30¢ 35¢, 40¢, 45¢ 46¢, 47¢, 48¢

Count. Write the total.

1\. 10 ¢, 20 ¢, 25 ¢, 30 ¢, 31 ¢, 32 ¢, 33 ¢ 33 ¢ total

2\. ____¢, ____¢, ____¢, ____¢, ____¢, ____¢, ____¢ ____¢ total

3\. ____¢, ____¢, ____¢, ____¢, ____¢, ____¢, ____¢ ____¢ total

4\. ____¢, ____¢, ____¢, ____¢, ____¢, ____¢, ____¢ ____¢ total

How much money?

5.   

Think
10¢, 15¢, 16¢

_____¢

6.    

_____¢

Write the amounts. Use >, <, or =.

7. **2** dimes = 20 ¢ **5** nickels = 25 ¢

2 dimes (<) **5** nickels

8. **6** nickels = _____¢ **3** dimes = _____¢

6 nickels ( ) **3** dimes

Quick Check

Fill in the missing month.

1. October, ______________ , December

How much money?

2.     

_____¢
total

Use >, <, or =.

3. **4** dimes ( ) **6** nickels

Name ____

I quarter	**I** quarter

25¢	**25¢**

Count. Write the total.

1.  

25 ¢, 30 ¢ 30 ¢ total

2.   

_____¢, _____¢, _____¢ _____¢ total

3.    

_____¢, _____¢, _____¢, _____¢ _____¢ total

4.   

_____¢, _____¢, _____¢ 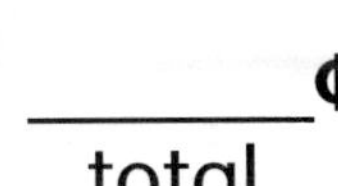 _____¢ total

How much money?

5.

Think 25¢, 35¢, 36¢

_______ ¢

6.

_______ ¢

7.

_______ ¢

8.

_______ ¢

9.

_______ ¢

10.

_______ ¢

★ Test Prep

How much money? Mark the space for your answer.

11

36¢	40¢	46¢	29¢
○	○	○	○

Name ____________________

Find the total cost. Ring the correct amount.

1.

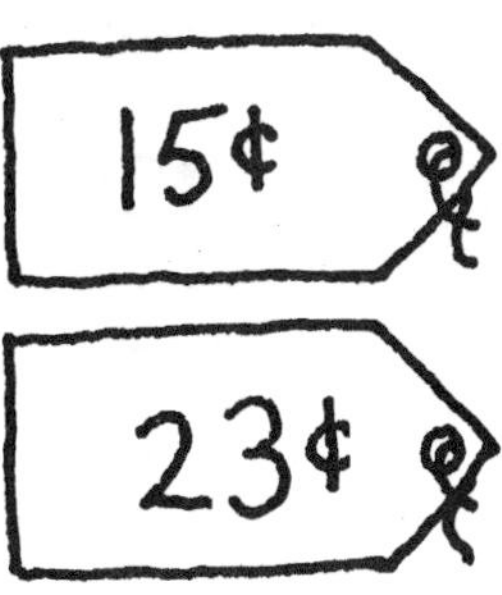

15¢
+ 23¢
38¢

2.

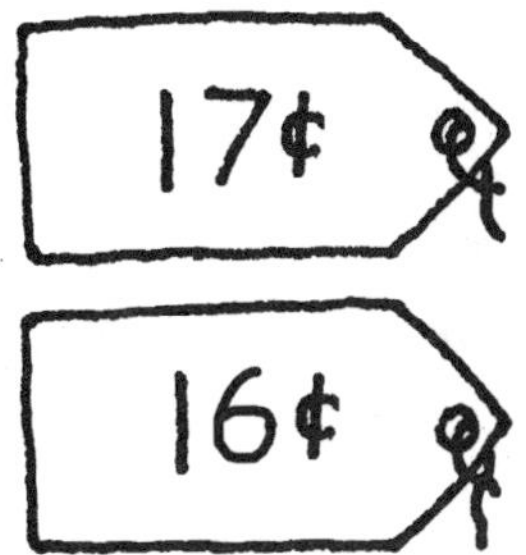

3.

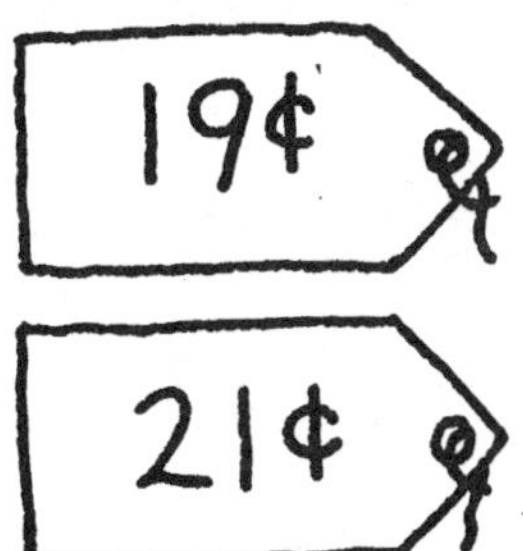

★ Test Prep

How much money? Mark the space for your answer.

4

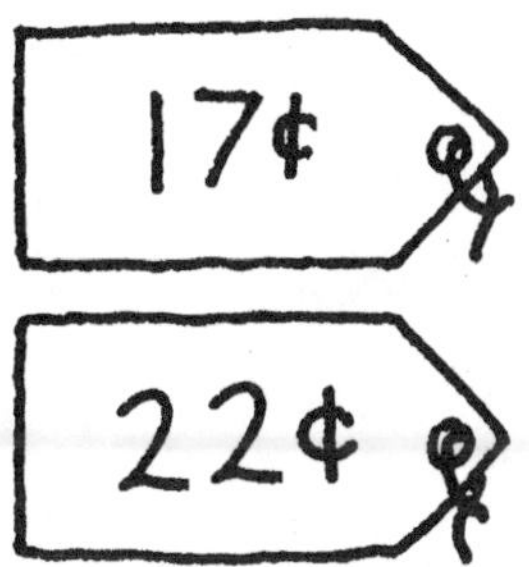

29¢ ○ 39¢ ○ 40¢ ○ 49¢ ○

How much change?

1. Elena had:

30¢

She bought:

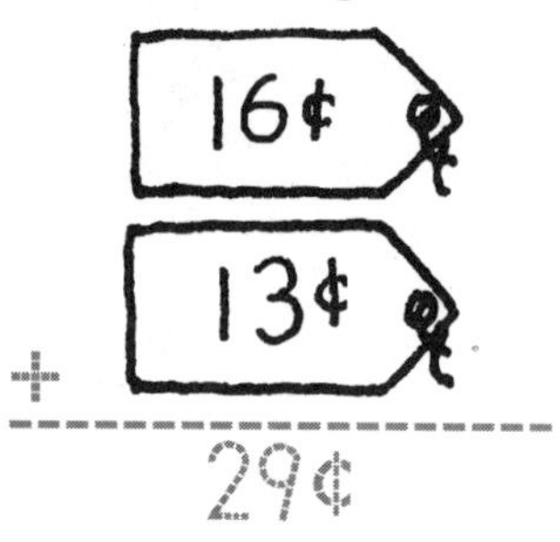

\+ 29¢

She got back:

30¢
−29¢
1¢

2. Had: 25¢

Bought:

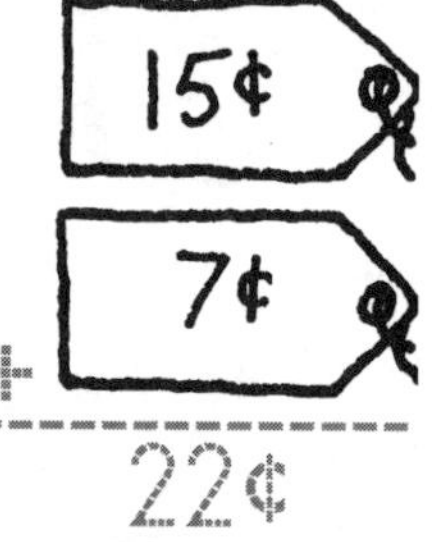

\+ 22¢

Got back:

3. Had: 40¢

Bought:

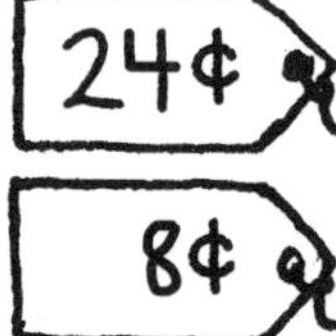

Got back:

 **Quick Check**

How much money?

1.

_______¢ total

Find the total cost.

2.

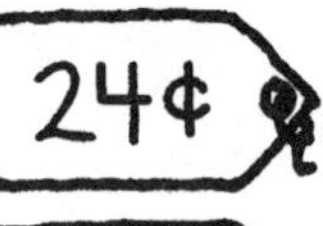

How much change?

3. Had: 45¢

Bought:

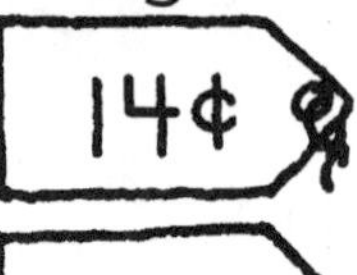

Got back:

STANDARD

Name ____________________

Problem

Lee has a bag of nickels and dimes.
How many different ways can he pay for a **45¢** pencil?

1 Understand

I need to find out how many different ways Lee can pay for a **45¢** pencil using only nickels and dimes.

2 Decide

I can make a list.

3 Solve

__4__ dimes and __1__ nickel
__3__ dimes and __3__ nickels
__2__ dimes and __5__ nickels
__1__ dime and __7__ nickels
__9__ nickels

There are __5__ different ways Lee can pay for a pencil worth **45¢**.

4 Look back

Did I find all the ways?

Make a list to solve.

1. Sari has pennies and nickels. How many different ways can she pay for a balloon that costs **17¢**?

Sari can pay for the balloon ____ different ways.

2. Duncan has a box full of change. How many different ways can he pay for a whistle that costs **35¢**, using at least **1** quarter?

Duncan can pay for the whistle ____ different ways.

3. Diane has a bag of pennies, nickels, and dimes. How many different ways can she buy a sticker worth **25¢**, using at least **1** dime?

Diane can pay for the sticker ____ different ways.

Name ______________________________ **Unit 8 Review**

Show the time on the clock. Draw the hands.

1\. 8:10

2\. 3:20

3\. 

12:05

4\. 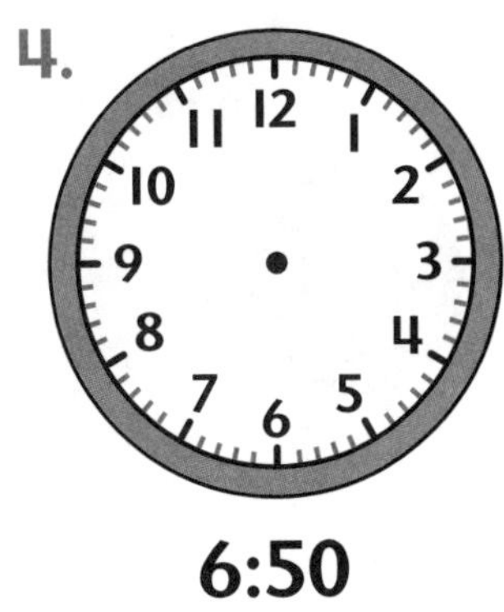

6:50

Fill in the blank.

5. There are ______ minutes in **1** hour.

6. There are ______ days in **1** week.

7. There are **24** hours in **1** __________.

8. There are **12** __________ in **1** year.

Write the time. Solve.

9. Billy played the drums from

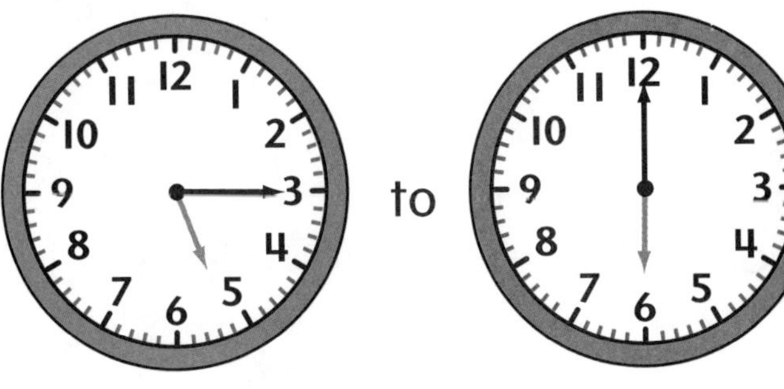

____:____ P.M. ____:____ P.M.

He played the drums for ______ minutes.

How much money?

10.

_____¢

11.

_____¢

12.

_____¢

Ring the correct amount.

13.

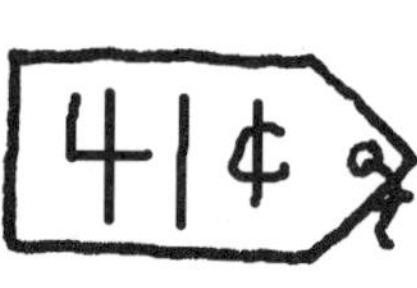

Write the amounts. Use >, <, or =.

14. **3** dimes = _____¢ **7** nickels = _____¢

3 dimes ◯ **7** nickels

15. **1** quarter = _____¢ **5** nickels = _____¢

1 quarter ◯ **5** nickels

Problem Solving Reasoning

Make a list to solve.

16. How many different ways can you make **30¢,** using only nickels and dimes?

_____ different ways

Name ______________________________

1

36	39	42		48	51

41 ○ 43 ○ 45 ○ 47 ○

2

 ○

○

 ○

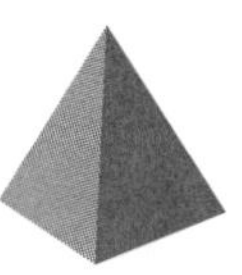 ○

3

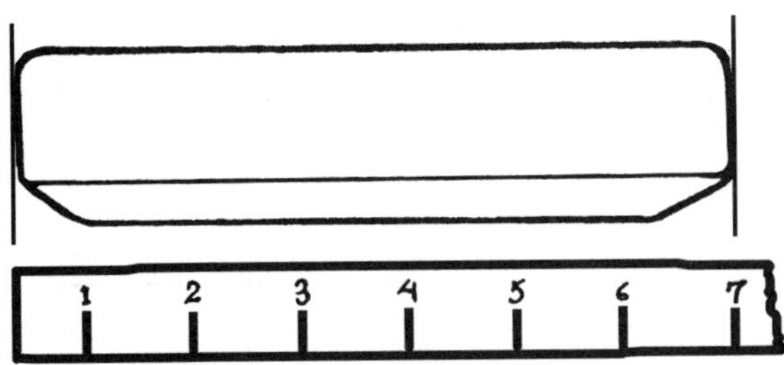

5 ○ 6 ○ 7 ○ 8 ○

4

○ **10** o'clock

○ quarter to **3**

○ half past **3**

○ quarter past **10**

5

1 minute = ______ seconds

24 ○ 30 ○ 60 ○ 90 ○

6

○ **3** dimes < **6** nickels

○ **4** dimes > **7** nickels

○ **2** dimes = **5** nickels

○ **1** quarter > **3** dimes

Decide on an answer. Mark the space for your answer.
If the answer is **not here**, mark the space for **NH**.

7. $8 + (4 + 4) = \square$

18	17	16	15	NH
○	○	○	○	○

8.

○ 30¢
○ 25¢
○ 21¢
○ 15¢
○ NH

9.

○ 42¢
○ 38¢
○ 33¢
○ 29¢
○ NH

10. $50 + 35 = \square$

75	80	85	90	NH
○	○	○	○	○

11. $90 - 25 = \square$

55	60	65	70	NH
○	○	○	○	○

12.

$$\begin{array}{r} 12 \\ 35 \\ +\ 24 \\ \hline \square \end{array}$$

○ 81
○ 71
○ 69
○ 61
○ NH

13.

$$\begin{array}{r} 74 \\ -\ 29 \\ \hline \square \end{array}$$

○ 65
○ 55
○ 54
○ 45
○ NH

UNIT 9 • TABLE OF CONTENTS

Data and Probability

We will be using this vocabulary:

line plot a diagram that shows how often each number occurs in a set of data
range the difference between the highest and lowest number in a set of data
mode the number in a set of data that occurs most frequently

Dear Family,

During the next few weeks our math class will be learning about data and probability.

You can expect to see homework that provides practice with data and probability.

As we learn about probability, you may wish to keep the following sample as a guide.

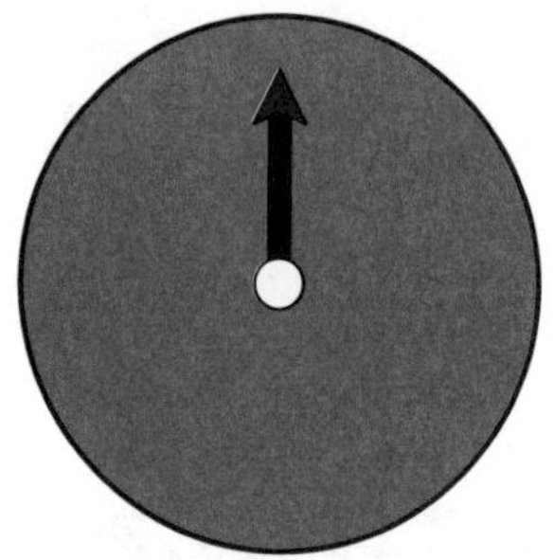

This spinner will always stop on red.

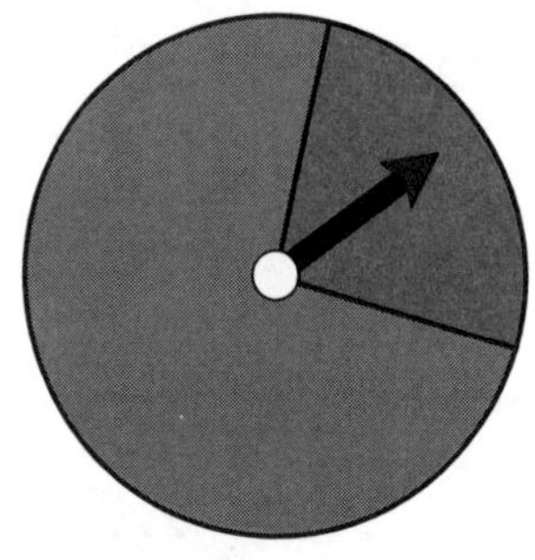

This spinner will sometimes stop on red.

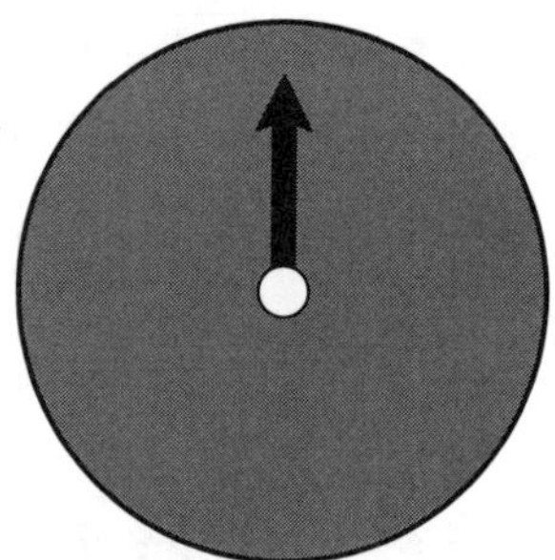

This spinner will never stop on red.

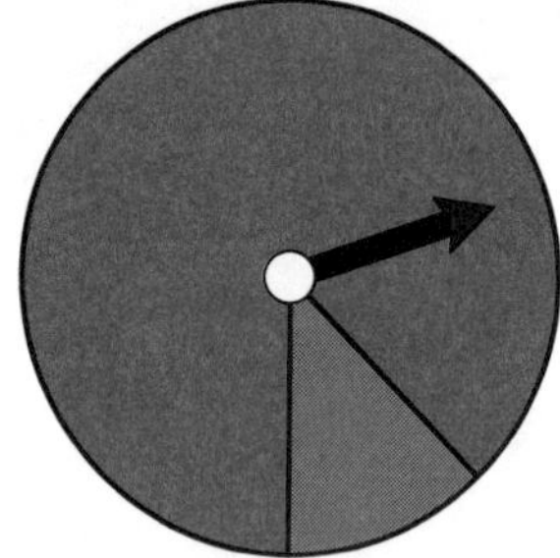

You are more likely to spin red on this spinner.

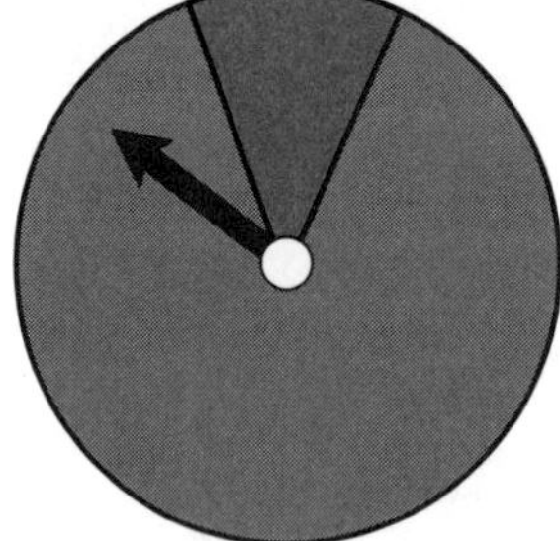

You are less likely to spin red on this spinner.

Sincerely,

Name ______________________________

Use the picture. Cross out as you count. Complete.

1. There are __5__ students reading.

2. There are ______ students writing.

3. There are ______ students in all.

4. There are ______ books on the top shelf.

5. There are ______ books on the middle shelf.

6. There are ______ books on the bottom shelf.

7. The top shelf has ______ more books than the bottom shelf.

8. There are ______ books in all.

9. What time does the clock say? ___:___

Look at the picture.
Cross out the objects in the picture as you complete the tally chart.
Remember that |||| stands for 5.

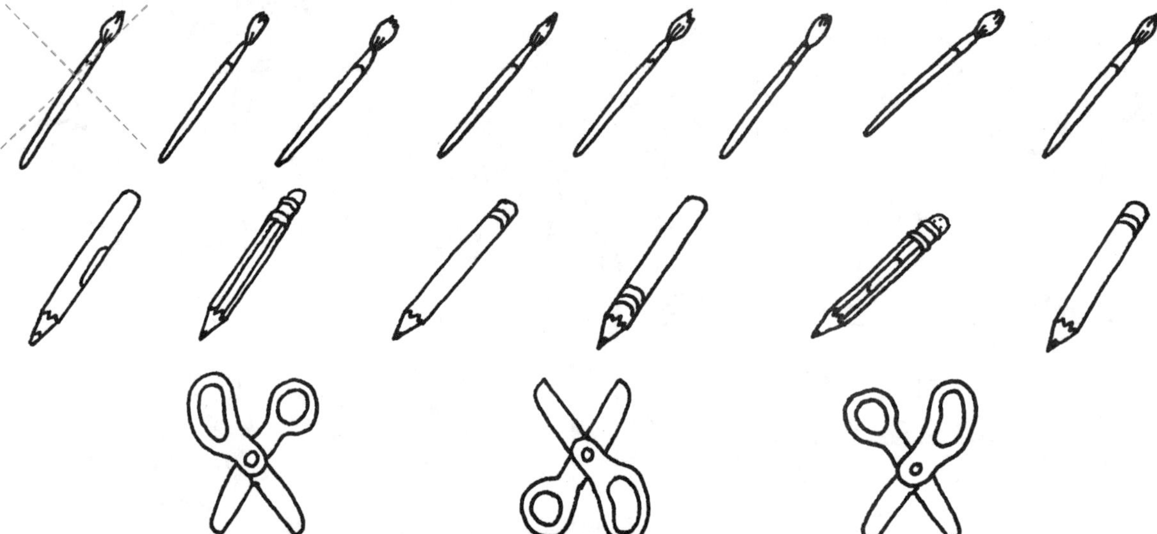

10.

Art Supplies	
paintbrush	|
pencils	
scissors	

Problem Solving Reasoning

Solve.

11. Are there more paintbrushes or scissors? ____________

How do you know? ______________________________

____

★ Test Prep

Mark under the number of tallies shown.

 |||| ||

4	5	6	7
○	○	○	○

Name ______________________________

Take a survey.

1. Ask 10 classmates to choose where they want to go on a field trip. Make tallies on the chart to record the data. Then write the total.

Field Trip Choices		
	Tally	**Total**
Farm		
Museum		
Factory		

Use the completed chart.

2. Which place do most of your classmates want to visit? ____________

3. Which place was chosen the least? ____________

Use your tally chart to complete the graph.
Fill in 1 box for every tally.

4.

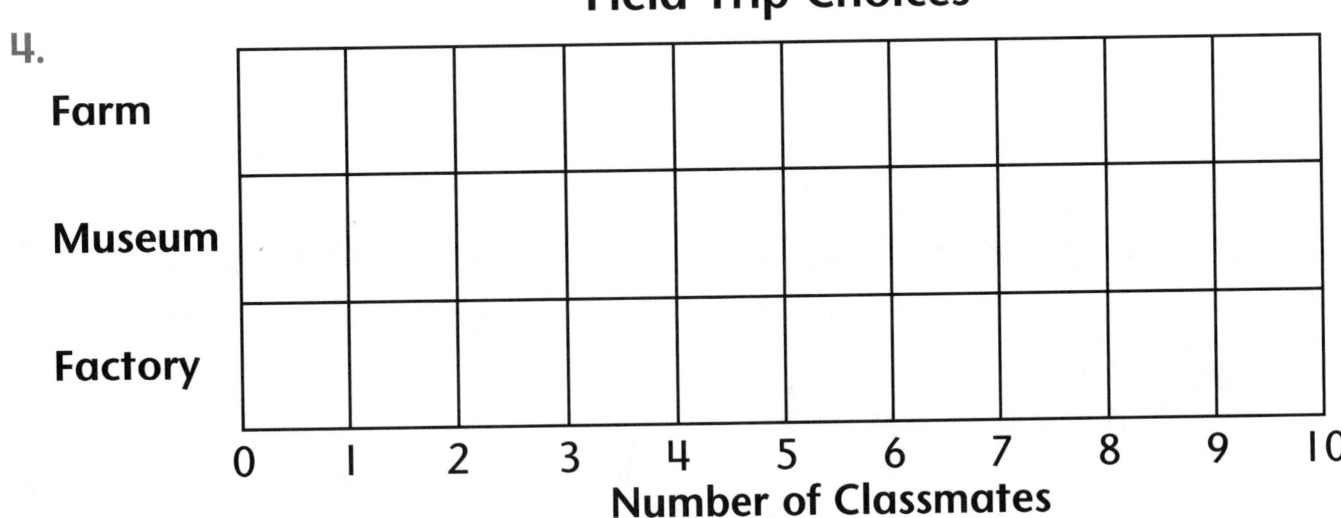

Take a survey.

5. Ask 15 classmates to choose their favorite school subject. Complete the tally chart.

Favorite Subjects		
	Tally	Total
Math		
Science		
Art		
Reading		

6. Which subject was chosen the most? ____________

7. Which subject was chosen the least? ____________

Problem Solving
Reasoning

8. Suppose you had asked all of your classmates to choose their favorite subject. Which subject do you think would be chosen the most? Why? ____________

____

____

★ Test Prep

Which drink was chosen the least? Mark the space for your answer.

9

Favorite Drink	
Juice	||||
Milk	𝍸 |||
Lemonade	𝍸 |
Water	𝍸

juice ○ milk ○ lemonade ○ water ○

Name ______________________________

Look at the tally chart.
Use the data to complete the graph.

Hits During the Season	
Kim	𝍸 𝍸 𝍸 𝍸 𝍸
Troy	𝍸 𝍸 𝍸
Lee	𝍸 𝍸 𝍸 𝍸

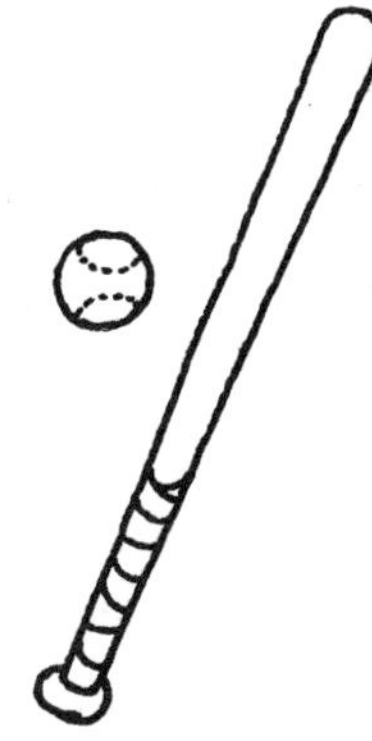

1.

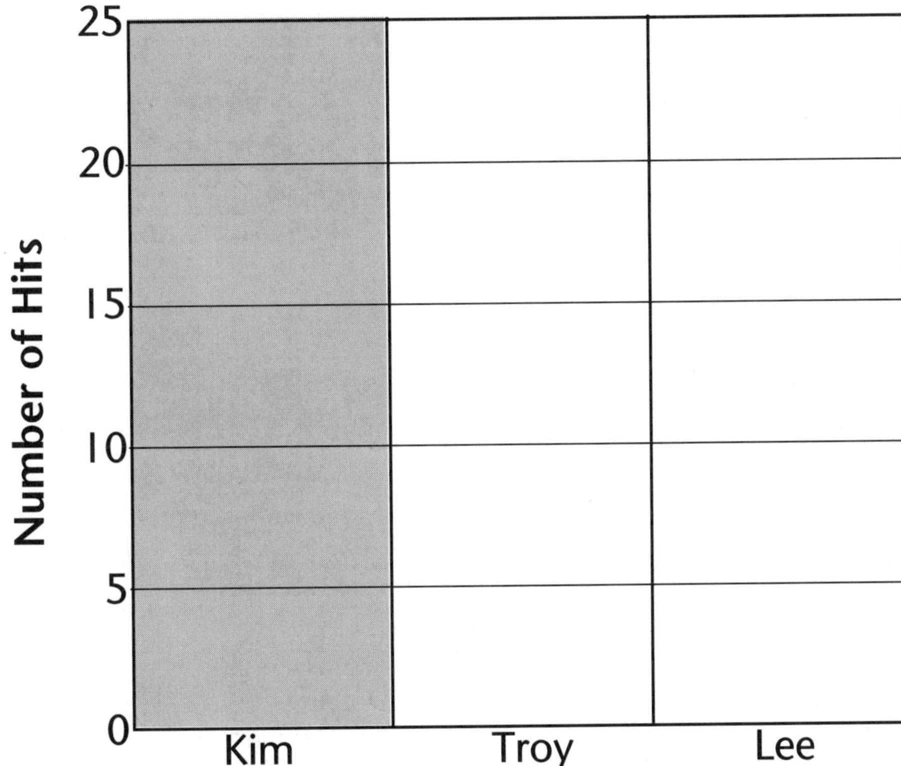

2. How many hits does Troy have? ______

3. Who has the most hits? ____________

Complete the graph.

4. Sue Linn played **10** games.
She made **8** hits for her team.
She struck out **6** times.
She walked **4** times.

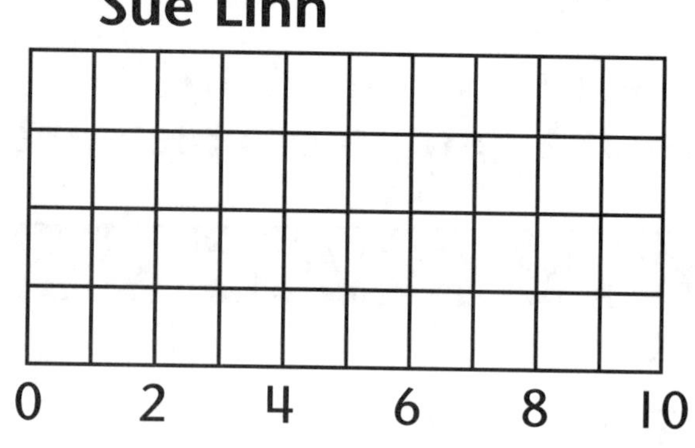

5. Jim played **9** games.
He had **6** hits.
He struck out **5** times.
He walked **3** times.

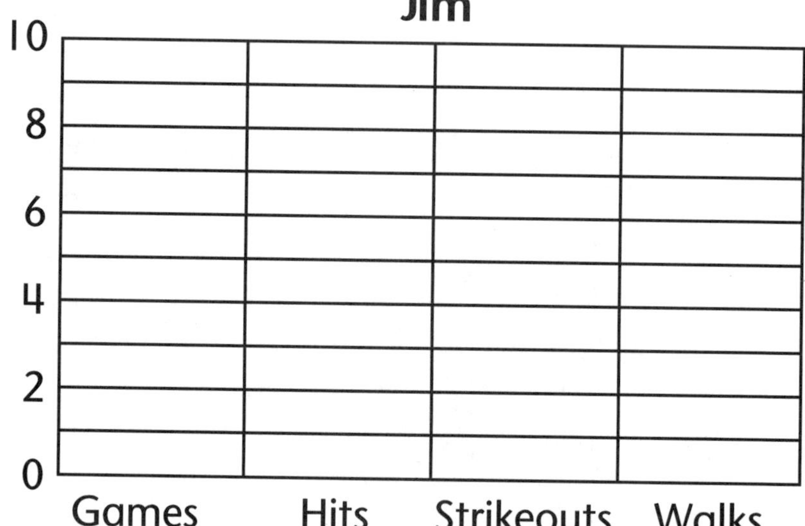

Problem Solving
Reasoning

6. Is it easier to see the information on the chart on page 235 or on the graph? Why? ____________________

✔ Quick Check

1. Mark the chart that shows the same information as the tally chart.

Favorite Pet	
dog	卌 卌 ||
cat	卌 卌

○

dog	12
cat	10

○

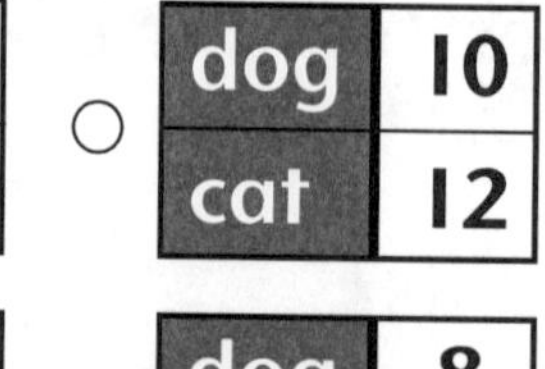

dog	10
cat	12

○

dog	10
cat	8

○

dog	8
cat	10

Name ______________________________________

The tally chart shows the ages of children at a day-care center.

Ages	Number of Children
1	||
2	|
3	||||
4	||
5	~~||||~~
6	|||

You can make a line plot of the data in the chart. Add X's to show the ages of the children.

1.

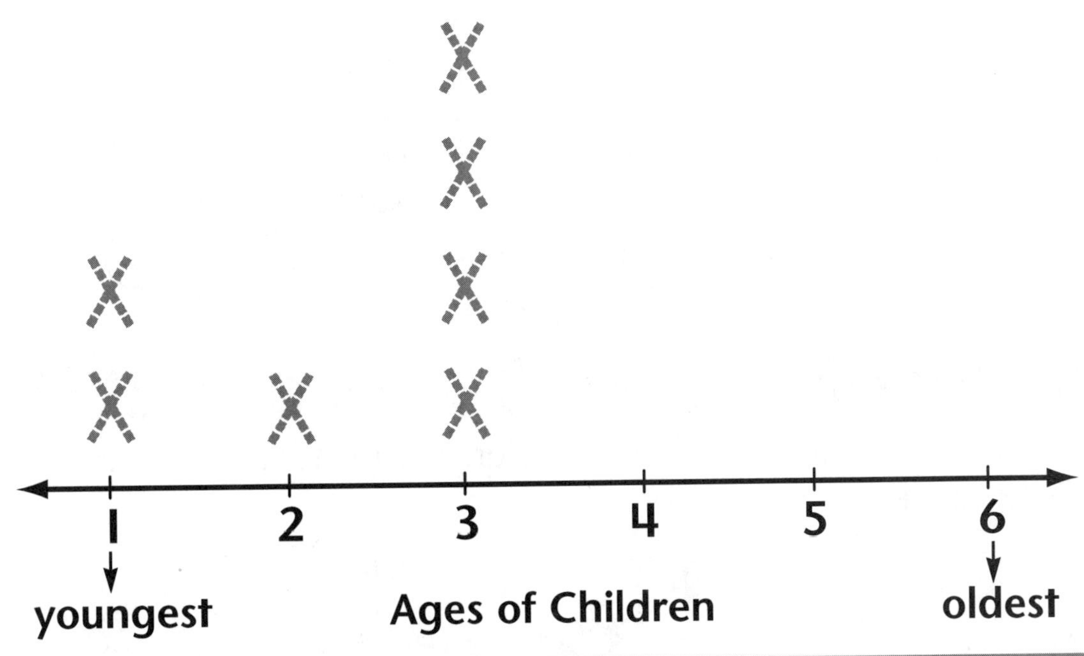

Count the X's to answer the questions.

2. How many children are **3** years old? ____

3. How many children are **6** years old? ____

The **range** is the difference between the least and the greatest numbers.

You can subtract to find the range.

The **mode** is the number that occurs most often.

Ages of Children

Use the line plot.

4. What is the oldest age? 6 ______

5. What is the youngest age? ______

6. What is the range? ☐ − ☐ = ☐

greatest least **range**

7. Which age has the most X's? ______? **mode**

★ Test Prep

What is the number with the greatest number of X's? Mark under your answer.

8

Class Favorite Numbers

5 ○ 4 ○ 3 ○ 2 ○

Name ______________________

STANDARD

Problem Solving Plan			
1. Understand	2. Decide	3. Solve	4. Look back

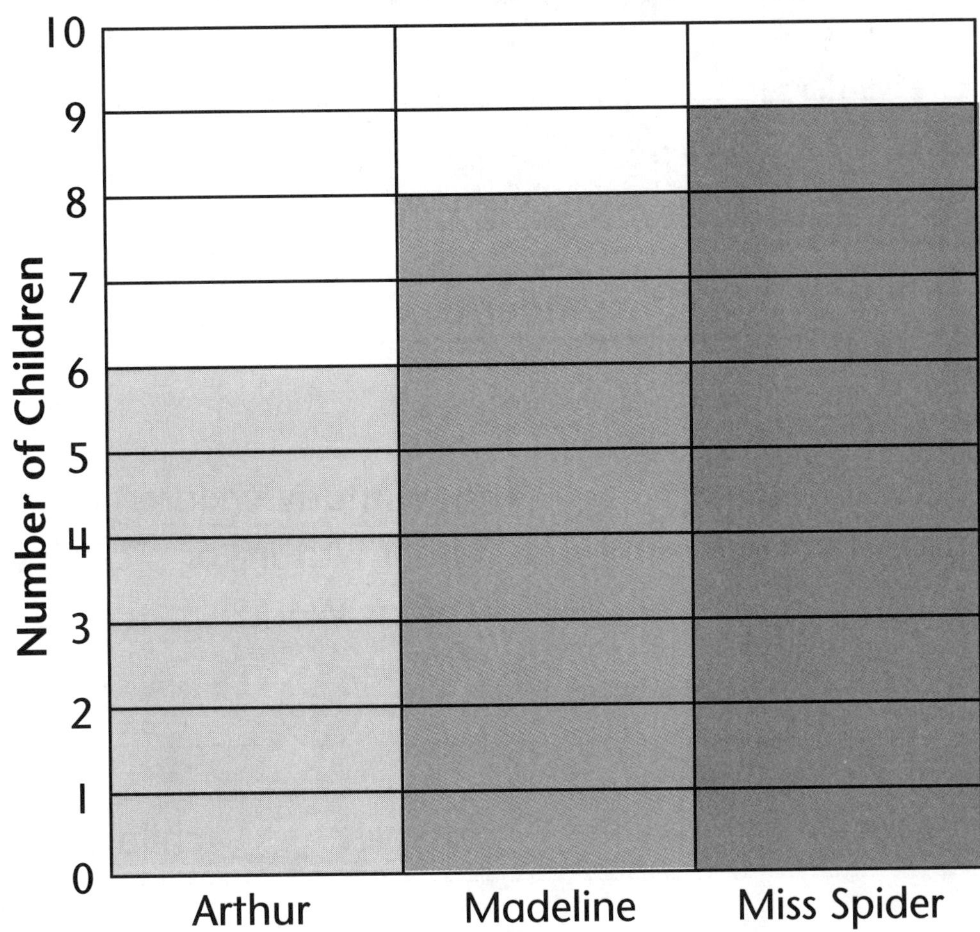

Use the graph.
Choose + or − to solve.

1. How many more children pick Madeline than Arthur?

Think Do you add or subtract? subtract

8 (−) 6 = 2

Answer 2 more children

2. How many children pick either Madeline or Miss Spider?

Think Do you add or subtract? ______

___ ◯ ___ = ___

Answer ___ children

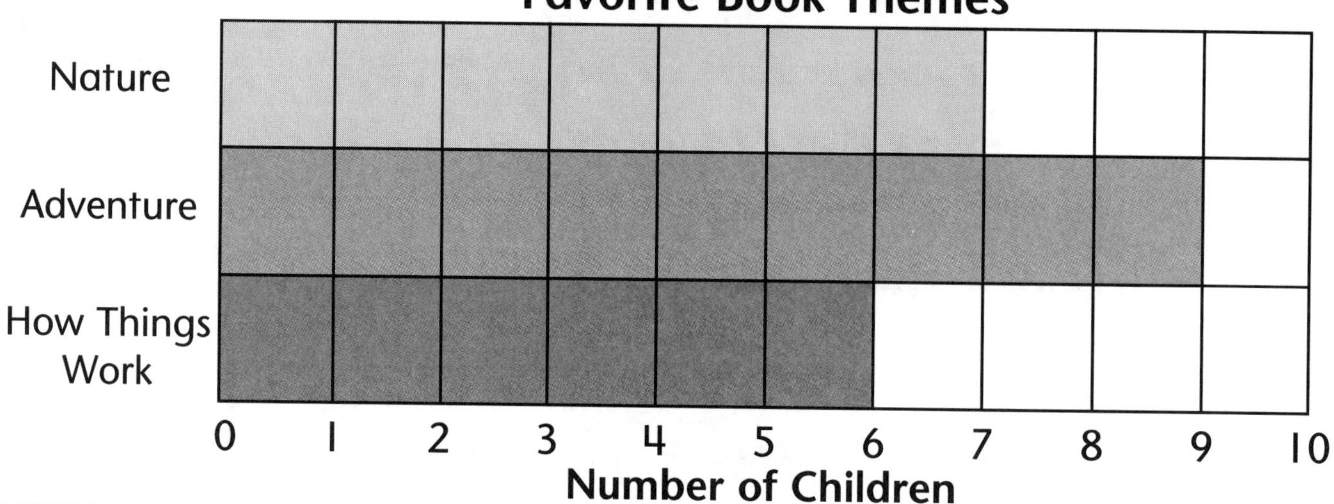

Use the graph.
Choose + or − to solve.

3. How many more children pick Adventure than pick How Things Work?

9 (−) 6 = 3

Answer 3 more children

4. How many children pick either Nature or pick How Things Work?

___ ◯ ___ = ___

Answer ___ children

5. How many more children pick Adventure than Nature?

___ ◯ ___ = ___

Answer ___ more children

6. How many fewer children pick How Things Work than Nature?

___ ◯ ___ = ___

Answer ___ fewer child

Extend Your Thinking

7. How could you solve problem 3 another way? ___

___

Name ____________________

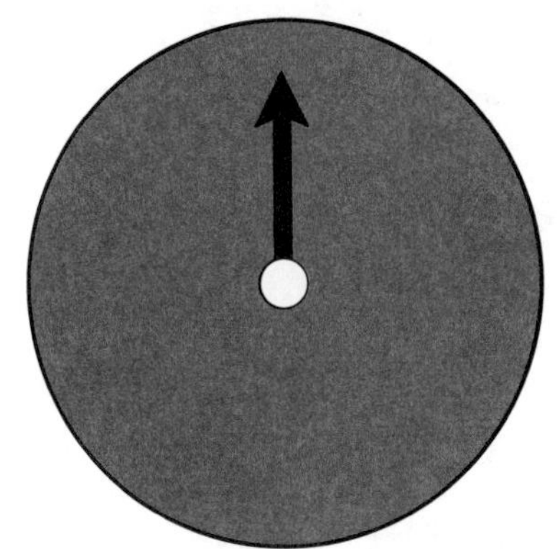

This spinner will **always** stop on red.

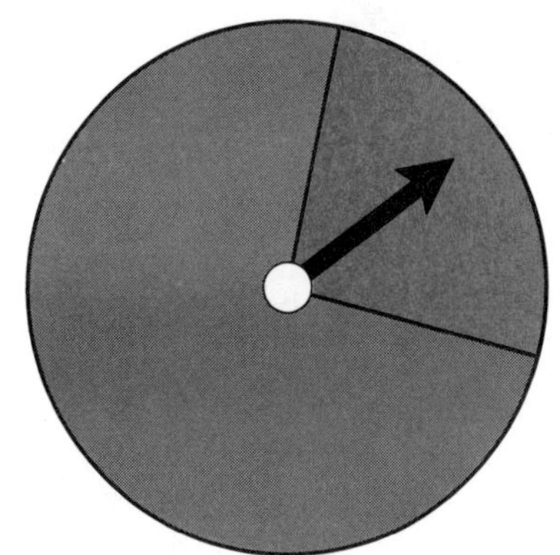

This spinner will **sometimes** stop on red.

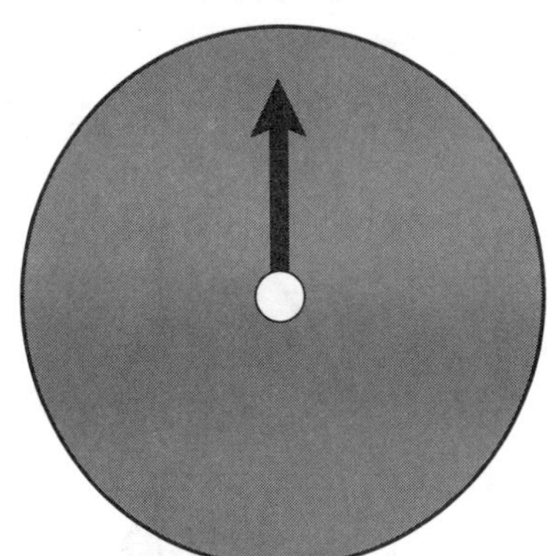

This spinner will **never** stop on red.

Ring whether the spinner will sometimes, always, or never stop on gray.

1.

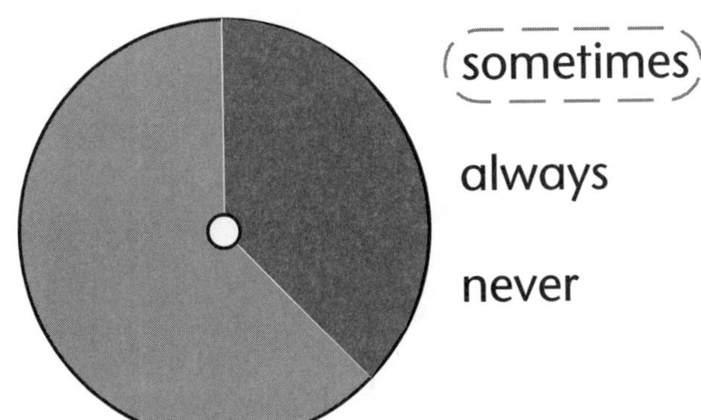

2.

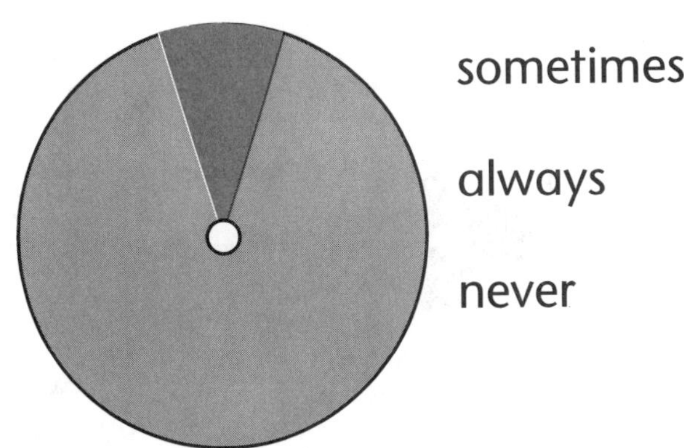

3.

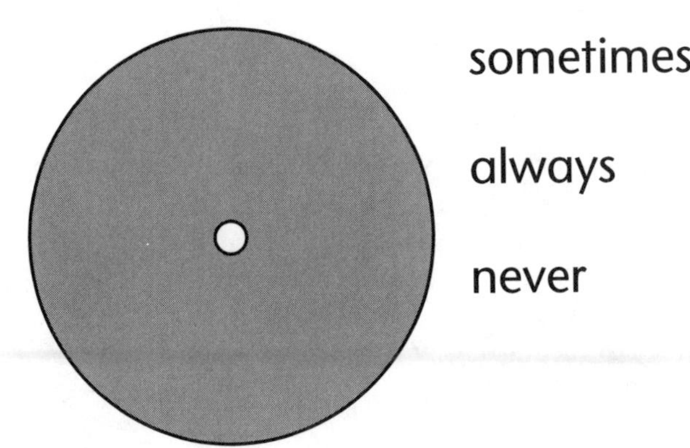

4.

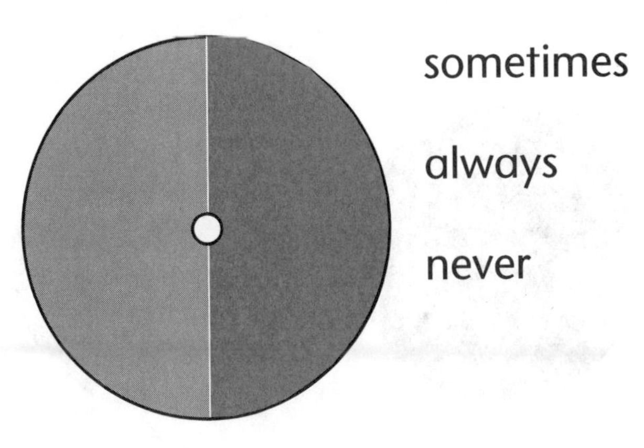

Ring whether you would sometimes, always, or never pick a red marble from the bag.

5.

sometimes always never

6.

sometimes always never

7.

sometimes always never

8.

sometimes always never

★ Test Prep

Mark under the spinner that would never spin red.

9

○

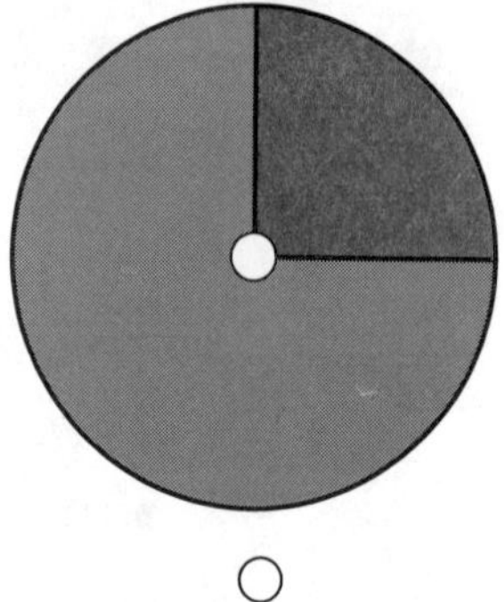

○

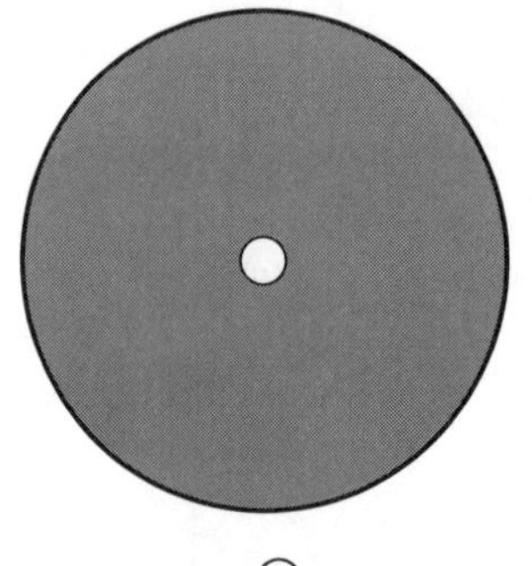

○

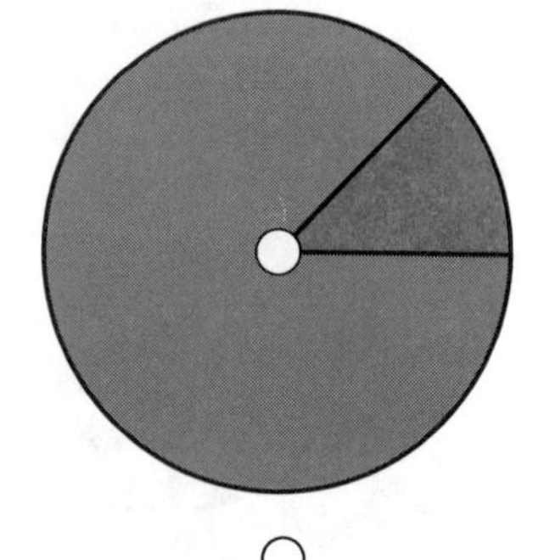

○

Name ____________________

Problem

Are you **more likely** or **less likely** to spin red?

1 Understand

I need to predict whether I am more or less likely to stop on red.

2 Decide

I will use a paper clip to spin. I will spin 10 times and record my results in a table. Then I will predict.

3 Solve

Try it.

Spinner Results	
red	
gray	

Ring your prediction. **Predict.** more likely

less likely

4 Look back

Does the answer make sense?

Are you more likely or less likely to land on gray?
Use a paper clip. Spin 10 times and complete the table.
Ring your predictions.

1.

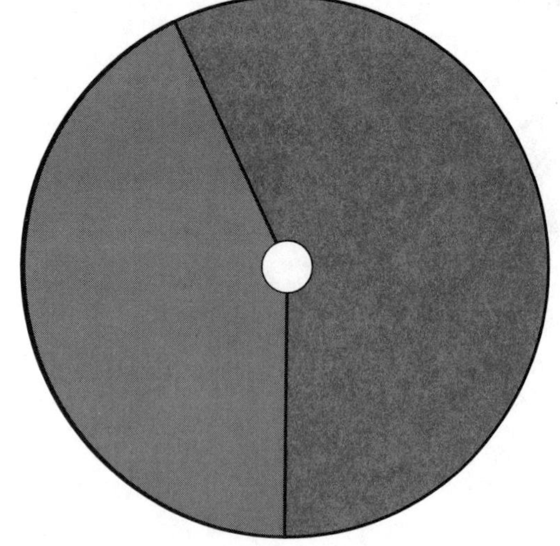

Spinner Results	
red	
gray	

Predict. more likely

less likely

2.

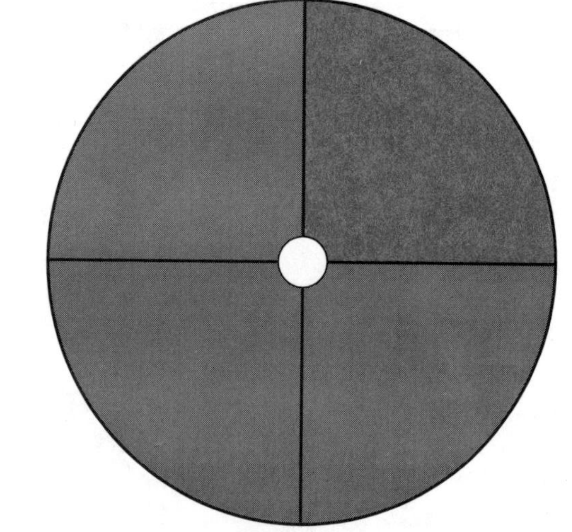

Spinner Results	
red	
gray	

Predict. more likely

less likely

3.

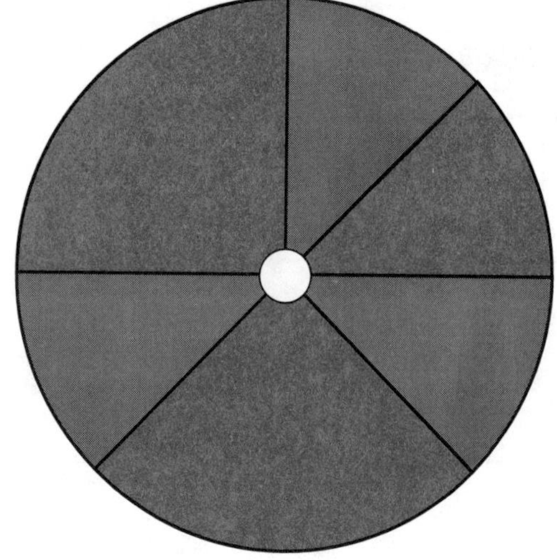

Spinner Results	
red	
gray	

Predict. more likely

less likely

Name ____________________

Use the tally chart to complete the graph. Answer the questions.

1.

Room 2's Favorite Fruit	
apples	卌 卌
bananas	卌 卌 II
grapes	卌 I

Room 2's Favorite Fruit

Number of Children	Apples	Bananas	Grapes
12			
10			
8			
6			
4			
2			
0			

2. How many children chose apples? ______

3. Which fruit got the most votes? ____________

Ring the answer.

4. Would you sometimes, always, or never pick a gray marble from the bag?

sometimes

always

never

5. Are you more likely or less likely to land on red?

more likely

less likely

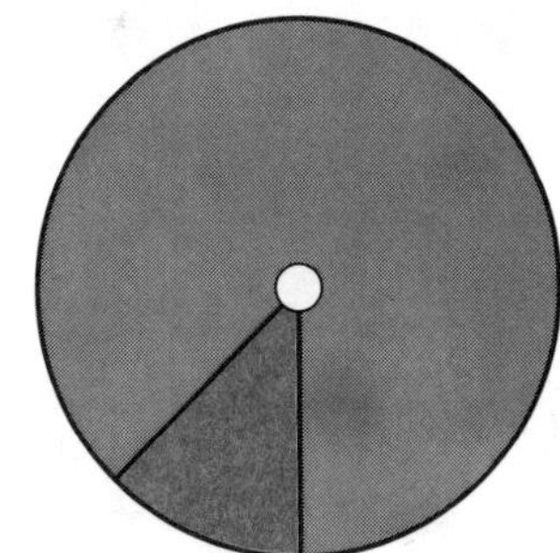

Problem Solving
Reasoning

Use the graph. Choose + or – to solve.

6.

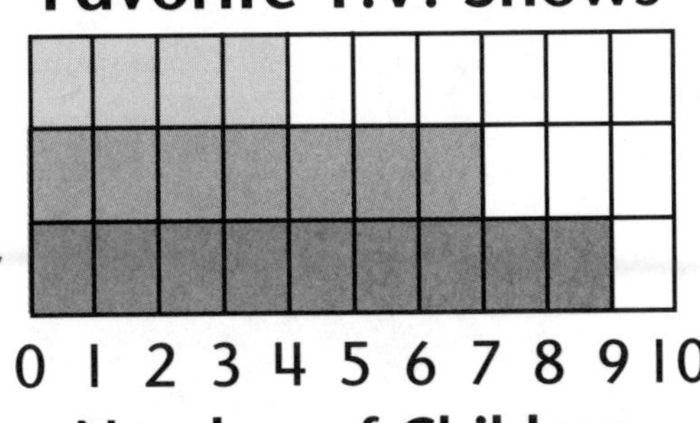

How many more children picked comedy than cartoon?

____ ◯ ____ = ____

____ more children.

Name ___________________________

1

8 + 9 = 17 ○ 18 − 9 = 9 ○ 17 − 9 = 8 ○ 8 + 8 = 16 ○

2

○ **8** nickels = **4** dimes

○ **5** nickels = **1** quarter

○ **1** quarter < **3** dimes

○ **6** nickels > **3** dimes

3

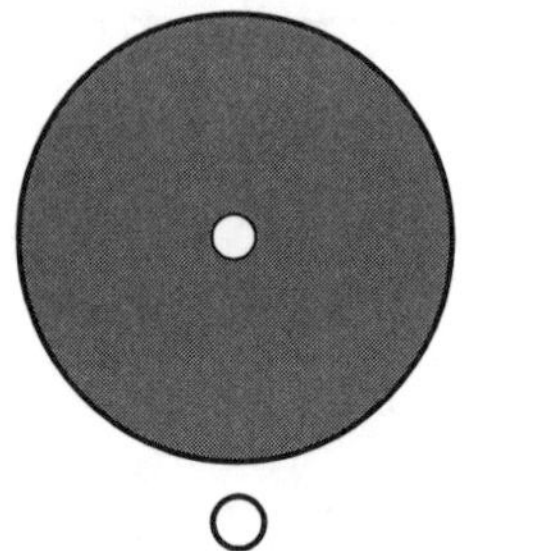
○

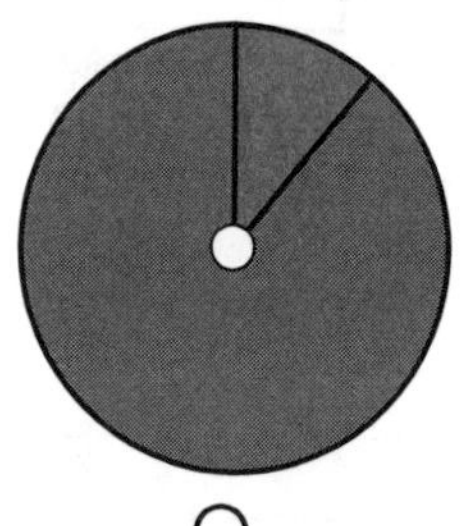
○

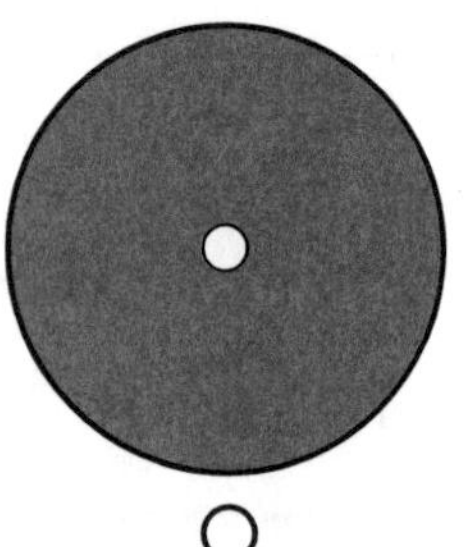
○

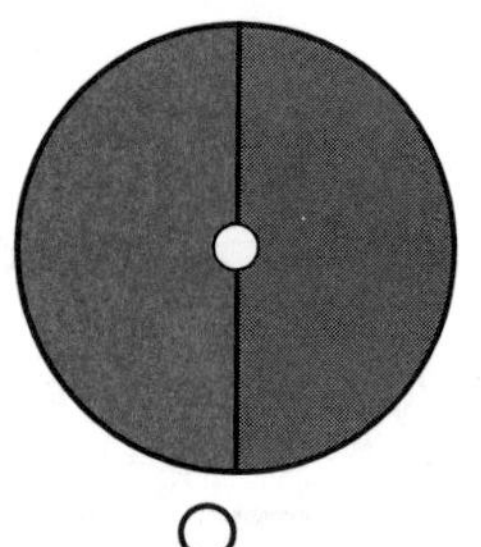
○

Decide on an answer. Mark the space for your answer.
If the answer is **not here**, mark the space for **NH**.

4

25 + 30 = ☐

45	60	55	50	NH
○	○	○	○	○

5

90 − 35 = ☐

65	35	60	45	NH
○	○	○	○	○

6

33¢	38¢	48¢	43¢	NH
○	○	○	○	○

UNIT 10 • TABLE OF CONTENTS

Place Value to 1,000

Dear Family,

During the next few weeks our math class will be learning about place value to 1,000.

You can expect to see homework that provides practice with reading, writing, and comparing numbers through 1,000.

As we learn about place value you may wish to keep the following sample as a guide.

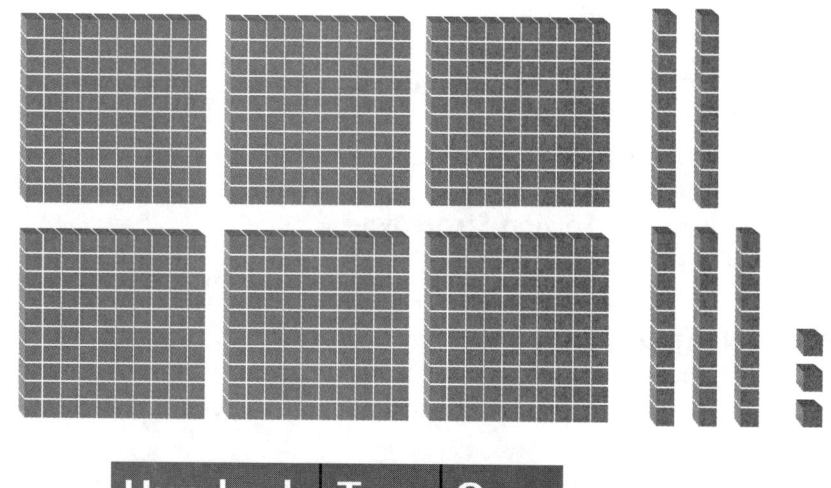

Hundreds	Tens	Ones
6	5	3

[6] hundreds [5] tens [3] ones

or

600 + 50 + 3

= 653

Sincerely,

Name ______________________________

10 tens in a group make 1 hundred.

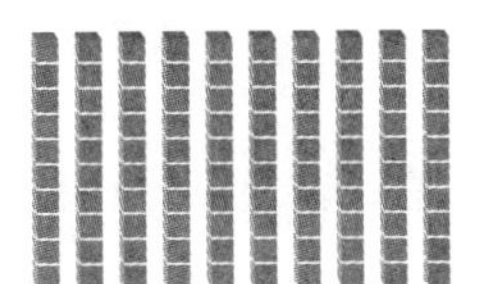 or 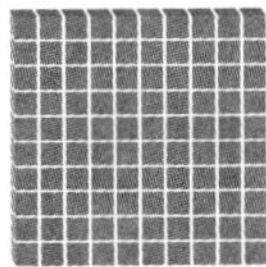

10 tens = one hundred

1 hundred and 0 tens and 0 ones = 100

Count by 100's. Write the missing numbers.

1.

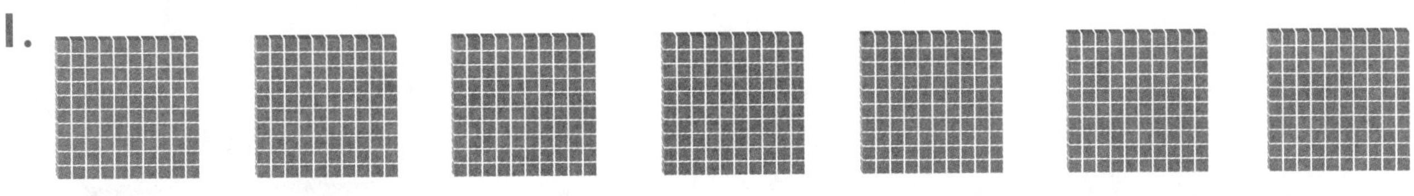

100, 200, ______, ______, **500**, **600**, ______,

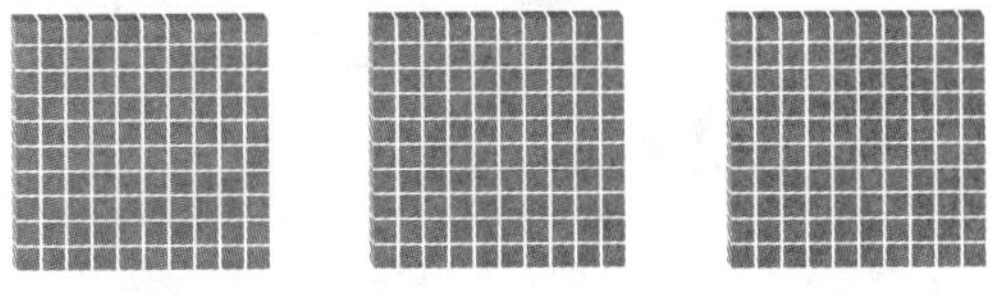

______, **900**, **1,000**

2. How many hundreds are in 1,000? ______ hundreds

Fill the blanks.

3. 4.

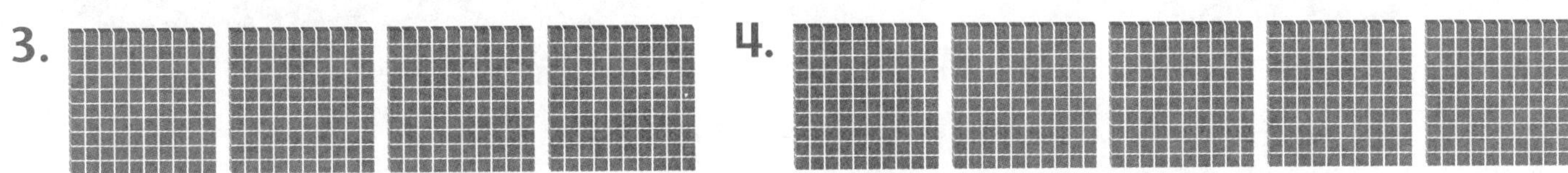

3.

Hundreds	Tens	Ones
4	0	0

4.

Hundreds	Tens	Ones

5. **800** is ____ hundreds ____ tens ____ ones.

6. **700** is ____ hundreds ____ tens ____ ones.

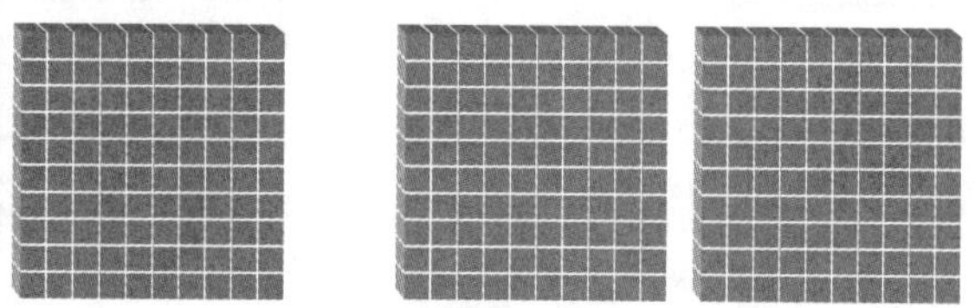

100 < 200
100 is less than 200

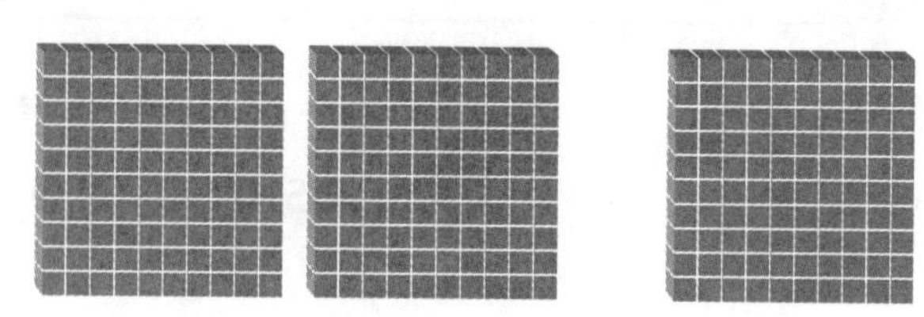

200 > 100
200 is greater than 100

Use >, <, or =. Look at the hundreds place.

7. 100 (<) 300
8. 500 ◯ 200
9. 100 ◯ 400
10. 400 ◯ 200
11. 600 ◯ 100
12. 300 ◯ 500

Write the number.

13. 6 hundreds 0 tens 0 ones 600

4 hundreds 0 tens 0 ones ____

1 hundred 0 tens 0 ones ____

9 hundreds 0 tens 0 ones ____

5 hundreds 0 tens 0 ones ____

Complete the table.

14.

	H	T	O
100	1	0	0
200			
300			
400			
500			

★ Test Prep

Decide on an answer. Mark the space for your answer.
If the answer is **not here**, mark the space for **NH**.

15

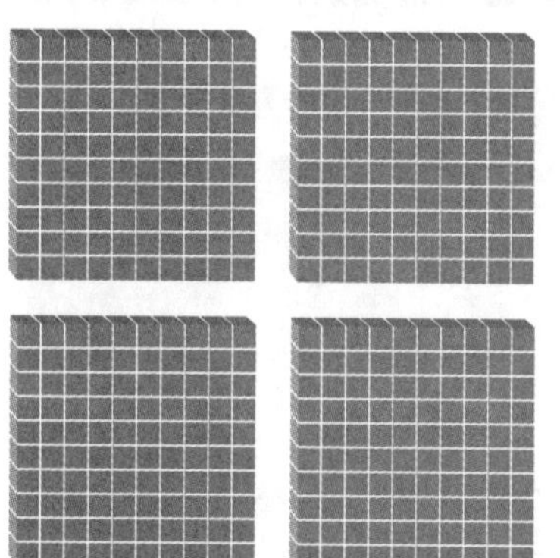

200 ◯ 300 ◯ 400 ◯ 500 ◯ NH ◯

Write the numbers.

1. 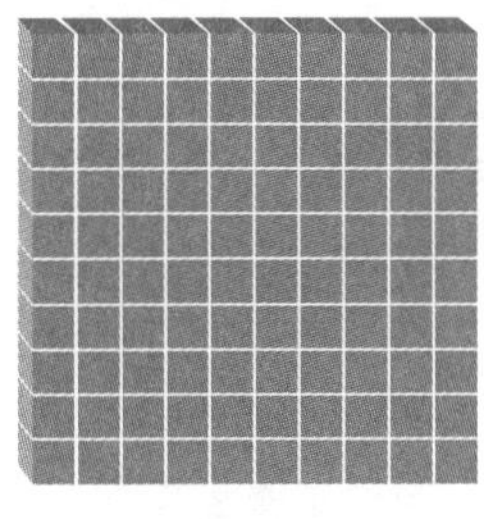

one hundred

Hundreds	Tens	Ones
1	0	0

100

2. 

one hundred seven

Hundreds	Tens	Ones

______

3. 

one hundred five

Hundreds	Tens	Ones

______

Complete.

4. **102** is 1 hundred 0 tens 2 ones, or 100 + 0 + 2 .

5. **106** is ____ hundred ____ tens ____ ones, or _____ + ____ + ____ .

Complete the number sentence.

6. **100 + 0 + 6 =** 106

7. **100 + 0 + 2 =** ☐

8. **100 + 0 + 1 =** ☐

9. **100 + 0 + 7 =** ☐

Write the missing numbers.

10. **101,** 102 **,103,** ______ , ______ **,106,** ______ **,108,** ______

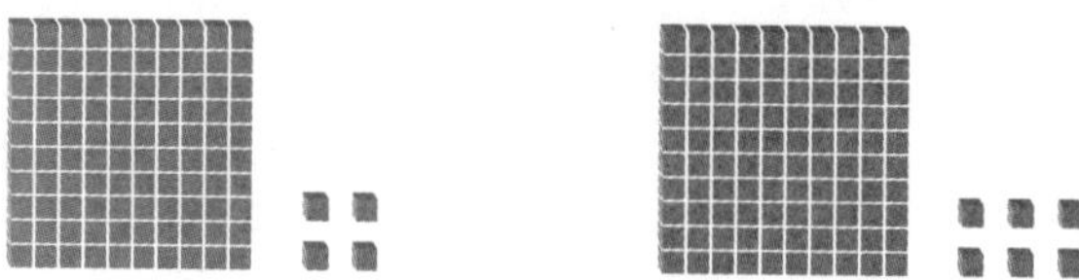

10<u>4</u> is less than **10<u>6</u>**.

10<u>4</u> < 10<u>6</u>

First compare the hundreds.
If the hundreds are the same, compare the tens.
If the tens are the same, compare the ones.

Use >, <, or =.

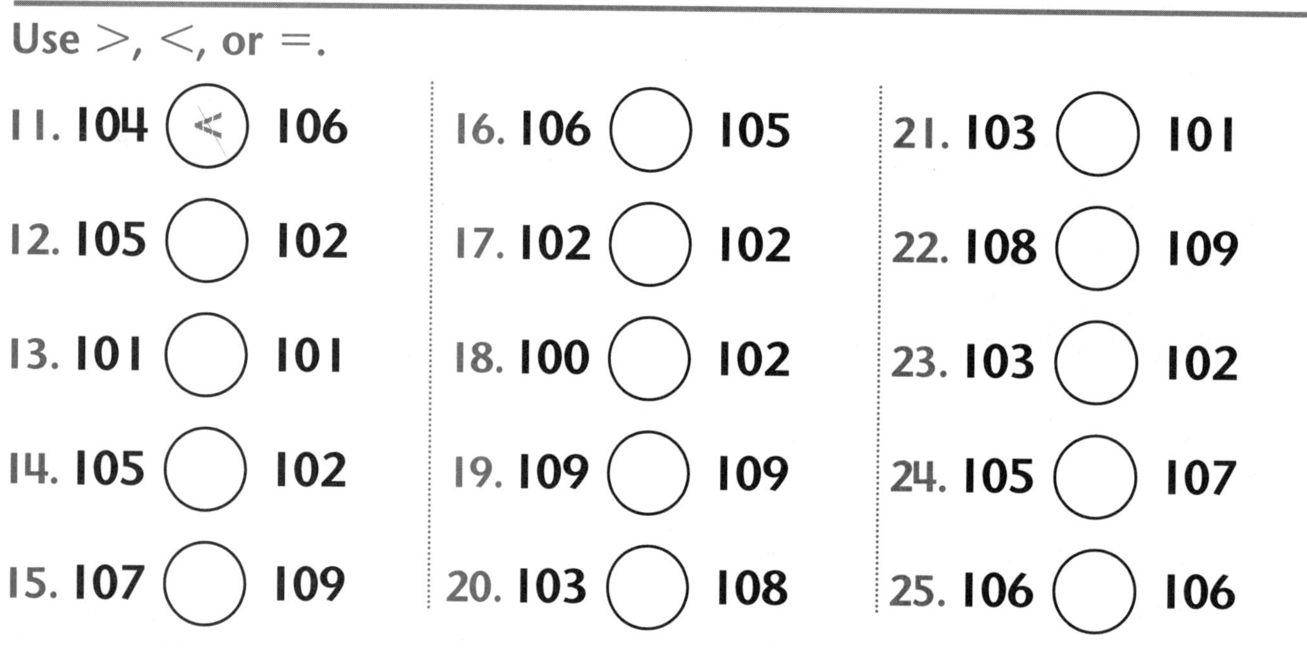

11. **104** (<) **106**
12. **105** ◯ **102**
13. **101** ◯ **101**
14. **105** ◯ **102**
15. **107** ◯ **109**
16. **106** ◯ **105**
17. **102** ◯ **102**
18. **100** ◯ **102**
19. **109** ◯ **109**
20. **103** ◯ **108**
21. **103** ◯ **101**
22. **108** ◯ **109**
23. **103** ◯ **102**
24. **105** ◯ **107**
25. **106** ◯ **106**

Problem Solving Reasoning Solve.

26. Dominic and Tony have marble collections. Dominic has **2** hundreds, **3** tens, and **6** ones. Tony has **2** hundreds and **2** tens, and **8** ones. Who has more marbles? ____________

★ Test Prep

Mark which one is not true.

27.
- ○ **106 > 104**
- ○ **107 < 109**
- ○ **103 > 104**
- ○ **100 < 101**

Name ______________________

Write the numbers.

1\.

Hundreds	Tens	Ones
1	2	0

100 + 20 + 0 = 120

one hundred twenty

2\.

Hundreds	Tens	Ones

______ + ______ + ______ = ______

one hundred thirty-five

Complete.

3\. **1** hundred **8** tens **5** ones is 185, or 100 + 80 + 5.

4\. **1** hundred **3** tens **4** ones is ______, or ______ + ______ + ______.

5\. **1** hundred **5** tens **9** ones is ______, or ______ + ______ + ______.

Complete the number sentence.

6\. **100 + 70 + 9 =** 179

7\. **100 + 40 + 1 =** ☐

8\. **100 + 30 + 6 =** ☐

9\. **100 + 90 + 7 =** ☐

Complete. Count from 100 to 200.

10.

100	110	120	130	140	150	160	170	180	190
101		121	131	141		161	171	181	191
	112		132	142	152	162	172	182	192
103	113		133	143	153	163	173	183	193
104		124	134	144	154	164		184	194
105	115	125	135			165		185	195
106	116		136	146	156	166	176	186	
107	117	127	137		157	167	177	187	197
108		128	138	148	158	168	178		198
109	119	129	139		159	169	179	189	199
									200

11. Shade all numbers that have **3** tens.

Use the chart to compare. Write >, < or =.

12. 134 ◯ 164

13. 141 ◯ 142

14. 127 ◯ 157

15. 159 ◯ 109

16. 172 ◯ 112

17. 199 ◯ 200

What comes before?

18. ______, 168

19. ______, 180

What comes between?

20. 145, ______, 147

21. 198, ______, 200

What comes after?

22. 159, ______

23. 109, ______

Quick Check

Write the missing numbers.

1.

100	200		400		600	700		

2. 103, ______, 105, ______, ______, 108

3. ______, ______, 189, ______, 191

Name ______________________________

Write the numbers.

1.

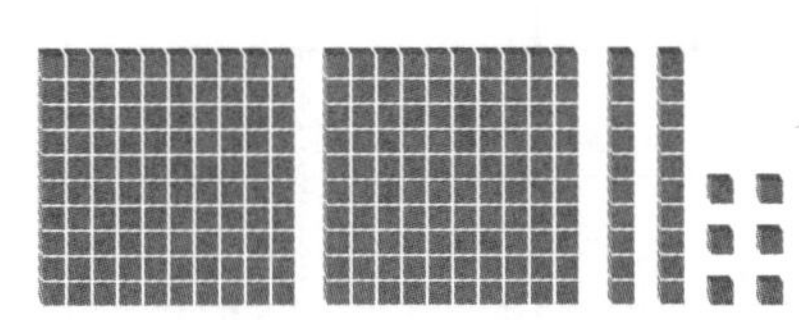

two hundred twenty-six

Hundreds	Tens	Ones
2	2	6

200 + 20 + 6 = 226

2.

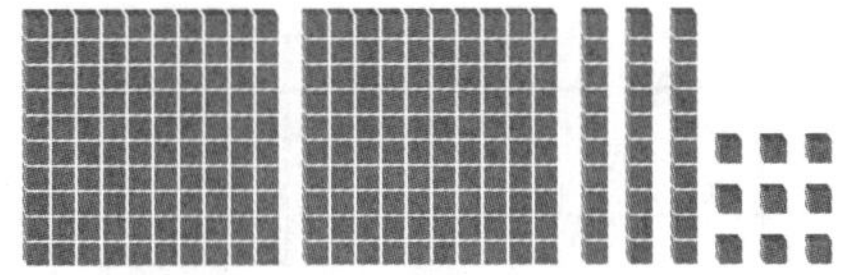

two hundred thirty-nine

Hundreds	Tens	Ones

_____ + _____ + _____ = _____

Complete.

3. **226** is 2 hundreds 2 tens 6 ones.
4. **241** is ____ hundreds ____ tens ____ one.
5. **201** is ____ hundreds ____ tens ____ one.
6. **210** is ____ hundreds ____ ten ____ ones.
7. **299** is ____ hundreds ____ tens ____ ones.
8. **300** is ____ hundreds ____ tens ____ ones.
9. **226** = 200 + 20 + 6 ⟶
10. **241** = _____ + _____ + ____ ⟶
11. **201** = _____ + _____ + ____ ⟶
12. **210** = _____ + _____ + ____ ⟶
13. **299** = _____ + _____ + ____ ⟶

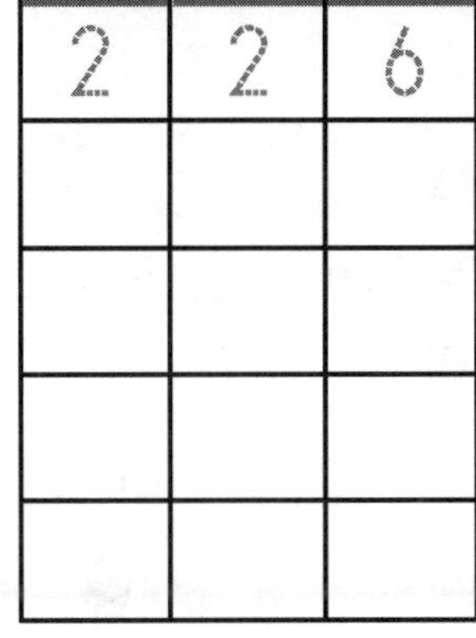

H	T	O
2	2	6

Complete. Count from 200 to 300.

14.

200	210		230			260		280	
201									
202									
					259				
									300

15. Shade all numbers that have **2** hundreds and **0** tens.

Write the missing numbers.

16. **207,** _____, _____, _____, **211,** _____, _____, **214**

17. **259,** _____, **261,** _____, _____, _____, **265,** _____

What comes before?

18. _____, **231**

19. _____, **280**

20. _____, **250**

What comes between?

21. **269,** _____, **271**

22. **298,** _____, **300**

23. **223,** _____, **225**

What comes after?

24. **250,** _____

25. **229,** _____

26. **279,** _____

★ Test Prep

Which number is between **279** and **281**? Mark the space for your answer.

27

Name ____________________

Write the numbers.

1.

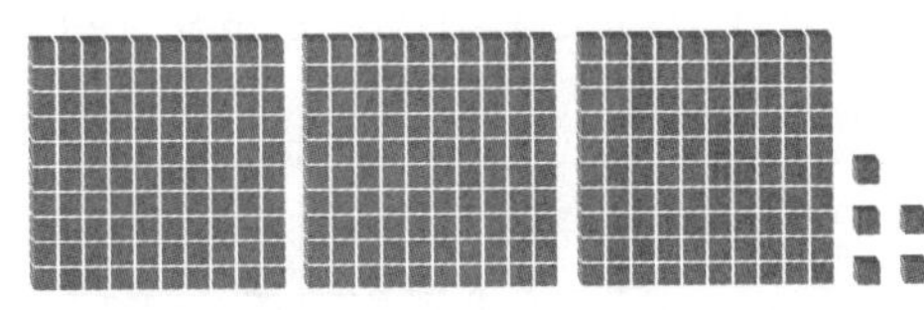

three hundred five

Hundreds	Tens	Ones
3	0	5

300 + 0 + 5 = 305

2.

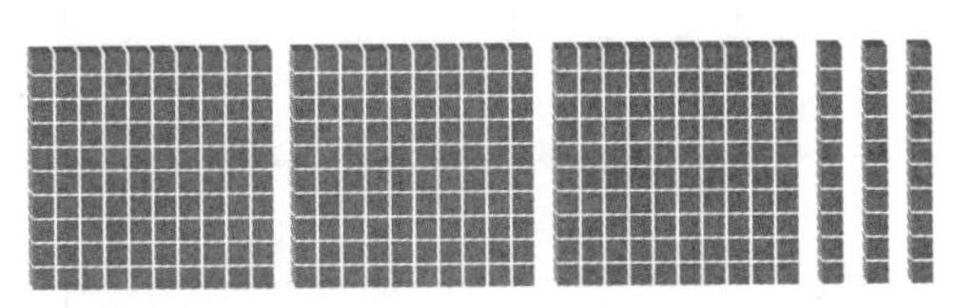

three hundred thirty

Hundreds	Tens	Ones

____ + ____ + ____ = ____

Complete.

3. **383** is 3 hundreds 8 tens 3 ones.

4. **328** is ____ hundreds ____ tens ____ ones.

5. **337** is ____ hundreds ____ tens ____ ones.

6. **379** is ____ hundreds ____ tens ____ ones.

7. **309** is ____ hundreds ____ tens ____ ones.

8. **400** is ____ hundreds ____ tens ____ ones.

9. **346** = 300 + 40 + 6 →

10. **392** = ____ + ____ + ____ →

11. **320** = ____ + ____ + ____ →

12. **311** = ____ + ____ + ____ →

13. **303** = ____ + ____ + ____ →

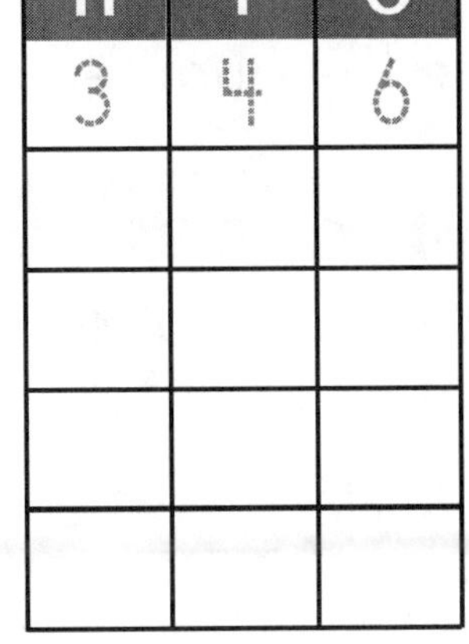

H	T	O
3	4	6

Complete. Count from 300 to 400.

14.

300			330					380	
301									
					359				
									400

15. Shade all numbers that have **3** hundreds and **4** ones.

Write the missing numbers.

16. **309,** ______ **,311,** ______ , ______ , ______ , ______ **,316**

17. ______ , ______ **,371,** ______ , ______ , ______ **,375,** ______

Problem Solving Reasoning Solve.

18. Draw 5 tens, 3 hundreds, and 6 ones.

Write the number. ______

★ Test Prep

What comes after? Mark the space for your answer.

327, ____

320	326	328	330
○	○	○	○

Name ____________________________________

Complete. Count from 400 to 500.

1.

400	410		430	440	450	460		480	490
	411	421	431	441	451	461		481	491
402		422	432		452		472	482	
403		423		443	453		473		493
	414	424	434	444		464	474	484	
405	415		435	445	455	465		485	495
406		426	436	446		466	476	486	
	417	427	437		457	467	477		497
408	418		438	448	458		478	488	
	419		439		459	469	479	489	499
									500

2. Shade all numbers that have 4 hundreds and 8 tens.

Write the numbers.

3.

Hundreds	Tens	Ones
4	6	7

400 + 60 + 7 = 467

four hundred sixty-seven

Write the numbers.

4. **417** = 400 + 10 + 7 →
5. **403** = ______ + ____ + ____ →
6. **500** = ______ + ____ + ____ →

H	T	O
4	1	7

Write the missing numbers.

7. 410, _____ , _____ , _____ , 414, _____ , _____ , _____ , 418

8. 453, _____ , 455, _____ , _____ , _____ , _____ , _____ , 461

What comes before?	What comes between?	What comes after?
9. _____ , 421	11. 477, _____ , 479	13. 456, _____
10. _____ , 466	12. 490, _____ , 492	14. 449, _____

Problem Solving Reasoning Ring all the ways to show 405.

15. 4 hundred and 5 ones

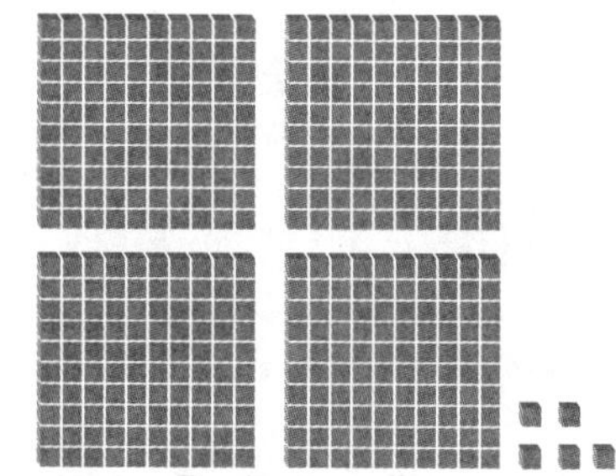

400 + 50

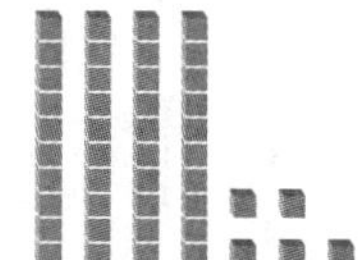

400 + 5

4 hundred and 5 ones

Quick Check

Write the missing numbers.

1. _____ , 238, _____ , _____ , _____ , 242, _____

2. 358, _____ , _____ , _____ , 362, _____ , 364

3. _____ , 495, _____ , 497, _____ , _____ , _____

Name ______________________

Complete.

1\.

Hundreds	Tens	Ones
6	5	3

[6] hundreds [5] tens [3] ones

or

600 + 50 + 3 = 653

six hundred fifty-three

2\.

Hundreds	Tens	Ones

[ ] hundreds [ ] tens [ ] ones

or

____ + ____ + ____ = ____

five hundred fifty-nine

3\.

Hundreds	Tens	Ones

[ ] hundreds [ ] tens [ ] ones

or

____ + ____ + ____ = ____

nine hundred twenty-nine

Complete.

4. **594 =** ____ hundreds ____ tens ____ ones →
5. **639 =** ____ hundreds ____ tens ____ ones →
6. **945 =** ____ hundreds ____ tens ____ ones →
7. **721 =** ____ hundreds ____ tens ____ one →
8. **539 =** ____ hundreds ____ tens ____ ones →
9. **674 =** ____ hundreds ____ tens ____ ones →

H	T	O

10. **200 + 30 + 5 =** 235
11. **400 + 50 + 8 =** ☐
12. **500 + 70 + 2 =** ☐
13. **700 + 90 + 7 =** ☐
14. **200 + 0 + 0 =** ☐
15. **300 + 60 + 4 =** ☐
16. **600 + 30 + 0 =** ☐
17. **800 + 0 + 6 =** ☐

Write the missing numbers. Count.

18. **900, 901,** ______, ______, ______, ______, ______
19. **118,** ______, ______, ______, ______, ______, ______
20. **732,** ______, **734,** ______, ______, ______, ______

What comes before?

21. ____, **431**
22. ____, **889**

What comes between?

23. **198,** ____, **200**
24. **131,** ____, **133**

What comes after?

25. **699,** ____
26. **489,** ____

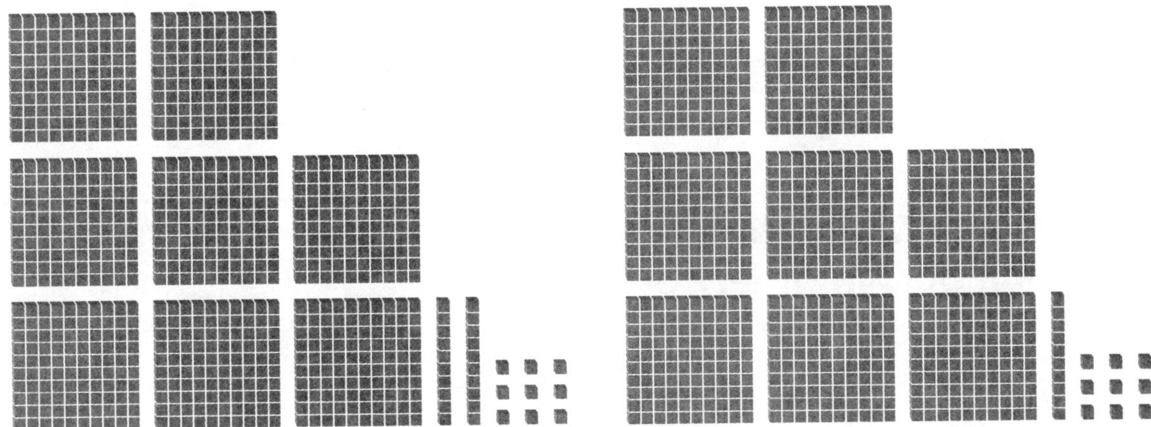

8<u>2</u>9 is greater than **8<u>1</u>9**.

8<u>2</u>9 > 8<u>1</u>9

The tens are not the same.

Remember: First compare the hundreds.
If the hundreds are the same, compare the tens.
If the tens are the same, compare the ones.

Use >, < or =.

27.	177 ◯ 361	301 ◯ 400	211 ◯ 321
28.	454 ◯ 454	413 ◯ 259	155 ◯ 205
29.	201 ◯ 110	396 ◯ 396	499 ◯ 319
30.	322 ◯ 207	246 ◯ 214	388 ◯ 499

Problem Solving Reasoning Solve.

31. Jacob and a friend play Guess My Number. Jacob's number has **4** ones, **6** hundreds, and **7** tens. What is his number? _______

Ring the greatest number.

32.

386	154	259	236

Ring the least number.

33.

173	626	418	132

Use the pictures. Write the number.
Write the numbers in order.

34.

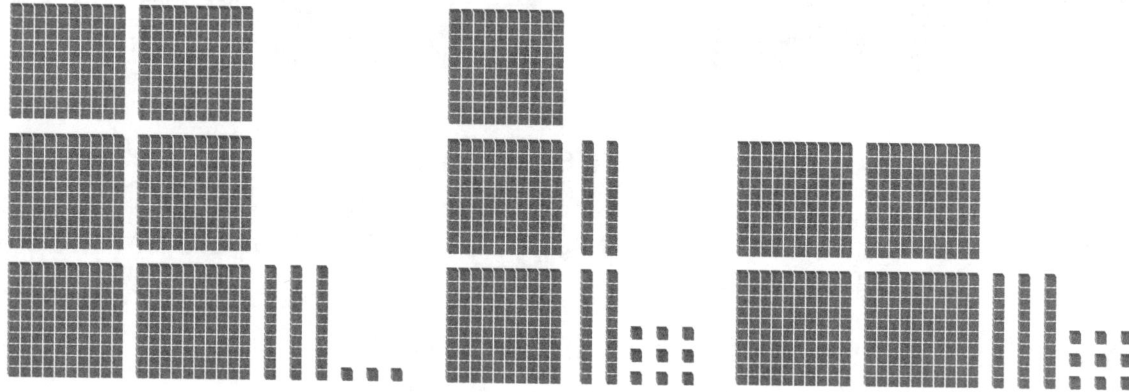

______ ______ ______

Answer ______ ______ ______
least greatest

Write the numbers in order.

35. 427 692 447

Answer ______ ______ ______
greatest least

★ Test Prep

Choose > or < .

604 ○ 597 | > ○ < ○

Name ____________________

Problem

Look at these numbers

150, 146, 142, 138, 134, 130, ___?___

What number is most likely to come next?

1 Understand

I need to find out what number is most likely to come next.

2 Decide

I can look for a pattern using a number chart.

3 Solve

I'll ring the numbers on the chart.

100	110	120	(130)	140	(150)	160	170	180	190
101	111	121	131	141	151	161	171	181	191
102	112	122	132	(142)	152	162	172	182	192
103	113	123	133	143	153	163	173	183	193
104	114	124	(134)	144	154	164	174	184	194
105	115	125	135	145	155	165	175	185	195
106	116	126	136	(146)	156	166	176	186	196
107	117	127	137	147	157	167	177	187	197
108	118	128	(138)	148	158	168	178	188	198
109	119	129	139	149	159	169	179	189	199

I see that each number is **4** less than the last.

I think **126** is most likely to come next.

4 Look back

Does my answer make sense? Why or why not?

What number is most likely to come next?
Ring the numbers.
Find a pattern to solve.

1. 322, 327, 332, 337, 342, 347, _______

300	310	320	330	340	350	360	370	380	390
301	311	321	331	341	351	361	371	381	391
302	312	322	332	342	352	362	372	382	392
303	313	323	333	343	353	363	373	383	393
304	314	324	334	344	354	364	374	384	394
305	315	325	335	345	355	365	375	385	395
306	316	326	336	346	356	366	376	386	396
307	317	327	337	347	357	367	377	387	397
308	318	328	338	348	358	368	378	388	398
309	319	329	339	349	359	369	379	389	399
									400

2. 229, 227, 225, 223, 221, 219, _______

200	210	220	230	240	250	260	270	280	290
201	211	221	231	241	251	261	271	281	291
202	212	222	232	242	252	262	272	282	292
203	213	223	233	243	253	263	273	283	293
204	214	224	234	244	254	264	274	284	294
205	215	225	235	245	255	265	275	285	295
206	216	226	236	246	256	266	276	286	296
207	217	227	237	247	257	267	277	287	297
208	218	228	238	248	258	268	278	288	298
209	219	229	239	249	259	269	279	289	299
									300

Name ________________________________

1¢	5¢	10¢	25¢	50¢

$.01	$.05	$.10	$.25	$.50

Write the amount two ways.

1.

55 ¢

$ .55

2.

_____ ¢

$ ___.____

3.

_____ ¢

$ ___.____

4.

_____ ¢

$ ___.____

Complete.

5. **$.01** = 0 dimes and 1 penny.
6. **$.02** = 0 dimes and ____ pennies.
7. **$.03** = ____ dimes and ____ pennies.
8. **$.04** = ____ dimes and ____ pennies.
9. **$.05** = ____ dimes and ____ pennies.
10. **$.06** = ____ dimes and ____ pennies.
11. **$.07** = ____ dimes and ____ pennies.
12. **$.08** = ____ dimes and ____ pennies.
13. **$.09** = ____ dimes and ____ pennies.

0 dimes and **4** pennies
4¢ or **$.04**

Write the amount two ways.

14. **0** dimes and **1** penny $.01 or 1¢
15. **0** dimes and **2** pennies ______ or ____
16. **0** dimes and **3** pennies ______ or ____
17. **0** dimes and **4** pennies ______ or ____
18. **0** dimes and **5** pennies ______ or ____

★ Test Prep

Choose >, <, or = . Mark the space for your answer.

19 **$.78** ◯ **78¢** | > ○ | < ○ | = ○

Name ____________________

10 dimes = $1.00

Complete.

1. two dollars = $ 2.00
2. eight dollars = $ ___.___
3. six dollars = $ ___.___
4. five dollars = $ ___.___
5. three dollars = $ ___.___
6. **6** dollars and **3** dimes = $ 6.30
7. **9** dollars and **6** dimes = $ ___.___
8. **8** dollars and **4** dimes = $ ___.___
9. **$5.50** = 5 dollars and 5 dimes
10. **$2.40** = ____ dollars and ____ dimes

Quick Check

Write the missing numbers.

1.

299		301	302	

Write the number.

2.

Hundreds	Tens	Ones
6	0	8

= ______

3.

Hundreds	Tens	Ones
4	2	0

= ______

Write the amount two ways.

4. **0** dimes and **7** pennies = ______ or ______¢

Write the amount.

5. **4** dollars and **5** dimes = $ ___.___

Complete. Use $.

1.

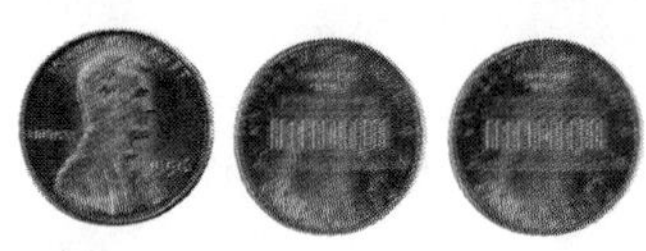

Dollars	Dimes	Pennies
2	0	9

= ☐

2.

Dollars	Dimes	Pennies

= ☐

Fill the blanks.

3. **$9.06** is __9__ dollars __0__ dimes __6__ pennies.

4. **$7.15** is ____ dollars ____ dime ____ pennies.

Write the amount.

5. **2** dollars **0** dimes **7** pennies is **$** __2.07__ .

6. **4** dollars **2** dimes **8** pennies is **$** ___.___ .

Problem Solving Reasoning Ring which is incorrect. Tell why.

7. **2.75¢** **$1.25** **$3.95**

★ Test Prep

How much money? Mark the space for your answer.

8

$1.03 ○ $1.30 ○ $1.21 ○ $1.12 ○

Name ______________________________

I half-dollar

$.50

2 half-dollars equal in value **$1.00**

Complete.

1. **I** half-dollar = $ ___.50___
2. **2** half-dollars = $ ___1.00___
3. **3** half-dollars = $ ___.___
4. **4** half-dollars = $ ___.___
5. **5** half-dollars = $ ___.___
6. **6** half-dollars = $ ___.___

Ring the groups that are worth $1.00.

7.

2 quarters equal in value a half-dollar

=

4 quarters equal in value **$1.00**

=

Use >, <, or = .

8. **25¢** (<) **$1.00**
9. **75¢** ( ) **$.50**
10. **$1.00** ( ) **4** quarters
11. **$1.50** ( ) **$2.00**
12. **$.25** ( ) **25¢**

Ring the greatest amount.

13. **$.75** **($1.25)** **$.50**
14. **$1.00** **$2.00** **$1.95**
15. **$4.25** **$4.00** **$4.50**
16. **50¢** **75¢** **$.55**
17. **$.25** **$.50** **$.75**

★ Test Prep

How much money? Mark the space for your answer.

18

○ 78¢ ○ 86¢ ○ 71¢ ○ 96¢

STANDARD

Name ____________________

Problem Solving Plan
1. Understand 2. Decide 3. Solve 4. Look back

Use the picture. Solve.

1. Which costs more, paper towels or beans?

Think How much do paper towels cost? $2.00
How much do beans cost? $1.48

$2.00 (>) $1.48

Answer ____________

2. Which costs more, oranges or light bulbs?

Think How much do oranges cost? ______
How much do light bulbs cost? ______

______ ◯ ______

Answer ____________

3. Which costs more, beans or sponges?

Think How much do beans cost? ______
How much do sponges cost? ______

______ ◯ ______

Answer ____________

4. Which costs less, peas or paper towels?

Think How much do peas cost? ______
How much do paper towels cost? ______

______ ◯ ______

Answer ____________

Use the picture. Solve.

5. Which costs less, the doll or the top?

____ ◯ ____

Answer ____________

6. Which costs more, the bowl or the book?

____ ◯ ____

Answer ____________

7. Which costs more, the ring or the book?

____ ◯ ____

Answer ____________

8. Which costs less, the plant or the ring?

____ ◯ ____

Answer ____________

Extend Your Thinking

9. How do you know you found the right answer in problem 8? Explain.

____

____

____

____

Name ______________________

What comes

before?	between?	after?
1. ______ , 550	3. 299, ______ , 301	5. 109, ______
2. ______ , 101	4. 909, ______ , 911	6. 980, ______

Ring the greatest number.

7. | 927 | 729 | 297 |
|---|---|---|

8. | 604 | 640 | 146 |
|---|---|---|

Ring the least number.

9. | 919 | 119 | 991 |
|---|---|---|

10. | 805 | 508 | 590 |
|---|---|---|

Complete.

11. 604 is ______ hundreds ______ tens ______ ones.

12. 352 is ______ hundreds ______ tens ______ ones.

Complete.

13. 500 + 30 + 0 = ☐

14. 900 + 0 + 8 = ☐

15. 400 + 0 + 0 = ☐

16. 700 + 60 + 5 = ☐

Write the amount two ways.

17.

______ ¢

$ ___ . ______

18.

______ ¢

$ ___ . ______

Problem Solving Reasoning

Use the picture. Solve.

19. Which costs more, the basket or the candle?

______ ◯ ______

Answer ______________

Name ____________________

Cumulative Review

★ Test Prep

1

3:40 ○ 8:30 ○ 8:15 ○ 9:15 ○

2

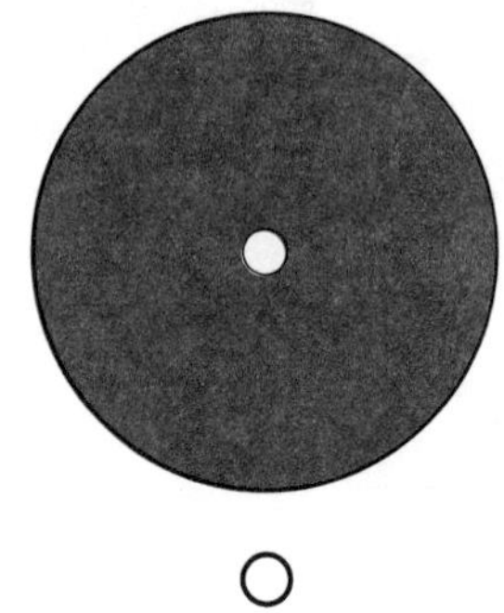 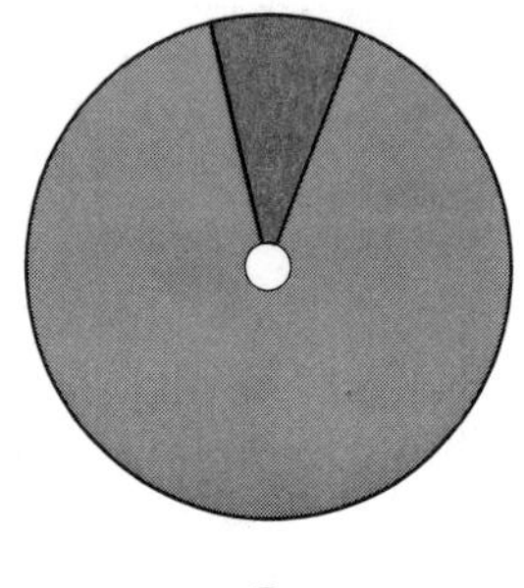 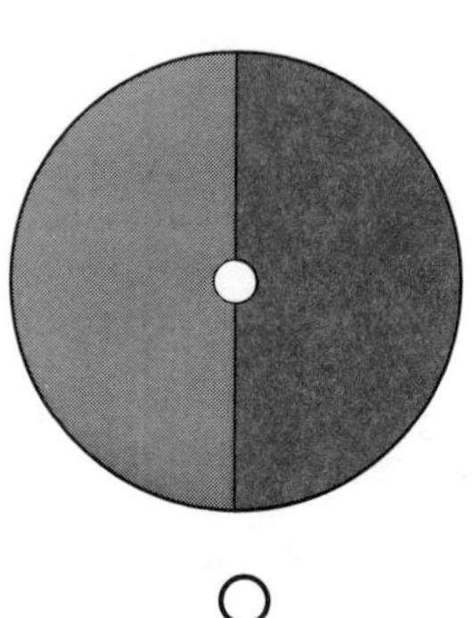 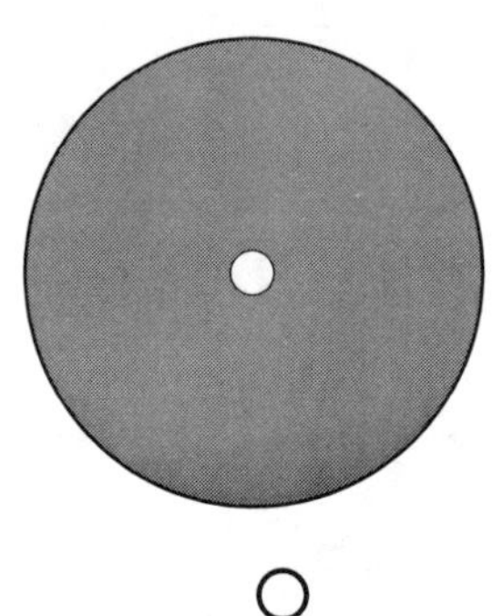

○ ○ ○ ○

3

50075 ○ 500705 ○ 575 ○ 5075 ○

4

847 ○ 487 ○ 408 ○ 87 ○

5

$30.05 ○ $3.50 ○ $3.15 ○ $3.05 ○

Decide on an answer. Mark the space for your answer.
If the answer is **not here,** mark the space for **NH.**

6

$$\begin{array}{r} 27 \\ 20 \\ +\ 36 \\ \hline \square \end{array}$$

○ 73
○ 84
○ 83
○ 74
○ NH

7

$$\begin{array}{r} 57 \\ +\ 19 \\ \hline \square \end{array}$$

○ 69
○ 76
○ 66
○ 75
○ NH

UNIT 11 • TABLE OF CONTENTS

3-Digit Addition and Subtraction

Dear Family,

During the next few weeks our math class will be learning about 3-digit addition and subtraction.

You can expect to see homework that provides practice with adding and subtracting 3-digit numbers.

As we learn about 3-digit addition and subtraction, you may wish to keep the following sample as a guide.

3-Digit Addition with Regrouping

	H	T	O
		1	
	4	5	2
+	1	3	9
	5	9	1

Remember to regroup.

11 ones = **1** ten **1** one

	H	T	O
		1	
	5	8	5
+	3	0	8
	8	9	3

Regroup.

13 ones = **1** ten **3** ones

3-Digit Subtraction with Regrouping

	H	T	O
		7	12
	5	~~8~~	~~2~~
−	2	5	9
	3	2	3

Remember to regroup a ten.

8 tens **2** ones = **7** tens **12** ones

	H	T	O
		8	11
	5	~~9~~	~~1~~
−	4	5	2
	1	3	9

Regroup a ten.

9 tens **1** one = **8** tens **11** ones

Sincerely,

Name ______________________________

Addition

H	T	O
3	2	4
+		3
3	2	7

$$\begin{array}{r} 324 \\ +\ \ 3 \\ \hline 327 \end{array}$$

Subtraction

H	T	O
9	5	8
−		6
9	5	2

$$\begin{array}{r} 958 \\ -\ \ 6 \\ \hline 952 \end{array}$$

Add or subtract.

1. $\begin{array}{r} 484 \\ -\ \ 0 \\ \hline 484 \end{array}$ $\begin{array}{r} 564 \\ +\ \ 3 \\ \hline \end{array}$ $\begin{array}{r} 846 \\ +\ \ 2 \\ \hline \end{array}$ $\begin{array}{r} 448 \\ -\ \ 7 \\ \hline \end{array}$ $\begin{array}{r} 678 \\ -\ \ 5 \\ \hline \end{array}$

2. $\begin{array}{r} 525 \\ +\ \ 4 \\ \hline \end{array}$ $\begin{array}{r} 931 \\ -\ \ 1 \\ \hline \end{array}$ $\begin{array}{r} 877 \\ -\ \ 2 \\ \hline \end{array}$ $\begin{array}{r} 762 \\ +\ \ 4 \\ \hline \end{array}$ $\begin{array}{r} 432 \\ -\ \ 2 \\ \hline \end{array}$

★ Test Prep

Solve. Mark the space for your answer.

$\begin{array}{r} 748 \\ -\ \ 6 \\ \hline \square \end{array}$

741	742	745	756
○	○	○	○

STANDARD

Name ______________________________

Addition

H	T	O
5	6	2
+	1	2
5	7	4

$$\begin{array}{r} 562 \\ +\ 12 \\ \hline 574 \end{array}$$

Subtraction

H	T	O
9	7	6
−	3	5
9	4	1

$$\begin{array}{r} 976 \\ -\ 35 \\ \hline 941 \end{array}$$

Remember to always start with the ones.

Add or subtract.

1. $\begin{array}{r} 813 \\ -\ 11 \\ \hline 802 \end{array}$ $\begin{array}{r} 403 \\ +\ 92 \\ \hline \end{array}$ $\begin{array}{r} 837 \\ -\ 25 \\ \hline \end{array}$ $\begin{array}{r} 429 \\ -\ 19 \\ \hline \end{array}$ $\begin{array}{r} 667 \\ -\ 42 \\ \hline \end{array}$

2. $\begin{array}{r} 737 \\ -\ 26 \\ \hline \end{array}$ $\begin{array}{r} 924 \\ +\ 63 \\ \hline \end{array}$ $\begin{array}{r} 890 \\ -\ 50 \\ \hline \end{array}$ $\begin{array}{r} 396 \\ -\ 63 \\ \hline \end{array}$ $\begin{array}{r} 773 \\ -\ 21 \\ \hline \end{array}$

3. $\begin{array}{r} 439 \\ -\ 25 \\ \hline \end{array}$ $\begin{array}{r} 899 \\ -\ 36 \\ \hline \end{array}$ $\begin{array}{r} 930 \\ +\ 25 \\ \hline \end{array}$ $\begin{array}{r} 430 \\ +\ 50 \\ \hline \end{array}$ $\begin{array}{r} 824 \\ -\ 13 \\ \hline \end{array}$

4. $\begin{array}{r} 754 \\ -\ 14 \\ \hline \end{array}$ $\begin{array}{r} 296 \\ -\ 73 \\ \hline \end{array}$ $\begin{array}{r} 762 \\ -\ 31 \\ \hline \end{array}$ $\begin{array}{r} 247 \\ +\ 32 \\ \hline \end{array}$ $\begin{array}{r} 524 \\ -\ 13 \\ \hline \end{array}$

★ Test Prep

Solve. Mark the space for your answer.

5. $\begin{array}{r} 876 \\ +\ 11 \\ \hline \square \end{array}$

○ 865 ○ 877 ○ 887 ○ 986

Name ____

Add or subtract.

1.

H	T	O
2	1	3
+ 1	6	2
3	7	5

H	T	O
2	4	0
+ 1	1	6

H	T	O
4	5	0
+ 3	4	1

H	T	O
4	5	2
+ 1	2	6

2.

H	T	O
6	6	5
− 3	2	4

H	T	O
8	6	2
− 4	3	0

H	T	O
8	0	5
+ 1	0	3

H	T	O
5	9	8
− 3	7	5

3.

H	T	O
3	9	3
− 1	7	0

H	T	O
9	1	6
− 5	0	1

H	T	O
4	4	1
+ 4	1	7

H	T	O
4	5	6
− 3	5	2

Now try these.

4.

785
+ 104
889

862
− 430

450
+ 341

665
− 324

393
− 173

5.

258
− 140

597
+ 102

345
+ 142

986
− 120

458
− 232

Add. Use mental math.

6. 256 + 100 = ____   683 + 300 = ____   212 + 300 = ____   441 + 200 = ____   500 + 196 = ____

Problem Solving
Reasoning

7. How does knowing your basic facts help you add in row 6?

____

Subtract. Use mental math.

8. 616 − 500 = ____   848 − 600 = ____   473 − 200 = ____   352 − 300 = ____   456 − 100 = ____

Problem Solving
Reasoning

9. How does knowing your basic facts help you subtract in row 8?

____

Quick Check

Add or subtract.

1. 652 + 7 = ____

2. 546 − 26 = ____

3. 314 + 543 = ____

4. 879 − 364 = ____

STANDARD

Name ______________________________

H	T	O
	1	
4	5	2
+ 1	3	9
5	9	1

Remember to regroup.

11 ones = 1 ten 1 one

H	T	O
	1	
5	8	5
+ 3	0	8
8	9	3

Regroup.

13 ones = 1 ten 3 ones

Add.

1.

H	T	O
	1	
8	3	7
+ 1	2	7
9	6	4

$$\begin{array}{r} 837 \\ +\ 127 \\ \hline 964 \end{array}$$

2.

H	T	O
5	4	5
+ 2	2	8

$$\begin{array}{r} 545 \\ +\ 228 \\ \hline \end{array}$$

3.

H	T	O
6	6	6
+ 3	2	6

$$\begin{array}{r} 666 \\ +\ 326 \\ \hline \end{array}$$

4.

H	T	O
8	2	3
+ 1	2	9

$$\begin{array}{r} 823 \\ +\ 129 \\ \hline \end{array}$$

5. $\begin{array}{r} 774 \\ +\ 218 \\ \hline \end{array}$ $\begin{array}{r} 137 \\ +\ 238 \\ \hline \end{array}$ $\begin{array}{r} 635 \\ +\ 136 \\ \hline \end{array}$ $\begin{array}{r} 342 \\ +\ 219 \\ \hline \end{array}$ $\begin{array}{r} 426 \\ +\ 368 \\ \hline \end{array}$

6. $\begin{array}{r} 369 \\ +\ 429 \\ \hline \end{array}$ $\begin{array}{r} 323 \\ +\ 259 \\ \hline \end{array}$ $\begin{array}{r} 842 \\ +\ 109 \\ \hline \end{array}$ $\begin{array}{r} 256 \\ +\ 306 \\ \hline \end{array}$ $\begin{array}{r} 648 \\ +\ 237 \\ \hline \end{array}$

7. $\begin{array}{r} 433 \\ +\ 239 \\ \hline \end{array}$ $\begin{array}{r} 567 \\ +\ 128 \\ \hline \end{array}$ $\begin{array}{r} 336 \\ +\ 247 \\ \hline \end{array}$ $\begin{array}{r} 811 \\ +\ 109 \\ \hline \end{array}$ $\begin{array}{r} 239 \\ +\ 119 \\ \hline \end{array}$

Add.

8.

H	T	O
4	6	7
+ 1	2	4
5	9	1

H	T	O
3	3	3
+ 6	5	9

H	T	O
6	5	4
+ 3	2	9

H	T	O
8	8	7
+ 1	0	7

Find the sum.

9. 448 + 249   449 + 339   729 + 169   638 + 258   277 + 619

10. 139 + 455   646 + 338   538 + 345   456 + 117   766 + 106

11. 665 + 119   346 + 515   234 + 228   428 + 415   518 + 364

Problem Solving
Reasoning

12. If you know that **379 + 363 = 742**, what is the sum of **363 + 379?** Explain. ____________________

____

★ Test Prep

Solve. Mark the space for your answer.

13. 456 + 228 = ☐

○ 228   ○ 674   ○ 684   ○ 685

Name ____________________

H	T	O
	7	12
5	~~8~~	~~2~~
− 2	5	9
3	2	3

Remember to regroup a ten.

8 tens **2** ones = **7** tens **12** ones

H	T	O
	8	11
5	~~9~~	~~1~~
− 4	5	2
1	3	9

Regroup a ten.

9 tens **1** one = **8** tens **11** ones

Subtract. Remember to regroup the tens and ones.

1.

H	T	O
	8	12
9	~~9~~	~~2~~
− 2	1	8
7	7	4

992
− 218
774

2.

H	T	O
	5	12
4	~~6~~	~~2~~
− 2	3	4
		8

462
− 234

3.

H	T	O
8	4	3
− 4	1	5

843
− 415

4.

H	T	O
8	8	2
− 5	1	8

882
− 518

5. 573 − 117   691 − 354   261 − 107   535 − 126   887 − 169

6. 226 − 109   158 − 109   666 − 227   455 − 137   888 − 269

7. 748 − 229   261 − 107   871 − 639   684 − 456   816 − 507

Subtract.

8.

H	T	O
	8	11
5	9	1
− 4	6	7

H	T	O
	8	12
9	9	2
− 6	5	9

H	T	O
9	8	3
− 6	5	4

H	T	O
8	9	4
− 1	0	7

Find the difference.

9. $\begin{array}{r} 697 \\ -\ 448 \\ \hline \end{array}$ $\begin{array}{r} 788 \\ -\ 339 \\ \hline \end{array}$ $\begin{array}{r} 898 \\ -\ 169 \\ \hline \end{array}$ $\begin{array}{r} 896 \\ -\ 638 \\ \hline \end{array}$ $\begin{array}{r} 896 \\ -\ 277 \\ \hline \end{array}$

10. $\begin{array}{r} 594 \\ -\ 455 \\ \hline \end{array}$ $\begin{array}{r} 984 \\ -\ 646 \\ \hline \end{array}$ $\begin{array}{r} 893 \\ -\ 538 \\ \hline \end{array}$ $\begin{array}{r} 573 \\ -\ 117 \\ \hline \end{array}$ $\begin{array}{r} 872 \\ -\ 766 \\ \hline \end{array}$

11. $\begin{array}{r} 784 \\ -\ 665 \\ \hline \end{array}$ $\begin{array}{r} 861 \\ -\ 515 \\ \hline \end{array}$ $\begin{array}{r} 462 \\ -\ 234 \\ \hline \end{array}$ $\begin{array}{r} 843 \\ -\ 415 \\ \hline \end{array}$ $\begin{array}{r} 882 \\ -\ 518 \\ \hline \end{array}$

Problem Solving
Reasoning

Solve.

12. There are **362** children and **245** adults at the theater. How many more children than adults are there?

_______ more children

★ Test Prep

Solve. Mark the space for your answer.

13 $\begin{array}{r} 635 \\ -\ 108 \\ \hline \square \end{array}$

○ 527 ○ 528 ○ 537 ○ 538

Name ________________________________

$$\begin{array}{r} \$2.43 \\ +\ 1.15 \\ \hline \$3.58 \end{array}$$

Add. Don't forget the $ and decimal point.

1. $\begin{array}{r} \$5.00 \\ +\ 2.00 \\ \hline \$7.00 \end{array}$ $\begin{array}{r} \$2.00 \\ +\ 5.00 \\ \hline \end{array}$ $\begin{array}{r} \$3.00 \\ +\ 5.00 \\ \hline \end{array}$ $\begin{array}{r} \$1.00 \\ +\ 4.00 \\ \hline \end{array}$ $\begin{array}{r} \$2.00 \\ +\ 6.00 \\ \hline \end{array}$

2. $\begin{array}{r} \$1.01 \\ +\ 2.05 \\ \hline \$3.06 \end{array}$ $\begin{array}{r} \$6.03 \\ +\ 2.04 \\ \hline \end{array}$ $\begin{array}{r} \$3.02 \\ +\ 3.03 \\ \hline \end{array}$ $\begin{array}{r} \$4.05 \\ +\ 2.03 \\ \hline \end{array}$ $\begin{array}{r} \$2.04 \\ +\ 1.05 \\ \hline \end{array}$

Subtract. Don't forget the $ and decimal point.

3. $\begin{array}{r} \$9.00 \\ -\ 5.00 \\ \hline \$4.00 \end{array}$ $\begin{array}{r} \$7.00 \\ -\ 3.00 \\ \hline \end{array}$ $\begin{array}{r} \$5.00 \\ -\ 4.00 \\ \hline \end{array}$ $\begin{array}{r} \$6.00 \\ -\ 2.00 \\ \hline \end{array}$ $\begin{array}{r} \$4.00 \\ -\ 1.00 \\ \hline \end{array}$

4. $\begin{array}{r} \$9.28 \\ -\ 8.16 \\ \hline \$1.12 \end{array}$ $\begin{array}{r} \$6.40 \\ -\ 4.20 \\ \hline \end{array}$ $\begin{array}{r} \$4.88 \\ -\ 3.62 \\ \hline \end{array}$ $\begin{array}{r} \$6.35 \\ -\ 4.11 \\ \hline \end{array}$ $\begin{array}{r} \$7.18 \\ -\ 7.08 \\ \hline \end{array}$

Problem Solving Reasoning

Show your work. Write the answer in a complete sentence.

5. Joe has **$6.00** in his bank. He takes **$3.00** out so that he can buy a present for his mother. How much does he have left in his bank?

$6.00
− 3.00
$

____

6. Akiko earns **9** dollars, **3** dimes, and **1** nickel, helping her sister on a paper route. She spends **3** dollars and **3** dimes of this money for a new bookmark and saves the rest. How much money does she save?

____

7. Ted's grandfather gives him **6** dollars, **4** dimes, and **2** nickels. He has **2** dollars, **2** dimes, and **3** nickels in his bank. How much does he have in all?

____

Quick Check

Add or subtract.

1. **639**
   + 232

2. **354**
   − 135

3. **$8.04**
   + 1.77

4. **$5.63**
   − 2.42

Name ______________________________

Problem

Jeff buys a large sandwich for **$4.15**.
He buys a shake for **$2.25**.
How much money does he spend?

1 Understand

I need to find out how much money Jeff spends.

2 Decide

I can use simpler numbers to help.

3 Solve

If I use simpler numbers the problem would read:

Jeff buys a large sandwich for **$4**.
He buys a shake for **$2**.
How much money does he spend?

I will add to find about how much Jeff spends.

$4 + $2 = $6

I think Jeff spends about **$6**.

Now I will add the amounts.

$$\begin{array}{r} \$4.15 \\ +\ 2.25 \\ \hline \$6.40 \end{array}$$

Jeff spends **$6.40**.

4 Look back

I know that my answer should be about **$6** and it is **$6.40**.

First solve the problem with simpler numbers. Use it to solve the next problem.

1. Ké has **$4**. He buys a large sandwich for **$2**. How much money does he have left?

   Ké has **$4.15**. He buys a large sandwich for **$2.12**. How much money does he have left?

2. Mary Lou buys a fish sandwich for **$2** and a small order of french fries for **$1**. How much does she spend?

   Mary Lou buys a fish sandwich for **$2.05** and a small order of french fries for **$.85**. How much does she spend?

3. Mark spends **$6**. Jenna spends **$5**. How much more does Mark spend than Jenna?

   Mark spends **$6.25**. Jenna spends **$5.35**. How much more does Mark spend than Jenna?

Name ______________________________

Problem Solving Plan			
1. Understand	2. Decide	3. Solve	4. Look back

Solve.

Answers

1. Jan has **$1.79**. She buys a marker for **$.68**. How much does she have left?

Think Jan starts with $1.79 .

How much does the marker cost? $ .68

Do you add or subtract? subtract

$1.79
– .68

2. Raul buys a toy car for **$4.29** and a truck for **$5.15**. How much money does he spend?

Think How much does the toy car cost? ____________

How much does the truck cost? ____________

Do you add or subtract? ____________

3. Leah has **8** dollar bills, **2** quarters, **2** dimes, **1** nickel, and **5** pennies. She buys a model airplane for **$5.36**. How much money does she have left?

Think: Leah starts with ____________ .

How much does the airplane cost? ____________

Do you add or subtract? ____________

Think about whether you need to add or subtract. Solve.

Answers

4. Eric has **$6.15**. He wants to buy a book that costs **$7.20**. How much more money does he need?

5. Mei-Mei wants to buy a doll that costs **$9.48**. She gives the clerk **9** dollar bills, **1** quarter, **2** dimes, and **1** nickel. How much money does the clerk give back to Mei-Mei?

6. Anthony wants to buy a toy airplane that costs **$4.79** and a bottle of glue that costs **$1.19**. How much money does he need?

Extend Your Thinking

7. Rachel has **$2.00** to spend. A pen costs **79¢**, a notepad **89¢**, and an eraser **49¢**.
What is the greatest number of pens Rachel can buy? Notepads? Erasers?

Workspace

_____ pens

_____ notepads

_____ erasers

Explain how you know the number of erasers you can buy.

____

Name ______________________________

Add or subtract. Watch the signs.
Remember to always start with the ones.

1. $\begin{array}{r} 261 \\ -\ 107 \\ \hline \end{array}$

2. $\begin{array}{r} 871 \\ -\ 256 \\ \hline \end{array}$

3. $\begin{array}{r} 784 \\ +\ 113 \\ \hline \end{array}$

4. $\begin{array}{r} 893 \\ -\ 166 \\ \hline \end{array}$

5. $\begin{array}{r} 573 \\ +\ 119 \\ \hline \end{array}$

6. $\begin{array}{r} 748 \\ -\ 219 \\ \hline \end{array}$

7. $\begin{array}{r} 229 \\ +\ 348 \\ \hline \end{array}$

8. $\begin{array}{r} 267 \\ +\ 126 \\ \hline \end{array}$

9. $\begin{array}{r} 685 \\ -\ 263 \\ \hline \end{array}$

10. $\begin{array}{r} 147 \\ +\ 237 \\ \hline \end{array}$

11. $\begin{array}{r} 519 \\ +\ 228 \\ \hline \end{array}$

12. $\begin{array}{r} 446 \\ +\ 223 \\ \hline \end{array}$

13. $\begin{array}{r} 234 \\ +\ 349 \\ \hline \end{array}$

14. $\begin{array}{r} 729 \\ +\ 169 \\ \hline \end{array}$

15. $\begin{array}{r} 728 \\ +\ 139 \\ \hline \end{array}$

Add or subtract.

16. $\begin{array}{r} \$1.48 \\ +\ 2.48 \\ \hline \end{array}$

17. $\begin{array}{r} \$8.37 \\ +\ 1.58 \\ \hline \end{array}$

18. $\begin{array}{r} \$4.49 \\ +\ 2.41 \\ \hline \end{array}$

19. $\begin{array}{r} \$6.88 \\ -\ 1.79 \\ \hline \end{array}$

20. $\begin{array}{r} \$5.47 \\ -\ 2.38 \\ \hline \end{array}$

Problem Solving Reasoning

Solve.

Answers

21. Martha buys a hat for **$6.27** and a pin for **$2.13**. How much money does she spend?

22. Hans has **9** dollar bills, **2** quarters, **1** dime, **3** nickels, and **6** pennies. He buys a baseball cap for **$8.50**. How much money does he have left?

Name ______________________________

★ Test Prep

1

I day = _____ hours

24	30	60	90
○	○	○	○

2

68	683	63	638
○	○	○	○

3

756	76	765	75
○	○	○	○

4

\$ .56	\$6.50	\$ .65	\$6.05
○	○	○	○

5

\$6.50 − 3.25 \$3.25	\$6.50 − 3.00 \$3.50	\$3.25 + 3.25 \$6.50	\$3.25 + 3.50 \$6.75
○	○	○	○

Decide on an answer. Mark the space for your answer.
If the answer is **not here**, mark the space **NH.**

6

$$\begin{array}{r} 74 \\ -\ 26 \\ \hline \square \end{array}$$

47	48	57	58	NH
○	○	○	○	○

UNIT 12 • TABLE OF CONTENTS

Multiplication and Division

We will be using this vocabulary:

array an arrangement of objects in rows
factor one of the numbers multiplied in a multiplication problem
product the result in a multiplication problem
order property of multiplication Changing the order of the factors does not change the product.
$2 \times 3 = 6$; $3 \times 2 = 6$

Dear Family,

During the next few weeks our math class will be learning about multiplication and division.

You can expect to see homework that provides practice with multiplication and division.

As we learn about multiplication, you may wish to keep the following sample as a guide.

3 groups of **2**

Write: $3 \times 2 = 6$ or

2	**factor**
× 3	**factor**
6	**product**

factor factor product

Sincerely,

Name ______________________________

Skip-count. Fill in the blanks.

1.

__2__ groups of **2**

__4__ in all

__2__, __4__

2.

_____ group of **2**

_____ in all

_____

3.

_____ groups of **2**

_____ in all

_____, _____, _____, _____

4.

_____ groups of **2**

_____ in all

_____, _____, _____

★ Test Prep

How many groups of **2**? Mark your answer.

1	2	3	4
○	○	○	○

STANDARD

Name ______________________

Fill in the blanks.

1. 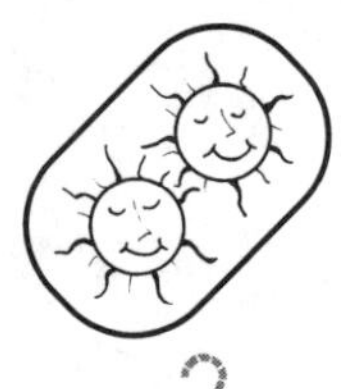  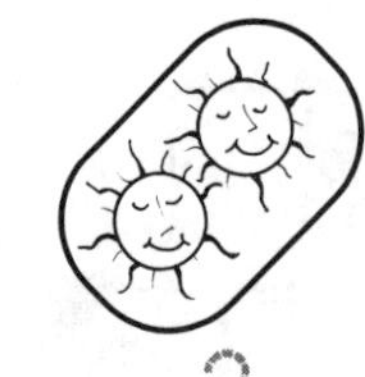 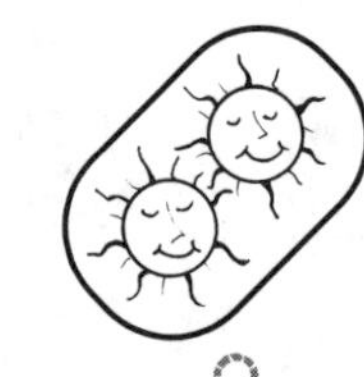

2 + 2 + 2 + 2

4 groups of 2

8 in all

2. 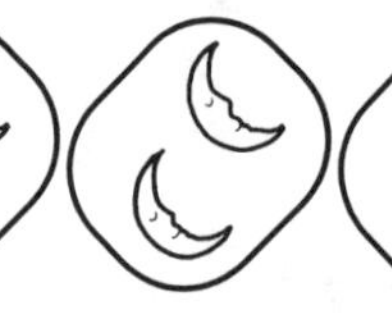 

___ + ___ + ___ + ___ + ___ + ___ + ___

___ groups of ___

___ in all

3.     

___ + ___ + ___ + ___ + ___

___ groups of ___

___ in all

4.

___ groups of 2

___ in all

5. 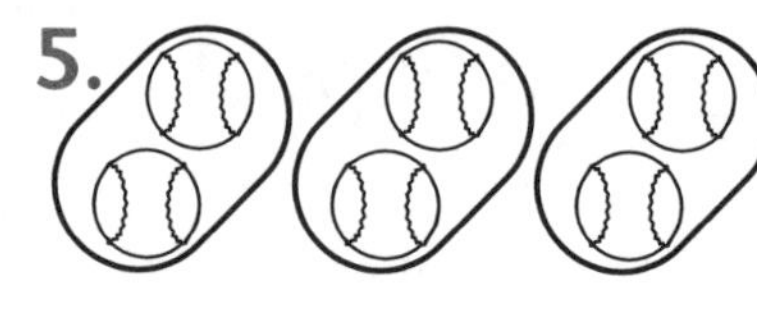 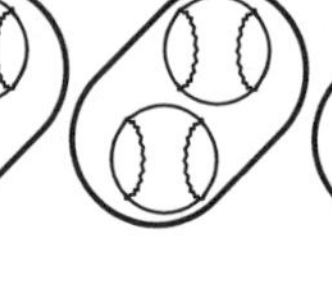 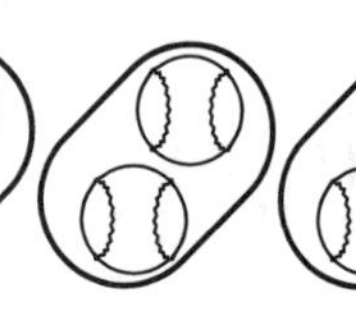 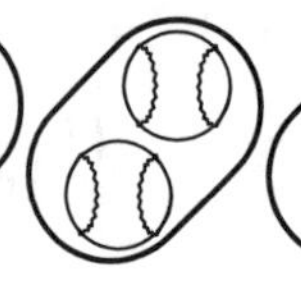 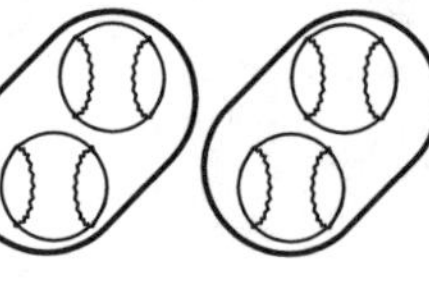 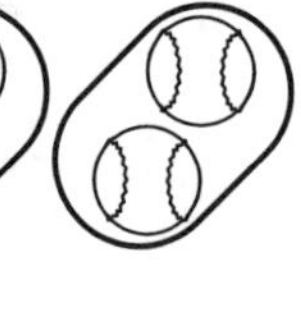

___ + ___ + ___ + ___ + ___ + ___ + ___ + ___

___ groups of ___

___ in all

★ Test Prep

How many in all? Mark the space for your answer.

6      

8 ○ 10 ○ 12 ○ 14 ○

Name ____________________

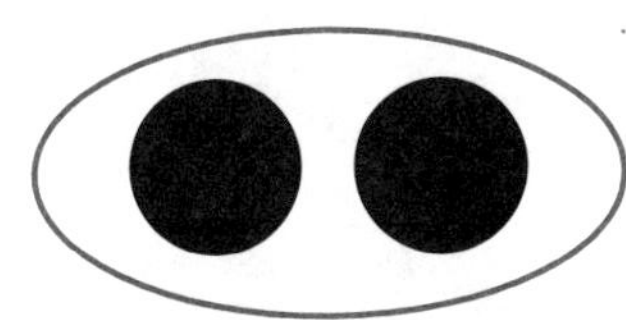 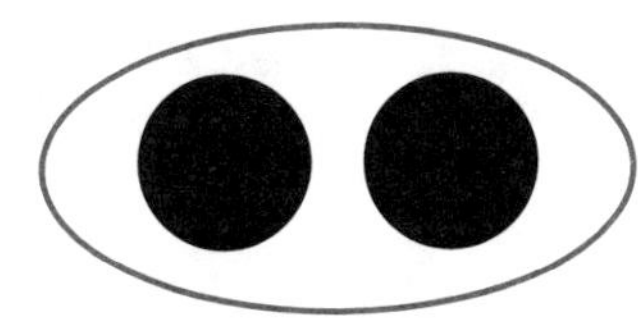 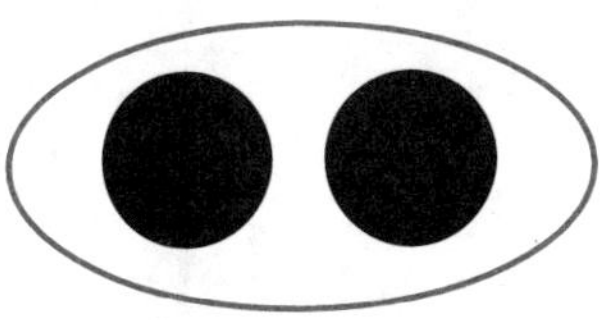

The picture shows **3** groups of **2**. There are **6** dots in all.

You say: **3** times **2** equals **6**.

You write: **3** × **2** = **6**

This sign tells you to multiply.

Draw groups of dots. Complete the number sentence.

1.   **1 × 2 =** 2

2.  **2 × 2 =** ____

3. **3 × 2 =** ____

4. **4 × 2 =** ____

5. **5 × 2 =** ____

6. **6 × 2 =** ____

7. **7 × 2 =** ____

8. **8 × 2 =** ____

9. **9 × 2 =** ____

The **array** has **3** rows of **2**.

Write: **3** × **2** = 6 or

$$\begin{array}{rl} 2 & \textbf{factor} \\ \times\ 3 & \textbf{factor} \\ \hline 6 & \textbf{product} \end{array}$$

factor **factor** **product**

Find the product.

10. $\begin{array}{r} 2 \\ \times\ 4 \\ \hline 8 \end{array}$

11. $\begin{array}{r} 2 \\ \times\ 5 \\ \hline \end{array}$

12. $\begin{array}{r} 2 \\ \times\ 6 \\ \hline \end{array}$

13. $\begin{array}{r} 2 \\ \times\ 7 \\ \hline \end{array}$

Quick Check

Skip-count. Fill in the blanks.

1. 

___ groups of **2**

____, ____, ____, ____ ___ in all

2. 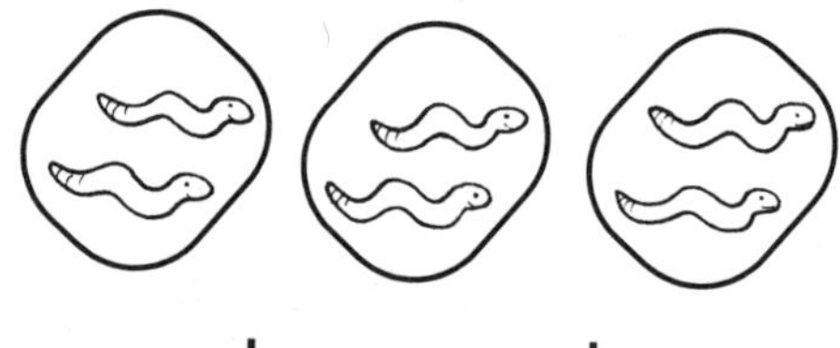

___ groups of **2**

____ + ____ + ____ ___ in all

Find the product.

3. 

$\begin{array}{r} 2 \\ \times\ 2 \\ \hline \end{array}$

Name ______________________

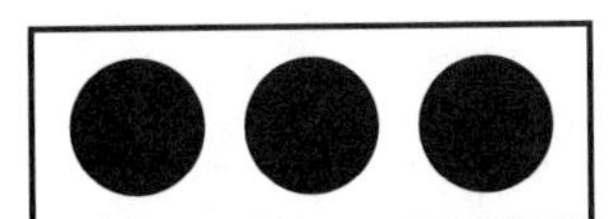 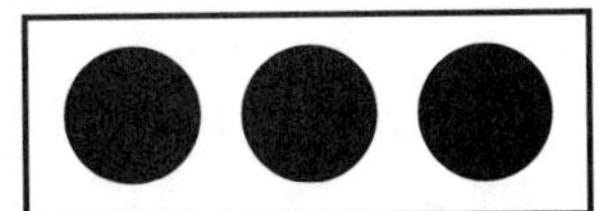

3, 6

There are **2** groups.
There are **3** objects in each group.
There are **6** objects in all.

Write: $2 \times 3 = 6$ or $\begin{array}{r} 3 \\ \times\ 2 \\ \hline 6 \end{array}$

Skip-count. Write the products.

1.   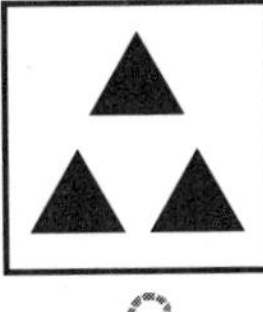

3, 6, 9

$3 \times 3 =$ 9

$\begin{array}{r} 3 \\ \times\ 3 \\ \hline 9 \end{array}$

2.

____, ____, ____, ____

$4 \times 3 =$ ____

$\begin{array}{r} 3 \\ \times\ 4 \\ \hline \end{array}$

3.   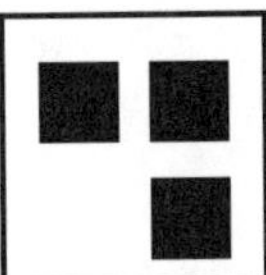  

____, ____, ____, ____, ____

$5 \times 3 =$ ____

$\begin{array}{r} 3 \\ \times\ 5 \\ \hline \end{array}$

4. 

____

$1 \times 3 =$ ____

$\begin{array}{r} 3 \\ \times\ 1 \\ \hline \end{array}$

5. 

$0 \times 3 =$ ____

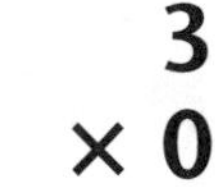

$\begin{array}{r} 3 \\ \times\ 0 \\ \hline \end{array}$

Find the product.

6.
1	8	2	3	3	2
× 2	× 2	× 2	× 1	× 0	× 7
2					

7.
7	3	1	2	2	6
× 2	× 3	× 3	× 6	× 8	× 2

8.
4	2	4	2	0	2
× 3	× 5	× 2	× 9	× 2	× 8

9.
0	3	3	5	3	2
× 3	× 2	× 4	× 3	× 6	× 3

10.
3	1	2	2	5	9
× 5	× 3	× 1	× 4	× 2	× 2

Problem Solving
Reasoning

11. If you multiply any number by 1, what is the product?
How do you know? ______________________

____

★ Test Prep

Multiply. Mark the space for your answer.

12.
6
× 3

○ 9 ○ 12 ○ 15 ○ 18

Name ____________________

Use repeated addition. Fill in the blanks.

1. 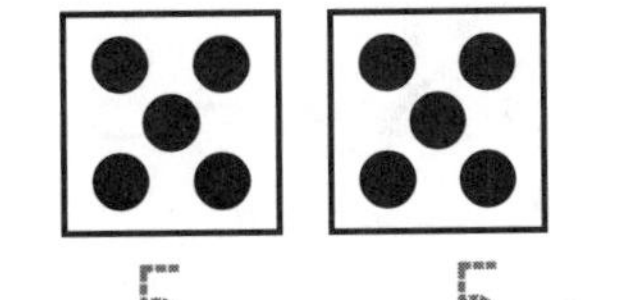

5 + 5 + = 10

2 groups of 5

10 in all

2. 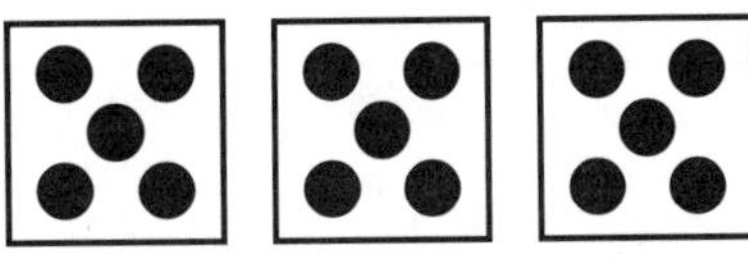

____ + ____ + ____ = ____

____ groups of ____

____ in all

3. 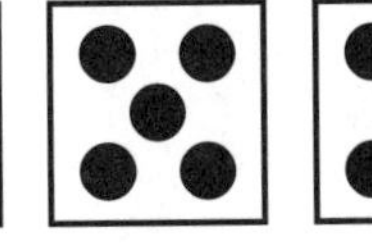 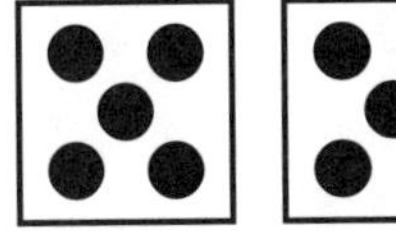

____ + ____ + ____ + ____ = ____

____ groups of ____

____ in all

4. 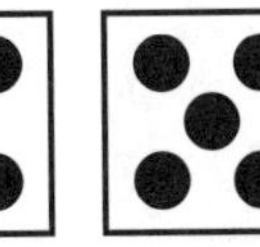 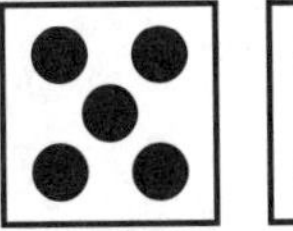 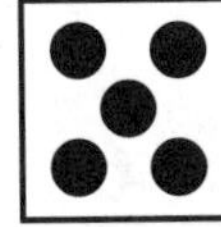  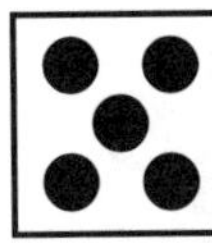

____ + ____ + ____ + ____ + ____ = ____

____ groups of ____

____ in all

Complete.

5. **0** groups of **5** = ____

6. **1** group of **5** = ____

7. **6** groups of **5** = ____

8. **7** groups of **5** = ____

Find the product.

9. 1 × 5 = 5

10. 0 × 5 = ____

11. 2 × 5 = ____

12. 5 × 3 = ____

13. 5 × 5 = ____

14. 5 × 4 = ____

Draw an array of 2 rows of 5.

15. $2 \times 5 =$ ______

Draw an array of 5 rows of 2.

16. $5 \times 2 =$ ______

Practice your facts. Solve.

17.

5	2	3	5	5	2	3	5
× 6	× 5	× 0	× 8	× 7	× 6	× 7	× 9

Problem Solving
Reasoning

18. If you multiply any number by **0**, what is the product? How do you know? ______________________

____

Multiply. Mark the space for your answer.

19

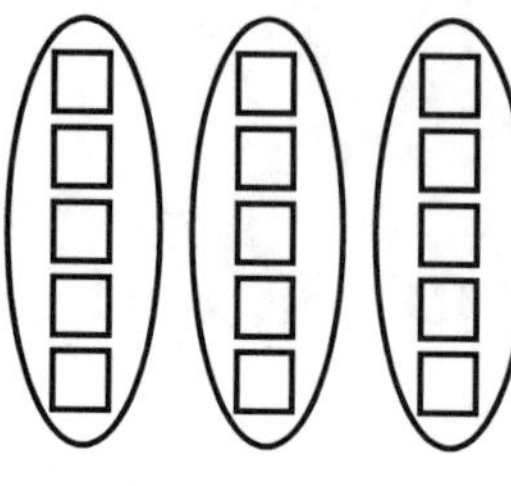

$3 \times 5 = \square$

18 ○ 15 ○ 12 ○ 8 ○

Name ______________________

Problem

Keith makes **2** piles of books on the shelf.
He puts **4** books in each pile.
How many books are there?

1 Understand

I need to find out how many books there are in all.

2 Decide

I can act it out.

3 Solve

I'll use counters instead of books.
I'll make **2** piles of **4** books.

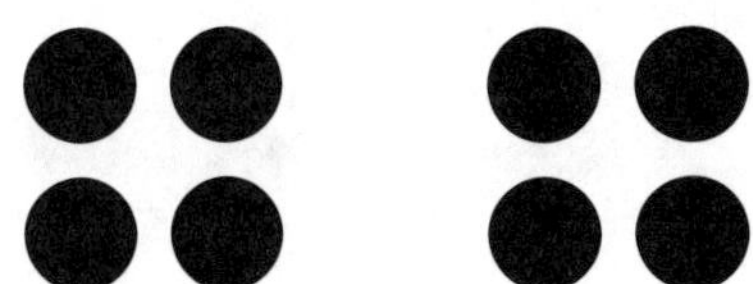

There are __8__ books.

4 Look back

I know **2** groups of **4** equal **8** or **2 x 4 = 8**.
My answer makes sense.

Use counters. Act it out to solve.

1. Toby sees **2** groups of girls playing. There are **3** girls in each group. How many girls does she see in all?

_____ girls

2. There are **4** girls. Each girl has **3** marbles. How many marbles do they have in all?

_____ marbles

3. Julie put **3** rows of papers on the desk. If she puts **3** papers in each row, how many papers does she put on the desk?

_____ papers

4. Pedro puts **3** rows of pencils on the table with **5** in each row. How many pencils does Pedro put on the table?

_____ pencils

5. In which problems did you put counters in arrays? Why? _____________

____

____

Name ______________________

Problem Solving Plan

1. Understand 2. Decide 3. Solve 4. Look back

Ring the operation.
Write the number sentence. Solve.

1. **1** bicycle has **2** wheels. How many wheels are there on **5** bicycles?

$2 \times 5 = 10$

10 wheels

Think

add subtract (multiply)

2. If **1** stool has **3** legs, how many legs are there on **6** stools?

____

_____ legs

Think

add subtract multiply

3. Ari has **3** books. Pam has **2** books. How many books do they have all together?

____

_____ books

Think

add subtract multiply

4. Ray needs **7** cans of juice. He already has **3** cans. How many more cans does he need?

____

_____ cans

Think

add subtract multiply

Ring the operation.
Write a number sentence. Solve.

5. **1** week has **7** days. How many days are there in **3** weeks?

____

add subtract multiply

_____ days

6. There are **30** days in April. There are **31** days in May. How many days are there in April and May?

____

_____ days

add subtract multiply

7. If **1** flower has **5** petals, how many petals are there on **9** flowers?

____

add subtract multiply

_____ petals

Extend Your Thinking

8. Choose one of the problems on this page. Show how you can check your answer to make sure it is correct.

Name ______________________________

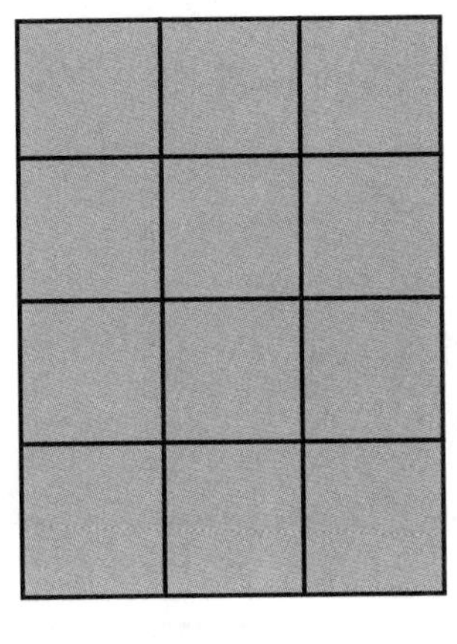

Turn the array on its side

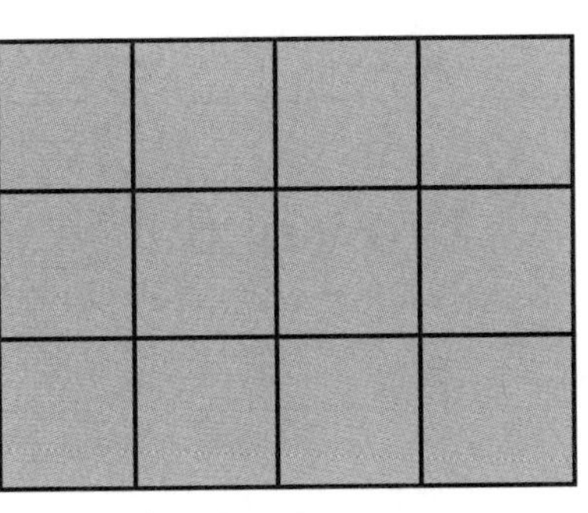

4 rows of 3
$4 \times 3 = 12$

or

3 rows of 4
$3 \times 4 = 12$

Use grid paper. Color squares to show the number in each row. Then turn the paper. Complete the number sentences.

1. 3 rows of 5 — 3 × 5 = 15 — or — 5 rows of 3 — ____ × ____ = ____

2. 4 rows of 1 — ____ × ____ = ____ — or — 1 row of 4 — ____ × ____ = ____

3. 0 rows of 3 — ____ × ____ = ____ — or — 3 rows of 0 — ____ × ____ = ____

4. 2 rows of 4 — ____ × ____ = ____ — or — 4 rows of 2 — ____ × ____ = ____

Continue using grid paper to complete the number sentences.

5. **5** rows of **4** **4** rows of **5**

______ × ______ = ______ or ______ × ______ = ______

6. **1** row of **3** **3** rows of **1**

______ × ______ = ______ or ______ × ______ = ______

Problem Solving
Reasoning

7. How is multiplying **3 × 2** the same as multiplying **2 × 3**?

Explain. ____

____

____

Quick Check

Multiply.

1.  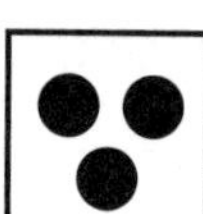 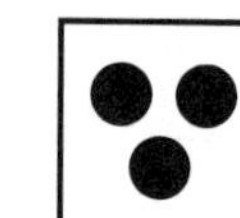 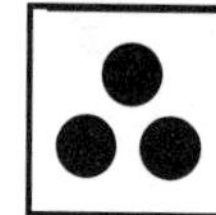 **4 × 3 =** _____

2. **6 × 5 =** _____

Write the number sentences.

3. **3** rows of **6** **6** rows of **3**

_____ × _____ = _____ or _____ × _____ = _____

STANDARD

Name ____________________

Skip-count. Fill in the blanks.

1. 10

1 group of 10

10 in all

2. 10, 20

____ groups of ______

______ in all

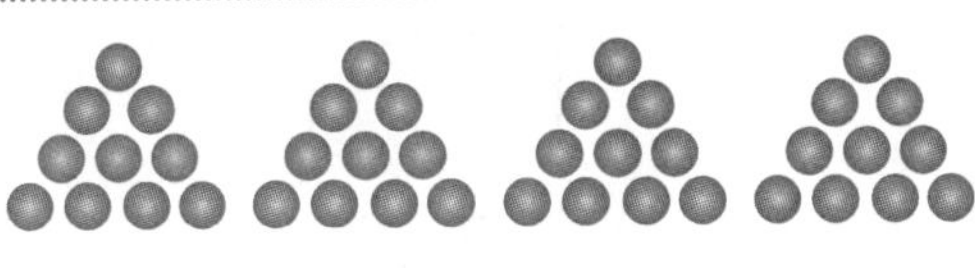

3. ____, ____, ____

____ groups of ______

______ in all

4. ____, ____, ____, ____

____ groups of ______

______ in all

5. ____, ____, ____, ____, ____

____ groups of ______

______ in all

Find the product.

6. 10×5 ____ 10×8 ____ 10×1 ____ 10×6 ____ 10×2 ____ 10×9 ____

★ Test Prep

Find the product. Mark the space for your answer.

7. $4 \times 10 = \square$

○ 30 ○ 14 ○ 40 ○ 6

STANDARD

Name ______________________________

A multiplication table shows the products of one factor and a series of other factors. Here's a multiplication table for **3**.

×	3
0	0
1	3
2	6
3	9
4	12
5	15
6	18

factor → 3 (top of second column); factor → 2 (left column); product → 6

Complete.

1.

×	2
0	0
1	2
2	4
3	6
4	
5	
6	
7	14
8	
9	18
10	

2.

×	5
0	
1	
2	
3	
4	
5	25
6	
7	
8	
9	
10	

3.

×	10
0	
1	
2	
3	
4	
5	
6	
7	
8	
9	
10	100

★ Test Prep

Find the product. Mark the space for your answer.

4. $2 \times 7 = \square$

12	16	14	9
○	○	○	○

Name ____________________

Birds Seen at White Lake

Each [bird] stands for **5** birds.

How many birds were seen by each person? Complete the number sentences.

1. Frank 2 × 5 = 10
2. Mae ___ × ___ = ___
3. Iris ___ × ___ = ___
4. José ___ × ___ = ___
5. Tim ___ × ___ = ___
6. Rosa ___ × ___ = ___

Solve.

7. How many birds did Mae and Iris see altogether?

   30 birds

8. How many birds did José and Tim see altogether?

   ___ birds

Cans of Juice Sold

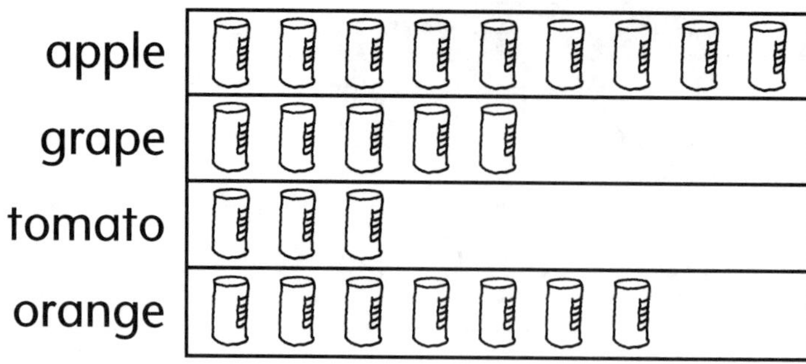

Each [can] stands for **10** cans.

How many cans of each type of juice were sold? Complete the number sentences.

9. apple 9 × 10 = 90

10. grape ____ × ____ = ____

11. tomato ____ × ____ = ____

12. orange ____ × ____ = ____

Problem Solving Reasoning

13. Write a number sentence that shows how many cans of grape juice and tomato juice were sold altogether. ________

Quick Check

Find the product.

1. **6 × 10 =** ____

Complete.

2.

×	5
0	
1	
	10
	15
4	

Solve.

3. **Balloons Sold**

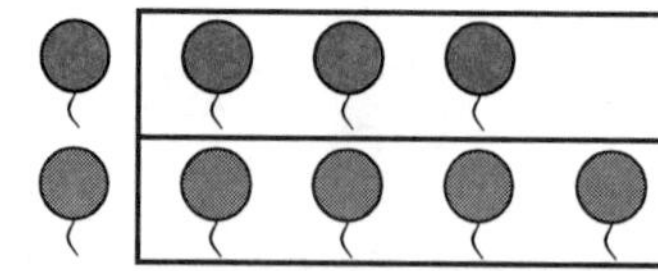

Each [balloon] stands for **5** balloons.

How many red balloons were sold?

____ × ____ = ____

STANDARD

Name ______________________________

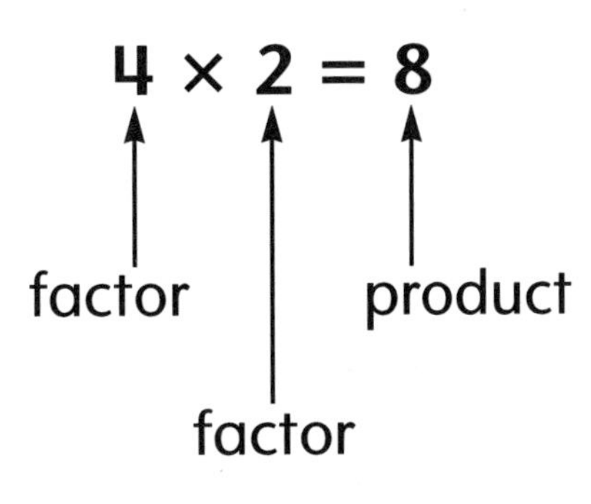

Find the missing factor.

1.   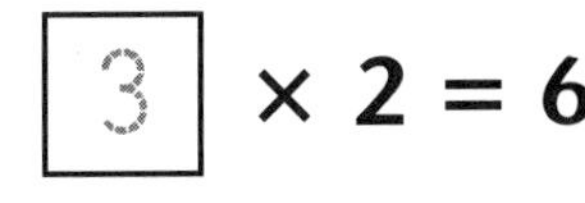 $\boxed{3} \times 2 = 6$

2.    $\square \times 2 = 8$

3. $\square \times 2 = 0$

4.    $3 \times \square = 6$

5.  $1 \times \square = 2$

6.   $\square \times 2 = 4$

7.     $4 \times \square = 8$

8. 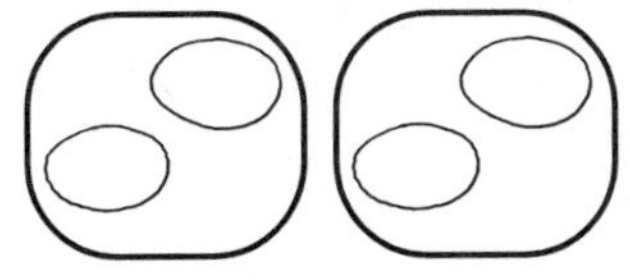 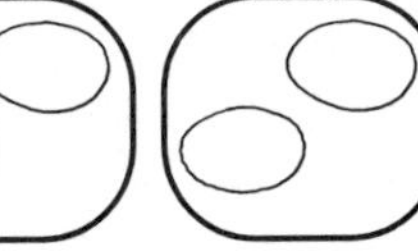  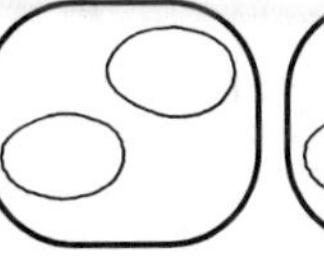 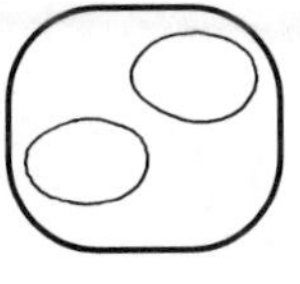 $\square \times 2 = 12$

Find the missing factor.

9. 

$\boxed{1} \times 2 = 2$

10.   

$\square \times 3 = 9$

11. 

$\square \times 5 = 20$

12.     

$\square \times 2 = 10$

13.      

$6 \times \square = 18$

14. 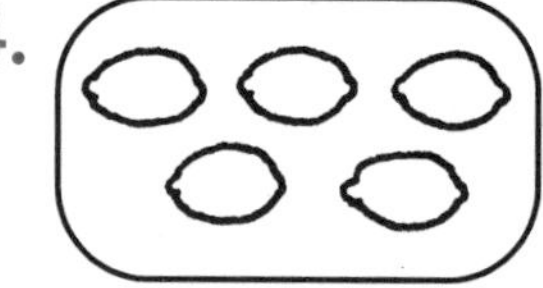 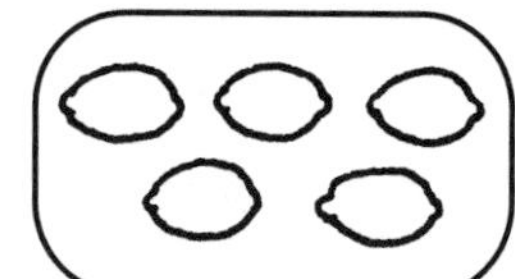

$2 \times \square = 10$

15.        

$8 \times \square = 24$

16.       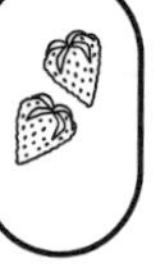  

$\square \times 2 = 18$

★ Test Prep

Solve. Mark the space for your answer.

17. $7 \times \square = 21$

2	3	5	4
○	○	○	○

STANDARD

Name ______________________________

Ring equal groups.
Write the number in each group.

1. 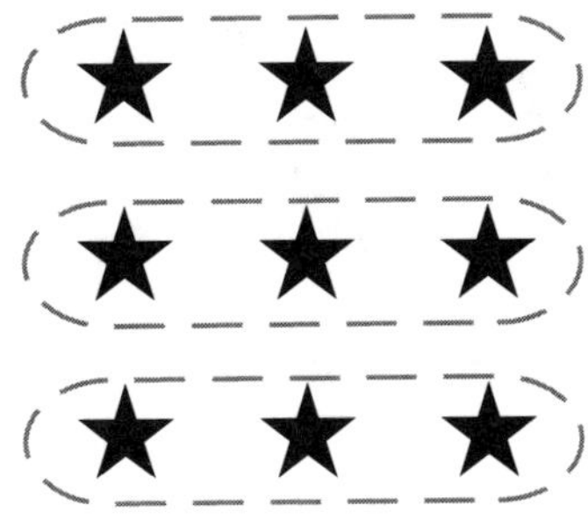

9 is **3** groups of 3.

2. 

8 is **2** groups of ____ .

3. 

15 is **5** groups of ____ .

4. 

16 is **4** groups of ____ .

5. ✱ ✱ ✱ ✱ ✱
✱ ✱ ✱ ✱ ✱
✱ ✱ ✱ ✱ ✱

15 is **3** groups of ____ .

6. 

10 is **5** groups of ____ .

7. 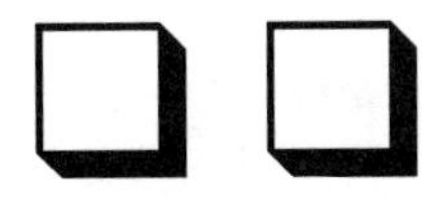

4 is **2** groups of ____ .

8. 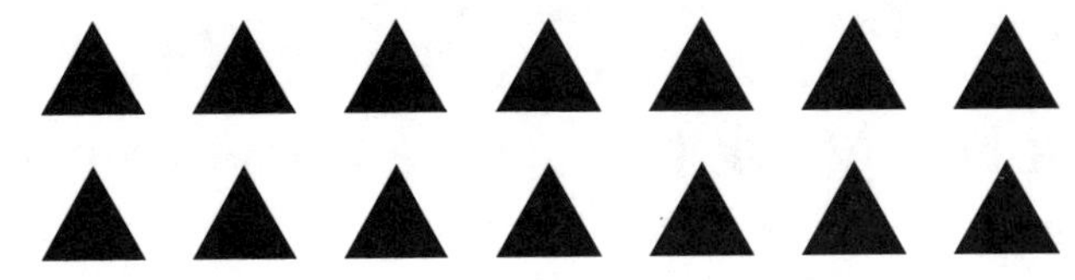

14 is **2** groups of ____ .

Ring equal groups.
Write the number in each group.

9.

8 is 4 groups of 2 .

10.

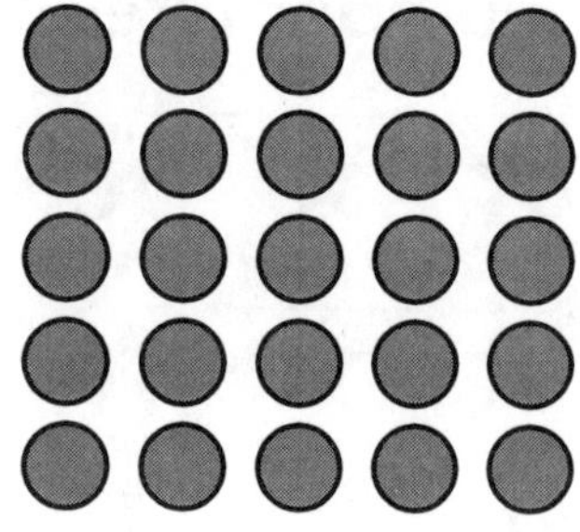

25 is 5 groups of ____ .

11.

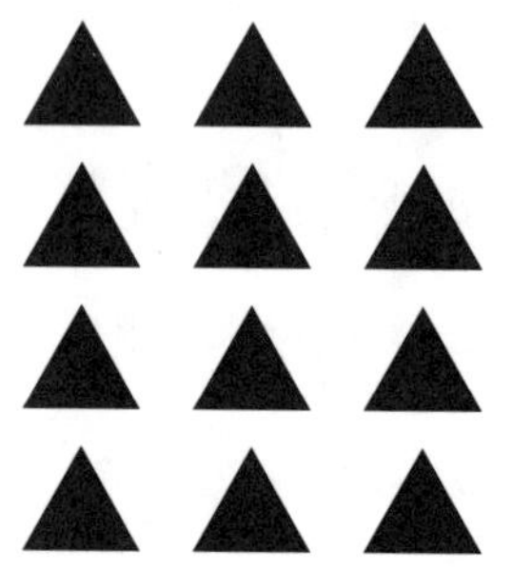

12 is 4 groups of ____ .

12.

12 is 2 groups of ____ .

13.

20 is 5 groups of ____ .

14.

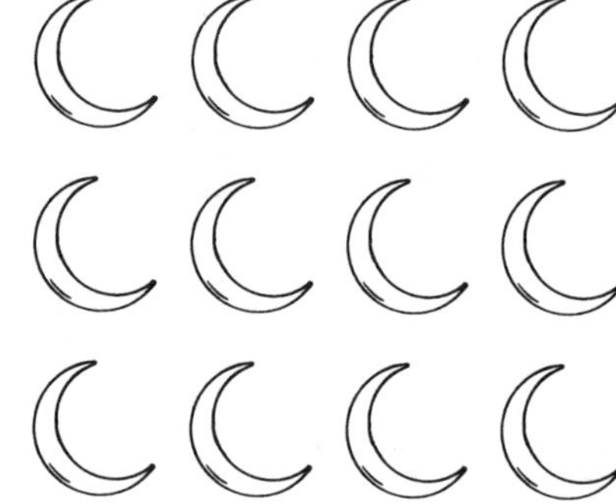

12 is 3 groups of ____ .

★ Test Prep

Solve. Mark the space for your answer.

15

10 is 2 groups of ☐

10	5	4	2
○	○	○	○

Name ______________________________

Tara has **8** shells.
She wants to give **2** shells to each friend.
How many friends will get shells?

$\begin{array}{r} 8 \\ -2 \\ \hline 6 \end{array}$ $\begin{array}{r} 6 \\ -2 \\ \hline 4 \end{array}$ $\begin{array}{r} 4 \\ -2 \\ \hline 2 \end{array}$ $\begin{array}{r} 2 \\ -2 \\ \hline 0 \end{array}$

You subtract **4** times.

4 friends will each get **2** shells.

Complete.

1. There are **10** children going sledding.
Each sled holds **2** children.
How many sleds do they need?

$\begin{array}{r} 10 \\ -2 \\ \hline 8 \end{array}$ $\begin{array}{r} 8 \\ -2 \\ \hline 6 \end{array}$ $\begin{array}{r} 6 \\ -2 \\ \hline 4 \end{array}$ $\begin{array}{r} 4 \\ -2 \\ \hline 2 \end{array}$ $\begin{array}{r} 2 \\ -2 \\ \hline 0 \end{array}$

You subtract __5__ times.

They need __5__ sleds.

2. Renée has **6** toy bears.
She wants to put **2** bears on each chair.
How many chairs will she use?

$\begin{array}{r} 6 \\ -2 \\ \hline 4 \end{array}$ $\begin{array}{r} 4 \\ -2 \\ \hline 2 \end{array}$ $\begin{array}{r} 2 \\ -2 \\ \hline 0 \end{array}$

You subtract _____ times.

Renée will use _____ chairs.

Complete.

3. Sam has **8** marbles.
He wants to give **2** to each friend.
How many friends will get marbles?

You subtract __4__ times.

_____ friends will each get **2** marbles.

Quick Check

Find the missing factor.

1.

3 × ☐ = **9**

Ring equal groups.
Write the number in each group.

2.

12 is **3** groups of _____ .

Complete the sentences.

3. Anika has **6** books.
She wants to put **2** books on each shelf.
How many shelves will she use?

You subtract _____ times.

Anika will use _____ shelves.

Name ______________________________

Fill in the blanks.

1. __10__ fish

Ring groups of **3**.

__3__ groups

__1__ left over

2. _____ birds

Ring groups of **5**.

_____ groups

_____ left over

3. _____ frogs

Ring groups of **2**.

_____ groups

_____ left over

4. _____ starfish

Ring groups of **3**.

_____ groups

_____ left over

Fill in the blanks.

5. _____ nests

Ring groups of **2**.

_____ groups

_____ left over

6. _____ dragonflies

Ring groups of **5**.

_____ groups

_____ left over

Problem Solving Reasoning Solve.

7. Mi Lee wants to store her marble collection in bags.
A shop sells bags that will hold up to **10** marbles.
Mi Lee has **38** marbles.
What are the fewest number of bags she needs to buy?

____

____

★ Test Prep

How many are left over? Mark the space for your answer.

8

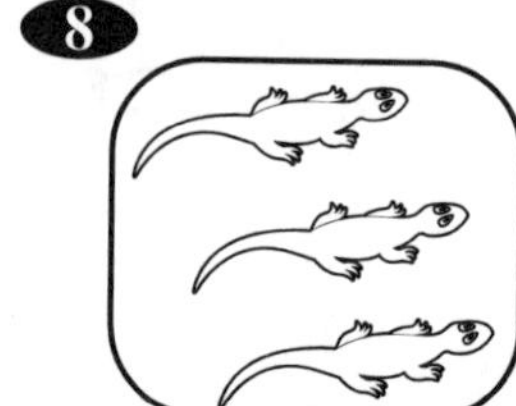
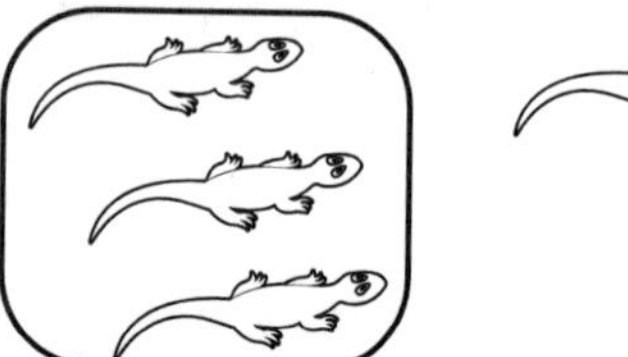
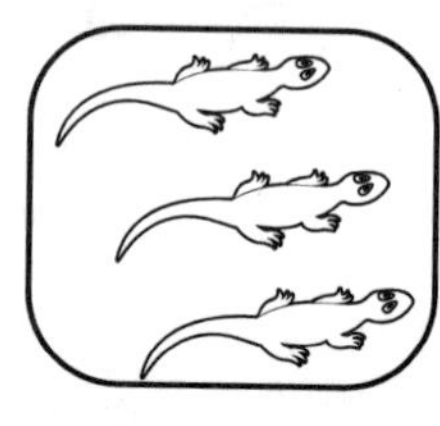

0	1	2	3
○	○	○	○

Complete the table to solve each problem.

One car has **4** wheels. Two cars have **8** wheels altogether.

cars	1	2	3	4	5			
wheels	4	8	12	16	20			

1. How many wheels are there on **5** cars? 20 wheels

2. How many wheels are there on **8** cars? ______ wheels

---

3 children can ride in one car.

children	3	6	9	12				
cars	1	2	3					

3. How many children altogether can ride in **6** cars? ______ children

4. How many children altogether can ride in **7** cars? ______ children

5. How many cars can take **15** children to the park? ______ cars

Complete the table to solve each problem.

Kenny reads **15** pages a day.

pages	15	30	45					
days	1	2	3	4				

6. How many pages will he read in **6** days? 90 pages

7. How many days will it take him to read **75** pages? _______ days

Leah puts **25** shells in each box.

shells	25	50				
boxes	1	2	3			

8. How many boxes hold **150** shells? _______ boxes

100 toys are made every **5** hours.

toys	100	200				
hours	5	10	15			

9. How many toys are made in **30** hours? _______ toys

★ Test Prep

Jenna buys **10** more stickers each day.

stickers	35	45	55		75	85
days	1	2	3	4	5	6

10 Mark how many stickers she has after **4** days.

70 ○ 50 ○ 60 ○ 65 ○

Name ______________________________

Skip-count. Fill in the blanks.

1.   

____, ____, ____

____ groups of ____

____ in all

2.    

____, ____, ____, ____

____ groups of ____

____ in all

3. 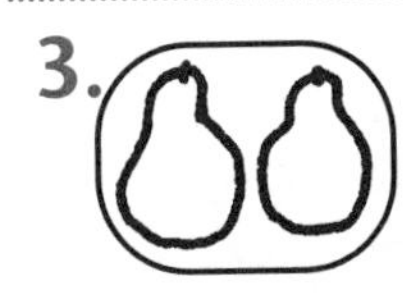  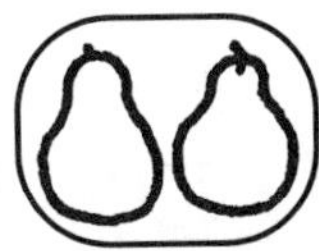  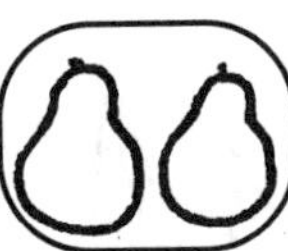

____, ____, ____, ____, ____

____ groups of ____

____ in all

Find the product.

4. $\begin{array}{r} 2 \\ \times\ 3 \\ \hline \end{array}$

5. $\begin{array}{r} 7 \\ \times\ 2 \\ \hline \end{array}$

Find the product.

6. $\begin{array}{r} 2 \\ \times\ 3 \\ \hline \end{array}$

7. $\begin{array}{r} 4 \\ \times\ 2 \\ \hline \end{array}$

8. $\begin{array}{r} 10 \\ \times\ 2 \\ \hline \end{array}$

9. $\begin{array}{r} 3 \\ \times\ 7 \\ \hline \end{array}$

10. $\begin{array}{r} 5 \\ \times\ 3 \\ \hline \end{array}$

11. $\begin{array}{r} 6 \\ \times\ 2 \\ \hline \end{array}$

12. $\begin{array}{r} 2 \\ \times\ 8 \\ \hline \end{array}$

13. $\begin{array}{r} 10 \\ \times\ 9 \\ \hline \end{array}$

14. $\begin{array}{r} 5 \\ \times\ 4 \\ \hline \end{array}$

15. $\begin{array}{r} 10 \\ \times\ 0 \\ \hline \end{array}$

16. $\begin{array}{r} 5 \\ \times\ 5 \\ \hline \end{array}$

17. $\begin{array}{r} 10 \\ \times\ 5 \\ \hline \end{array}$

Ring equal groups.
Write the number in each group.

18.

9 is **3** groups of ____ .

19.

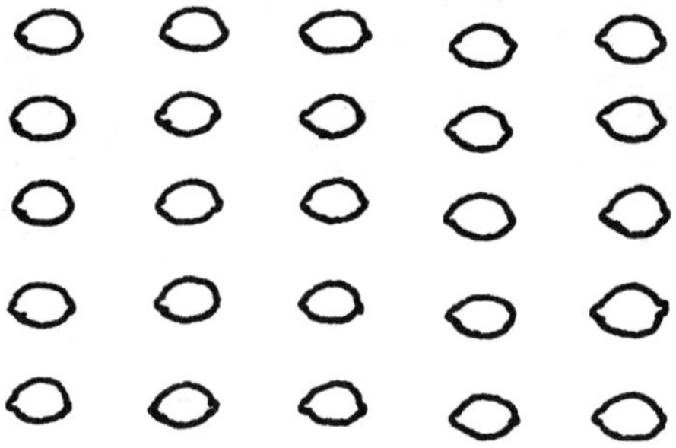

25 is **5** groups of ____ .

20.

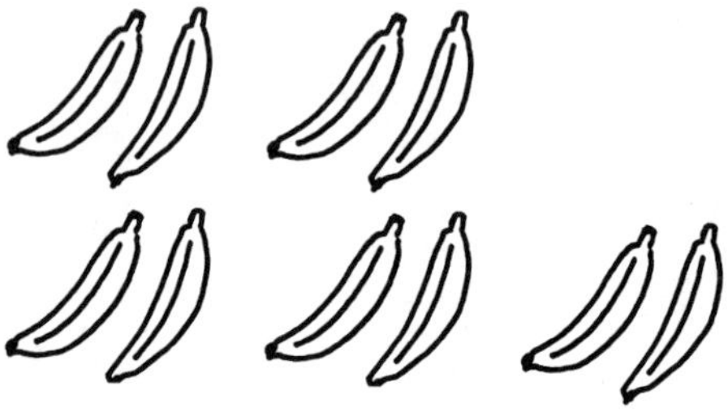

10 is **5** groups of ____ .

21.

16 is **2** groups of ____ .

22.

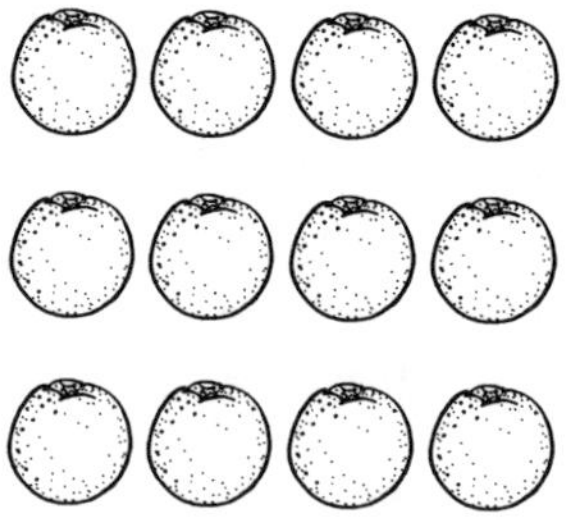

12 is **3** groups of ____ .

23.

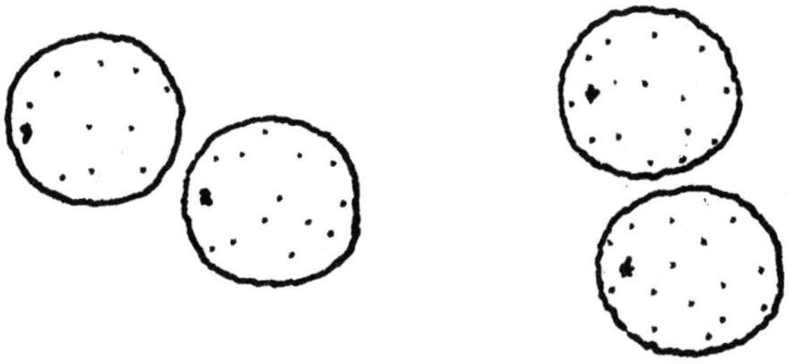

4 is **2** groups of ____ .

Problem Solving Reasoning

Ring the operation.
Write a number sentence. Solve.

24. One cat has **4** legs.

How many legs are there on **3** cats?

____

____ legs

add   subtract   multiply

Name ________________________________

1

○ 9 o'clock ○ quarter past 4

○ quarter to 4 ○ quarter past 9

2

I year = _____ months

6	12	24	30
○	○	○	○

3

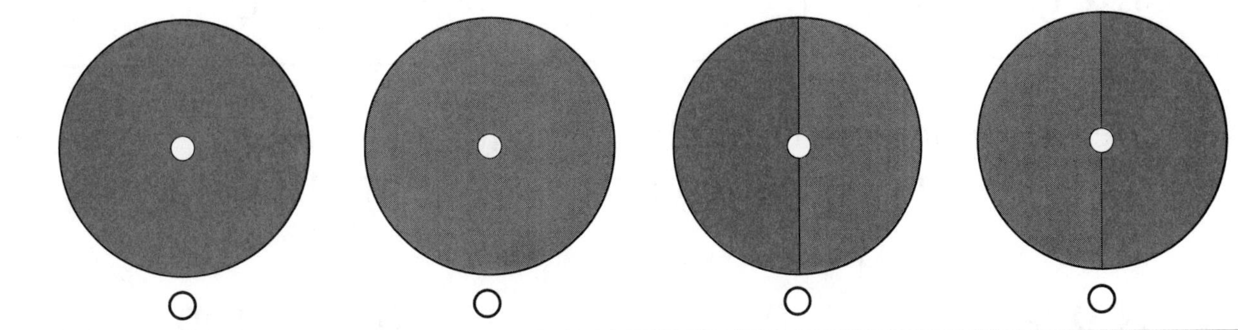

○ ○ ○ ○

4

248	2048	200408	20048
○	○	○	○

5

639	60309	60039	600309
○	○	○	○

6

$8.95	$5.98	$5.908	$5.89
○	○	○	○

7

23 ◯ 18 = 5

+	−	$>$	$<$
○	○	○	○

8

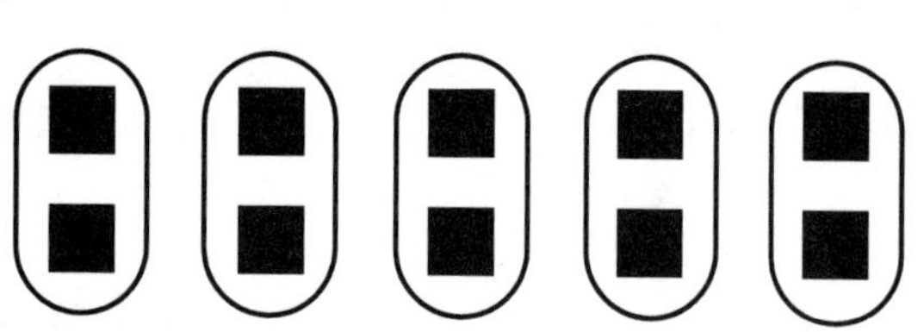

5 groups of **2** or ☐ in all.

2	5	10	20
○	○	○	○

9

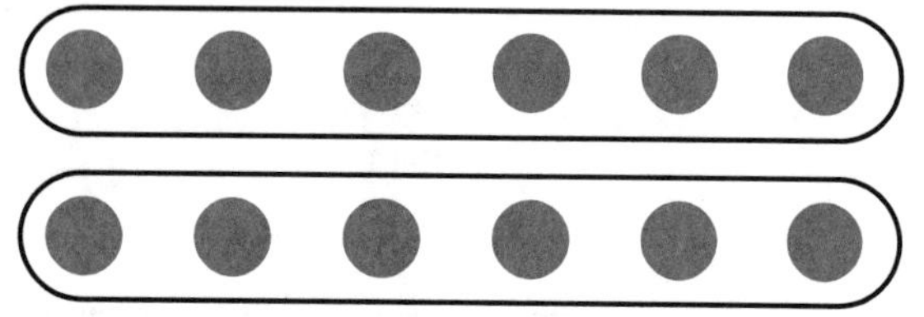

12 is **2** groups of ☐.

12	8	6	5
○	○	○	○

10

Decide on an answer. Mark the space for your answer.
If the answer is **not here**, mark the space for **NH**.

10 × 0 = ☐

0	1	10	100	NH
○	○	○	○	○

11

$$\begin{array}{r} 35 \\ +\ 57 \\ \hline \square \end{array}$$

○ **83**
○ **82**
○ **93**
○ **92**
○ NH

12

$$\begin{array}{r} 73 \\ -\ 54 \\ \hline \square \end{array}$$

○ **29**
○ **28**
○ **19**
○ **18**
○ NH

add

3 + 4 = 7

between

35, 36, 37

36 is between 35 and 37.

addend

3 + 5 = 8

addends

cent (¢)

= 1¢

after

39, 40

40 is after 39.

centimeter a metric unit of length

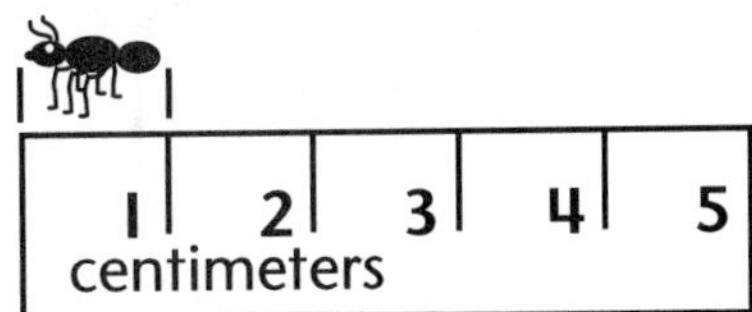

bar graph

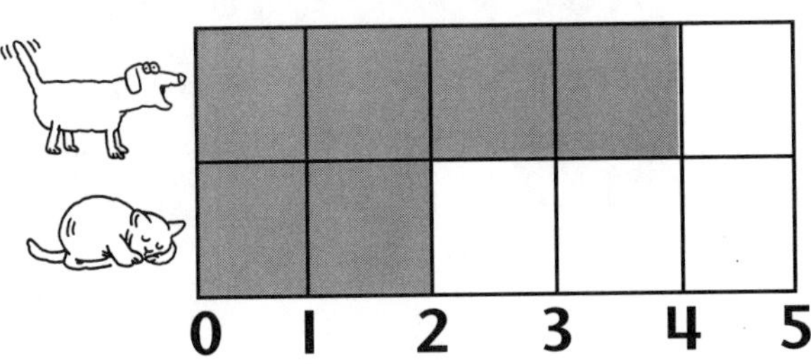

circle

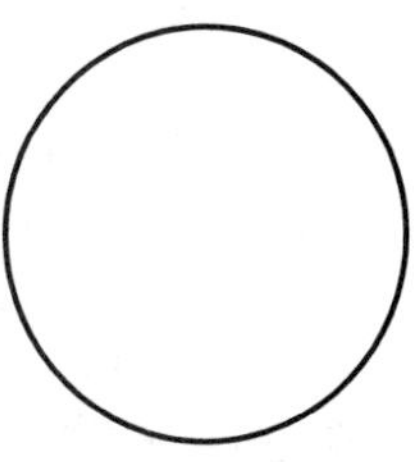

before

33, 34

33 is before 34

cone

congruent

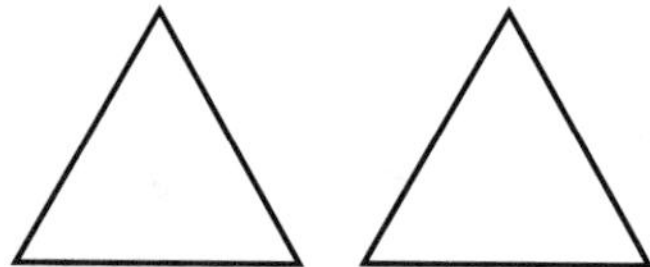

These triangles are congruent.
They are the same size and shape

corner

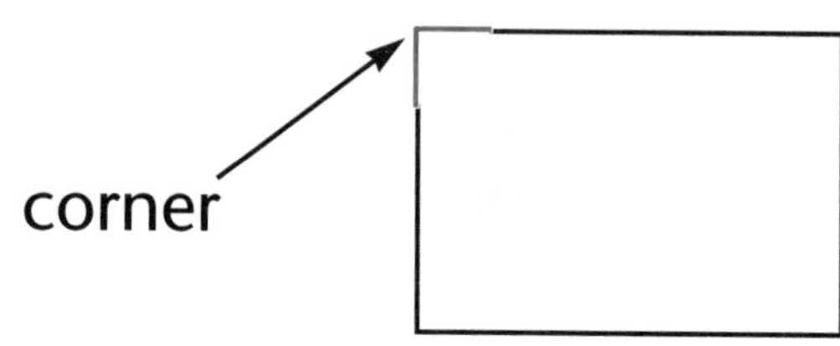

cube

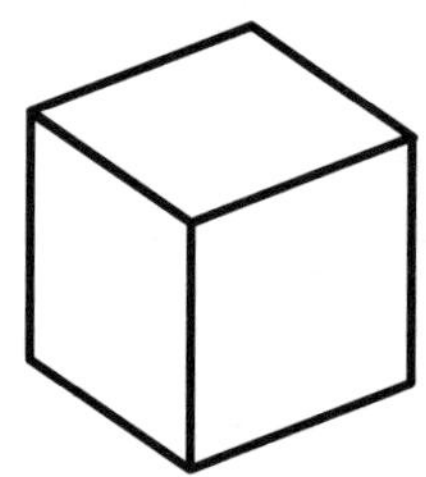

cup a customary unit of capacity

cylinder

day

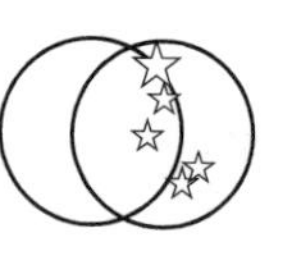

8:00 AM 8:00 PM 8:00 AM

There are 24 hours in a day.

difference

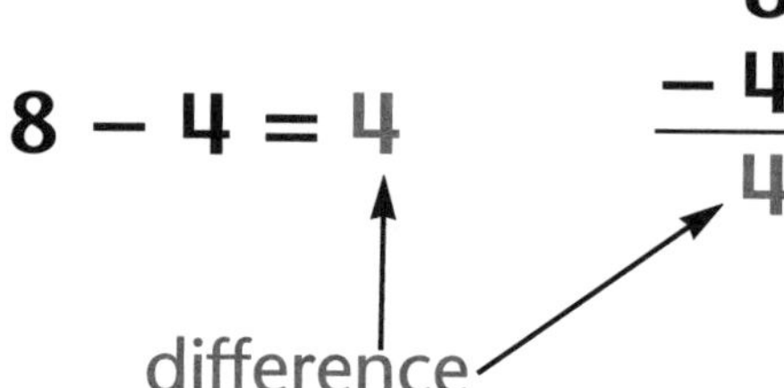

digit

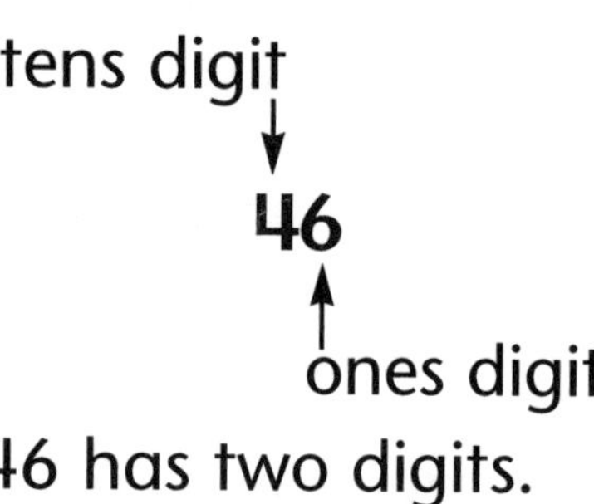

46 has two digits.

dime

10¢ **10** cents

dollar

100¢ or $1.00

edge

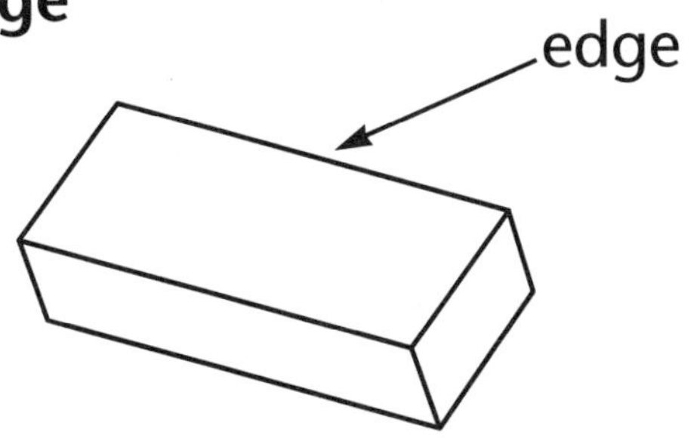

is equal to

4 = 4

4 is equal to 4.

estimate

about 20 shells

expanded form

245 = 200 + 40 + 5

face

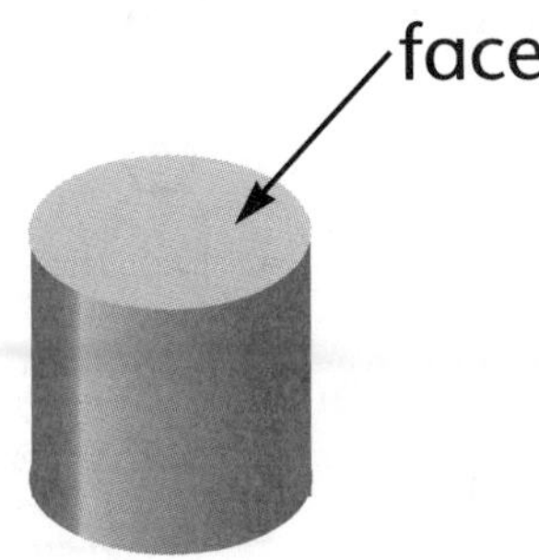

fact family

3 + 6 = 9   6 + 3 = 9

9 − 3 = 6   9 − 6 = 3

foot a customary unit of length

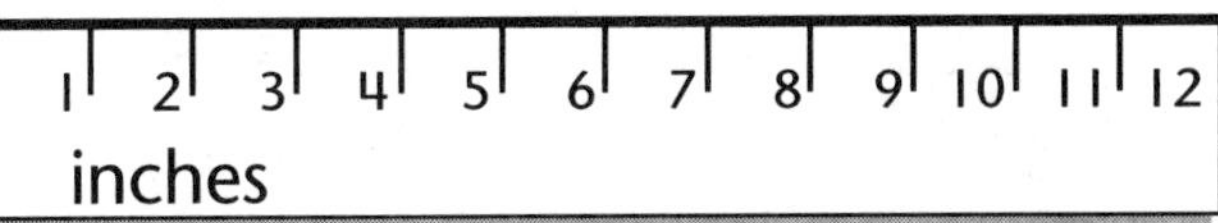

12 inches equal 1 foot.

factor

3 × 2 = 6

factors

fourths

$\frac{1}{4}$	$\frac{1}{4}$
$\frac{1}{4}$	$\frac{1}{4}$

4 fourths equal a whole.

fraction

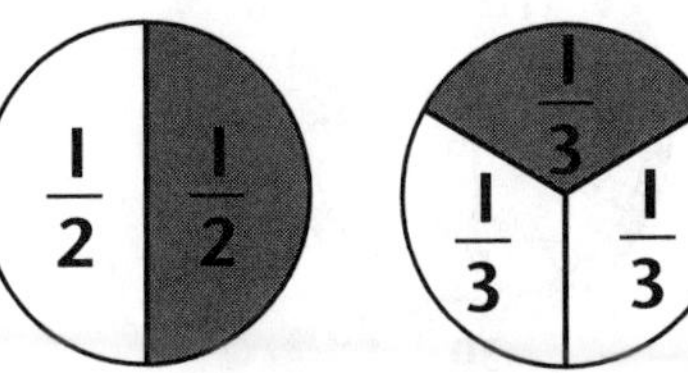

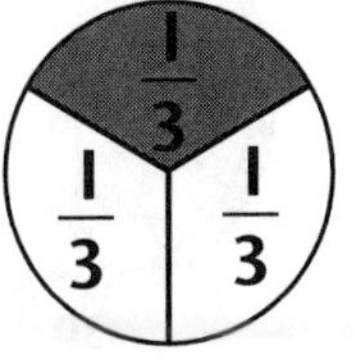

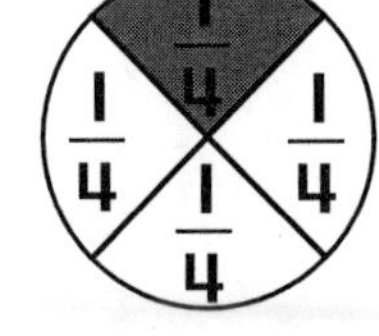

one-half   one-third   one-fourth

gallon a customary unit of capacity

4 quarts equal **1** gallon.

halves

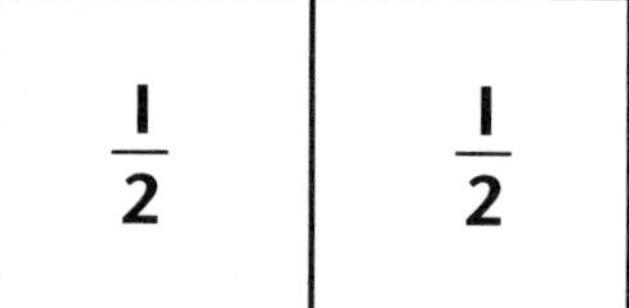

2 halves equal a whole.

is greater than

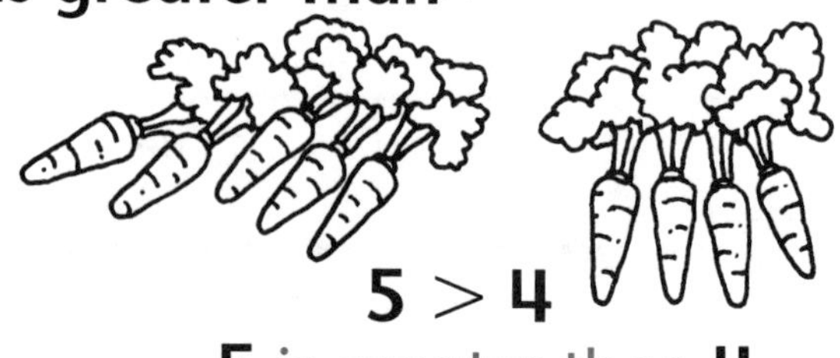

5 > **4**

5 is greater than **4**

hour

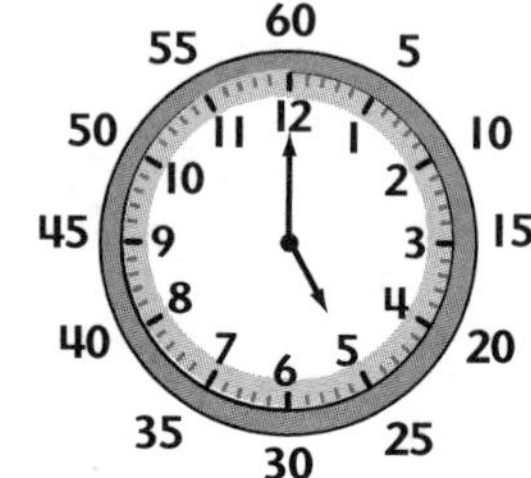

There are 60 minutes in an hour.

grouping property

3 + (2 + 3) = **8**

(3 + 2) + **3** = **8**

hundreds

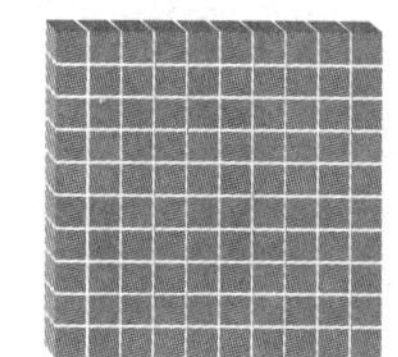

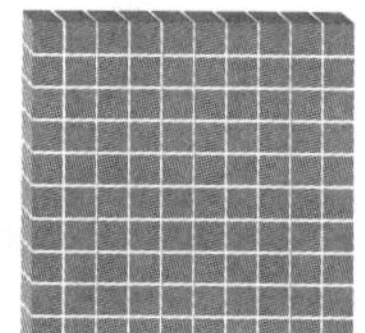

3 hundreds

half dollar

50¢ **50** cents

inch

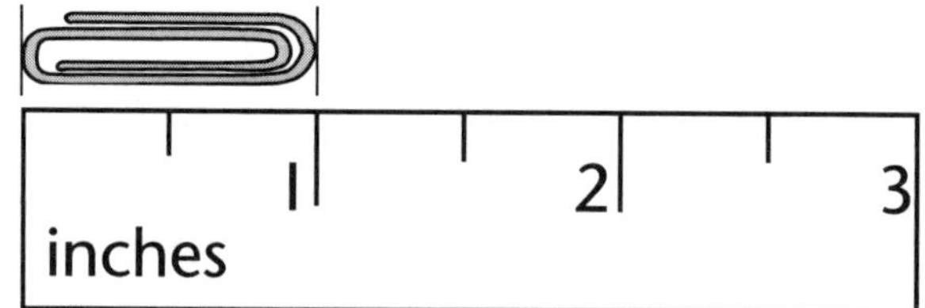

half hour

30 minutes equals **1** half hour.

kilogram a metric unit of mass

The book is about **1** kilogram.

is less than

3 < 5

3 is less than **5.**

line of symmetry

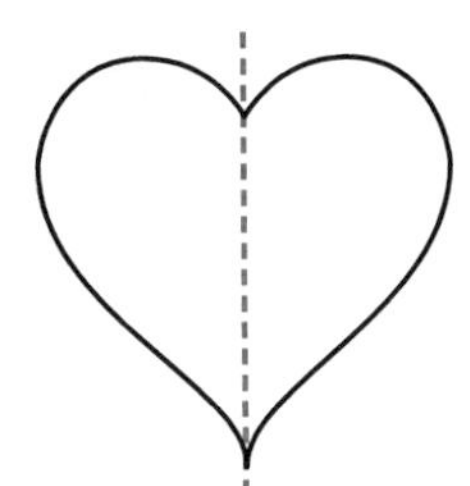

liter (L)

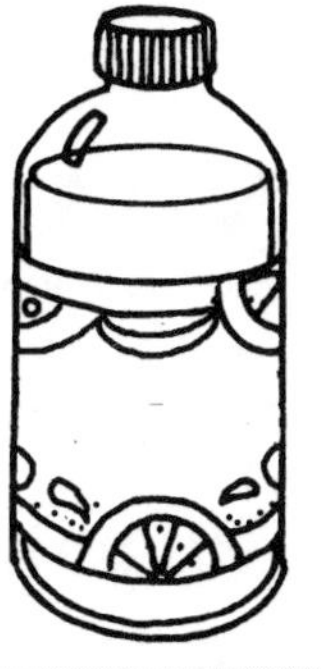

meter a metric unit of measurement

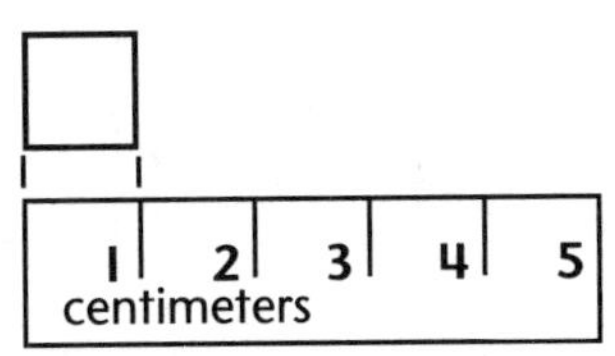

100 centimeters equal **1** meter.

minute

There are **60** seconds in a minute.

mode the number that occurs most often

1 2 2 3 4 5

2 is the mode.

month

There are 12 months in a year.

multiplication sentence

6 × 3 = 18

multiply

4 × 2 = 8

nickel

5 cents

number sentence

8 + 2 = 10

6 − 4 = 2

picture graph

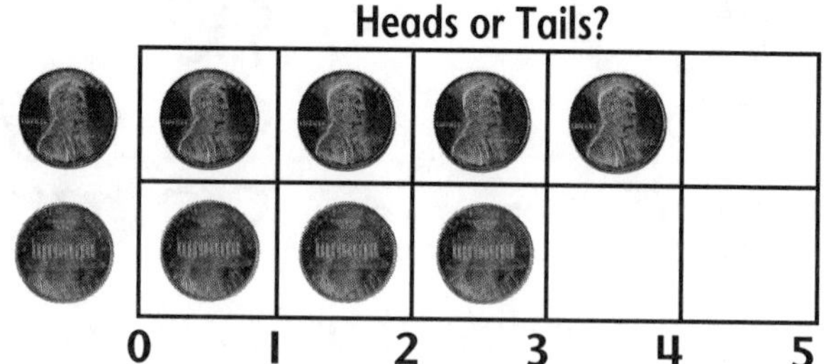

ones

5 ones

pint a customary unit of capacity

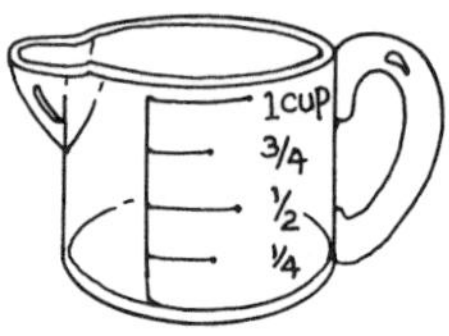

2 cups equal 1 pint.

order property

3 + 4 = 7

4 + 3 = 7

place value the value of each place

Tens	Ones
3	4

In 34 the digit 3 is in the tens place.

pattern

3, 5, 7, 9, 11, __?__

pound a customary unit of weight

The butter weighs about 1 pound.

penny

1¢   1 cent

product

5 × 3 = 15

$$\begin{array}{r} 3 \\ \times\ 5 \\ \hline 15 \end{array}$$

product

quart a customary unit of capacity

2 pints equal **1** quart.

quarter

25¢

25 cents

quarter past

quarter past **11** or **11:15**

quarter to

quarter to **4** or **3:45**

range the difference between the least and the greatest numbers

1 2 3 4 5 6

6 − 1 = 5 ← range

rectangle

rectangular prism

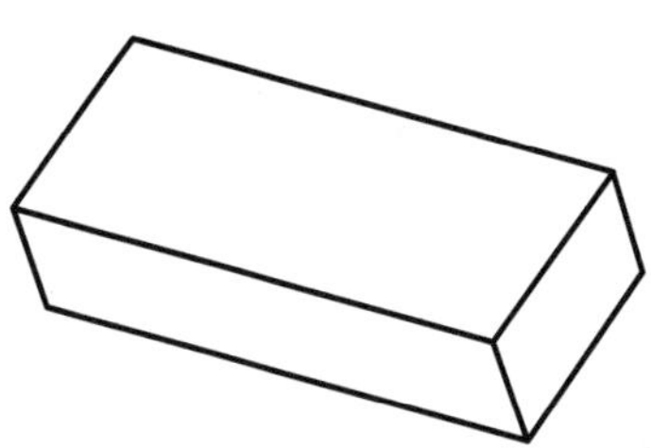

regroup

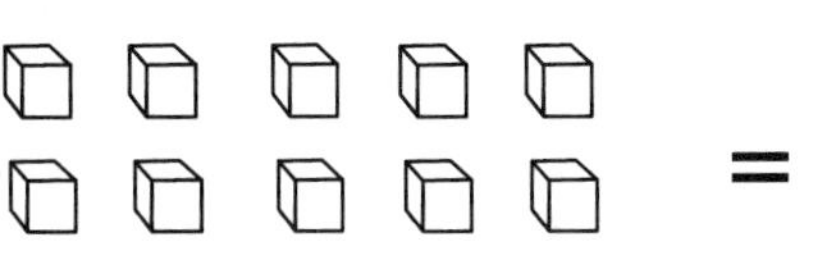

=

10 ones equal **1** ten

related facts

9 + 1 = 10

10 − 1 = 9

second

It takes about **1** second to snap.

skip-count

2 4 6 8

sum

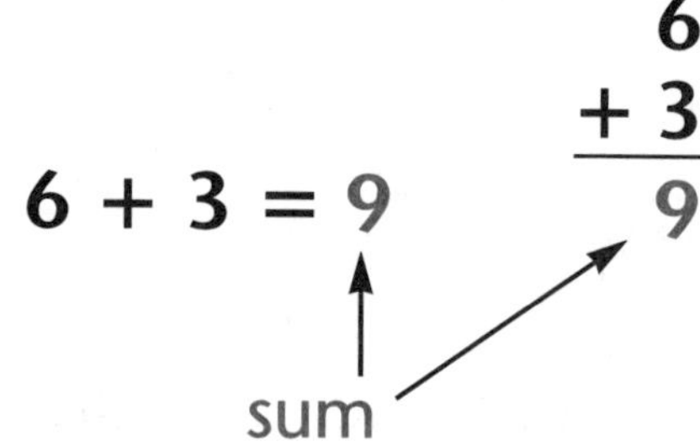

sphere

tens

4 tens

square

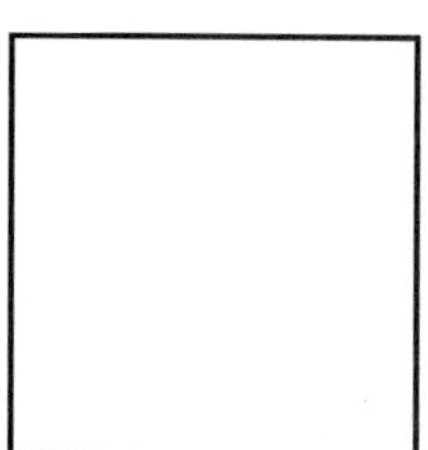

thirds

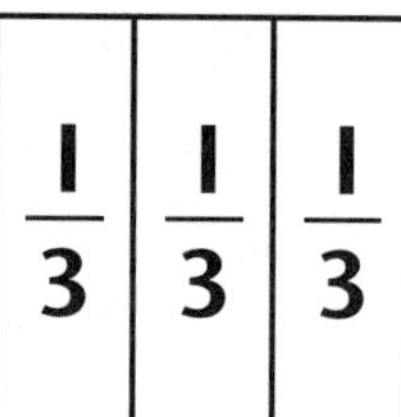

square pyramid

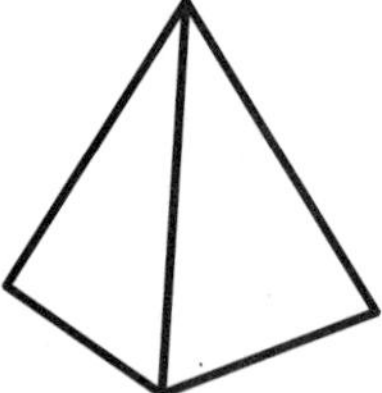

triangle

subtract

$5 - 2 = 3$

week

Sunday, Monday, Tuesday, Wednesday, Thursday, Friday, Saturday

There are **7** days in a week.